Understanding Canada

Building on the New Canadian Political Economy

EDITED BY

WALLACE CLEMENT

McGill-Queen's University Press
Montreal & Kingston • London • Buffalo

© McGill-Queen's University Press 1997
ISBN 0-7735-1502-X (cloth)
ISBN 0-7735-1503-8 (paper)

Legal deposit first quarter 1997
Bibliothèque nationale du Québec

Printed in Canada on acid-free paper

Canadian Cataloguing in Publication Data

Main entry under title:
    Understanding Canada: building on the new Canadian
    political economy
    Includes bibliographical references.
    ISBN 0-7735-1503-8 (pbk.)
    ISBN 0-7735-1502-X (bound)
    1. Canada – Economic conditions – 1991–   2. Canada
    – Economic policy – 1991–   I. Clement, Wallace.
    HC115.U52 1997   330.971'0647   c96-990070-8

This book was typeset by Typo Litho Composition Inc.
in 10/12 Baskerville.

Understanding Canada
Building on the New Canadian Political Economy

As corporations are restructured, governments cut back spending, and the international economy is transformed, there is an increasing need to understand the economic and political forces involved, evaluate their implications, and develop strategies to modify them to meet society's interests. In light of the current situation, the study of political economy is more relevant than ever.

Understanding Canada examines a variety of topics from viewpoints ranging from the established to the interdisciplinary. Contributors look at issues such as gender, Native peoples, race, ethnicity and migration, globalization, foreign policy, the welfare state, regulation, communications, popular culture, and space and the environment, as well as the more traditional subjects of economic growth, resources and manufacturing, labour, regionalism, Quebec, and the character of the Canadian state.

The new Canadian political economy has emerged from its infancy and is now regarded as a respected and innovative field of scholarship. *Understanding Canada* furthers this tradition by focusing on current issues in an accessible and informative way.

WALLACE CLEMENT is director of the Institute of Political Economy, Carleton University.

Contents

Preface

Since publishing *The New Canadian Political Economy* in 1989, Glen Williams and I have maintained contact about the project with Philip Cercone, executive director of McGill-Queen's University Press. We thought about a second edition, but the timing was never quite right. Eventually it became evident, through discussions with colleagues, that instead of a second edition we needed an entirely new volume directed to middle and senior undergraduate students. *The New Canadian Political Economy* had been used as a text for such students, though it had been conceived as more of a graduate reference work. Having attained a "place" in the literature as a statement of its time, it was not readily "up-datable."

Thus I designed *Understanding Canada: Building on the New Canadian Political Economy* to capture the interest of undergraduates through a focus on issues relevant to them. It was meant to demonstrate for students the value of political economy insights. Instead of focusing on the founders and practitioners of political economy, the present volume aims to "build on" the tradition and its new links to more disciplines and area studies.

This volume, as the title suggests, goes beyond the original collection edited by Glen Williams and me, concentrating less on the roots of Canadian political economy and more on the current questions, puzzles, and problems that motivate current thinking in the field. It aims to do so in an accessible and informative way, emphasizing mainly the issues rather than the authors engaged in the new Canadian political economy. This collection stands on its own and is, in a sense, liberated by the availability of its predecessor for those seeking more about the foundations of the tradition.

Glen Williams was unable to complete the editorial work needed for this new undertaking because of other professional and personal commitments. I wish to thank him, however, for his contribution to the formation of this project. Fortunately, we were able to write a chapter together. As the sole editor, this time I have had a closer relationship with each of the authors and pieces in this book. The project has had its rewards. The evident vibrancy of the tradition, and the impact it has had on social science scholarship, have been impressive. Not only has a new generation of scholars become engaged with political economy, but the political economists of old have also evolved.

Understanding Canada: Building on the New Canadian Political Economy has half again as many chapters as *The New Canadian Political Economy* because new areas have been added (feminist political economy, foreign economic relations, foreign policy, space and the environment, the welfare state, regulation, and popular culture) and an earlier joint chapter has been separated into two subjects (Native people and race, ethnicity and migration). Other areas have been consolidated (resources and industrialization).

I wish to thank Elaine Rouleau, administrator of the Institute of Political Economy at Carleton University, for her assistance with administrative aspects of this project. Elsie Clement has assisted with my contributions; as always, I thank her. Philip Cercone and the people at McGill-Queen's University Press have continued to offer solid support. Finally, I wish to acknowledge the twenty-five authors of these seventeen chapters for contributing their talent and time to make this project possible. I think the next generation of political economy students, who will carry us into the next millennium, will benefit by the accessibility and insights of these chapters.

Wallace Clement
Director
Institute of Political Economy
Carleton University

Contributors

Frances Abele, School of Public Administration, Carleton University

Gregory Albo, Department of Political Science, York University

Isabella Bakker, Department of Political Science, York University

Janine Brodie, Department of Political Science, York University

Wallace Clement, Department of Sociology and Anthropology and Institute of Political Economy, Carleton University

William Coleman, Department of Political Science, McMaster University

Richard Gruneau, Department of Communications, Simon Fraser University

Jane Jenson, Departement de science politique, Université de Montréal

Meg Luxton, Women's Studies, Atkinson College, York University

Laura Macdonald, Department of Political Science, Carleton University

Ted Magder, Department of Social Science, York University

Heather Jon Maroney, Department of Sociology and Anthropology, Carleton University

Mark Neufeld, Department of Politics, Trent University

Paul Phillips, Department of Economics, University of Manitoba

Daniel Salée, Department of Political Science, Concordia University

Liora Salter, Osgoode Hall Law School, York University

Rick Salter, Pape and Salter, Toronto, Ontario

Katherine Scott, Policy Associate, Canadian Council on Social Development

Rob Shields, Department of Sociology and Anthropology, Carleton University

Daiva Stasiulis, Department of Sociology and Anthropology, Carleton University

Iain Wallace, Department of Geography, Carleton University

Mel Watkins, Department of Economics, University College, University of Toronto

David Whitson, Department of Political Science, University of Alberta

Sandra Whitworth, Department of Political Science, York University

Glen Williams, Department of Political Science, Carleton University

1 Introduction: Whither the New Canadian Political Economy?

WALLACE CLEMENT

Political economy is a holistic approach to understanding society from a materialist perspective. Political economy, at its best, connects the economic, political, and cultural/ideological moments of social life. Rather than seeking explanations through narrowly constructed disciplines, it tries to build from a totality which includes the political, economic, social, and cultural, where the whole is greater than its parts. Its claim is that to understand each of the political, economic, social, and cultural requires contextualization of each with the other.

By "materialist" is meant a perspective that begins with the assumption that the relations between people are fundamentally shaped by the way a society reproduces itself. How people make a living – for example, as use-value producers, commodity producers for sale, or wage earners – strongly influences how they are formed as social beings. The points of production and reproduction are starting places for a materialist analysis, but understanding does not stop with the way a society meets its basic economic needs. A materialist analysis recognizes that how the production, distribution, and consumption of goods and services is organized in a society is inherently social and political. Such organization needs to be justified and be made to seem legitimate. Political economy, as an integral part of society, has an understanding of the cultural and ideological aspects of society. Moreover, political economy is historical and dynamic, since it seeks to locate the motion of society in the forces of change as production and reproduction transform. It seeks out tensions and contradictions within society that produce struggles and resistance to the prevailing order. Such a critical account is integral to political economy.

Ideas have an important place within political-economic accounts, but, unlike idealist approaches, which begin with values, beliefs, or attitudes and from these explain society's workings, the materialist approach contends that the realm of ideas itself requires explanation. That is not to say that ideas stand "outside" the material. On the contrary, the ideological and cultural are embedded in the economic base and are an integral part of the reproduction of society. Political economy seeks out the underlying structures and patterns that inform the way ideas are developed.

The cultural/ideological within political economy includes the meaning that people attach to their lives, especially what is now popularly referred to as "identities." The way they understand and justify what they do and who they are, including the guidelines they use for their behaviour, is the essence of the cultural/ideological. It is both inherited and created, covering religion, cultural traditions, sexism, racism, class consciousness, values, attitudes, interests, and ideals. These factors are not autonomous forces within political economy. They arise out of and help to shape people's material existence. Identities are dynamic and integral features of political and economic realities.

Also at the heart of political economy is an inherent interest in social change. Materialism is never static, uniform, or timeless, so there is always a historical dimension. Particularly central is the unfolding of social and technical change, but so too are political and cultural struggles. Besides being historical, political economy is also always spatial – consciously located in particular territories, which are themselves relationally specified by both domestic and international relations.

As part of this concern with social change, examination of human agency emphasizes the importance of the actions of people in shaping the course of history. Politics within political economy is to do not simply with governments but with all power relations, whether involving nations, workers, or households. Politics contains the notions of tensions and contradictions, plus the struggles and resistance that form part of the dynamic of society. What occurs within the workplace, in unions, in social movements, or between the sexes is as political as elections. All involve struggles for control and seek to assert what is "right, just, and proper." Such an approach to politics expands the notion of democracy to the way people organize, coordinate, and are controlled in all aspects of their lives.

The goal of the new political economy is to explain "the economy" and market forces so that political and social interventions can direct economic processes. "Markets" are not only economic; they can also be social and political in their direction. Exclusively economic adjustment without political and social limitations and agendas is not possible or sustainable. The economy is both political and social, with the social embodying both cultural and ideological aspects and the political embodying both military and democratic features. Each moment of the economic, political, and social operates at a variety of levels of abstraction and has many types (politics, for example, can be fascist, conservative, liberal, social democratic, or socialist). The economy itself has both structure and agency – that is, capital and capitalists or labour and labourers who are both abstract and concrete (meaning real people with races, ages, sexes, not only abstractions as neo-classical economists imagine). These 'agents' are all located in time and space (local, national, and international contexts). The new political economy seeks most of all to prevent the political and social aspects of life from being marginalized by a strictly economic logic. Its goal is to reveal the political agendas of economic practices and to assert the importance of the social.

For political economy, the economic provides the context, but the political, ideological, and cultural write the text of history and specify the particulars for each nation and the possibilities for the future. The script is one in which human actors have significant freedom of action within the limits of the structures that political economy seeks to identify.

Within political economy there are several tendencies. In Canada, it has been inclusive of various ideological orientations, whereas in other countries, such as Sweden, it is dominated institutionally by a neo-classical market liberal tradition that has traditionally located itself against socialist and social-democratic alternatives. The overarching tradition in Canada is one that investigates the relationship between the economy and politics as they affect social and cultural life. Within neo-conservative political economy, primary emphasis is on free trade, unfettered markets for capital, and minimal state intervention outside its coercive responsibilities (the military abroad and penal institutions at home). Liberal political economy places the determinant weight on the political system and markets, with stress on culture and technology. Within social-democratic political economy, electoral party politics and alliances with the labour movement are primary, with tensions, social organization, and distribution of social resources emphasized. Socialist political economy grants primacy to the economic system and classes and places more emphasis on contradictions, ideology, and resistance. Within feminist political economy, reproduction and gender are forefront, with popular politics and identity struggles emphasized. The key methodological insight that binds these theories is the importance of totalities understood from a materialist perspective. In each, social relations are located within the context of the economic, political, and cultural/ideological, on the one hand, and dimensions of time and space, on the other. Each seeks out tensions or contradictions within society as political economy supports struggles and resistance. To know how societies are, and can be, transformed is the primary goal of political economy. How we think and act can change the material organization of society. In other words, politics matter, and the economy is not simply abstract forces but that which is imbedded in relations between people. Once that is understood, it becomes clear that "the economy" both affects people and is affected by their actions.

CANADIAN POLITICAL ECONOMY

In Canadian political economy, the 1920s through the early 1950s were the classic period, with staples production and issues of place (in their international and regional contexts) made central by the work of Harold Adams Innis. The tradition then entered the doldrums, experiencing a revival in the early 1970s, focusing on response to U.S. domination of Canada's culture and economy, primarily within a "dependency" paradigm.[1] In the 1980s, the new Canadian political economy began to broaden and deepen these concerns.[2]

The New Canadian Political Economy predicted development of fresh directions, building on the solid foundation examined in its primarily reflective articles. That collection concentrated on the roots of the tradition. Whereas it looked back to the classic, Innisian tradition and described itself as building on but distinct from that way of seeing the world, the current volume seeks to examine contemporary issues in light of their trajectory and look forward, at the emerging directions in scholarship and practice. The earlier book established a foundation and practice. This one claims a body of scholarship that expands the classic boundaries, engages more fields, and regards more issues as central to its viewpoint. This approach is reflected in authorship and discipline, both of which have been broadened by inclusion of both established scholars and "young Turks." As a "way of seeing" more than as a "subject," political economy is truly interdisciplinary.

In the life of Canadian political economy, we are now in a period of solid scholarship that possibly lacks the heat and light of the 1970s and 1980s but certainly has a more solid base and greater rigour. The new tradition has penetrated many disciplines and been adopted there as its own: sociology, political science, law, history, geography, women's studies, Canadian studies, international affairs, public administration, communications, social work, cultural studies, and labour studies all have political economy streams within them.

And the new Canadian political economy has itself been transformed by its association with these disciplines and area studies. There
is an ongoing dialectic evident in many of the pieces gathered here. As
we find ourselves past the mid-point of the 1990s, Canadian political
economy, in a revised guise, and with greater diversity and broader
directions, continues its vibrancy. It is defined by its drive to explore
the changing relationships between the economy and politics as reflections of the social and cultural life of society.

Canadian political economy remains a diverse and fairly eclectic
gathering point for a variety of projects, issues, and concerns. While
possibly still too narrow for some, *Studies in Political Economy*, the flagship journal of the revised tradition in Canada which just published its
fiftieth issue, illustrates the tremendous range of the field. Certainly
the boundaries are pushed further by some of the contributors to this
volume. Many of the authors represented here are on the frontiers of
Canadian political economy in the 1970s and 1980s. Even those contributors who appeared in the earlier volume reflect major changes
in their subjects; examples include Frances Abele's piece on Native
peoples (chapter 6); Daiva Stasiulis on race, ethnicity, and migration
(chapter 7); Albo and Jenson on the state (chapter 10); Salée and
Coleman on Quebec (chapter 12); and Ted Magder on communications (chapter 15). In other pieces there is a much stronger dialogue
between Canadian political economy and other relevant fields; examples include Luxton and Maroney on women's studies (chapter 5);
Laura Macdonald on international relations (chapter 8); Neufeld and
Whitworth on foreign policy (chapter 9); Whitson and Gruneau on
popular culture (chapter 16); and Wallace and Shields on environmental studies (chapter 17).

At Carleton University's Institute of Political Economy, which offers
the country's only master's degree in political economy, three streams
are identified for heuristic purposes: Canadian, international, and
comparative political economies. Each reflects a distinguishable tradition, set of assumptions, and literature. Yet all are called on by many
practitioners of political economy. Canadian political economy has as
one of its hallmarks the international context of Canada's history and
existence. The place of the "external" in Canada's "internal" development has long been at the core of all the traditions within Canadian
political economy. Similarly, much of Canadian political economy has
been comparative, whether implicitly or explicitly. There have been
the "traditional" comparadors – the United Kingdom and the United
States. Then came the "settler colonies" of Australia, New Zealand,
Argentina, and Uruguay (as with Philip Ehrensaft and Warwick

Armstrong).[3] More recently, "late industrializers," such as Sweden, have become a familiar comparison (for example, Gordon Laxer).[4] Canada has also been compared and contrasted in a continental (with the United States) and Nordic (Sweden, Finland, and Norway) context (by Clement and Myles).[5] Political economy in Canada encourages all three traditions. This book is about Canadian political economy, but the other "streams" of political economy are well represented here: for example, the chapters by Laura Macdonald on foreign economic relations and by Neufeld and Whitworth on foreign policy are both located in the international tradition, while the chapter by Bakker and Scott (13) on the welfare state is in the comparative mode, which also provides the backdrop for the chapters by Albo and Jenson on the state and Salter and Salter (14) on state regulations. The other chapters are far from insular: Paul Phillips on labour (chapter 4), Daiva Stasiulis on race and ethnicity, Wallace and Shields on space and the environment, Ted Magder on communications, and Whitson and Gruneau on popular culture, all built on a command of international scholarly literature as applied to the political economy of the Canadian case.

CONTENTS

The collection opens with a chapter (2) on economic growth and crisis by the dean of the Canadian political economy tradition, Mel Watkins. Watkins has had the strongest links to the Innisian tradition and has been a major interpreter of Innis. Three seminal articles by Watkins mirror the path of this tradition: the classical re-interpretation,[6] the dependency approach,[7] and the neo-marxist version.[8] He also contributed the lead article in *The New Canadian Political Economy*. The present piece demonstrates his continued vitality and engagement with the field as he revisits the staples thesis and debates around dependent industrialization. Watkins presents the foundations and international context of the political economy tradition, especially the "cycles" growth theory and staples approaches. Much of his emphasis is on time as a key variable in political economy: booms and busts, recoveries and recessions, waves and cycles. He is also sensitive to the unfolding of Canada in its international context, casting an eye on implications for employment and social services. Following a clear presentation of linkages and competing visions of staple growth in Canada, he directs his placement of Canada in time and space towards an understanding of contemporary issues. Watkins asks the "large questions" about Canada's economy and the importance of political determinants, addressing such issues as resource dependence and truncated manufacturing (taken up again in Clement and William's chapter, which follows), regionalism, Native people, and gender (each of which become subjects for later chapters).

The chapter (3) by Wallace Clement and Glen Williams on resources and manufacturing is a backdrop to the special features of Canada's industrial economy. Each author represents a somewhat distinct approach to these issues. Clement is most widely known for *The Canadian Corporate Elite* and *Continental Corporate Power*, while Williams's *Not for Export: Toward a Political Economy of Canada's Arrested Industrialization* has recently been released in its third edition. Canada's industrialization is characterized by the pervasiveness of foreign direct investment, the centrality of resource extraction for exports, its branch-plant structure, and its place in the international division of labour. This chapter locates the current economic situation of Canada in a series of past practices and decisions by economic and political leaders. It traces political actions and public perceptions towards foreign ownership and explains how and why resource exports became such a defining feature. Of special importance is the explanation of the "debt trap" and overdevelopment of resource megaprojects in the past two decades. This factor is especially relevant as an account of government debt that offers an alternative to one that blames social services. Also touched on is the environmental cost of Canada's industrial practices – a theme developed in the final chapter by Wallace and Shields. The discussion of Canada's international trade agreements is further pursued in the chapter by Laura Macdonald.

Paul Phillips, like Mel Watkins an economist by training, is widely known for his scholarship on labour history, regionalism, women's work, and his efforts to revive the writings of H. Clare Pentland. Phillips edited and wrote the introduction to Pentland's *Labour and Capital in Canada, 1650–1860*, a classic text, which was written during the doldrums of Canadian political economy but not published until twenty years later.

Phillips, in chapter 4, provides a compelling background to the shame of unemployment – a responsibility that should be borne by those in control of the labour market rather than its victims. He addresses the Canadian government's practices to control labour and diminish citizens' entitlements, undercutting the "accord" engineered between labour and capital following the Second World War. Phillips carefully locates the ideological struggles that have accompanied these attacks and directly addresses the characterizations that orthodox economics has made of the current period of restructuring. While providing an important bridge with the classical traditions of Innis and Pentland, Phillips offers the reader a primer on contemporary economics in a clear, comprehensible way by identifying the distinctiveness of the new Canadian political economy tradition as a way of seeing Canada and of the alternatives that it poses. In this tradition, labour is an actor in the transformation of the labour process, not simply an abstraction, as in the orthodox approach.

Meg Luxton and Heather Jon Maroney edited *Feminism and Political Economy: Women's Work, Women's Struggles* (1987), an important collection, which, like *Politics of Diversity: Feminism, Marxism and Nationalism* (1986), edited by Roberta Hamilton and Michele Barrett, challenged the practice of Canadian political economy in some fundamental ways. Maroney and Luxton here (chapter 5) trace developments since their earlier statement. In their continued opposition to the ghettoization of "women's issues," they see the new Canadian political economy as a means, through its holistic approach, to break these barriers. They illustrate contentious past relations between socialist-feminism and Canadian political economy. Materialism provides some common ground, especially around issues such as pay equity and the impact of public-sector cutbacks and private-sector restructuring.

Luxton and Maroney convincingly argue that "feminism has reshaped the core issues of traditional political economy." At the same time, feminism itself has been reshaped as a social movement, and women as political subjects and identities. The issues of race, ethnicity, and nation have re-entered political economy through feminism in a way reminiscent of how the earlier tradition was challenged by the relations of class and gender. Again, it is the integrated (holistic) analysis that provides the common ground. This chapter raises many specific issues for political economy, such as the place of households and family forms in the new Canadian political economy and the issues of immigration and new work forms, especially housework.

Abele and Stasiulis contributed a joint, path-breaking piece to *The New Canadian Political Economy*. This time, each was allocated her own chapter. Frances Abele has just concluded several years as deputy director of research with the Royal Commission on Aboriginal Peoples, an experience that clearly informs her chapter (6). She interrogates the complex past and very real present of indigenous peoples in Canada. Their political struggles and economic transformation are directly located in their cultural and ideological context.

Abele also provides important methodological insights on the intersection between biography and history. She addresses issues of sources and the quality of "evidence" posed by representations of indigenous peoples. Contrary to traditional depictions of these people as a "dying race," she documents their renewed political, economic, and cultural presence. Their activism is especially prominent concerning land claims, land settlements, and self-government (as well as environmental issues; see chapter 17, by Wallace and Shields). Such struggles and resistance are testament to human agency's ability to move apparently immobile political objects (see the chapter by Salter and Salter, which includes discussion of land claims). Indigenous peoples are clearly not homogeneous in their communities, economies, or political goals, but Abele provides a clear introduction to a political-economic understanding.

In a challenging and poignant chapter (7), Daiva Stasiulis locates Canada as an immigrant society, the source of which has shifted significantly in the past decade away from Europe to Asia. This Asian migration itself is highly diverse, ranging from Indochinese refugees to Hong Kong investors. Stasiulis challenges the "two founding nations," hegemonic representation of contemporary Canada, at the heart of Canadian culture, ideology and politics. At this especially crucial juncture of "nation-building," she challenges, current "multicultural" discourse. This chapter is an exemplar of the complexity and nuance of the interaction of material conditions with cultural and ideological factors. Stasiulis builds a revised account and periodization of the history of settlement and colonization, emphasizing the "mode of incorporation" of migrants into the labour force. She documents how Anglo conformity and the construction of British hegemony have been the defining model of nation-building. Contrary to conventional views, she contends that there has been a major place for "unfree" labour in Canada's immigrant experience, including current agricultural- and domestic-labour arrangements. She directly addresses racism in Canadian public policies. Stasiulis includes an assessment of current issues of race and migration associated with contemporary restructuring and "globalization," offering a strong link into the next two chapters.

Chapters 8 and 9 are firmly rooted in the international political economy tradition, which emphasizes the relations between nations, first in the economic sense, then in the political one. Laura Macdonald's accessible account of foreign economic relations in chapter 8 locates Canada in the world economy. She demonstrates the traditional connection between the external and the internal while identifying the forces of regionalism and globalization. She presents a balanced assessment of both policies and perspectives on "the international" in her views on global political economy. In a way that is distinct from classical political economy, she calls for the new Canadian political economy to "go global" in its standpoint and perspective. Macdonald provides a penetrating rendition of international agreements and their impact on Canada, including an evaluation of "free trade" with the United States and Mexico. In so doing, she calls for a rethinking of "space" and the place of Canada and Canadian political economy within it, using the experience of transnational responses to the North American Free Trade Agreement by tri-national (Canada/United States/Mexico) social movements.

Mark Neufeld and Sandra Whitworth, young scholars like Laura Macdonald, examine the Canadian state's role "on the world stage" of geopolitics in chapter 9. They evaluate the "image" of Canada in political, diplomatic, and military terms, which they find grounded in the historical British Empire and Commonwealth and its weaning process around the Second World War. They bring the reader through the defiant Diefenbaker era under u.s. hegemony, Pearson's peacekeeping tradition and "quiet diplomacy," and Mulroney's slipping under the covers with Ronald Reagan. The post–Cold War complexity and rapid changes faced by Jean Chrétien's government are viewed as having dropped the traditional "middle power" identity. It is towards the current conjuncture that their analysis and advocacy is directed. Their perspective is located in the Robert Cox tradition of Canada's middle-power role in the context of declining American hegemony (in the world, not Canada, where its grip is being intensified). They examine a set of images of Canada on the international stage, as "loyal ally," "loyal opposition," and "extra-parliamentary opposition." The piece is impressive for the way in which it contextualizes the role of "ideas" in their material existence while using those same ideas to imagine alternative futures.

Gregory Albo, a recent doctoral graduate from Carleton University's Political Science Department and co-editor of *A Different Kind of State? Popular Power and Democratic Administration*, and Jane Jenson, co-author of *Crisis, Challenge and Change: Party and Class in Canada Revisited*, team up once again. In chapter 10, they examine challenges to the legitimacy of "the state" in Canada (by Quebec nationalism and claims for Native self-government). What role has the state had through social programs, they ask, in moderating "market discipline"? Is the Canadian state in the process of dismantling itself? These relevant questions are addressed in the context of another, even more basic, question: what is the capacity of the state to act, especially under the forces of globalization? At this time, when even the most fundamental features of the state are subject to challenge and transformation, they wish to know how best to understand state formations. They do so by locating the place of "the state" in various political economy traditions, concluding with their own version of the themes "production, space, and identity" within the new Canadian political economy.

Janine Brodie is one of Canadian political economy's foremost authorities on politics and spacial questions as author of *The Political*

Economy of Canadian Regionalism and co-author of *Crisis, Challenge and Change: Party and Class in Canada Revisited.* She addresses, in chapter 11, the "where" questions about how accounts of territory and province are constructed as being contentious not only for political economy but in geographic, economic, political, cultural, and ideological terms. She critically evaluates geographic accounts and those based on federalism and institutions. Instead, she builds on the insights of Innis and Vernon Fowke. Brodie uses the device of "national policies" to periodize spatial relations, including the current era of "hemispheric economic integration" and its attendant implications for provinces and the federal state. She develops the theme of the erosion of the welfare state, which is picked up as well in the chapters by Salter and Salter and by Bakker and Scott. The transfer of debt load is weakening the provinces by reducing transfers from the federal level for primary health and education, leaving the provinces to do less with less. Balkanization and a diminished role of the state become themes in this new Canadian reality.

William D. Coleman, author of *The Independence Movement in Quebec 1945–1980,* and Daniel Salée, co-author of *The Shaping of Quebec Politics and Society*, take on the long-standing "Quebec question" in an original and provocative chapter (12). They document the building of a "counter paradigm" in Quebec since the "Quiet Revolution," beginning in 1960. Key elements have included development of a francophone business class, a large public sector, and a strong, independent labour movement. A central issue has been the creation of social space through struggles over the politics of language. This "counter paradigm" has been characterized by the authors as a movement from a "nationality" to a "society" – that is, from identification as French Canadians to identification as Québécois, challenging the "place" of Quebec within a confederation of "equal" provinces under the rubric of a multicultural Canada.

Salée and Coleman tie their analysis to the diminishing of federal powers through the collapse of the Keynesian welfare state, which was once used to redistribute wealth (see chapter 13, by Bakker and Scott), and implimentation of international trade agreements as part of capitalist transformation (as discussed by Macdonald in chapter 8). These developments have led to the regime of accumulation based on unregulated continentalism and monetarism adopted by the Parti Québécois in a kinder, gentler form not possible by a crippled federal state. In Quebec, as the counter-paradigm argument goes, a more solidaristic social formation can produce social democracy, especially through employment policies, only under sovereignty. Salée and Coleman challenge the gap between social-democratic promises and actual welfare-state erosion, identifying a series of "unresolved issues" for a sovereign Quebec. They provide some original, new visions of Quebec and its future, tackling the issue of competing identities in the context of both sovereigntist and globalizing forces, including an insightful look at immigrant experiences relevant to the discussion by Stasiulis.

Isabella Bakker, editor of *The Strategic Silence: Gender and Economic Policy*, and Katherine Scott, a doctoral candidate in York University's Political Science Department, write in chapter 13 about the welfare state within the comparative political economy tradition by locating Canada in the context of other welfare states and how they have been transformed since the Second World War. They evaluate the Keynesian welfare state as a set of economic, political, and social policies for development in liberal democracies – that is, seeing the state as moderating and guiding market-driven levels of unemployment and consumption through fiscal policy. The chapter sketches the evolution of the Canadian welfare state and provides a clear account of the principles for eligibility and coverage contained in various programs. They see Canada as a liberal welfare regime, but more uneven than other liberal states, given its (until now) strong universal public education and health insurance provisions. The authors make insightful observations about the gendered nature of the welfare state and address the current debate about the fate of Canada's welfare state. They not only describe but offer an explanation for the way the welfare state's transformation can be understood. Their account leads directly into the next chapter.

Liora Salter has been an activist concerning standards and regulations and is the author of *Mandated Science*, and Rick Salter is a lawyer who has long been a participant in struggles for Yukon and BC Aboriginal self-government. Chapter 14 contends that the welfare state is being replaced by regulatory boards and agencies as a reconstituted infrastructure. They examine five traditional areas of state activity infused by new regulatory regimes (often characterized as "deregulation") – namely, the environment, broadcasting, telecommunications, standards, and medicine, plus an alternative example of Native self-government. From these cases they draw some directions and identification of forces affecting the welfare state. Specifically, they analyse how the state operates in various "markets" and the "new international reality" – that is, how the Canadian state is transforming itself with "globalization." They contrast North American and European experiences with new regulatory forms. The main contrast, however, is a detailed analysis of the process and participants in Aboriginal self-government and Yukon land- claims negotiations. They look to the future in terms of prospects and possibilities, raising complex issues of participation, process, and interests. These are classic concerns of democracy in the wider sense used by C.B. Macpherson, including the role of elected officials, independent regulators, and those who are deemed to be "participants" or "interests" identified with the issues. Salter and Salter provide an innovative account that contests the public-private divide of state and civil society so important for most political economists.

Ted Magder's contribution (chapter 15) extends the article he wrote on communications in *The New Canadian Political Economy*, also raising the issues of democracy and participation in public discourse. He is the author of *Canada's Hollywood: The Canadian State and Feature Films*. Magder situates his chapter in the historical development of the press in Canada and discusses the traditional political economy issues of ownership and processes governing major media outlets, including their implications for content, covering newspapers, television, cable, and film. But he examines more than the "ownership and control" of mega-media complexes. He also addresses the commodification of culture and the influence of advertising, both linked to issues of regulation (as do Salter and Salter in their chapter). Magder looks at the future of rapidly changing technologies of communications and their implications for democratic practices of access and diversity.

David Whitson and Richard Gruneau, authors of *Hockey Night in Canada: Sport, Identities, and Cultural Politics*, examine popular culture spectacles in chapter 16. Leisure and entertainment have become vast transnational "service" industries, with an importance for consumption. Whitson and Gruneau situate their political economy vis-à-vis cultural studies and the importance of their perspective for theory. Their empirical focus is on sports industries and their professionalization, commercialization, and conglomeration. North American popular culture has produced an enormous market, with its own draw, demands, and political-economic logic. There is a vast network of franchising and close connection with the media. Whitson and Gruneau examine the relationship between public subsidies and private ownership, especially concerning facilities, whereby municipalities are compelled to compete continentally for teams. They analyse particularly how these forms of consumption are embedded in contemporary Canadian political economy, and their ideological implications. This chapter is a most welcome expansion of political economy's earlier boundaries.

Taking in a different direction the theme of space explored in several earlier chapters, as well as issues of culture and the environment, Iain Wallace and Rob Shields deal in chapter 17 with resource over-exploitation and the limits to nature. They note changes in popular perceptions of the environment and its elevation to a "moral social space." The chapter offers an account of why the new environmentalism arose in the late 1980s and how "sustainable development" priorities were elevated to the national and international levels. Popular views on the environment have brought them more in line with those of Native peoples, who have been key actors in projecting the environment into political economy – through, for example, the Berger Inquiry and James Bay resistance. The environment has become a new site of resistance. "Nature" is an object of resource exploitation, a value in itself for environmentalists, and a homeland for Native people. The authors locate the environment within theories of the state, capitalism, and social movements, understanding the environment as a material reality that is threatened in its reproduction both immediately and in the long term.

Whither the new Canadian political economy? The chapters that readers are about to encounter speak well to the variety and vibrancy of this tradition. It has not become doctrinaire or bogged down in dead-end debates, nor has it settled into an intellectual corner to develop its own orthodoxy. Instead, it has become appropriated into traditional disciplines and been a major promoter of interdisciplinary dialogue. It has become part of the discourse of public-policy advocates and been popularized by such fine journalists as Linda McQuaig in books such as *The Quick and the Dead, The Wealthy Banker's Wife,* and *Shooting the Hippo?* Feminism, environmentalism, and cultural studies have all "challenged" political economy over the past decade. Political economy has not repelled these challenges so much as it has been transformed by them, to become richer and more interdisciplinary. And the traditional disciplines, at their best, have welcomed political economy streams into their folds. The notable exception may be most economics departments, but increasingly we find acceptance by more economists in other academic units, such as international affairs, public administration, history, communications, social work, women's studies, and Canadian studies. The most interdisciplinary of economists are drawn out of economics departments. The more common instance, however, is in departments such as geography, political science, and sociology, where political economy has become a core stream within the discipline.

Are there material conditions at the base of political economy's intellectual relevance? One would think so. As corporations restructure, governments cut back, and the international economy transforms, there is wider and greater demand to understand the forces at work, to comprehend their implications, and develop strategies to change them in ways that put people, as bearers of society and culture, first.

NOTES

1 The initial revival is documented in Clement and Drache, compilers, *Practical Guide.*

2 Consolidation of the new Canadian political economy tradition is evident in Drache and Clements, eds., *The New Practical Guide*, and Clement and Williams, eds., *The New Canadian Political Economy*. See Marchak's remarkably insightful "Canadian Political Economy" for the origins and practices to that time, with special reference to the debates, critiques, and puzzles in the tradition, and Mahon's conceptualization in "New Canadian Political Economy."

3 Ehrensaft and Armstrong, "Formation of Dominion Capitalism."

4 Laxer, *Open for Business.*

5 Clement and Myles, *Relations of Ruling.*

6 Watkins, "A Staple Theory of Economic Growth."

7 Watkins, "The Staple Theory Revisited."

8 Watkins, "Innis Tradition."

REFERENCES

Albo, Greg, Langille, David, and Panitch, Leo, eds. *A Different Kind of State? Popular Power and Democratic Administration.* Toronto: Oxford University Press, 1993.

Clement, Wallace, and Drache, Daniel, compilers. *A Practical Guide to Canadian Political Economy.* Toronto: James Lorimer and Company, 1978.

Clement, Wallace, and Williams, Glen, eds. *The New Canadian Political Economy.* Montreal: McGill-Queen's University Press, 1989.

Clement, Wallace, and Myles, John. *Relations of Ruling: Class and Gender in Postindustrial Societies.* Montreal: McGill-Queen's University Press, 1994.

Drache, Daniel, and Clement, Wallace, eds. *The New Practical Guide to Canadian Political Economy.* Toronto: James Lorimer and Company, 1985.

Ehrensaft, Philip, and Armstrong, Warwick. "The Formation of Dominion Capitalism: Economic Truncation and Class Structure." In *Inequality: Essays on the Political Economy of Social Welfare.* A. Moscovitch and G. Drover, eds. Toronto: University of Toronto Press, 1981.

Laxer, Gordon. *Open for Business: The Roots of Foreign Ownership in Canada.* Toronto: University of Toronto Press, 1989.

Mahon, Rianne. "The 'New' Canadian Political Economy Revisited: Production Space, Identity." In J. Jenson, R. Mahon, and F. Bienefeld, eds., *Production Space, Identity: Political Economy Faces the 21st Century.* Toronto: Canadian Scholars' Press, 1993.

Marchak, Patricia. "Canadian Political Economy." In *Canadian Review of Sociology and Anthropology*, 22 no. 5 (1985), 673–709.

Watkins, Mel. "The Innis Tradition in Canadian Political Economy." In
   Canadian Journal of Political and Social Theory 6 (Winter–Spring 1982), 12–34.
– "A Staple Theory of Economic Growth." In *Canadian Journal of Economics and
   Political Science,* 29 (May 1963), 141–58.
– "The Staple Theory Revisited." In *Journal of Canadian Studies,* 12 (Winter
   1977), 83–95.

2 Canadian Capitalism in Transition

MEL WATKINS

Why are some countries rich, some countries poor, and others in between? Why, even in the rich countries, are some years good, with the economy booming, and other years bad, with the economy stagnating or even falling back? These matters have concerned the great political economists, from Adam Smith in the eighteenth century to Karl Marx in the nineteenth to John Maynard Keynes and Joseph Schumpeter in the twentieth.

As well, countries grow and suffer crises in different ways – not totally different, of course, but at least somewhat. In the best of circumstances, the result will be an indigenous political economy tradition that grasps the nettle of that distinctiveness. Such has been the Canadian experience, from the old political economy earlier this century, led by Harold Adams Innis and W.A. Mackintosh, to the new political economy of recent years, with myriad contributors.[1]

Questions abound. Canada is a rich country, unambiguously so by global standards (which does not mean that there are no poor people in Canada, for there are many – indeed, indefensibly so, given that overall level of affluence). How did it get that way? Canada is noted for the abundance of its natural resources, or staples, and its reliance on their export. Has that situation given a particular character, or specificity, to the economy, while providing an important clue as to how growth has taken place, at least initially and perhaps even down to the present day? (How much does history count? How much does an economy's condition depend on where it was? In fact, economists who study economic growth do talk increasingly about "path dependency.")

Staple exports have tended to set the pace for the economy, sometimes fast and sometimes slow. How have different staples left their distinctive stamp on Canadian society?

Canada is an industrialized country: its prime minister is allowed to attend the prestigious annual economic summit of the seven leading industrial nations of the world. But does the flip side of the staples cast of the Canadian economy give it the least-rounded industrial structure of the seven? (The now-defunct Science Council of Canada called the nation's industrial structure "truncated" and was abolished for such frank talk.)

Canadian political economists since Innis have been at pains to expose the branch-plant character of this pattern of dependent industrialization. The means of production in Canada are predominantly in private hands, but many of those hands are foreign. Canada is a capitalist country, and its capitalist, or business, class is dominant. But what is the nature of that class? Is it predominantly commercial or industrial? independent or dependent?

A striking feature of the half-century of economic history since the Depression and Second World War, both globally and in Canada, is the long boom of the 1950s and 1960s down into the 1970s and the generalized crisis thereafter. Political economists in general, and the Canadian practitioners in particular, have been much preoccupied with this phenomenon. There have for years been those (such as the Russian economist N.D. Kondratieff and Joseph Schumpeter) who saw such long waves, of some fifty to sixty years, going back to Britain's Industrial Revolution more than two centuries ago.[2] Mackintosh's post-Confederation economic history of Canada was premised on recurring booms and crises associated with the changing fortunes of staples exploitation[3] – what Innis graphically called "cyclonics." The question for the nineties: is the last crisis over, or has the next boom begun?

STAPLE THEORY OF ECONOMIC GROWTH

Canada was founded in the modern period of history as an offshoot of Europe; the Aboriginal people were already present, of course, but their rights were respected only to the extent that the imperial and, in the long run, settlers' interests were served. Though initially merely an impediment on the route to the rumoured riches of Cathay, Canada soon came to be valued in its own right for its resources (fish, fur, and so on), which were exported to the mother country, first France and later Britain; an industrializing Britain, for its part, was able to export its surpluses of manufactures, capital, and people. These self-evident truths are the building blocks of a staple theory of economic growth relevant to Canada (and to other new countries/regions, notably the American colonies, Australia, New Zealand, and, with modifications, South Africa, the Caribbean, and Latin America).

Economic growth is a process by which one thing leads to another – or fails to do so.[4] The export of a staple has potential spread effects or linkages to other sectors at home (at the margin) or abroad (at the metropolitan centre). The staple can be subjected to further processing or manufacturing, such as fur into hats or wheat into flour; these are forward linkages. Inputs can be produced for use by the staple sector. Such backward linkages can be further subdivided into infrastructure (railways to move wheat) and capital goods (mining machinery). The building of infrastructure in its turn can then have further and powerful spread effects, potentially exceeding the original linkage from the staple itself and leading to pervasive industrialization; the central importance of Canadian railways for both staple production and industrialization has long been understood.[5]

The disposition of the incomes generated in the export sector creates final demand linkage. It too can be further subdivided, into consumption (spending on a range of consumer goods, from cotton textiles to colour television sets) and fiscal linkage (appropriation by the state of economic rent or surplus generated in the resource sector, over and above all costs, including a normal return to capital, and *its* disposition). Eric Kierans's estimates of the massive rents generated by metal mining in Manitoba, captured mostly by foreign owners rather than by the provincial state, and the contrasting reality of the Alberta Heritage Fund, accumulated from economic rents in oil and gas, show the potential of this fiscal linkage to creation of further linkages. As well, the failure of the state to capture rents may simply mean that private capital becomes sloppy and inefficient and fails to generate them.[6]

Growth of a more diversified character around the export base will be facilitated by the availability of labour via immigration and of capital via borrowing. Demand for the staple sets the pace, but the extent to which economic growth takes place around it depends as well on supply responses, both institutional and technological. Alexander Dow, after detailed research on the metal-mining industry, finds "Canadian entrepreneurship and innovation without which the industry would not, most likely, have succeeded as it did." John Fogarty, drawing on the historical experiences of Argentina and Australia as well as Canada, likewise argues against the demand bias of the staple theory, insisting that it is entrepreneurship, both private and public, that counts. Carl Solberg's careful comparison of the wheat economies of Canada and Argentina demonstrates that it is public entrepreneurship – government policies on agricultural research and education, rail transportation, and the grading, storing, and marketing of wheat – that enabled Canada to reap the larger benefits in the long run.[7]

In all cases – and not only with respect to fiscal linkage – responses can be the result not only of the operation of markets but also of state policies, both at the margin and at the centre, which can help or hurt. These state policies in their turn can be powerfully conditioned by the specific social formations that emanate from exploitation of specific staples. Hence, for example, the family farm in the Canadian prairies, itself a consequence of government homestead policy, facilitated the cooperative movement and the agrarian protest politics that then pushed the government in positive ways.

It is helpful to be more explicit about the spatial dimension in two senses – namely, whether linkages are reaped at home or abroad, and whether by domestic or foreign capital. First, how much production takes place locally? Second, of that local production, how much is controlled by local capitalists and how much by external capitalists? The first issue concerns the quantity of production and the extent of growth; the second, the extent of indigenous ownership and control – that is, the independence and maturity of the resulting capitalist development.[8]

In forward linkage, resources can be processed at the point either of production or of consumption (or even at somewhere in between, as in the case of bauxite, which is processed where electric power is cheap). Encouragement to process resources within Canada has been called "the manufacturing condition"; it has been consciously pursued by provincial governments, from Ontario's "little National Policy" in the late nineteenth and early twentieth centuries to Alberta's "province-building" in the postwar years.[9] A recurring theme in the Canadian literature is the limited nature of forward linkages. Canada has persistently tended to export relatively unprocessed resources and certainly shown no ability to make a quantum leap from supplying a range of critical inputs for industrialization to having an advanced industrial structure.[10]

It seems reasonable to infer that foreign ownership of the resource industry will exacerbate the tendency of forward linkages to be weak, particularly when the foreign owner is a vertically integrated corporation using the resource as an input into its metropolitan operations. Perhaps the most striking example of weak and ineffectual linkage – actually of all linkages – is Sudbury, long the site of some of the the world's richest nickel mines but now dependent for jobs on a government decision to locate the processing of tax returns there.

Backward linkage and, above all, consumption linkage define a range of market demands. In the nature of things – mostly transport costs – from the outset some, even many, of these opportunities will lead to home production in the new country. But also in the nature of things – the newness of the hinterland and the politics of the imperial connection, which favours industry at the centre over that at the margin – there will be substantial reliance on imports at the outset, for manufactures in general and for more sophisticated goods such as machinery in particular. The greater the leakage into imports, the less the growth locally around the export base.

The propensity to import capital goods may persist indefinitely. The reliance on substantial imports of machinery down to the present day – even in the mining sector, where Canada has been a major producer for a century – brands Canada's industrial structure as not fully developed.

Within the broader manufacturing sector, the process of import substitution tends to proceed inexorably as local producers try to pre-empt markets defined by imports; this switch to domestic sourcing is actually facilitated by the import houses themselves. It is to be expected that manufacturers will further attempt to aid and abet that process by resort to protection. The resulting tariff is no aberration and, notwithstanding orthodox economic theorizing, has its benefits. It enhances consumption linkage and, with supplies of labour and capital available from abroad, accelerates the overall growth of the economy. Historically, the tariff not only had this protectionist effect in Canada, it also generated higher revenues during periods such as the early-twentieth-century export boom, when significant volumes of imports continued; these revenues were then used to build more railways, which generated further rounds of linkage effects. The tariff, then, also contributes to growth via fiscal linkage and infrastructure linkage. (There really was no end to the process: railways built through solid rock in outlandish places in northern Ontario led to discoveries of minerals faster than would otherwise have been the case, unleashing yet further linkages. One should not underestimate the role of luck in economic history.)[11]

There was yet one further consequence of the tariff that links our two spatial dimensions. Unable to export to Canada, some foreign producers, particularly from the United States, jumped the high tariff wall after 1879 and set up branch plants in Canada. To that extent, Canada got industrial production – beyond that which it already had from the 1850s on – but not under the control of indigenous Canadian capital; it got its own industry, but not, to the same extent, its own industrial capitalists; it industrialized, but dependently and incompletely. The propensity of branch plants to import parts lessened linkage effects.

It would be wrong, however, to attribute this situation simply to the tariff. The tariff made it more attractive for foreign capital to come to

Canada, but it can hardly be credited with creating the fresh, expansionist urges of foreign capital. (The next section melds this aspect of capitalist development into the story of staples growth, to explain how a staples economy comes to be characterized by dependent industrialization and a comprador business class.)

Conceptually, what is described to this point is centrally a modified Keynesian, macro model of economic growth, in which exports rather than domestic investment are the leading sector; so, too, exports are the leading source of instability. Mackintosh grasped this point early on and by marrying staple theory and Keynesian theory provided the rationale for Canada's post–Second World War strategy of economic growth (see below). In effect, a National Policy, which used the tariff to increase linkage effects from staple exports, was stood on its head; if Canada wanted assured access to foreign markets for its exports (largely staples) it had to provide easier access into its domestic market for imports. Canada became a leader in pushing for liberalized trade, albeit at the risk of entrenching its staple status.[12]

A persistent theme in the writings of the new political economists is that there are two variants of the staples thesis – a more optimistic version (going back to Mackintosh) of growth around a staples export base, culminating in a mature diversified economy, and a more pessimistic version (going back to Innis) of staples exploitation generating "rigidities" that reproduce economic vulnerability and dependence.[13] While it is possible to overstate the difference between Innis and Mackintosh (and lose the nuances in both), the point at issue is crucial: how mature has the Canadian economy become? Can it still sensibly be described as a staples economy?

In fact, these queries beg a prior question that must be frankly faced: to what extent does the emphasis on staples capture the totality of the Canadian growth experience since the beginning? The answer is that there has always been much by way of "local growth" that escaped the net, but staples such as fish and fur "dominated" the early economic history of Canada.[14] The economy of what is today Canada has been from its Euro-Canadian beginnings an integral part of a larger North Atlantic economy and has tended to grow and fluctuate with it;[15] the edge that has made the difference (good and bad) has been the varying fate of the staple trades and industries. Yesterday's "local growth" (home production for home markets) has become, in the modern era of free trade, export-dependent manufacturing and service industries (a point to be dealt with below). Comparatively, Canada has done better than staples-biased economies such as Argentina and Australia, in part because of an abundant endowment of hydro-electric potential and fossil fuels, plus the ability to shift from agricultural staples such as wheat to industrial staples such as minerals and news-print.[16]

Still, a recent overview of Canadian political economy, after citing the apparent importance of manufacturing and tertiary activities, con-cludes:

This is not to say that the Canadian economy is now any less reliant on natural resource–based production to generate its wealth than it was in the past. Much of Canada's manufacturing base consists of processing resource–based com-modities such as lumber, pulp and paper, and various mineral and oil-based products ... In all, resource and resource-based activities generate as much as fifty cents out of every dollar produced in this country. This continued reliance of the Canadian economy on primary resources and resource-based manufac-turing puts it at odds with the situation in many other large nation-states and has important consequences for the operation of the Canadian political econ-omy.[17]

The new political economy is arguably a marriage of Innis and Marx, of staples and class.[18] The staples bias affects the capitalist class (as we see below); it also affects the rest of the class structure. A distinction must be made between the earlier staples – trades – and the later ones – industries.[19] The direct producers in the staple trades are not a work-ing class, or proletariat proper, but independent commodity produc-ers, varying from Indian bands in the days of the fur trade to family farmers producing wheat. Conflict takes place around the terms of the exchange of the staple for trade-goods and interest paid on debts incurred by the direct producers; surplus is appropriated by capital via mechanisms of unequal exchange. The protest movements of western grain farmers are ample evidence of these conflicts, from which flowed important political and economic effects. In contrast, the staple indus-tries, such as mining and newsprint production, are industries proper, with workers who are paid a wage over which they typically bargain collectively through a union, with surplus value being appropriated in the customary, Marx-described manner. From these conflicts emerge important consequences for wage structures and hence for living standards and for technological change; as an example, high wages create a larger domestic market for consumer goods while encour-aging labour-saving innovation and (frequently) the import of capital goods.

It should not be forgotten, however, that whether the staple activity is a trade or an industry, capitalism makes the struggle of the direct pro-ducers with capital unequal. Canadian capital has not been able to for-mulate a full-fledged industrial strategy (see below); not surprisingly, neither Canadian farmers nor Canadian workers, separately or together, have been able to assume that task in its stead.[20] The project becomes truly daunting when allowance is made for the divisiveness of the intense regionalism characteristic of the Canadian economy; that regionalism seems to inhere in the strung-out, bi-national Canadian economy, but it is further exacerbated by the uneven development associated with specialization in staples. The result has been, typically, to divide people, or popular forces, more than capital.

The distinction between staple trades and industries can be pushed one step further by examining the consequences for social or class formation of the particular mode of production associated with each staple. Like Innis, one would keep one's eye on the staple and its mode of production and the pervasive consequences; like Marx, one would systematically explore the relationships between the mode of production and class structure.[21] The American development economist Albert Hirschman calls this approach micro-Marxism.[22]

In the process one could, following Hirschman, judge the staples in terms of whether their impact for growth and development have been good or bad. Of course, what happens depends in some part on the environment, physical and political, within which the staple has its impact; fish created both the "aggressive commercialism" (Innis) of New England and the staple trap in which contemporary Newfoundland is mired now that the fish have disappeared (but from which it may be rescued by new staples; see below). As Ommer reminds us in her superb study of the historic Jersey–Gaspé cod fishery, the staple that leaves the colony underdeveloped can create development in the metropole; indeed, as in her case study, the two go together.[23] Still, some staples do seem mostly good from the perspective of the margin (such as wheat and the family farm and the egalitarian society and the progressive politics that flows therefrom),[24] while others seem mostly bad (as with oil, which produces instant, unearned wealth and giant companies and right-wing politics and pollution).[25]

But assessment of goodness or badness also very much depends on where one is situated within the social formation. Consider the fate of Aboriginal peoples. From their perspective it is arguable that only the fur trade has a claim to have treated them tolerably well; all subsequent staples, from wheat to hydro, have taken their home lands and rendered them dysfunctional. Some staples, like hydro megaprojects, may simply be genocidal and intolerable, but others might well be beneficial to Aboriginal peoples if they took place within the context of a land-claims settlement that granted genuine self-governance and created a different institutional framework; the Berger Inquiry in the 1970s can be seen as exploring the possibility that even a giant gas pipeline might be acceptable to the Dene of the Mackenzie Valley under those circumstances.[26]

Consider also the consequences for women of the effects of different staples. In traditional historical writings, including that of the old political economy, women hardly existed, yet we know that Aboriginal women played a key role in the fur trade and that the "family" of the "family farm," which grew the crops for consumption at home and abroad, self-evidently included women and their unpaid labour. As well, the single-industry resource communities that dot the Canadian hinterland (the pulp towns, the mining towns) provide limited opportunities for women to work at well-paying jobs.[27]

DEPENDENT INDUSTRIALIZATION

How does a staples economy come to be characterized by dependent industrialization? Begin with a general argument about early industrialization that has been made with respect to Britain and to continental Europe.[28] There are two paths to industrialization: one that emerges out of artisanal beginnings in the hands of new capitalists, and one based on the extension of pre-existing merchant capital into the new industrial sphere. The first is the strong path, which leads to a mature industrial structure; the second is a weak one, where industrial capital never comes fully to dominate financial capital.

Can this line of reasoning be applied to Canada? There are two problems in doing so. First, Canada's economy was dominated in its pre-industrial phase not simply by commerce and finance but specifically by trade in staples. Second, Canada industrialized later, after capitalism had transformed itself from a competitive mode to a monopoly mode as a result of the rise of the large corporation, including its multinational variant.

Canada ends up on the weak path.[29] Merchant-cum-financial capital remains dominant and tolerates, indeed invites in, foreign industrial capital to produce a weak path of dependent industrialization. Canadian financial capital may even be antagonistic towards indigenous industrial capital. But the critical point is the rise next door of the American industrial corporation; it is born multinational and, as the agent of foreign monopoly capital, creates barriers to entry for smaller, indigenous industrial firms. Previously the technique of the more advanced United States had moved to Canada (or British North America) via the migration of individual American businessmen, who then become permanent residents, even founders of great Canadian families such as the Masseys; now it came in institutional corporate form. The result was to stifle indigenous Canadian development, which, emulating the United States, had been proceeding, with a lag, along the strong path. Canada was shunted onto the weak path. The villain of the piece becomes American industrial capital, though Canadian capital can be seen as an accomplice.

The path of dependent industrialization was, for reasons we have seen, one of import substitution, of producing for the protected domestic market rather than taking on world markets in manufactures. While we may see that as second best, we risk missing the point that Canadian capital pioneered the import substitution industrialization (ISI) model – it is in fact known elsewhere, particularly in Latin America, as the "Canadian model" – and that Canada has done remarkably well out of it in conjunction with the large domestic market associated with a succession of staple exports.[30]

The result is not an alliance within Canada between indigenous financial and industrial capital (creating, in Marxist terminology, finance capital), with industrial capitalists as the dominant, or hegemonic, fraction within the capitalist class. Rather, there is an alliance between Canadian financial capital and American industrial capital. Because of the size and power of the United States, the resulting alliance is (in Clement's felicitous phraseology) an "unequal alliance," with Canadian capital a junior partner. Within Canada, the hegemonic fraction remains financial capital.

This is almost, but not quite, the full story. Because Canada is a staple economy, we should distinguish within industrial capital between staple industries, or primary manufacturing, and secondary manufacturing proper. The former can be, and in fact are, more powerful than the latter. The hegemonic fraction is made up of financial capital and of staple capital, foreign and domestic, which is in alliance with American industrial capital. This "staples fraction," in fact, is disproportionately represented within the Business Council of National Issues (the highly influential organization that consists of the chief executive officers of the 150 largest private-sector corporations) and the structures of the state. As a consequence, the secondary manufacturing interest is weak in Canada, and it is difficult to develop an industrial strategy. Though Canada is industrialized, industry is in important respects immature and the country remains a staples economy – a pattern that has been called "advanced resource capitalism."[31]

Canadian capital has accepted a division of labour both sectorally and geographically. Historically, it has been able to dominate in commerce and finance, including infrastructure and real estate, but not in industry proper. In the staple sector the story is mixed, with the majority of resource industries under foreign control well into the postwar period. In those sectors where capital is able to dominate at home, it will have a base to try to become "world class" and operate abroad. This phenomenon exists in Canada, but the division of labour that constrains Canadian capital is its tendency to see only the American market, not the whole world as its oyster.

There is clearly a close, symbiotic relationship between the nature of the domestic business class and the extent of foreign ownership of the economy; the weaker the former, the stronger the latter, and vice versa. (Canadian policy has been to let the foreigner in to undertake the tasks that Canadian business cannot do; Japan's policy has been not to let the foreigner in until Japanese business has demonstrated that it can compete.) And just as other class forces could not "get their act together" concerning the tariff (see above), neither were they sufficiently strong and united to force Canadian capital to perform better than it did; in explaining the origins and persistence of foreign ownership in Canada, Gordon Laxer indicts the whole Canadian class structure![32]

Foreign ownership became an important political issue in Canada in the 1960s – under the leadership of the Liberal economic nationalist Walter Gordon – and the debates about it were central to the emergence of the new political economy.[33] Yet the ink had hardly dried on this literature when (as we now know) there was a considerable decrease after 1970 in foreign (mostly American) ownership and control of the Canadian economy relative to Canadian ownership and control. This outcome raises the possibility that the Canadian capitalist class is now – and perhaps long has been? – more impressive than some of us have thought.[34]

Canadian ownership within the resource sector has increased (relatively) as domestic capital has been attracted by the large rents that can be appropriated. This development shows some maturing of Canadian capital, but towards becoming more efficient as rentier capital, rather than as industrial capital. Perhaps, as well, Canadian capital became more confident in its dealings with American, as the latter struggled to maintain its international hegemony vis-à-vis Japanese and European capital. While increasing Canadian control in the past quarter-century has mostly been relative to American, it has made Canada a base for continental rather than for global capital. And while dependence via foreign ownership decreased, dependence via trade increased, with the latter definitely rising under free trade and the former no longer falling (see below). In short, Canada did not transcend its staple-biased, semi-industrial status, nor its pervasive Americanization (and all that follows therefrom) in matters economic, political, social, cultural, and military.

Research on Canadian class structure in a comparative context bears out these propositions. Canada's industrial and occupational

composition – with fewer workers in manufacturing and a larger resource proletariat than the average industrialized country – bears the
imprint of truncated development. But Canada has also incorporated
distinctively American practices for the organization of capitalist production, deploying a disproportionate amount of labour power in
control and surveillance of other workers, particularly in sectors traditionally dominated by American capital.[35]

An unexpected vindication of the political economy view of foreign
ownership in particular and the Canadian economy in general is to be
found in the so-called Porter Report, named after Professor Michael
Porter of the Harvard Business School and co-funded by the Business
Council on National Issues and the Mulroney government. The Canadian economy, we are told, has an abnormal bias to the export of
unprocessed resources, a high and increasing reliance on the u.s.
market, a high level of foreign ownership, and a tendency among subsidiaries of foreign firms not to be efficient exporters. The report rec-
ommends policy directed towards transforming subsidiaries into more
autonomous and efficient "home bases"[36] – but the exact opposite
may be happening under free trade (see below).

BOOMS AND CRISES

An important problem facing social scientists and historians, and
hence political economists, is the choice of the proper spatial and temporal units for study. On the spatial dimension, our (materialist) argument relies on the reach of the commodity and the corporation;
the Canadian experience is therefore comprehensible only within a
centre–margin, or imperial frame of reference.[37] With respect to the
temporal dimension, social scientists tend to be almost obsessively
present-minded and uninterested in history, while historians tend to
reify politics, even politicians, or rely on arbitrary periods, such as centuries. Political economists need to take both economics and history
seriously and define politics broadly.

There is merit in relying on long waves as the temporal unit for
study.[38] Just as a fundamental characteristic of capitalism is that it has
developed unevenly over space (centres and margins), another is that
it has unfolded unevenly over time (booms and crises). As well as having shorter recessions and recoveries, the post-1945 experience has
lent new credibility to the view that longer cycles, or long waves, of
boom and crisis, also seem to inhere in the evolution of industrial capitalism. In so far as each phase seems to encapsulate a broad range of
economic, political, and social phenomena that encompasses both
institutions and technology, and to be common to linked economies,

it is highly useful as a discrete entity for the study of political economy.[39]

Take the most recent long wave (which may or may not be over as I write or as you read this). The global boom of the late 1940s, 1950s and 1960s has been called the Golden Years (Hobsbawm) and hailed as the greatest period of economic growth and prosperity in the history of capitalism. The boom was very strong in Canada, being comparable to the great wheat boom that lasted from the mid-1890s to the First World War. It was based on large-scale exports of resources to the United States, with inflows of American capital providing funds to expand staple sectors – including such new staples as oil and gas, iron ore, uranium, and potash – and with markets secured by foreign ownership ties; its essence was neatly captured in the title of a book of that time, Hugh Aitken's *American Capital and Canadian Resources*.[40] Cheap energy, notably oil, fuelled the global boom; Canada, as a major consumer and exporter of energy, stood to gain, whatever the price. Demographically, the "baby boom" and waves of immigration fed consumption and investment.

Both the staples bias of the economy and the pattern of dependent industrialization persisted, though altering in ways beneficial to Canadian economic growth at that time. With the decline of the British Empire, Canada moved wholly into the American empire at a time when the United States was the undisputed hegemonic power of the capitalist world. The close American embrace created clear benefits for Canada, while entrenching its staples status. It also caused some problems, notably in the military and automotive sectors, where imports systematically outran exports. U.S. policy towards Canada, however, was largely benign; special-status arrangements such as the Defense Production Sharing Agreement (DPSA) of 1958 and the Auto Pact (1965) locked Canada into a pattern of dependent industrialization that was nevertheless significantly beneficial to Canada. The DPSA allowed Canada to cash in on the Pentagon spending, magnified by the Vietnam War, that played a key role in the American boom, while the Autopact permitted auto factories in Canada to achieve the economies of scale of the so-called Fordist production model of the postwar world.

Demand-led Keynesianism came to Canada but, notwithstanding its apparent potential to produce greater emphasis on the domestic market as the prime source of growth, did little to alter the staples bias of Canadian economic policy. But in Canada, as elsewhere, it did legitimize a much expanded welfare state (to provide a safety net and to maintain demand and hence employment) and underlay a new accord between capital and labour, in which workers were allowed increased rights to unionize and to share in productivity gains in return for abandoning any radical demands for widespread nationalization or workers' control.

Sometime around 1970 this greatest of booms petered out. Demand for Canadian staples slowed, and the birth rate fell, lessening the demographic push on demand. The United States lost the war in Vietnam and in 1971 had to devalue its dollar; it was no longer the hegemonic power it had been, having to give ground to Germany and Japan industrially and to the Organization of Petroleum Exporting Countries (OPEC) on the setting of the price of oil. The United States could no longer afford to be so benign, even to Canada; in the face of its troubles, Washington, as part of its broader policy of detente, first gave Canada more room to manoeuvre in the 1970s – leading to the modest economic nationalism of the Trudeau era – and then, with Reagan and the new Cold War, forced Canada to abandon such policies in the 1980s.[41] With the election of the Mulroney government in the mid-80s, Canada was ready to "buy into" the U.S. neo-conservative agenda of free trade and no economic nationalism.

The pressure from workers to increase both their wages and the social wage (the benefits of the welfare state) while companies tried to maintain their profit rates and the well-to-do their privileged position led to inflation that persisted even in recessionary times; the resulting "stagflation" broke the Keynesian compromise. The leap in globalization that resulted from the long boom increased the mobility of capital – both lessening the ability of any national state to tax it and pushing up interest rates in order to prevent its flight. But labour remained mostly immobile and the state retained its ability to tax it. At the same time, workers in high-wage countries such as Canada were increasingly subjected to low-wage competition from abroad.

The good times for the many were over. Recessions became deeper and longer. Unemployment became persistent, and inflation was kept under control by the threat, and reality, of its increase. First, the private sector "down-sized" – a process greatly facilitated by the burgeoning electronic technology; in the new post-Fordist world of flexible specialization, economies of scale were replaced by economies of scope, pyramidal structures tended to erode, and there was devastation in labour markets. Second, in the face of accumulating deficits and debt consequent on the poor performance of the private sector, the public sector shrank and began to dismantle the welfare state. From the 1980s into the 1990s, a new, right-wing consensus emerged, insisting that if the "fundamentals" were put right (in all senses of that term), the economy could again prosper.[42]

Less writing has been done on prior long waves in Canada, but enough is known to suggest their existence and the value of further study of them. Three prior long waves have been detected since Britain's Industrial Revolution: good years from the 1780s to c. 1815 and bad ones to c. 1850; a good phase from c. 1850 to the early 1870s and a bad one thereafter to the mid-1890s; and good years from the mid-1890s to the First World War and bad ones until the Second World War. For Canada, the second and third waves seem to have applied. The boom of the 1850s, associated with exports of lumber and wheat and the building of railways, marked the beginning of real industrialization in British North America, while the Canadian economy slowed perceptibly in the 1870s and 1880s and into the 1890s, awaiting settlement of the west and the surge of prairie wheat exports. With the turn of the century came the wheat boom and the Klondike Gold Rush, floods of capital and people and railways galore, and a major surge in industrialization. The interwar years were troubled times, from the uncertainties of the 1920s to the Depression of the 1930s, as Canada made the difficult adjustment from the "old industrialism" of coal and iron, wheat and railways, to the "new industrialism" of oil and autos, hydro, newsprint, and minerals.[43] And then the last long wave – and the question: is it over?

THE SITUATION TODAY

By the early 1980s, the Canadian economy seemed to have reached an impasse. Its staple bias and dependent, often inefficient industrial structure were impossible to ignore. Keynesian policy was passé. The Trudeau government toyed with post-Keynesian policies, not only of wage and price controls, but also of an activist energy policy and industrial strategy. Free-market, neo-conservative policies had triumphed in Britain under Margaret Thatcher and in the United States under Ronald Reagan. With the election of the first Mulroney government in 1984 they came to Canada.

The core of right-wing policies in Canada was free trade, first the Canada–United States Free Trade Agreement of 1989 and then the North American Free Trade Agreement of 1993. Sold as an industrial strategy that would make Canadian manufacturing efficient, it may well be entrenching the staples status of the Canadian economy. The removal of barriers to trade permits each country to pursue more fully its comparative advantage. For Canada, already strong sectors (such as staples) grow further, while weak sectors (such as secondary manufacturing) shrink. Certainly the latter has happened, though a good part of that has to be attributed to the serious recession of the early 1990s and a misguided monetary policy that led to an overvalued Canadian dollar. Significantly, bilateral trade disputes between the United States and Canada, which were supposed to go away, have not. American interests still try to block rising resource imports from Canada. Predictably, the volume of two-way trade has taken a quantum leap upwards.

Cross-border investment flows have likewise increased; the two-decade decline in the level of foreign (American) ownership of the Canadian economy seems to have ended. American-based multinationals have tended to meld their previously separate Canadian production operations into a u.s.-based North American division; head offices of subsidiaries have been shut down in Canada, and jobs lost. Overall, the Canadian economy has been further and decisively integrated into the American economy; the result has been an increased economic dependence of Canada on the United States that may result in greater political and cultural dependence.

In the face of its declining hegemony globally, the United States has moved to increase its hegemony continentally and now hemispherically; Canada is almost certainly more tightly tied than before. At the same time, greater continental economic integration has increased strains on the Canadian federation by increasing the potential for separate regions to "go it alone"; free trade has arguably advanced the cause of Quebec separatism.

If staples remain critical for Canada's fate, we need to know the prospects for staples. Resource "megaprojects" – significantly, the word is a Canadianism – seem to be facing increasing objection from environmentalists and Aboriginal peoples; James Bay II is a case in point. There has also been some concern that the best Canadian resources have been found and the Third World is the new frontier,[44] but recent years have seen discoveries of vast amounts of nickel-cobalt-copper in Labrador, of diamonds in the Northwest Territories, and of Hibernia-like oil-fields off the west coast of Newfoundland.

The era of the Keynesian consensus – of the Keynesian welfare state (KWS for short; actually, the "w" does double-duty, standing also for warfare) – is dead. What is taking its place? It is apparently being replaced, according to the British writer Bob Jessop, by the Schumpeterian workfare state (SWS).[45] For Schumpeter, entrepreneurship and innovation were central to economic growth. They were the creative side of the "creative destruction" that inhered in the process of capitalist development; "competitiveness," the buzz-word of our times, conjures up both the good (the drive for efficiency) and the bad ("down-sizing" and low-wage competition). Keynesianism legitimized larger, positive government; Schumpeterianism delegitimized government. Keynesianism was consistent with assistance for the unemployed and the poor; Schumpeterianism wants to replace "welfare" with "workfare."

If that is indeed what is happening, the emerging arrangement is hardly a thing of beauty.[46] But that is not the crux of the matter. Rather: will it work? Is the world economy stable in the absence of a hegemon? Is the story of the mid-1990s the collapse of the Mexican peso, or the fact that the collapse was contained? Has the inflation that destroyed the KWS finally been brought under control?[47] If that has been done by permanently driving up unemployment, then how does the SWS deal with that? If income distribution becomes more unequal, will there be enough purchasing power to buy the cornucopia of goods? Will the SWS deliver enough of the goods to enough of the people to be viable long enough to constitute another long boom? (A question for the student reader: are your job prospects becoming more or less miserable?) Beyond all this, is it possible that the computer is an innovation on a par with the printing press, with effects that will hardly be sorted out quickly? Is it also possible that the environmental consequences of past industrial growth have already begun to place limits on further economic growth?

As for Canada, the historian Donald Creighton wrote a long time ago of "the embarrassments peculiar to a staples-producing economy." The moral of this chapter is that we have hardly seen the last of those. Still, we must not overstate our problems; as too many people in this world know, there are fates much worse than embarrassment.

NOTES

1 For a collection of Innis's writings, see Drache, ed., *Staples*. For Mackintosh, see in particular Mackintosh "Economic Factors" and *Economic Background*. The bibliography of the present volume, with its predominance of items published since 1970, is a testament to the size of the new political economy.

2 The great Marxist historian Eric Hobsbawm has organized his brilliant new book on the twentieth century, *Age of Extremes*, around these waves. He writes: "[A] succession of 'long waves' of about half a century in length has formed the basic rhythm of the economic history of capitalism since the late eighteenth century" (p. 268).

3 Mackintosh, *Economic Background*.

4 See my "Staple Theory of Economic Growth."

5 The concepts of forward and backward linkage were first put forward by Hirschman in his *Strategy*. He updated these concepts – identifying infrastructure linkage, plus others noted below – in "A Generalized Linkage Approach." On the dual contribution of railways to Canadian economic development, see in particular Pentland, *Labour and Capital*.

6 The distinction between consumption and fiscal linkages is made by Hirschman in "Approach." For Kierans's work, see his *Report,* prepared for Manitoba's NDP government and, regrettably, now out of print. The failure of rents even to be generated in the absence of a proper tax-and-royalty regime is a point made in Gunton's "Manitoba's Nickel Industry."

7 I played down this supply-side dimension in my "A Staple Theory." Dow has been diligent in correcting this omission in his writing on metal mining. For the quote, see his "Prometheus in Canada." See also Fogarty, "Staples," and Solberg, *The Prairies and the Pampas.*

8 In "Approach," Hirschman makes a different distinction between inside linkage (further activity undertaken by those already in the original activity) and outside linkage (by newcomers or those outside the existing activity).

9 See Nelles, *The Politics of Development,* and Pratt, "The State and Province-Building."

10 See research done under the auspices of the Science Council of Canada: Bourgault, *Innovation.*

11 Hirschman ("Approach") refers to the tariff in the export-led economy as indirect fiscal linkage. Of contemporary writers, Naylor has been particularly conscious of the revenue effects of the National Policy tariffs; in the past, so were Mackintosh and Innis.

12 See Mackintosh, "Canadian Economic Policy." Mackintosh's role in bringing Keynes's ideas to Canada has been emphasised by David Wolfe in his writings on the politics of postwar Canadian economic development; see in particular "The Delicate Balance," chap. 5.

13 See especially the voluminous writings of Drache on Innis, notably "Harold Innis"; the most recent is his "Introduction" to Drache, ed., *Staples.* See also Spry, "Overhead Costs."

14 See Harris, "Preface."

15 This point has largely escaped Canada's historians who write as if Canada were a self-contained entity; perhaps the major moral of the staples approach – where Canada is necessarily a margin to an imperial centre – is that Canadian history cannot usefully be written that way.

16 Schedvin, "Staples."

17 Howlett and Ramesh, *Political Economy.*

18 For an attempt to reduce Canadian political economy to Marx alone, see McNally, "Staple Theory" and "Technological Determinism." The two articles fail to generate a single fresh insight about Canadian political economy. For a reply to McNally's first article, see Parker, "Commodity Fetishism."

19 The distinction is to be found in Innis; for its fuller articulation, see Phillips, "Staples."

20 For an analysis of such problems associated with the tariff in the earlier period, see Craven and Traves, "Class Politics." In general see Gordon Laxer, *Open for Business.*

21 This is precisely what Clement has done in his studies on nickel mining (*Hardrock Mining*) and the fisheries (*The Struggle to Organize*).

22 Hirschman, "Approach."

23 Ommer, *From Outpost to Outport*. Ommer has also contrasted the "success" of Iceland around fish with the relative "failure" of Newfoundland in her "What's Wrong?"

24 See my "Wheat."

25 As I write (summer 1995), there are stories in the press about how, with oil prices falling, the "oil-rich superpower" of Nigeria, "riddled with corruption," is "a nation committing suicide."

26 See in particular Waldram, *As Long*; Watkins, "From Underdevelopment to Development"; and Berger, *Northern Frontier*.

27 See in particular Fox, "Women's Role"; Van Kirk, "*Many Tender Ties*"; Cohen, "*Women's Work*"; and Luxton, *More*.

28 Notably by the Marxist historian Maurice Dobb in *Studies*.

29 There are two main writers on this matter, R.T. Naylor and Wallace Clement. While there are differences between them, together they are responsible for the Naylor-Clement thesis, which is the idea that launched the new Canadian political economy. Of the voluminous writings of each of these authors, see in particular Naylor, *History*, 2 vols., and Clement, *Continental Corporate Power*.

30 Williams, *Not for Export*.

31 The term is Drache's; see his "Staple-ization." See also Mahon, *Politics*; Langille, "The Business Council" and Atkinson and Coleman, *The State*.

32 Laxer, *Open for Business*.

33 See Canada, Privy Council Office, *Foreign Ownership* (Watkins Report), prepared under the tutelage of Walter Gordon; and Levitt, *Silent Surrender*.

34 See Niosi, "The Canadian Bourgeoisie"; Carroll, *Corporate Power*; and Resnick, "Maturing."

35 This paragraph is a précis, mostly in the authors' words, of Black and Myles, "Dependent Industrialization"; see also Clement and Myles, *Relations*, particularly chap. 4.

36 Porter and Monitor Co., *Canada*.

37 The subtitle of Innis's *The Cod Fisheries* is *The History of an International Economy*.

38 See Gordon, Edwards, and Reich, *Segmented Work*. especially chap. 2.

39 This is what F.W. Burton had in mind when he wrote, in 1934: "In Canada … we must think of business fluctuations not simply as 'credit cycles', that is, as rhythmic and purely monetary phenomena, but also as chapters in our national economic development" ("The Business Cycle," 144.)

40 See also Clark-Jones, *A Staple State*.

41 Clarkson, *Canada*.

42 There is a large literature on the postwar long wave. See in particular Wolfe, "Rise" and "Crisis"; Campbell, *Grand Illusions*; Strain and Grant, "Social

Structure"; Jenson, " 'Different' "; Drache and Glasbeek, *The Changing Workplace*, particularly chap. 2; and McBride, *Not Working*, especially chap. 3.

43 The terms are Innis's. For the post-Confederation period to the 1930s, see Mackintosh, *Economic Background* and "Economic Factors"; for the longer period see Maurice Lamontagne, *Business Cycles*, particularly chap. 4. See Burton ("The Business Cycle"): "The expansion of staple production and of transportation facilities has been rapid in good times; with a reversal of conditions, the distress of the staple industries has been severe" (p. 153).

44 See Phillips, "New Staples."

45 Jessop, "Towards."

46 In August 1995 the United Nations rated Canada the world's number-1 country – at a time when the unemployment rate hovered around 10 per cent and one of five Canadian children lived in poverty.

47 The role of inflation, and the "necessity" of fighting it, undermined the Keynesian attempt to "pump-prime" the French economy in the early 1980s and helped in the 1990s to push Sweden – with its highly developed KWS – into abandoning the central commitment to full employment; see Glyn, "Social Democracy."

REFERENCES

Aitken, Hugh G.J. *American Capital and Canadian Resources.* Cambridge, Mass.: Harvard University Press, 1961.

Atkinson, Michael M., and Coleman, William D. *The State, Business, and Industrial Change in Canada.* Toronto: University of Toronto Press, 1989.

Berger, T.R. *Northern Frontier, Northern Homeland: The Report of the Mackenzie Valley Pipeline Inquiry.* Ottawa: Department of Supply and Services, 1977; rev. ed., Toronto: James Lorimer, 1988.

Black, Don, and Myles, John. "Dependent Industrialization and the Canadian Class Structure: A Comparative Analysis of Canada, the United States and Sweden." *Canadian Review of Sociology and Anthropology,* 23 no. 2 (May 1986), 157–81.

Bourgault, Pierre L. *Innovation and the Structure of Canadian Industry.* Science Council of Canada Special Study No. 23. Ottawa: Information Canada, 1972.

Burton, F.W. "The Business Cycle and the Problem of Economic Development." In H.A. Innis and A.F.W. Plumptre, eds., *The Canadian Economy and Its Problems,* 143–58. Toronto: University of Toronto Press, 1934.

Campbell, Robert M. *Grand Illusions: The Politics of the Keynesian Experience in Canada 1945–1975.* Peterborough, Ont.: Broadview Press, 1987.

Canada, Privy Council Office. *Foreign Ownership and the Structure of Canadian Industry* (Report of the Task Force on the Structure of Canadian Industry, or Walkins Report). Ottawa: Queen's Printer 1968.

Carroll, William. *Corporate Power and Canadian Capitalism.* Vancouver: University of British Columbia Press, 1986.

Clark-Jones, Melissa. *A Staple State: Canadian Industrial Resources in Cold War,* Toronto: University of Toronto Press, 1987.

Clarkson, Stephen. *Canada and the Reagan Challenge: Crisis in the Canadian-American Relationship.* Toronto: James Lorimer, 1982; rev. ed., 1985.

Clement, Wallace. *Continental Corporate Power: Economic Elite Linkages between Canada and the United States.* Toronto: McClelland and Stewart, 1977.

– *Hardrock Mining: Industrial Relations and Technological Change at Inco.* Toronto: McClelland and Stewart, 1981.

– *The Struggle to Organize: Resistance in Canada's Fishery.* Toronto: McClelland and Stewart, 1986.

Clement, Wallace, and Myles, John. *Relations of Ruling: Class and Gender in Postindustrial Societies.* Montreal: McGill-Queen's University Press, 1994.

Cohen, Marjorie Griffin. *Women's Work, Markets, and Economic Development in Nineteenth Century Ontario.* Toronto: University of Toronto Press, 1988.

Craven, Paul, and Traves, Tom. "The Class Politics of the National Policy, 1872–1933." *Journal of Canadian Studies* (autumn 1979), 14–38.

Dobb, Maurice. *Studies in the Development of Capitalism,* rev. ed. New York: International Publishers, 1964.

Dow, Alexander. "Prometheus in Canada: The Expansion of Metal Mining, 1900–1950." In Duncan Cameron, ed., *Explorations in Canadian Economic History: Essays in Honour of Irene M. Spry,* 211–28. Ottawa: University of Ottawa Press, 1985.

Drache, Daniel. "Harold Innis and Canadian Capitalist Development." *Canadian Journal of Political and Social Theory,* 6 (winter-spring 1982), 35–60.

– "Staple-ization: A Theory of Canadian Capitalist Development." In Craig Heron, ed., *Imperialism, Nationalism and Canada,* Toronto: New Hogtown Press, 1977, 15–33.

– ed. *Staples, Markets, and Cultural Change: Selected Essays of Harold Innis.* Montreal: McGill-Queen's University Press, 1995.

Drache, Daniel, and Glasbeek, Harry. *The Changing Workplace: Reshaping Canada's Industrial Relations System.* Toronto: James Lorimer, 1992.

Fogarty, John. "Staples, Super-Staples and the Limits of Staple Theory: The Experiences of Argentina, Australia and Canada Compared." In D.C.M. Platt and Guido di Tella, eds., *Argentina, Australia and Canada: Studies in Comparative Development 1870–1965,* 19–36. London: Macmillan Press, 1985.

Fox, Bonnie. "Women's Role in Development." In Gordon Laxer, ed., *Perspectives on Canadian Economic Development,* 333–52. Toronto: Oxford University Press, 1991.

Glyn, Andrew. "Social Democracy and Full Employment." *New Left Review,* 211 (May-June 1995), 33–55.

Gordon, David M., Edwards, Richard, and Reich, Michael. *Segmented Work, Divided Workers: The Historical Transformation of Labor in the United States.* Cambridge, England: Cambridge University Press, 1982.

Gunton, Thomas. "Manitoba's Nickel Industry: The Paradox of a Low-Cost Producer." In Thomas Gunton and John Richards, eds., *Resource Rents and Public Policy in Western Canada*, 89–117. Halifax: Institute for Research on Public Policy, 1987.

Harris, R. Cole. "Preface." In R. Cole Harris, ed., *Historical Atlas of Canada*, Vol. I: *From the Beginning to 1800*. Toronto: University of Toronto Press, 1987.

Hirschman, Albert. "A Generalized Linkage Approach to Development with Special Reference to Staples." *Economic Development and Cultural Change*, 25 Supplement (1977), 67–98.

– *Strategy of Economic Development*. New Haven, Conn.: Yale University Press, 1958.

Hobsbawm, Eric. *Age of Extremes: The Short Twentieth Century 1914–1991*. London: Michael Joseph, 1994.

Howlett, Michael, and Ramesh, M. *The Political Economy of Canada: An Introduction*. Toronto: McClelland and Stewart, 1992.

Innis, H.A. *The Cod Fisheries: The History of an International Economy*. First published 1954. Rev. ed. Toronto: University of Toronto Press, 1978.

Jenson, Jane. " 'Different' but not 'Exceptional': Canada's Permeable Fordism." *Canadian Review of Sociology and Anthropology* (Feb. 1989), 69–94.

Jessop, Bob. "Towards a Schumpeterian Workfare State? Preliminary Remarks on Post-Fordist Political Economy." *Studies in Political Economy*, 40 (spring 1993), 7–39.

Kierans, Eric. *Report on Natural Resource Policy in Manitoba*. Winnipeg: Queen's Printer, 1973.

Lamontagne, Maurice. *Business Cycles in Canada: The Postwar Experience and Policy Directions*. Toronto: Canadian Institute for Economic Policy and James Lorimer, 1984.

Langille, David. "The Business Council on National Issues and the Canadian State." *Studies in Political Economy*, 24 (autumn 1987), 41–86.

Laxer, Gordon. *Open for Business: The Roots of Foreign Ownership in Canada*. Toronto: Oxford University Press, 1989.

Levitt, Kari. *Silent Surrender: The Multinational Corporation in Canada*. Toronto: Macmillan, 1970.

Luxton, Meg. *More than a Labour of Love: Three Generations of Women's Work in the Home*. Toronto: Women's Press, 1980.

McBride, Stephen. *Not Working: State, Unemployment, and Neo-Conservatism in Canada*. Toronto: University of Toronto Press, 1992.

Mackintosh, W.A. "Canadian Economic Policy from 1945 to 1957 – Origins and Influences." In Hugh G.J. Aitken et al., *The American Economic Impact on Canada*, 51–68. Durham, NC: Duke University Press, 1959.

– *The Economic Background of Dominion-Provincial Relations*. Appendix III of the Royal Commission Report on Dominion-Provincial Relations. Edited and with an Introduction by J.H. Dales. Carleton Library No. 13. Toronto: McClelland and Stewart, 1964.

– "Economic Factors in Canadian History." *Canadian Historical Review*, 4
     (1923), 12–25; reprinted in M.H. Watkins and H.M. Grant, eds., *Canadian
     Economic History: Classic and Contemporary Approaches*, Ottawa: Carleton
     University Press, 1993.

McNally, David. "Staple Theory as Commodity Fetishism: Marx, Innis and
     Canadian Political Economy." *Studies in Political Economy*, 6 (autumn 1981),
     35–64.

– "Technological Determinism and Canadian Political Economy: Further
     Contributions to a Debate." *Studies in Political Economy*, 20 (summer 1986),
     161–70.

Mahon, Rianne. *The Politics of Industrial Restructuring: Canadian Textiles.*
     Toronto: University of Toronto Press, 1984.

Naylor, R.T. *The History of Canadian Business 1867–1914.* 2 vols. Toronto: James
     Lorimer, 1975.

Nelles, H.V. *The Politics of Development: Forest, Mines and Hydro-Electric Power in
     Ontario, 1840–1941.* Toronto: Macmillan, 1974.

Niosi, Jorge. "The Canadian Bourgeoisie: Towards a Synthetical Approach."
     Canadian Journal of Political and Social Theory, 7 no. 3 (fall 1983),
     128–49.

Ommer, Rosemary E. *From Outpost to Outport: A Structural Analysis of the Jersey-
     Gaspé Cod Fishery 1767–1886.* Montreal: McGill-Queen's University Press,
     1991.

– "What's Wrong with Canadian Fish?" *Journal of Canadian Studies*, 20 no. 3
     (fall 1985), 122–42.

Parker, Ian. "Commodity Fetishism and 'Vulgar Marxism': On 'Rethinking
     Canadian Political Economy'." *Studies in Political Economy*, 10 (winter 1983),
     143–72.

Pentland, H. Clare. *Labour and Capital in Canada 1650–1860*, ed. P. Phillips.
     Toronto: James Lorimer, 1981.

Phillips, Paul. "New Staples and Megaprojects: Reaching the Limits to
     Sustainable Development." In Daniel Drache and Meric Gertler, eds., *The
     New Era of Global Competition: State Power and Market Power*, 229–46. Montreal:
     McGill-Queen's University Press, 1991.

– "Staples, Surplus, and Exchange: The Commercial Industrial Question
     in the National Policy Period." In Duncan Cameron, ed., *Explorations in
     Canadian Economic History: Essays in Honour of Irene M. Spry*, 27–43. Ottawa:
     University of Ottawa Press, 1985.

Porter, Michael E., and the Monitor Company. *Canada at the Crossroads: The
     Reality of a New Competitive Environment.* Ottawa: Business Council on National
     Issues and Ministry of Supply and Services Canada, 1991.

Pratt, Larry. "The State and Province-Building: Alberta's Development
     Strategy." In Leo Panitch, ed., *The Canadian State: Political Economy and
     Political Power*, 131–64. Toronto: University of Toronto Press, 1977.

Resnick, Philip. "The Maturing of Canadian Capitalism." *Our Generation*, 15 no. 2 (fall 1982), 4–24.

Schedvin, C.V. "Staples and Regions of Pax Britannica." *Economic History Review*, 43 no. 4 (1990), 533–59.

Solberg, Carl E. *The Prairies and the Pampas: Agrarian Policy in Canada and Argentina, 1880–1930.* Stanford, Calif.: Stanford University Press, 1987.

Spry, Irene M. "Overhead Costs, Rigidities of Productive Capacity and the Price System." In William M. Melody, Liora Salter, and Paul Heyer, eds., *Culture, Communication and Dependency: The Tradition of H.A. Innis*, 155–66. Norwood, NJ: Ablex Publishing Corp., 1981.

Strain, Frank, and Grant, Hugh. "The Social Structure of Accumulation in Canada, 1945–1988." *Journal of Canadian Studies* (winter 1991–92), 75–93.

Van Kirk, Sylvia. *"Many Tender Ties": Women in Fur Trade Society 1670–1870.* Winnipeg: Watson and Dwyer, 1980.

Waldram, James B. *As Long as the Rivers Run: Hydroelectric Development and Native Communities in Western Canada.* Winnipeg: University of Manitoba Press, 1988.

Watkins, Mel. "From Underdevelopment to Development." in Mel Watkins, ed., *Dene Nation: The Colony Within*, 84–102. Toronto: University of Toronto Press, 1977.

– "A Staple Theory of Economic Growth." *Canadian Journal of Economics and Political Science*, 29 (May 1963), 141–8; reprinted in M.H. Watkins and H.M. Grant, eds., *Canadian Economic History: Classic and Contemporary Approaches*, 19–38. Ottawa: Carleton University Press, 1993.

– "Wheat as a Staple." *Business History Review* (spring 1993), 280–7.

Williams, Glen. *Not for Export: Toward a Political Economy of Canada's Arrested Industrialization.* 3rd ed. Toronto: McClelland and Stewart, 1994.

Wolfe, David. "The Crisis in Advanced Capitalism: An Introduction." *Studies in Political Economy*, 11 (summer 1983), 7–26.

– "The Delicate Balance: The Changing Economic Role of the State in Canada." 2 vols. Doctoral thesis, University of Toronto, 1980.

– "The Rise and Demise of the Keynesian Era in Canada: Economic Policy, 1930–1982." In M.S. Cross and G.S. Kealey, eds., *Modern Canada, 1930–1980's*, 46–80. Toronto: McClelland and Stewart, 1984.

3 Resources and Manufacturing in Canada's Political Economy

WALLACE CLEMENT AND
GLEN WILLIAMS

Canadian political economy cut its teeth on interpreting the historical pattern of Canadian resource and industrial development. So penetrating has been its analysis that nearly every Canadian has been exposed at some level to its insights. Political economy tells us that the particular way Canada meets its economic requirements – that is, how the production of goods and services is organized – is inherently a political and social process sustained by, and shaping, its culture and ideologies.

In the political economy tradition both the historical (how things dynamically transform over time) and spatial (regional/provincial, national, and international boundaries and relations) are integral to an understanding of change in Canada. The economy is not simply a set of inanimate corporations or trade figures shaped by anonymous markets, as it has become in neo-classical economics. In political economy there is an assumption of the role of human agency – the actions of people in shaping of history. The economy provides the context, but the political and cultural/ideological write the text of history, identifying the particulars of each nation and the possibilities for the future.

We wish to highlight four themes in examining Canada's resource and industrial development:

- foreign direct investment and control of Canadian production at levels unmatched anywhere else in the world;
- the resource-extraction base of Canada's foreign trade;
- the branch-plant organization of Canadian manufacturing and the Canadian domestic market by parent u.s. industries; and
- Canada's unique role in the international division of labour.

While there has been consensus on the centrality of these four issues in political economy analysis, we see below that practitioners have frequently disagreed on their meaning. Nowhere is this more true than when Canada's position in the international political economy is assessed.

FOREIGN DIRECT INVESTMENT (FDI)

Foreign investment has a long history of charting the course of Canada's economic development. The ready availability of massive infusions of foreign capital for investment has pushed and pulled at the shape of resource and industrial development by defining economic logic and profitability for governments, business firms, and individuals.

During the ninteenth and early twentieth centuries, British investment in Canadian canals and railways facilitated the export of Canada's resources to Europe. Canada, with a population of only 7.2 million in 1911, accounted for more than 10 per cent of British overseas investment and was greater in value than British investment in India. This was mainly portfolio investment, or loans, repayable over time by the companies and governments that had negotiated them.

Early-twentieth-century U.S. investment, in contrast, tended to take the form of ownership shares of productive enterprises such as manufacturing factories, mines, and forestry concerns. Unlike portfolio investment, direct investment usually arrived in Canada to stay. From owning less than one-fifth of Canadian industry in 1914, foreign (mostly U.S.) investors owned three-fifths of Canada's manufacturing and mining in 1971, and more than two-fifths today. No other advanced country has ceded so much influence over its economic direction to foreign firms.

By both absolute and relative measures, the greatest expansion of FDI in Canada took place in the quarter-century following the end of the Second World War. Believing that it was largely responsible for the postwar economic boom, politicians and senior bureaucrats generally applauded this growth. FDI was also very popular with the public. In 1956, 68 per cent of Canadians believed that U.S. investment had been good for Canada. As late as 1963, though about one-half of Canadians believed that their country was more dominated by the United States than it had been a decade before, a greater number thought this was "a good thing" than otherwise. Some 56 per cent still judged that U.S. investment had well served Canada's interests.[1]

These attitudes and perceptions began to shift dramatically in the late 1960s. Government studies had revealed that foreign enterprises had generally employed Canadian capital to expand their resource and manufacturing concerns rather than bringing new capital into the country to fund growth. Worse, foreign control of the Canadian economy had led to an overall emphasis on resource extraction over manufacturing and had immobilized the innovative and competitive capacity of domestic industry.[2]

By the late 1970s, most Canadians felt that there was too much foreign investment in their economy and were prepared to endorse a buyback of 51 per cent of U.S. companies in Canada even if this were to reduce living standards.[3] Policies that represented a mild challenge to foreign capital emerged under the Liberal government, such as the Foreign Investment Review Agency (FIRA), which monitored new FDI, and the National Energy Program (NEP), which increased the space for Canadian capital in the energy sector. These initiatives were bitterly contested by both foreign capital and its domestic allies in Canada. Overall, federal politicians and the bureaucratic elite thought it wise to dodge the increasingly nationalist public mood on this question.

A severe economic recession in the early 1980s put an end to any further policy experimentation with economic nationalism by Ottawa. The Conservative party achieved a landslide victory in the 1984 election in part by blaming Canada's economic difficulties on the supposed hostility of the Trudeau government to American investors. By the mid-1980s, over three-fifths of Canadians wanted to "encourage" FDI, while only one-fifth sought to "discourage" it. A majority now disapproved of any 51 per cent buyback.[4] In this climate, Brian Mulroney's Conservatives were able to dismantle both FIRA and the NEP without provoking major controversy.

Debate over FDI re-emerged with the 1987 Canada–United States. Free Trade Agreement (FTA). Several of the FTA's clauses bound Ottawa's hands in dealing with American investors. U.S. firms were guaranteed "national treatment" in Canada. This meant that discrimination between U.S. and Canadian firms in respect to establishment, investment, operations, and sale was forbidden. For resource firms, export taxes and export restrictions were prohibited. In manufacturing, Canada promised never to impose performance requirements, such as export or domestic sourcing quotas, on U.S. branch plants.

Many Canadians believed, and emotionally argued, that the terms of the FTA went too far by stripping Ottawa of its capacity to compensate for the harmful effects of American resource and manufacturing investment. The political elite was split over the FTA in 1988, with the leadership of the Liberal and New Democratic parties arguing that Canada's economic sovereignty had been compromised. In the end, a plurality of Canadians opposed the FTA before both the 1988 and

1993 elections. By 1995, however, the studied ambiguity of Canadians in regard to U.S. FDI had once again come into view. While a plurality favoured the FTA's successor, the North American Free Trade Agreement (NAFTA), three-fifths thought that the United States was benefiting most from the treaty while only 5 per cent believed that Canada had been the biggest beneficiary.[5]

RESOURCE DEPENDENCE

Canada's economy began as a source of commercial commodities for European masters, including the classic staples of fish in the form of salt cod, fur (especially beaver), square timber, gold (obtained through placer mining), and wheat. Later, in the industrial era, new resources became the raw materials demanded by the swelling U.S. economy, including the industrial staples of fish in the form of frozen cod blocks, pulp and paper, minerals, and energy (oil, gas, and hydro power). A staple is any natural resource developed for export; resources developed for manufacturing or consumption in Canada would not be staples. Much of Canada's resource development, however, has been with export in mind. Even today well over half of Canada's forest products are exported, as are four-fifths of its mineral products (such as nickel, copper, zinc, iron, and potash). Because resources are developed for export, the infrastructure of the economy, as in its transportation networks, is constructed to serve this purpose. Thus ports, railways, pipelines, and energy grids have been shaped by resources. One need only be reminded of the importance of wheat in these respects. Today three-fifths of all Canadian freight by rail and half its shipping is dedicated to the export of minerals.

Canadian industrial raw materials are prominent within the continental marketplace. Resource companies dominate lists of Canada's top exporters (see Table 1). In 1992 Canada supplied over one-third of U.S. copper imports, one-half of its imported nickel, three-fifths of imported zinc, and almost three-quarters of its imported aluminium. Canada was also the source for all of its imported electricity and nearly all its imported natural gas. Four-fifths of U.S. imports of forest products were from Canada.[6] For minerals such as asbestos, gypsum, iron ore, nickel, potash, silver, and zinc, imports from Canada constitute a remarkably large share of total U.S. consumption.[7]

The top 25 exporting companies for 1992, as identified by the *Globe and Mail Report on Business*, are listed in Tables 1 and 3. Table 3 focuses on the automobile industry, which is discussed separately. Table 2 covers all the top 50 companies identified by the same source, focusing on their main activities. As can be seen, 30 of the top 50 companies

Table 1
Canada's top non-auto exporters, 1992

Company	Exports	Exports	Ownership	Main activity
IBM Canada	3,907	62	IBM, USA 100%	Computers
Noranda	3,389	41	Brascan 40% (15% foreign)	Minerals, forestry
Canadian Pacific	2,418	24	(29% foreign)	Minerals
Canadian Wheat Board	2,310	66	Federal government	Grain
Inco	1,354	45	(23–55% foreign)*	Nickel
Alcan Aluminium	1,300	17	(31–57% foreign)*	Aluminium
Fletcher Challenge	1,200	67	FC, New Zealand	Forest products
Pratt & Whitney	1,195	85	United Tech, USA 98%	Aerospace
Amoco Canada	1,180	29	Amoco, USA 100%	Energy
TransCanada Pipelines	1,126	36	BCE 49%	Energy
Mobile Oil Canada	1,100	63	Mobile, USA 100%	Energy
Falconbridge	1,098	62	Noranda 50% Trelleborg, Sweden, 50%	Mining
Bombardier	1,084	35	Bombardier family	Engineering
Shell Canada	913	19	Shell, Netherlands, 100%	Energy
Abitibi-Price	880	31	Olympia & York 82%	Forest products
Alberta & Southern	820	88	Pacific Gas & Electric, USA, 100%	Energy
Nova	816	27	†	Energy
Cominco	808	61	Pine Point Mines 28%	Mining
XCan Grain	664	92	Wheat Pools	Grain
Canfor	637	77	Matthew-Cartier Holdings 41%	Forest

Sources: "Canada's Export Stars," *Globe and Mail Report on Business*, April 1993, 71; "Canada's Largest Corporations," *Financial Post Magazine*, May 1993.
* Reported share of foreign ownership/control varies by sources.
† Hong Kong interests control 52% of Husky Oil, Nova's main petroleum asset.

are concentrated in four resource activities: mining/minerals, forest products, energy, and grain. These 50 companies generate half of Canada's export value.[8]

Table 2
Canada's top 50 exporters by sales, 1992

Main activity	No. of firms
Mining/minerals	9
Forest products	9
Energy	8
Engineering/aerospace	6
Auto makers/parts	5
Computers/office equipment	3
Chemicals	3
Grain	3
Steel	2
Food	1
Consumer goods	1
Total	50

Source: Calculated from "Canada's Export Stars," *Globe and Mail Report on Business Magazine*, April 1993, 71.

Also evident from Table 1 is the importance of foreign ownership in many of the largest exporting companies. There are not many manufacturing multinationals identified here because for most of this century u.s. branch plants operating in Canada were restricted by their American parents to the Canadian domestic market.[9] Notable exceptions are IBM Canada, which moves products within an international network of intracompany transfers; Pratt & Whitney, an aerospace company that operates in a continental-contract structure; and the American automobile companies, which have operated in a continentally integrated industry for more than three decades. The key energy exporters are also foreign-owned: Amoco (which took over Dome Petroleum, once touted as Canada's flagship energy company), Mobile Oil, Shell, Alberta & Southern Gas, and Husky Oil. There are also several important Canadian-based, international minerals giants: Brascan, Canadian Pacific, Inco, Alcan, and Noranda.

How is it that resources continue to have such an important place in Canada's export economy and that multinationals (or branch plants) are so prominent in their ownership structures? Much of the explanation lies in the period from the end of the Second World War through

the Korean War. During this time of rapid expansion, Canadian resource ownership declined from 62 per cent (in 1946) to 30 per cent
(in 1957). In the course of a decade U.S. ownership came to dominate
Canada's resources boom, and resources were exported in less processed form than they had been earlier.

The United States emerged from the Second World War as the clear
economic giant of the capitalist world. Its leaders sought to ensure
access to crucial raw materials to protect its position. To this end a U.S.
presidential commission was struck, reporting in 1952 with *Resources
for Freedom* (Paley Report), which specified twenty-two "key" materials
required from outside the United States. Canada was identified as the
primary secure source for thirteen of these: aluminium, asbestos, co-
balt, copper, iron ore, lead, natural gas, newsprint, nickel, petroleum,
sulphur, titanium, and zinc. Soon thereafter Canada experienced
a massive boom in these resources and an influx of U.S. companies
eager to develop them.[10] Canada's economy, and particularly its politicians, became "addicted" to resource exports as the means to development. Kenneth Taylor, Canada's deputy minister of finance at the
time, is quoted as saying about the Paley Report, "I keep it in my
desk, and every time I get depressed about the future, I take it out
and read it."[11]

Consistent with the traditional shaping of transportation systems
based on the demands of resource exports, the Paley Commission encouraged U.S. participation in the St Lawrence Seaway construction so
that Labrador iron ore could have passage to the U.S. interior.[12] The
United States implemented the report's recommendations by creating
stockpiles of strategic resources. This process distorted resource development in Canada by creating an artificially high demand for specific
products. U.S. agencies then used the generated surplus to bring demanding producers to heel. This demand-side discipline removed any
leverage that "scarce resources" might have given Canada. These policies and practices were a strategic part of U.S. military-industrial control. They give lie to the liberal notion of "markets" and reveal the
importance of human intervention into apparently invisible forces.

Well after it became evident that Canada had been alarmingly drawn
into the intimacy of U.S. resource demands and overcommitted to a
single market, Liberal politicians began to respond. Mitchell Sharp,
then secretary of state for external affairs, issued a policy paper in
October 1972 outlining a "third option" promoting diversified trading
partners. This strategy required an industrial policy supporting high
technology and manufacturing. It failed, as Stephen Clarkson tells
us, because "it was more than many politicians and bureaucrats felt
appropriate in an export-led capitalist economy heavily centred on the

exploitation of staples resources."[13] The federal government launched in its place more of the old resource strategy, this time concentrating on resource megaprojects. At the centre of its original plan was the National Energy Program, predicated on high energy costs and scarcity of petroleum, which centralized control federally and intensified resource exports. The program collapsed, however, as the price of oil fell, leaving heavy debt, broken trust with provincial governments, and a void in industrial strategies. The Liberal government never recovered, losing the general election of 1984 to Mulroney's neo-conservatives, who proceeded to launch the most aggressive continental integration in Canada's history. The national economy had faltered. Each region of the country was compelled to turn southward to market its resources.

More intensively than ever before, Canadian capitalists took their investments abroad, primarily to the United States. Under the Liberals from 1980 to 1984 the net capital abroad increased by $4.8 billion annually, but under the Conservatives between 1984 and 1991 this escalated to $10.5 billion annually. By the end of 1991, FDI in Canada stood at $130 billion, double its level of a decade earlier. Under the Mulroney government foreign ownership reversed its gradual decline from the Trudeau years, increasing from 48 to 52 per cent for manufacturing and from 38 to 43 per cent for resources. There ceased to be even the pretence of a national industrial strategy and an internally driven, internally logical set of policies. Setting of pace and direction was abdicated to the United States. Canadian capitalists, being quite mobile, joined multinational capital in the centre.

From the American point of view, energy became the main resource to be coveted in the 1980s. The Three-Mile Island disaster in 1979 caused its nuclear-reactor program to be frozen, leaving a gap in U.S. energy requirements. The demand was to be filled by natural gas from western Canada and hydro from Quebec. Until this time hydro power exports from Canada had been incidentally generated surplus. Now projects were being constructed, especially near James Bay, for "firm power" contracts; in other words, hydro power had become a staple. It also became virtually the sole economic platform throughout Liberal Robert Bourassa's second period as premier of Quebec. Resistance to such strategies came from Native peoples, whose homelands were expropriated for flooding, and from activists, who reminded us that the diversion of waterways, exploration in the High Arctic, and transmission by pipelines and powerlines all took their toll on the environment. Karl Froschauer tells us that there is no complete east–west network of powerlines in Canada, with only 35 interprovincial lines compared to the 100 connected to the United States.[14]

The FTA prohibits Canada from restricting its resource exports to the United States or charging beyond domestic prices for its energy exports. The Canadian debt load is swelled through financing of expensive energy megaprojects, such as Hibernia on the continental shelf of Newfoundland, Beaufort Sea oil and gas in the Arctic, and heavy-oil upgraders at Lloydminster, Alberta. Interest payments on loans to cover these debts amount to an annual drain of $13 billion, leaving the Canadian state in a form of staples debt trap. In the summer of 1994, for example, the federal and Alberta governments finally withdrew from the Lloydminster megaproject at a combined loss of $1 billion. Investment had been announced by the Conservatives as part of the 1988 federal election campaign. While Ottawa loses $558 million and Alberta $425 million, the construction companies gained as the project went $400 million over projected construction costs. Ottawa's withdrawal follows another $400-million loss in the NewGrade heavy-oil upgrader in Regina. The Liberal government is also attempting to escape Ottawa's "investment" in Hibernia. And people wonder where the national debt comes from.[15]

Staples are the key policy instrument for export-led growth; the state assumes infrastructure costs (such as railways, ports, pipelines, and hydro projects) and foreign debts. To pay the debt, more staple extraction is required, and fewer manufacturing conditions are applied. Short-term solutions appear to work because the construction phase is labour-intensive and welcomed by local capitalists, especially construction firms, but in the longer term they produce structures of dependence and debt, for which social programs incur the blame, and leave few jobs behind.

Resources are soft sands on which to build an economy unless developed with extraordinary care. Resource depletion is a mounting problem throughout Canada's forestry industry, and problems in the east-coast fishery have become legion. The traditional fishery has collapsed because of stock depletion, and instead of shipping exports, Fisheries Products International, Canada's largest fish company, is processing imported fish.[16] Nor does resource richness mean exclusivity or monopoly power. Mineral-resource giants in Canada are not limited to Canadian sources. Inco, the world's largest producer of nickel, has built its Indonesian nickel mine into the world's fourth-largest operation (behind only a Russian mine in Norilsk and Inco's own in Sudbury and Thompson). It has overcome a major limitation by gaining access to a nearby hydro plant, making the Indonesian cost of production considerably lower than Canada's (when the cost of labour, environmental controls, taxes, and minimal royalties are factored-in). Inco owns 58 per cent of the company, 20 per cent is held by Sumitomo

Metal Mining of Japan, and 20 per cent is traded on Indonesian stock exchanges.[17] In resource development planning does take place, but inside multinational corporations, which have a private, international agenda that is not identical with the interests of Canadian workers, taxpayers, or consumers.

THE MANUFACTURING COUNTER-EXAMPLE: AUTOMOBILES

The five automobile companies from Table 2, a summary of the top 50 exporters, are listed in Table 3, which is dominated by "Big Three" u.s. branch plants: General Motors, Ford, and Chrysler. The new age is represented by Honda, the Japanese giant. Canadian content is supplied by Frank Stronach's Magna Corp. a parts supplier, notorious for moving large segment of its operations to the u.s. south and Mexico.

Automobiles are at the heart of manufacturing industries throughout advanced capitalist societies, and Canada is no exception. What is exceptional about Canada, however, is the Canada–United States Automotive Products Trade Agreement (Auto Pact) of 1965, which organizes trade and production of automobiles on a continental basis. There is full integration; four-fifths of the vehicles assembled in Canada are destined for the u.s. market, while seven-tenths of the Canadian market is supplied by u.s.-assembled vehicles.[18] These transactions are intracompany transfers of products, not exchanges within a market between buyers and sellers.

The Auto Pact means different things to each country. As Jon R. Johnson tells us, "From the us perspective, the Auto Pact was a sectoral free trade arrangement permitting the three major us automobile manufacturers to rationalize their Canadian and us operations. From the Canadian perspective, the Auto Pact was a market-sharing arrangement ... ensuring that a certain share of the North American automotive industry remained in Canada."[19] For the United States, it meant free trade; for Canada, managed trade. The difference, of course, rests in the fact that the industry is u.s.-controlled. In exchange for some assurances of production in Canada, the Canadian industry was surrendered to u.s. companies.

Conditions in the automobile industry have changed dramatically since 1965. Under competition from Japan, the North American industry restructured in the 1980s, closing many plants and investing in modernized operations. Throughout this time Canadian operations fared well because their costs of production have been lower by 30 per cent. Most of the difference is attributable to the lower value of the Canadian dollar, but part is the result of the lower cost of employee

Table 3
Canada's top auto exporters, 1992

Company	Exports ($million)	Exports (% of sales)	Ownership	Main activity
GM Canada	13,000	67	100% GM, USA	Automakers
Ford Canada	7,780	64	94% Ford, USA	Automakers
Chrysler Canada	7,055	85	100% Chrysler, USA	Automakers
Honda Canada	2,000	80	50.2% Honda Japan 49.8% Honda USA	Automakers
Magna	953	40	51% F. Stronach	Autoparts

benefits, especially health insurance premiums.[20] On the labour-union front, the Canadian Auto Workers broke from the U.S. parent, the United Auto Workers, with the Auto Pact providing some level of legislative protection for jobs in Canada.[21]

What does the future hold for the automobile industry in Canada? The FTA has significantly altered the Auto Pact, despite Canadian politicians claiming otherwise. The FTA does not affect Canada's obligations under the Auto Pact, but "US obligations have been subsumed under the FTA ... [The] incentive for vehicle manufacturers in Canada to meet Auto Pact requirements has been weakened and further expansion of the Auto Pact prohibited."[22] This means that the FTA excludes Japanese auto companies from the Auto Pact. The only thing keeping automotive jobs in Canada now is the lower cost of production, a condition that could change with Mexico's entry into NAFTA.

ARRESTED INDUSTRIALIZATION

Resource-intensive, relatively low-technology production has eclipsed higher-technology manufacturing in Canada, thereby standing the logic of twentieth-century economic development on its head. In an international marketplace where high- and medium-technology manufactured products have seized a dominant place in world trade, Canada has upheld its traditional focus on resource-based exports. Overall, Canada's trade deficit in fully manufactured end products for the five years between 1990 and 1994 totalled an overwhelming $156 billion.[23] While it is common for the most economically developed industrial countries to have three-fifths or more of their exports made up of finished manufactures, Canada can manage only slightly in excess of two-fifths of its exports in this key category. When automotive trade is removed from the calculation, the proportion plummets to just over one-quarter.

The wellspring of international competitiveness in high- and medium-technology manufactures can be found in the process of research and development (R&D) of new industrial commodities. Canada similarly lags behind in this crucial activity. With a rate of business-enterprise investment in R&D only two-thirds the average of the European Union and less than one-half the rate of Germany, Japan, and the United States, Canada is poorly positioned to improve its competitive position in fully manufactured end products.[24]

Failure to innovate and to export is reflected in the comparatively small share claimed by manufacturing in Canada's gross domestic product (Table 4). When interpreting the full extent of Canada's performance deficiencies here, we must remember that a significant portion of Canada's total manufacturing output comes from resource-based enterprises operating in the relatively low-technology wood and minerals sectors rather than from the medium- or high-technology producers characteristic of manufacturing in other industrial countries. Table 5, showing that Canadian manufacturing has a lower-than-normal share of manufacturing jobs in its employment profile, underscores the human cost of emphasizing resource production over trade in fully manufactured goods.

As in the resource industries, the considerable structural anomalies of Canadian manufacturing are directly related to FDI and continental economic specialization. The base for Canada's current industrial structure was established in the boom years of the 1890s through 1914 behind the National Policy tariffs. In that era, the prairie wheat staple was sovereign. According to Buckley's estimates, 42 per cent of Canada's gross capital formation from 1901 to 1915 was poured into railway construction, most of it in the west, and prairie farms. Less than 7 per cent was left for investment in the industrial machinery required for launching modern manufacturing.[25] Nothing more could reasonably be expected from industry's meagre share than provision of a useful supplement to the resource-export economy by generation of some manufacturing employment in central Canada and westbound cargo for the new transcontinental railway.

The industrial strategy employed by early Canadian manufacturers was an early form of "import-substitution industrialization" (ISI). It was characterized by unchallenged dependence on foreign production technology and lack of interest in manufacturing for anywhere beyond the domestic market. The federal government was involved through setting tariff levels high enough to make feasible domestic production

Table 4
Percentage share of manufacturing in GDP

	1970	1989
Canada	19.8	17.5
Japan	36.0	28.9
Germany	38.4	31.2
Sweden	25.0	19.7*
United States	25.2	18.9

Source: OECD, *Industrial Policy in OECD Countries*, Annual Review. (Paris 1993), Table 7.
* 1990.

Table 5
Percentage share of manufacturing jobs in total civilian employment

	1970	1992
Canada	22.3	14.6
Japan	27.0	24.4
Germany	49.3	30.4
Sweden	27.6	18.9
United States	26.4	17.0

Source: OECD, *Labour Force Statistics* (Paris, various years).

of goods that would otherwise be imported – that is, import substitution. Canadian manufacturers, seeking a cheap and effective shortcut, licensed U.S. industrial processes rather than developing their own. In contrast to the situation of industrialists in other countries who initially borrowed technology and then assimilated, adapted, and innovated from this knowledge base, use of foreign machinery and production processes became a permanent part of the early Canadian industrial pattern, thus tying it structurally to the evolution of U.S. industry.

With geographic proximity to the United States, a tariff-protected domestic market, and concessionary tariff privileges within the British Empire, Canada was an obvious location for American branch plants. Through take-overs of existing Canadian manufacturing firms (often already linked to them through licensing arrangements) and establishment of new subsidiaries, American industrialists consolidated their prominence in Canada's most dynamic industrial sectors by the 1920s. Canadian-owned manufacturing became concentrated in such techno-logically backward and less capital-intensive industries as textiles, cloth-ing and footware, food processing, and furniture manufacturing.

Three production patterns have marked the seven decades of hege-mony for u.s. manufacturing branch plants in Canada. None of these production patterns has broken the original mould that we have seen cast Canadian industries as mere ancillaries to staples-resource extrac-tion. All three have contributed to a spatial division within North American manufacturing that accounts for the failure of Canadian industry to become internationally competitive. The first period, from the 1920s to the late 1940s, consolidated the worst features of the previous import-substitution behaviour of Canadian-owned industries. u.s. firms established a Canadian presence in order to gain access to a tariff-protected market for products they would otherwise have shipped from their southern u.s. factories. There was no provision in their Canadian branch plants for development of distinct product lines for world markets, save for transfer of some export business from their u.s. operations to take advantage of Canada's preferential access to Great Britain and the dominions.

The second period, from the late 1940s to the mid-1970s, further institutionalized import substitution and, with it, Canada's industrial role in the continent. With the collapse of imperial preference, Cana-dian branch plants lost even this limited export role. Increasingly, American firms viewed the Canadian market as part of their domestic operations. Typically, an administrative division of the North Ameri-can market would establish a Canadian "satellite" plant to satisfy regional demand in this country, just as, say, a Chicago plant would fill demand in the u.s. midwest, while R&D and exports were centred in the u.s. parent plant.

Production from the late 1970s to the present has continued to be organized on a continental basis. Instead of "satellite" plants, which produced a large range of miniature-replica lines for Canada only, most successful Canadian branch plants have now become "rational-ized," specializing in production of a more limited range of lines for the entire continent.

Continental rationalization was modelled on developments in the automotive sector following signing of the Auto Pact. A turning point for the North American production regime, the pact was a by-product of successive rounds of post-1945 tariff liberalization under the Gen-eral Agreement on Tariffs and Trade (GATT). In order to strengthen the competitiveness of this linchpin North American industry in the face of a stiff challenge from off-shore producers, u.s. automakers, as well as the Canadian and American governments, agreed to forsake miniature-replica assembly through implementation of sectoral free trade. Though the Auto Pact did not prevent Japanese and European firms from seizing a sizable share of the continental market, it was judged a success, providing a valuable brace for this sector against the swelling trade storm.

A debate then began in earnest on Canada's most appropriate strategy for adjusting to the major transformations taking place in the international production regime. Nationalists wanted an industrial strategy to challenge directly the power of the foreign owners of Canada's truncated industries – to get them to sell their factories to Canadians or oblige them to operate more clearly in the national interest by doing more R&D in Canada and exporting Canadian manufactures to foreign customers. Continentalists argued that inefficient Canadian factories could survive in the liberalized GATT environment only through general adoption of the Auto Pact model of rationalized continental production. Canadian-U.S. free trade, they said, either under GATT or by bilateral treaty, was the only way forward.

As discussed above, the public leaned towards the nationalist position during the 1970s. Continentalism, however, was dominant among Canada's bureaucratic and political elites as well as big business.[26] As a result, Canadian-U.S. tariffs were reduced under the Kennedy and Tokyo rounds of GATT to the point where it was anticipated that by 1987 over 90 per cent of cross-border trade would face tariffs of 5 per cent or less. By the mid-1980s just one Canadian manufacturer in five foresaw contraction of its business from introduction of Canadian-U.S. free trade.

Complementing tariff reduction in the process of continental rationalization of Canadian industry was devaluation of Canada's dollar in relation to the U.S. dollar. Figure 1 shows that the Canadian dollar is now worth some 30 per cent less than it was in the early 1970s. Devaluation cushioned the fall in tariff protection for Canadian manufacturers, by making imports more expensive, and gave Canadian factories a favourable cost-locational advantage in North America by reducing Canadian labour rates in relation to American workers in the same industry. Nowhere has the effect of devaluation been more keenly felt than in the auto industry, whose exports currently make up nearly one-quarter of Canada's total export trade. In testimony before a House of Commons committee in 1993, Buzz Hargrove, president of the Canadian Auto Workers, estimated that Canadian auto plants had an "advantage" of $9 per hour per worker (with the Canadian dollar then at $0.79 U.S.) because of their lower real wages, as compared to U.S. plants. This meant, he submitted, that "for every four workers it costs

Figure 1
Value of the Canadian dollar in relation to the U.S. dollar, selected years, 1974–94
Source: Bank of Canada, *Review* (various years).

the industry, whether it bc Japanese transplants or American industry to hire in the United States, they can hire five in Canada, an additional worker for nothing."[27]

Canada's manufacturing sector had proceeded far along the road of continental rationalization through tariff reduction and devaluation by the early 1980s. Merchandise-trade surpluses with the United States had begun to balloon, and a chronic deficit in automotive trade was turning into a chronic surplus. Despite these apparent successes, Canada remains a mainly resource-producing industrial backwater in North America. In the reshuffling of the continental manufacturing system to keep pace with changes in the international production regime, Canadian branch plants continue to be technologically dependent and constrained by administrative policies established by American head offices. This means that their economic competitiveness is not underwritten primarily by economic factors but is politically contingent upon Canada's continued open access to the U.S. market, as well as maintenance of a relatively lower standard of living for Canadians, as reflected in the devaluation policy.

Canada's vulnerability is well illustrated in the economic record of the Mulroney years. In the early 1980s, business became concerned that the investments it had already made, or planned to make, in continental rationalization would be endangered by a flood of American non-tariff barriers erected by Congress at the urging of disgruntled regional interests. What was required, they told Ottawa, was a free-trade agreement that would guarantee Canada exemption from such obstructions. In the end, the FTA, though it removed the few remaining tariffs between the two countries, achieved little more than cosmetic relief from American non-tariff barriers. Canadian business, deeply disappointed, nevertheless offered key and energetic support to the Conservatives in the 1988 election because they feared that defeat of the FTA would deliver the policy initiative in Ottawa to the nationalists.

After their success in the 1988 free-trade election, the Tories soon became entangled in the currency question. For what appear to be mainly ideological reasons, related to monetarist orthodoxy concerning interest rates, inflation, and a "strong" currency, they, and the Bank of Canada, orchestrated a rise in the value of the dollar of some 20 per cent between 1986 and 1991 (see Figure 1). This revaluation had the immediate effect of making Canadian products far less competitive in American markets already shrunk by the force of a major economic recession. Ironically, the Tories' high-interest-rate/high-dollar policies worked at cross-purposes with the FTA by seriously undermining one of Canada's principal locational advantages in continental rationalization. In 1990, 80 per cent of members of the Canadian Exporters' Association reported that the appreciation of the Canadian dollar had hurt their businesses.[28] Business felt betrayed by the Tories and complained in terms that lay bare the political vulnerability of Canadian branch-plant manufacturers under continentally rationalized production. Take, for example, these remarks by P. Koenderman, president and chief executive officer of Babcock and Wilcox Canada:

During the days of the free trade debate in Canada we were very enthusiastic supporters of such an agreement. We were, within our corporation within North America, the low cost producer, and compared to our U.S. sister manufacturing organizations we stood to benefit greatly from a free trade agreement in that more work would be shifted to Canada ... Given the appreciation of the Canadian dollar relative to the U.S. and other currencies, the situation today is very much different, in that within our company we are now the high-cost producer within North America and we are struggling to remain competitive. It is a very, very serious situation. We are virtually cut off from work that we would get from our parent company in the U.S. ... [W]ithin our corporation we are sensing a great loss in Canada as a good place to do business and make major investments.[29]

CANADA'S ROLE IN THE INTERNATIONAL DIVISION OF LABOUR

Canada's position in the international division of labour has been the subject of heated debate in the study of Canadian political economy.[30] Despite the marked contrast in interpretations, the two principal approaches hold the common premise that the Canadian economy has never acquired the authentic attributes of a bona fide national economy. Rather, in this century, and as far back as the initial European colonization, Canada's economy has been a subordinate adjunct, or satellite, of more developed economies. As we have seen, this view is grounded in three considerations: unmatched levels of FDI and foreign control of production; the resource-extraction base of foreign trade; and the branch-plant organization of manufacturing by parent U.S. industries.

Working from this common premise, the first approach stresses the economic, social, and political limitations inherent in Canada's development model. It holds that Canada is being underdeveloped or economically destabilized by its external relationships. It stresses the exploitative character of FDI, resource specialization, and branch-plant industrialization. This approach has generally dominated the new Canadian political economy. The preceding chapter, by Mel Watkins, is an articulate expression of this position.

While also highlighting the distorting effect of continental economic linkages on Canadian development, the second approach features a less gloomy analysis. Opportunities as well as obstacles are said to be characteristic of the pattern of Canadian growth. While foreign capital, staple-resource extraction, and branch-plant industries all present fundamental structural problems for policy makers, highly developed political and economic institutions provide the flexibility necessary to draw benefits from otherwise adverse circumstances. Canada's unique relationship with more advanced economic centres thereby confirms its developed status rather than placing it in danger of decline. This approach was dominant in the classic period of liberal political economy in Canada but has also been reflected within the new Canadian political economy, as articulated below by Laura Macdonald, in chapter 8.

This approach would argue that the FTA and NAFTA represent ongoing attempts by the Canadian economic and political elites to institutionalize politically Canada's relatively favoured regional position within the international division of labour as a mainly resource-producing region within the North American economy. Canada has not been deindustrialized by the FTA or NAFTA. On the contrary, these treaties come near the end of a two-decades-long process of reindustrialization (continental rationalization) designed to make industries more congruent with deep structural changes in the international production regime driven by trade liberalization and the rise of the newly industrialized countries. It has even been suggested that we should look beyond capital's neo-liberal NAFTA project (to circumscribe the national state's ability to intervene in the international economy), as well as labour's rejectionist position on NAFTA (in favour of national social democracies), to recognize that NAFTA, with the addition of appropriate political and bureaucratic structures, could represent an opening towards greater economic and political democracy throughout the Americas.[31] Much remains contested concerning Canada's resources and manufacturing within the new global economy.

NOTES

1 Canadian Institute of Public Opinion (CIPO), *Gallup Poll*, 6 July 1963. F.J. Fletcher and R.J. Drummond, *Canadian Attitude Trends*, 1960–1978, Working Paper No. 4, Institute for Research on Public Policy, Montreal, August 1979, Table 13, p. 38.

2 See Canada, Privy Council Office, *Foreign Ownership*, and Canada, *Foreign Direct Investment*.

3 CIPO, *The Gallup Report*, 16 June 1988.

4 Ibid., 3 June 1985 and 16 June 1988.

5 Gallup Canada, *The Gallup Poll*, 31 Aug. 1993 and 13 March 1995.

6 Calculated from United States, National Trade Data Bank, International Trade Administration, *U.S. Foreign Trade Highlights*, and Canada, *Summary of External Trade*, Dec. 1992.

7 See Clement, "Political Economy," Table 4, p. 49.

8 *Globe and Mail Report on Business Magazine*, April 1992, 34.

9 See Williams, *Not for Export*.

10 See Clement, "Political Economy"; the process has been thoroughly documented by Clark-Jones, *A Staple State*.

11 Quoted by Kenny, "Getting the Lead Out," 47.

12 Ibid., 46n.

13 Clarkson, "Disjunctions," 107–8.

14 See Froschauer, "Provincial Hydro Expansions," 40.

15 See "$1-billion Oil Stake Abandoned," *Globe and Mail*, 5 Aug. 1994, A1.

16 See Kevin Cox, "Sea Change," *Globe and Mail*, 17 May 1994, B24.

17 See John Stackhouse, "Inco Bets on Indonesia," *Globe and Mail Report on Business*, 19 May 1994, B1–2.

18 See Holmes, "Globalization," 156.

19 Johnson, "The Effect," 256.

20 See Holmes, "Globalization," 166–7; Holmes, "From Three Industries to One," 35.

21 See Yates, "Autoworkers' Response," 132.

22 Johnson, "The Effect," 256.

23 Computed from Statistics Canada, *Summary of Canadian International Trade* (Ottawa: various years).

24 OECD, *Main Science and Technology Indicators*, I, (Paris, 1993), Table 25.
25 Computed from Buckley, *Capital Formation*, 22, 132, 135.
26 See, for example, McCall and Clarkson, *Trudeau*, chap. 3–7.
27 Canada, House of Commons, Subcommittee on International Trade of the
   Standing Committee on External Affairs and International Trade, 4 Feb.
   1993, 30:27.
28 J.D. Moore, vice-president, policy, Canadian Exporters' Association, "Canada's Competitiveness and Export Performance," *Parliamentary Weekly
   Quarterly Report*, 1 no. 3 (Sept. 1992), 27.
29 Canada, House of Commons, Committee on Finance, 24 May 1990,
   126:19.
30 See Williams, "Canada."
31 See Williams, *Not For Export*, chap. 8; and Macdonald, below, chap. 8.

REFERENCES

Buckley, K. *Capital Formation in Canada, 1896–1930*. Toronto: University of
   Toronto Press, 1955.
Canada. *Foreign Direct Investment in Canada* (Cray Report). Ottawa: Information
   Canada, 1972.
Canada, Privy Council Office, *Foreign Ownership and the Structure of Canadian
   Industry*. Report of the Task force on the Structure of Canadian Industry
   (Watkins Report). Ottawa, 1968.
Clark-Jones, Melissa, *A Staple State: Canadian Industrial Resources in Cold War*.
   Toronto: University of Toronto Press, 1987.
Clarkson, Steven. "Disjunctions: Free Trade and the Paradox of Canadian
   Development." In D. Drache and M.S. Gertler, eds., *The New Era of Global
   Competition: State Policy and Market Power*, 103–26. Montreal: McGill-Queen's
   University Press, 1991.
Clement, Wallace. "A Political Economy of Resources." In W. Clement and
   G. Williams, eds., *The New Canadian Political Economy*, 36–53. Montreal:
   McGill-Queen's University Press, 1991.
Froschauer, Karl, "Provincial Hydro Expansions: Required to Serve Industrial
   Development in Canada and Continental Integration (1960–1987)."
   PhD thesis, Sociology, Carleton University, 1992.
Holmes, John, "From Three Industries to One: Towards an Integrated North
   American Automobile Industry." In M.A. Molot, ed., *Driving Continentally:
   National Policies and the North American Auto Industry*, 23–62. Ottawa:
   Carleton University Press, 1993.
– "The Globalization of Production and the Future of Canada's Mature Indus-
   tries: The Case of the Automotive Industry." In D. Drache and M.S. Gertler,
   eds., *New Era of Global Competition*, 153–80. Montreal: McGill-Queen's
   University Press, 1991.

Johnson, Jon. R., "The Effect of the Canada-u.s. Free Trade Agreement on the Auto Pact." In M.A. Molot, ed., *Driving Continentally: National Policies and the North American Auto Industry*, 255–89. Ottawa: Carleton University Press, 1993.

Kenny, Jim, "Getting the Lead Out: State, Capital and Society and the Development of New Brunswick's Base Metal Industry, 1952–1972." PhD thesis, History, Carleton Univeristy, 1994.

McCall, C., and S. Clarkson, *Trudeau and Our Times: The Heroic Delusion* (vol. ii). Toronto: McClelland and Stewart, 1994.

Williams, Glen. *Not for Export: The International Competitiveness of Canadian Manufacturing*, 3rd ed. Toronto: McClelland and Stewart, 1994.

Williams, Glen, "Canada in the International Political Economy." In W. Clement and G. Williams, eds., *The New Canadian Political Economy*, 116–37. Montreal: McGill-Queen's University Press, 1991.

Yates, Charlotte, "North American Autoworkers' Response to Restructuring." In M. Golden and J. Pontusson, eds., *Bargaining for Change: Union Politics in North America and Europe*, 111–45. Ithaca, NY: Cornell University Press, 1992.

4 Labour in the New Canadian Political Economy

PAUL PHILLIPS

Arguably, labour should be the central focus of any political economy. The reason is readily apparent. People are the subject of political-economic analysis, and people spend the largest single part of their time on earth working, either in the labour market (the formal economy) or in the domestic (informal) economy. Work, or lack of it, shapes people's identity and provides both the material and, to some extent at least, creative basis of existence. Many people without work decay, in mind, spirit, and body. Thus labour, the human expression of work, is the essential object of concern for the study of society. In the Canadian economy today, wracked by high unemployment, rising inequality, falling real wages, and a collapsing welfare state, it is labour that is at the centre of the political and economic storm.

HISTORICAL CONJUCTURE: THE CURRENT ECONOMIC CRISIS

The Second World War brought to an end the "Great Depression" in Canada, an economic collapse that threatened, had it continued much longer, the continued existence of the capitalist system. Wartime expenditures, mobilization of the country's material and human resources, and extensive government intervention in the economy, however, brought rapid recovery and, with it, the threat of war-induced inflation. The federal government's first response was to control labour and suppress the reinvigorated unions' quest for collective bargaining and higher wages, but by 1944 it had become obvious that industrial cooperation from labour in the war effort and countering of the rising popularity of the socialist CCF required that the government recognize the legitimate demands of organized labour for the right to recognition by employers and to guaranteed access to "free" collective bargaining. This was done through a wartime order-in-council, the justly famous PC1003 of 1944, which after the war was incorporated into both federal and provincial labour legislation.

The granting of compulsory recognition and collective bargaining did not initially bring industrial peace to Canada. Many of the large corporations continued to resist, but a series of union break-throughs and epoch-making strikes in the years just after the war resulted in an unofficial truce, which in the United States has been called the postwar "labour-management accord" – a set of expectations and understandings accepted by both sides. The central element of this compromise was the understanding that "through colective bargaining, unions would obtain for their members relative job security and regularly rising real wages based on sharing the gains made available through increases in productivity. In exchange, corporations would retain a free hand to introduce new technology, to reorganize production as they saw fit, and to invest wherever they pleased. The accord was intended to give workers a fair deal and employers a free hand."[1]

The feared postwar depression, of course, never happened. Pent-up consumer demand, American investment, welfare-state expenditures, resource exports, and, in the United States, military-industrial (rearmament) expenditures on the Cold War and to extend American hegemony over the international economy all acted to buoy demand in the economy. As well, governments made commitments to fiscal and monetary policies to maintain consumer demand and, in Canada, to develop resource exports to satisfy American strategic demand and, particularly in the 1960s, to extend the welfare state.[2] This combination of economic and policy factors produced a prolonged boom characterized by rising real incomes and a profusion of consumer goods never previously available to the majority of the working class. Most conspicuous in this new consumerism were houses, automobiles, appliances, and home electronics.

The postwar boom, marred only by relatively minor recessions when unemployment crept higher, continued through to the late 1960s. Orthodox economists, elated by the prolonged period of growth, declared the business cycle dead and an end to ideological disputation about political economy. Indeed, political economy was declared dead. But already by the late 1960s commodity prices were rising and productivity growth slowing. When the OPEC oil cartel quadrupled the price of oil in 1973, the contradictions in the world capitalist economy in which Canada was completely integrated as a matter of policy became manifest in stagflation – the combination of economic and productivity stagnation with rapidly rising prices.

What followed through the 1970s was a competitive conflict for income shares among labour, domestic and foreign capital, and money lenders. One critical element of the postwar accord had been regularly rising real wages out of the productivity dividend. But productivity stagnated, and increasing shares of output were being claimed by oil producers both within and outside Canada. Labour faced not only the bargaining power of capital demanding its share from domestic production but also demand from oil-producing regions and countries for a larger share of economic output. Canada and the rest of the Western world entered a period of inflation based on class and regional conflict over distributive shares of national income.

The Canadian state directed its response at labour. The federal government appointed a Prices and Incomes Commission to pursue a "voluntary" wage-restraint program. The inflationary pressures that followed the oil-price shock of 1973–4, however, brought the heavy hand of compulsory wage controls in the form of the Anti-Inflation Board (AIB) (1975–78). It is debatable just how effective the AIB was in reducing wages and prices, though the general consensus among economists was that it reduced wages and prices by a few percentage points over its three-year life.

A renewal of class conflict–induced inflationary pressures after expiry of the AIB was fairly soon suppressed by the rise of unemployment in the deep recession of 1981–83, which resulted from deliberate introduction of monetarist policies (strict control of money supply and high interest rates) in both Canada and the United States.[3] To supplement the de facto private-sector wage control that resulted from employers' increased bargaining power caused by the rise in unemployment, Ottawa also introduced wage controls into the public sector with its "6 & 5" program (1982–84), limiting wage increases to 6 per cent for 1982–83 and 5 per cent for 1983–84. Most of the provinces followed suit.

The attack by government and employers on labour and labour income was not limited to restrictive fiscal and monetary policies and wage controls. It extended to a sustained assault on unions and on the collective bargaining process.[4] Ad hoc restrictions on the right to strike and to collective bargaining increased steadily through the 1970s and 1980s and became encoded in legislation. Meanwhile, employers, facing falling profits resulting from rising international competition, stagnant productivity and markets, and increased resource prices, demanded consessions from labour and government. The state's response, in addition to restrictive labour legislation, was to

shift the burden of taxation from capital to labour by reducing corporate taxation and shifting the burden onto individual income taxes of
middle-income earners (wage and salary workers) and onto consumption taxes and to begin the process of eroding the welfare state and the
social wage. Both the shift in taxation and the erosion of the social
wage and safety net accelerated in the 1980s under Brian Mulroney's
Conservative government. However, the election of a Liberal government in 1993 did not change government policy. In fact, in their first
two years in office, the Liberals cut the social wage far more than had
the Conservatives in the previous nine years.

Thus, all the elements of the postwar accord had been severely
eroded by the 1980s. The results for labour have been ominous. Some
have been the focus of political debate, such as the continuing high
levels of unemployment and underemployment and the repeated reductions in unemployment insurance coverage and eligibility, pension
entitlement, family allowances, health and education expenditures,
and minimum wages. A few of the debates have not been closely identified with the ongoing economic crisis and its effects on labour, such as
the battles between the "greens" trying to save the environment from
ecological disaster and loggers and fishers trying to save their jobs,
though these conflicts originate in the lack of alternative economic
opportunities engendered by the crisis. Some of the effects have been
manifest in concessions on wages and working conditions that many
unions have been forced to concede, and indeed in the decreasing
portion of the labour force that is organized in unions, though the
decline in Canada has been just a fraction of what it has been in the
United States.

Some of the results just appear as statistics in the numerous studies
from Statistics Canada and the (now-disbanded) Economic Council of
Canada on the labour market – widening income disparities between
"rich" (higher wage and salary earners) and poor; a decline in real
wages, particularly after tax, and especially for new entrants to the
labour market, for whom starting wages fell by a quarter over the last
decade or so; a rising proportion of involuntary part-time work alongside a growing proportion of involuntary overtime and work weeks of
over fifty hours; and declining access to careers or job ladders.[5] And,
of course, others appear in the fiscal crisis of the state, which manifests
itself in major cutbacks in expenditures and employment in the social
sector, particularly in health and education.

There is an ideological battle under way at both the political and
the intellectual levels to interpret what is happening to labour in the
current crisis and to assess labour's role in that crisis. Orthodox economics, which dominates in elite, business, government, and media
circles, holds labour responsible for its own problems – a blame-the-

victim analysis. The new Canadian political economy (NCPE) sees labour, in Canada and elsewhere, as bearing the burden of a major adjustment in the world capitalist economy, the result of a historic and ongoing process of capital accumulation under capitalist property relations. Before developing this comparative analysis, it is important that we link the NCPE with the Canadian political economy tradition dating back to Harold Innis and the institutionalists in the early years of this century, as informed and influenced by Marxist and radical political economy.[6]

LABOUR IN TRADITIONAL CANADIAN POLITICAL ECONOMY

One of the elements that distinguishes political economy analysis from orthodox economics is that political economy does not treat labour as an abstract commodity producing an invariable quantity of work, as does neo-classical economics. Rather, a worker, whether self-employed or waged labour, embodies a potential to do work. This potential Marx called "labour power." The actual work performed or extracted, or re-alized labour, depends on the way the work is organized and the extent to which potential labour is extracted at the workplace. This process of organizing and extracting labour is known as the labour process. These concepts – labour power, labour process, and realized labour – give us a powerful framework for analysing the political economy of labour in both historical and contemporary contexts.

It has become conventional to divide Canadian history into a number of periods or stages based on the labour process and on the status of labour (that is, whether workers are independent producers or waged labour).[7] The earliest period is usually referred to as pre-industrial Canada, or the age of primitive accumulation. This phase lasts until the early-to-mid-nineteenth century, ignoring the differentiation between the era before European contact and the period when what is now Canada was gradually incorporated into a world (mercantile) capitalist system through development of a succession of staple (raw-material) export industries. What is clear now is that the economic organization of pre-contact Aboriginal societies was far more complex and diverse than is commonly perceived. However, from a labour perspective, the "domestic mode of production" (to use Sahlin's terminology), based on the sexual division of labour, production for use, and small-scale, reproducible technology, generally prevailed.[8]

Arrival of the Europeans and contact with the Native population, primarily through the fur trade, modified the Native economic organization, but not until this century did the capitalist mode of production completely overcome and destroy the domestic (or subsistence) mode, which had persisted among the Aboriginal population. This interaction and modification of both the Aboriginal and European modes of production is referred to as the "articulation of modes of production"[9] and has only quite recently become an area of research concentration.[10]

European labour was also affected by this articulation, though this issue was largely unexplored by Innis and the early practitioners of Canadian political economy, who generally ignored class as an analytical category in favour of the sorts of exchange relationships and technological and geographical determinism integral to Innis's staple approach.[11] What the staple approach did emphasize, however, was how a series of staple trades and industries introduced labour to mercantile and then industrial capital and labour processes, thus fragmenting the labour experience. The way in which European labour was integrated into the mode of production characteristic of the staples of the mercantilist period was first explored in depth by Pentland.[12] He emphasized the interdependence of labour and mercantile capital, which made the worker dependent on the employer for survival in an economy where labour demand was unstable and intermittent and made the employer dependent on the worker when labour was scarce and unreliable. The resulting labour relations defined a legal and social relationship of master-servant that he termed "paternalist."

Pentland is better known for his work on the evolution of a capitalist wage-labour market and the "making" of the Canadian working class in the second period of Canadian labour history, the first industrial revolution in the mid-and-later nineteenth century. This is also the period of Canadian labour that received early attention from the younger generation of social historians. They were concerned with how the work experience in industrializing Canada in the nineteenth and early twentieth centuries, with the dominance of the skilled worker in the labour process, shaped working-class culture and class and gender relations.

Around the turn of the century, the North American economy began a process of structural and institutional change which has also been referred to as the second industrial revolution. The most important aspect of this transformation was organizational – the emergence of monopoly capital and the labour process that accompanied it. It involved the move from extensive growth of production – more workers using more capital in traditional processes controlled by skilled workers – to intensive production, employing more and specialized capital to replace skilled labour and utilizing unskilled and work-skilled on production lines involving minute division of labour.[13] At the management level, emergence of large-scale monopoly capital necessitated the growth of corporate bureaucracy. The accompanying expansion of demand for low-wage clerical work opened the white-collar market for women, launching the "feminization" of the office.[14]

Labour responded both collectively and individually to this degredation of labour through unionism, the rise of socialist political parties, high turnover, and industrial sabotage. In this opposition to monopoly capitalism, labour was joined by farmers and small business. Capital was on the defensive until the First World War, when, in combination with the state, it was able virtually to destroy the protest movement. The turning point in Canada was the Winnipeg General Strike in 1919, but this was merely the best-known Canadian confrontation. The suppression of opposition to monopoly capital was continent-wide, and by the early 1920s the voices of labour, farmers, and small business were "muted and meaningless," while those of monopoly capitalists "appeared triumphant."[15]

The collapse of organized labour, the fall in the ratio of skilled to unskilled labour, and the resulting constraints on workers' incomes and consumption power, however, had their price. Canada and the United States had barely recovered from the sharp postwar depression (1920–23) when the collapse of international trade, domestic consumption, and, as a consequence, investment produced the Depression of the 1930s. This decline set the stage for wartime recovery and the postwar boom and subsequent stagnation described above – a period variously labelled "Fordism" or the "era of segmentation."[16]

Traditional political economy in Canada was rooted in the staples and staples-dependence approach to Canadian economic development. The early staples and later agricultural staples were controlled by commercial capital, and labour was dominated by independent commodity producers (farmers, fishers, independent loggers, Native trappers). Expropriation of surplus produced by these primary producers took place through unequal exchange and market power and usually accrued to a distant metropole region or to a comprador commercial-financial class in such trade and banking centres as St John's, Halifax, Saint John, Montreal, Kingston, Toronto, and later Winnipeg and Vancouver.[17] This process was reinforced by the repeated waves of ethnically differentiated immigration that fragmented labour's historical consciousness. This fragmentation was further strengthened by the different and isolated nature of work and labour control in the various staple industries that separated their work experience. Thus labour consciousness often took a populist and spatial (or regional) form rather than a class-conscious form.

The rise of industry and domestic manufacturing and an industrial-based working class and unionism in central Canada presented a challenge to the staple interpretation, as noted by both social historians and by Marxist-informed political economists who rejected the primacy of commercial over industrial capital inherent in the traditional staples approach. In fact, it is necessary to blend both interpretations into a regionally differentiated political economy, since, as has been demonstated, the staple approach remains relevant to large regions and industries in Canada.[18]

CONTEMPORARY ANALYTICAL PERSPECTIVES

Orthodoxy: Blaming the Victim

Late-nineteenth- and twentieth-century development has also led to a challenge to traditional political economy from orthodox economics which has characterized growth over this period as "neoclassical" – by which is meant an incremental and continuous increase in capital, technology, labour, human capital, and resources producing a (more-or-less) sectorally balanced economic growth under the control of self-regulating markets.[19] The obvious conclusion that proceeds from this perspective is that the economic stagnation that characterizes the current crisis is the result of market imperfections. According to this position, at the centre of imperfect markets are labour markets and the welfare state.

It is not easy to summarize briefly the orthodox analysis of the economic stagnation, high and persistent unemployment, government deficits, and tendency to inflation since the 1970s. However, the orthodox view can be stated as a number of propositions frequently advanced by establishment economists and neo-liberal (a neo-conservative) government spokespersons.[20] Perhaps the economic agencies most persistently and explicitly espousing these views are the American-dominated International Monetary Fund and World Bank and the European Union–dominated OECD.[21]

The first proposition is that Canadians (Americans, Britons, Germans, or even Slovenians) "are living beyond their means." That is, real wages and social wages (government transfers and social expenditures) are too high and must be reduced through declining wages and lowered minimum wages and reduced government expenditures on the social safety net (such as unemployment insurance) and on social programs (such as medicare). A variant of this premise is that Canadian industry is "not competitive" because of overpaid (and underworked) workers, restrictive work rules, and environmental and safety over-regulation. This stance leads to advocacy of "free trade" to force wages and working and environmental standards down to a level competitive with producers in the Third World.

The second is that productivity is stagnant because of "labour-market inflexibility." This means that unions should be curtailed, labour standards and work rules relaxed, and more power given to employers to allocate labour at their discretion, including more freedom to fire or lay off workers without restriction or reference to seniority. One other manifestation of this position is the call for greater inequality in wages and salaries, including managerial incomes, to increase incentives.

The third proposition is that the "natural" rate of unemployment – the minimum rate of unemployment considered to be consistent with stable prices – has doubled since the 1950s and 1960s.[22] The primary reason for the shift, in this view, is the increased percentage of women in the labour force who are more selective about which jobs they will accept and the generosity of the unemployment-insurance system, which allows workers extended job search before accepting work. The answer to this problem is both to accept a higher unemployment rate and to reduce unemployment-insurance entitlement and benefits.

The fourth is that productivity has stagnated because the level of investment has been curtailed by excessive regulation and too-low profit levels. The solution is seen in reduction of corporate taxation, privatization of profitable public-sector enterprises, deregulation of industries, and a shift in the distribution of income from labour to capital.

This is not the place to attempt to challenge these propositions on either theoretical or empirical grounds. Suffice it to say that they are based on a large, complex, sophisticated but consistent body of neo-classical economic theory, which is a-historical (that is, considers the economy independent of the past) and considers market-determined values superior to human or political values. In contrast, the political economy approach incorporates in its body of theory both the historical evolution of the economy and the values existing in social and economic institutions. Thus its analysis leads to a very different set of propositions about the current economic crisis.

The Political Economy Perspective: Structures of Accumulation

The first proposition of the political economy analysis is that all capitalist countries have gone through a series of long waves, or swings, in economic activity.[23] These are comprised of expansionary or growth periods, averaging around twenty-five years and interrupted only by short, shallow economic slowdowns, followed by equally long periods of relatively slow and uneven growth marked by frequent, long, and deep downturns, or depressions. In Canada, since its industrial revolution, there have been three such periods of relative slowdown and recurring depressions or deep recessions – 1873–96, 1920–40, and from around 1970 to the 1990s. (The dates for the United States are more or less the same.) Typically, as well, the expansionary phases of these long waves in Canada are associated with resource booms: the period before 1873, with agricultural expansion in Ontario; 1897–1920, with the "wheat boom" in the prairies and the mining, lumbering, and pulp-and-paper booms in southern British Columbia and northern Ontario, Quebec, and further east; and after 1945, with the boom in mineral, energy, and forest resources in response to American demand. It is this association – of economic expansion with resource booms and of stagnation with depressed international markets or prices for resource commodities – that has reinforced the staple interpretation of Canadian development in the industrial period.

However, the political economy approach must look beyond just the role of resources. It must also examine the roots of economic crises and the importance of institutions of production and accumulation in generating these long swings. This approach is embodied in the social models of capitalist development represented by the (American) "social structures of accumulation" (SSA) and the (French) "regulation theory" (RT) schools of political economy. Though the two schools differ, each postulates that every long-wave period of accumulation is characterized by specific labour-market and labour-process institutions (social structures or regimes of accumulation) that, in the expansionary phase, provide an environment conducive to growth (accumulation) but which, as the process takes place, become increasingly restrictive of further accumulation, thereby producing stagnation and eventually crisis.[24]

This leads to the second proposition of the political economy approach. In applying this general analysis to Canadian labour since 1945, certain commonalities with the regimes and social structures in other industrial capitalist countries must be recognized. The postwar period, commonly referred to as the regime of Fordism, combined for its macroeconomic balance mass production for mass consumption with its microeconomic foundations, production-line (segmented) work organization and a segmented labour market. The institutional form of this labour-process and labour-market segmentation was the collective agreement between unions and employers in the primary labour market, which embodied segmented pay structures, work organization, and job ladders (known as internal labour markets) and the unconstrained right of employers to introduce technological change and increased capital intensity (organic composition of capital) in legally enforceable contracts.

Workers in this primary labour market were disproportionately male, white, and in the age groups from 25 to 50 years. In industries and occupations where mass production was not feasible, where high division of labour and the "scientific management" subdivision of tasks could not be combined with capital-intensive production techniques, or where specialized knowledge or on-the-job acculturation to bureaucratically controlled work organization was not required, labour-market conditions and legal barriers to union recognition relegated workers to a segmented, unregulated, secondary labour market. These workers were disproportionately women, visible minorities and immigrants, and young people, all groups thought to have a secondary attachment to the labour market.

The Fordist regime of the postwar labour-management accord, the union structures and the collective bargaining system embodied in the accord, and the supporting state policies provided a favourable institutional framework and the consumer demand necessary for corporate capital accumulation through to the 1960s. Even by then, however, contradictions in the accumulation process and rising conflicts between labour and capital were threatening both the macro- and microeconomic elements of balance in the regime and the institutions that assured their compatibility and moderated their conflictual characteristics.

The third proposition of the political economy approach is that these contradictions and conflicts undermined the profitability of capital, leading to a fall in investment and, with it, technological stagnation. Capital, aided by the resulting unemployment, responded through intensification of work and lower wages and with demands for lower taxes on business, reduction in the social wage, and increased competition (deregulation) in input markets. The agency to achieve these goals was "globalization" – reducing barriers to movement of goods, services, and capital across national boundaries so as to open vast pools of low-wage, non-unionized labour in low-tax jurisdictions where there were minimal levels of social wage.

This results in the fourth postulate of contemporary political economy. However successful such a strategy was at the micro- level of the global firm, at the macro- level the resulting stagnation in real wages and the rise in unemployment limited labour's ability to consume. In order to maintain demand, governments were forced to offset reduced business investment and wage earners' consumption through increased spending and transfers and corporate tax cuts, which resulted in rising government deficits. Efforts to combat these deficits through increases in consumption taxes and cuts in social, education, and health programs merely added to unemployment and further decreased consumption. At the same time, increased international competition brought a restructuring of global capital and a shift of investment to low-wage, developing countries.

The threat to labour, unions, and social democracy in this restructuring process is obvious. Unemployment, the disappearing middle stratum of jobs in goods production and the expanding lower stratum of service jobs, falling wages, reductions in the social wage, declines in private-sector unionization, greater inequality, and increased nonstandard forms of work (part-time, subcontract, involuntary self-employment, home work) are all manifestations of this process that bode ill for the working class. Labour and social democracy have been forced on the defensive and have generally proven unsuccessful in maintaining past gains, with their voices indeed "muted and meaningless" once more.

Contemporary Relevance: The Importance of Perspective

The relevance of the current economic crisis for labour is obvious in the headlines in the daily newspapers and in the media news bulletins regarding unemployment, declining labour incomes and social-security protection, a growing secondary labour market, and increasing economic and social inequality. It is manifested in the policies being enacted by legislatures worldwide, reducing social expenditures, restricting union organizing and bargaining rights, deregulating labour markets, and redistributing income from labour to capital.

Descriptions of what is happening differ little between proponents of orthodox economics and those operating from a political economy perspective. Differences arise, however, in the analysis of the cause of the crisis and, therefore, in the policy prescriptions. The orthodox neo-liberal analysis presents labour as the cause of the crisis, and therefore the burden of adjustment must, and should, fall on labour. The political economy approach, in contrast, approaches the crisis as a systemic problem that can be resolved only by adjustments to the system. How these adjustments take place will determine the distribution of the burden of adjustment between labour and capital. This distribution in turn depends on the balance of power of class forces – a subject little considered in orthodox analysis.

The structure-of-accumulation analysis presented above immediately rules out some of the policy options frequently advanced as answers to Canada's current woes. First, the "staple option," or reliance on expansion of resource-based industries, is no longer feasible, on both economic and ecological grounds. Quite simply, Canada has reached, if not passed, the limits of sustainable resource exploitation.[25] Second, the option of "humanizing" the economic decline of Canadian labour – the view associated with the "neo-socialists" – accepts the neo-liberal economic analysis and its policy prescriptions and in practice merely attempts to devise policies to soften the adjustment and make it less brutal for the lower segments of the working class.[26] However successful it may be in softening the process of restructuring, it does little to change the end results.

The political economy schools have argued that the new institutions (social structures of accumulation or modes of regulation) that are constructed in the process of generating a new phase of long-wave expansion are in part determined by working-class struggle in the previous period of stagnation. "Although workers respond to and resist capitalists' explorations, the most promising forays, shaped by the impact of workers' struggles, are gradually consolidated."[27] This suggests that how labour responds to the current restructuring process will help determine its welfare and influence in the evolving regime or social structure of accumulation – for the next half-century.

Historical political economy in Canada has taught us, first, that unregulated markets lead to inequality, not only between labour and capital but also between the centre and the periphery. The increased globalization of the capitalist economy therefore presents particular problems for Canada and the Canadian worker. While Canada is a developed and industrialized country and has its own global corporations, it is at the periphery of the capitalist centre, and the crisis of Fordism intensifies as one moves from the centre to the periphery.[28]

Canadian political economy has taught us, second, that developmental linkages do not occur naturally, through a self-regulating market, but rather through the intermediation of either, or both, the state and corporate bureaucracy. For example, the majority of Canadian (and world) trade is accounted for by intracorporate transfers, not by market exchange. Thus macroeconomic, labour-market, interest, and exchange-rate policies may have less effect on national economic performance and response to globalization than do internal corporate planning mechanisms and competitive strategies. Under Fordism, a mode of national regulation, economic linkages, and employment could be encouraged by national-state policies and labour-market regulation. This is not possible in a global system where national regulatory measures are prohibited by a mode of international regulation embodied in treaties such as the Canada–United States Free Trade Agreement (FTA), the North American Free Trade Agreement (NAFTA),

and the General Agreement on Tariffs and Trade (GATT). The decay
of Fordism is thus integrally connected to the decline of the nation-
state as an independent, policy-making unit.

STRATEGIC IMPLICATIONS

There have been two strands of thought among political economists
about appropriate policy response to these developments in the economy. One advocates replication at the international level of the labour-
market regulatory institutions prevailing at the national level. The second argues that international regulation is probably unattainable and
that labour should turn its attention to restructuring the labour-capital
relation in the domestic economy so that labour attains greater control
of the location, rate, and form of accumulation.

The first strand was succinctly developed in a 1994 opinion editorial in the *Globe and Mail*, "Wanted: A GATT Agreement That Covers
Workers":[29]

Trying to help the lot of the worker in an open system is like trying to heat a
house in the middle of winter with all the windows open. It's futile. To heat a
house, you must either close the windows or equalize temperatures with the
outside environment.

'Closing the windows' means some form of protectionism, which is not a
realistic option for smaller economies ... [T]he most attractive alternative is a
world agreement on jobs ... The second-best option, then, is a sort of "GATT
for Jobs," which would extend the current General Agreement on Tariffs and
Trade to include the establishment of a global safety net, thus (to switch meta-
phors) levelling the international playing field.[30]

The difficulties in achieving such a system may be seen in the failure of
even the United States (with lukewarm Canadian backing) to achieve a
meaningful labour side-agreement to NAFTA. Neither financial nor
industrial capital has any interest in the international regulation of
labour markets. Indeed, the major international agencies of capital,
led by the IMF, are pressing for, and achieving, deregulation of labour
markets throughout the world. Furthermore, the elites in the developing countries are adamantly opposed to any minimum standards in
labour markets or on the environment that would reduce their competitive advantage in attracting capital investment and, with it, jobs.

The alternative – international union action to extend minimum
standards through industrial action – faces insummountable obstacles,
not least the willingness of governments of developing countries and
regions to suppress unionization through legislative restrictions or

even through force.[31] There is also the long-standing problem of promoting international working-class solidarity in a capitalist system which pits country against country in their search for jobs. This, of course, is no reason to discourage or oppose international union cooperation, as is beginning to develop among Canada, the United States, and Mexico to deal with common interests affected by NAFTA, though the effectiveness of this cooperation will depend to some extent on the success of Mexican labour in freeing itself from the control of the business-dominated government.

Furthermore, the nature of the labour and capital markets created by NAFTA precludes the social-charter and labour-mobility protections provided for labour in the European Union. American, Mexican, and Canadian capital explicitly opposes any form of mandatory minimum social safety net or any income transfers like those provided in the European Union under provisions such as the Common Agricultural Plan (CAP). Given this opposition, reopening NAFTA to include such provisions would appear to be impossible. In addition, a major motivation for the Americans in negotiating NAFTA was to prevent migration of Mexican labour to the United States by encouraging U.S. capital to relocate within Mexico. Thus the idea of a common labour market is equally unrealistic. In any case, given the differences in levels of development, increased labour mobility would only put further downward pressure on wages in Canadian and American labour markets, where labour still gets some protection from low-wage competition because of the location advantages or the non-tradeability of services.

The second strategy is to limit control of accumulation, in particular location of investment, by international capital. One thrust of this option has been popularized by Piore and Sabel, who have advocated revival of a craft-based, flexible specialization, where economies of scope and flexibility would provide protection from low-wage competition.[32] Mahon, in contrast, has criticized this model on grounds that it ignores the macroeconomic balance, "between changes in production and the structure of consumption," and argues that continuation of extensive, well-paid social services and of core, unionized industries is necessary for maintenance of high levels of consumption.[33]

This leads to a redirection of emphasis towards repatriating control of capital to local communities. This implies a labour strategy of increasing influence in controlling those property rights of ownership that materially affect labour directly – in particular, the rights of usufruct (use), to manage, and to destroy, relocate, or dispose of capital.[34] In turn, this leads to strategies such as worker-owned industrial cooperative complexes such as the successful Mondragon Co-ops in Spain[35] and to wage-earner investment funds such as those devised but never implemented (except in an ineffectual, watered-down form) in Sweden.[36] In any case, the election of a conservative government in Sweden led to the abolition of the wage-earner funds in the early 1990s. Nevertheless, such moves to industrial democracy, if widely achieved, could pose an enormous challenge to global corporate capital by changing the central institutions and structures of political economy regulation.

THE IMPORTANCE OF POLITICAL ECONOMY

Many observers of North American labour in the current crisis have called either for a labour campaign for shorter hours to spread the diminished amount of available work or, at the other extreme, the divorce of income entitlement from work entirely. The outline of today's political economy of labour developed above raises questions about the viability of either strategy, however useful it may be in raising consciousness of the issues. Spreading available work may lower unemployment but will do little to halt polarization of society, restore the real wages of the new entrants to the labour market, or improve those of the increased numbers in the secondary labour market. At the same time, the mobility of global capital towards low-tax jurisdictions makes it inconceivable for national governments to attempt to redistribute income on a non–labour-market basis. Besides, such change would demand a revolution not only in the forms of property rights but also in the hearts and minds, or, in Veblen's terms, the ingrained instinct of workmanship, of Canadians.

NOTES

1 Bowles and Edwards, *Understanding Capitalism*, 218.

2 The federal government in 1945 announced its commitment in the White Paper on Employment and Income to combining its acceptance of Keynesian-type demand management through fiscal and monetary policies with support for a continued role for Canada as an exporter of natural resources – "a rather unique synthesis of the traditional Canadian staples-led approach to economic development with the Keynesian theory of demand management and fiscal stabilization" (Wolfe, "Rise and Demise," 55). For other analyses of the export-led boom see Clark-Jones, *A Staple State*; Aitken, *American Capital*; and Kent, "Structure," 102–3. With respect to the welfare state, unemployment insurance was introduced in 1940, family allowances in 1945, a universal old-age pension in 1951, and medicare (following Saskatchewan's lead), the Canada Pension Plan, the Canada Assistance Act, and the Guaranteed Income Supplement in the 1960s.

3 In fact, monetarism had been introduced first by the Bank of Canada in 1975, along with income controls.

4 Panitch and Swartz, *Assault*; Drache and Glasbeek, *The Changing Workplace.*

5 Picot, Myles, and Wannell, *Good Jobs*; Picot and Wannell, *Job Loss*; Myles, Picot, and Wannell, *Wages and Jobs*; Myles and Fawcett, *Job Skills*; Morrisette, Myles, and Picot, *What Is Happening?*; Morissette and Sunter, *What Is Happening?*; Betcherman et al., *Employment*; Economic Council of Canada, *Good Jobs*; and Krahn and Lowe, *Young Workers.*

6 Innis began his influential writings in the 1920s, but he was strongly influenced by people such as Thorstein Veblen, who wrote at the turn of the century and was in turn influenced by Marx. See Innis, "Work."

7 Kealey, "Structure"; Heron, *Canadian.*

8 Sahlins, *Stone Age Economics.*

9 Beal, *Money*, 37ff. See also Tough, *Native People.*

10 In addition to the works of Beal and Tough cited above, see Ray, *Indians*; Ray and Freeman, '*Give*'; van Kirk, '*Many*'; Usher, "Aboriginal"; and collections of Fur Trade Conferences. A review of some of the issues involved can be found in Abele and Stasiulis, "Canada."

11 The following is largely a highly condensed version of my "Through."

12 Pentland, *Labour*, chaps. 1–2.

13 The common term used for this change in the labour process is "scientific management," which actually refers to the system advocated by one of the pioneers of the organizational changes, F.W. Taylor.

14 Lowe, *Women.*

15 Edwards, *Contested Terrain*, 38–9.

16 Fordism is the term coined by the French regulation school. (See Aglietta, Theory; Lipietz, *Mirages*; and Boyer, *Search*). The "segmentation of labour" terminology originated with the American social-structures-of-accumulation school. (Gordon, Edwards, and Reich, *Segmented Work*; Bowles, Gordon, and Weisskopf, *After*). The regulation school strongly informs one of the most significant recent publications in Canadian political economy, Drache and Gertler, eds., *The New Era*, particularly the chapter by Mahon, 316–52.

17 Phillips, "Staples."

18 Clark-Jones, *A Staple State*; Phillips, "New Staples."

19 See, for example, Drummond, *Progress.*

20 It has become common in Canada to label as "neo-conservative" the policies of retrenchment, privatization, deregulation, and control of labour that have dominated since the 1970s, particularly because they have been associated with conservative governments such as Margaret Thatcher's in Britain, Ronald Reagan's in the United States, and Brian Mulroney's in Canada. However, from an economic-theory point of view, they are more

accurately "neo-liberal," since they embody the ideology of nineteenth-century economic liberalism. Nor is this ideology restricted to bourgeois parties, as is evidenced by the introduction of neo-liberal policies in Ontario by Bob Rae's NDP government.

21 See, for example, the IMF *Survey*, 16 May 1994, 153–6, for an elaboration of this position.

22 The Bank of Canada usually estimates the "natural" rate at around 8 per cent. In the United States in 1994, the Federal Reserve Bank (the U.S. central bank) appeared to begin to raise interest rates in anticipation of inflationary pressure whenever the unemployment rate fell near to 6 per cent, indicating that it considers that figure to be the "natural" rate.

23 The concept of long waves or swings goes back to the nineteenth century, but interest in it waned in the long boom of the 1950s and 1960s. Stagflation in the 1970s brought renewed interest even from orthodox economists, who tend to emphasize the technological basis of long waves. For a Canadian analysis, see Lamontagne, *Business Cycles.*

24 For a fuller development of these social models see Lipietz, *Mirages*; Bowles, Gordon and Weisskopf, *After*; and, for a Canadian perspective, Mahon, "Post-Fordism."

25 Phillips, "New Staples."

26 This approach was first identified with the views and policies of Roger Douglas, finance minister in New Zealand's Labour government in the 1980s. In Canada it has been typified by Bob Rae's NDP government in Ontario and its "social contract." A more successful variant is the Labour government in Australia from 1983 to 1996, which administered the restructuring process through a series of labour-government accords. The most prominent academic guru of neo-socialism in Canada is John Richards of Simon Fraser University's Commerce Department.

27 Gordon, Edwards, and Reich, *Segmented Work*, 11–12.

28 See Lipietz, *Mirages,* for an elaboration of this argument.

29 Valaskakis, "Wanted."

30 Ibid.

31 Such legislative restriction is not limited to developing countries. Witness the "right-to-work" states in the United States – mostly in the South – which limit unionization in their pursuit of jobs, regardless of the quality of these jobs.

32 Piore and Sabel, *The Second*, 258–308.

33 Mahon, "Post-Fordism," 321.

34 The importance of these is discussed in Phillips, "Functional Rights."

35 Whyte and Whiyte, *Making Mondragon.*

36 Olsen, *Struggle.*

REFERENCES

Abele, Francis, and Stasiulis, Daiva. "Canada as a 'White Settler Colony': What about Natives and Immigrants?" In Wallace Clement and Glen Williams, eds., *The New Canadian Political Economy*, 240–77. Montreal: McGill-Queen's University Press, 1989.

Aglietta, Michel. *A Theory of Capitalist Regulation*. London: New Left Books, 1979.

Aitken, H.G.J. *American Capital and Canadian Resources*. Cambridge, Mass.: Harvard University Press, 1961.

Beal, Carl. "Money, Markets and Economic Development in Saskatchewan Indian Reserve Communities 1870–1930s." PhD thesis, Department of Economics, University of Manitoba, 1994.

Betcherman, Gordon, et al. *Employment in the Service Economy*. Ottawa: Economic Council of Canada, 1991.

Bowles, Samuel, and Edwards, Richard. *Understanding Capitalism*. New York: Harper and Row, 1985.

Bowles, Samuel, Gordon, David, and Weisskopf, Thomas. *After the Wasteland*. Armonk, NY: M.E. Sharpe, 1990.

Boyer, Robert. *The Search for Labour Market Flexibility*. Oxford: Clarendon Press, 1988.

Clark-Jones, Melissa. *A Staple State*. Toronto: University of Toronto Press, 1987.

Drache, Daniel, and Gertler, Meric, eds. *The New Era of Global Competition*. Montreal: McGill-Queen's University Press, 1991.

Drache, Daniel, and Glasbeek, Harry. *The Changing Workplace*. Toronto: Lorimer, 1992.

Drummond, Ian. *Progress without Planning*. Toronto: University of Toronto Press, 1987.

Economic Council of Canada. *Good Jobs, Bad Jobs: Employment in the Service Sector.* Ottawa, 1990.

Edwards, Richard. *Contested Terrain*. New York: Basic Books, 1979.

Fur Trade Conference Papers:
– D.L. Morgan et al. *Aspects of the Fur Trade*. St Paul: Minnesota Historical Association, 1967.
– Malvina Bolus, ed. *People and Pelts*. Winnipeg: Peguis, 1972.
– Carol Judd and Arthur K. Ray, eds., *Old Trails and New Directions*. Toronto: University of Toronto Press, 1980.
– Thomas Buckley, ed., *Rendezvous*. St Paul; Minn.: North American Fur Trade Conference, 1984.
– Bruce Tigger et al. eds. *Le castor fait tout*. Montreal: Lake St Louis Historical Society, 1987.

Gordon, David, Edwards, Richard, and Reich, Michael. *Segmented Work, Divided Workers*. Cambridge: Cambridge University Press, 1982.

Heron, Craig. *The Canadian Labour Movement.* Toronto: Lorimer, 1989.

Innis, Harold. "The Work of Thorstein Veblen." In Harold Innis, *Essays in Economic History,* 17–26. Toronto: University of Toronto Press, 1956.

Kealey, Gregory. "The Structure of Canadian Working-Class History." In W.J.C. Cherwinski and Gregory Kealey, eds., *Lectures in Canadian Labour and Working-Class History,* 23–36. St John's, Nfld: New Hogtown and Committee on Canadian Labour History, 1985.

Kent, Tom. "The Structure of Canadian Regional Programs." In Paul Phillips, ed., *Incentives, Location and Regional Development,* 101–9. Winnipeg: Manitoba Economic Development Advisory Board, 1975.

Krahn, Harvey, and Lowe, Graham. *Young Workers in the Service Economy.* Ottawa: Economic Council of Canada, 1990.

Lamontagne, Maurice. *Business Cycles in Canada.* Toronto: Lorimer for the Canadian Institute for Public Policy, 1984.

Lipietz, Alain. *Mirages and Miracles: The Crisis of Global Fordism.* London: Verso, 1987.

Lowe, Graham. *Women in the Administrative Revolution: The Feminization of Clerical Work.* Toronto: University of Toronto Press, 1987.

Mahon, Rianne. "Post-Fordism: Some Issues for Labour." In Daniel Drache and Meric Gertler, eds., *The New Era of Global Competition,* 316–32. Montreal: McGill-Queen's University Press, 1991.

Morrissette, Rene, Myles, John, and Picot, Garnett. *What Is Happening to Earnings Inequality in Canada?* Analytic Studies Branch Research Paper No. 60, Statistics Canada, Ottawa, 1993.

Morrissette, René, and Sunter, Deborah. *What Is Happening to Weekly Hours Worked in Canada?* Analytic Studies Branch Research Paper No. 65, Statistics Canada, Ottawa, 1994.

Myles, John, and Fawcett, Gail. *Job Skills and the Service Economy.* Ottawa: Economic Council of Canada, 1990

Myles, John, Picot, Garnett, and Wannell, Ted. *Wages and Jobs in the 1980s.* Analytic Studies Branch Research Paper No. 17, Statistics Canada, Ottawa, 1988.

Olsen, Gregg. *The Struggle for Economic Democracy in Sweden.* Aldershot: Avebury, 1992.

Panitch, Leo, and Swartz, Donald. *The Assault on Trade Union Freedoms.* Toronto: Garamond, 1993.

Pentland, Claire. *Labour and Capital in Canada, 1650–1860.* Toronto: Lorimer, 1981.

Phillips, Paul. "Functional Rights: Private, Public and Collective Property." *Studies in Political Economy,* 38 (summer 1992), 61–84.

– "New Staples and Mega-Projects: Reaching the Limits to Sustainable Development." In Daniel Drache and Meric Gertler, eds., *The New Era of Global Competition,* 229–46. Montreal: McGill-Queen's University Press, 1991.

– "Staples, Surplus and Exchange: The Commercial-Industrial Question in the National Policy Period." In Duncan Cameron, eds., *Explorations in Canadian Economic History*, 27–43. Ottawa: University of Ottawa Press, 1985.

– "Through Different Lenses: The Political Economy of Labour." In Wallace Clement and Glen Williams, eds., *The New Canadian Political Economy*, 77–98. Montreal: McGill-Queen's University Press, 1989.

Picot, Garnett, Myles, John, and Wannell, Ted. *Good Jobs, Bad Jobs and the Declining Middle*. Analytical Studies Branch Research Paper No. 28, Statistics Canada, Ottawa, 1990.

Picot, Garnett, and Wannell, Ted. *Job Loss and Labour Market Adjustment in the Canadian Economy*. Analytic Studies Branch Research Paper No. 5, Statistics Canada, Ottawa, 1987.

Piore, Michael, and Sabel, Charles. *The Second Industrial Divide*. New York: Basic Books, 1984.

Ray, A.J. *Indians in the Fur Trade*. Toronto: University of Toronto Press, 1974.

Ray, A.J., and Freeman, D.B. "*Give Us Good Measure*". Toronto: University of Toronto Press, 1978.

Sahlins, M. *Stone Age Economics*. New York: Aldine Publishing, 1972.

Tough, Frank. "Native People and the Regional Economy of Northern Manitoba, 1870–1930s." PhD thesis, Department of Geography, York University, 1987.

Usher, Peter. "Aboriginal Property Systems in Land and Resources: Lessons for Socialists." In Jesse Vorst, Ross Dobson, and Ron Fletcher, eds., *Green on Red: Evolving Ecological Socialism*, 93–102. Winnipeg/Halifax: Society of Socialist Studies/Fernwood Publishing, 1993.

Valaskakis, Kimon, "Wanted: A GATT Agreement that Covers Workers." *Globe and Mail*, 22 April 1994.

Van Kirk, Sylvia. *"Many Tender Ties": Women in Fur Trade Society 1670–1870*. Winnipeg: Watson and Dwyer, 1980.

Whyte, William, and White, Kathleen. *Making Mondragon*. Ithaca, NY: IRL Press, 1988.

Wolfe, David. "The Rise and Demise of the Keynesian Era in Canada: Economic Policy, 1930–1932." In M. Cross and G. Kealey, eds., *Modern Canada*, 46–78. Toronto: McClelland and Stewart, 1984.

5 Gender at Work: Canadian Feminist Political Economy since 1988

HEATHER JON MARONEY AND MEG LUXTON

INTRODUCTION

In a 1994 interview for the journal *Studies in Political Economy (SPE)*, Judy Rebick, past president of the National Action Committee on the Status of Women (NAC), assessed the importance of political economy for feminist politics.

SPE: What this emphasises is how much political economy is a women's issue, right?

Judy: Absolutely, there's no question. It's very hard to introduce that notion into the debate because when you talk about women's issues, immediately it's the more narrowly defined women's issues: abortion, pay equity etc. ... [I]t took us two years to get the credibility to be heard on other issues within the Constitution.

I think the deficit debate is very important for women. ... The net effect [of the framework of deficit reduction] is to completely marginalize women's issues, because, of course, most concerns of women either require government expenditure or intervention and both things are really out of fashion right now. So we have to develop strategies of dealing with it, an analysis of why it is there.[1]

Rebick's cautious assessment illustrates both the appeal of political economy as a guide for action and some of the problems in breaking through the political and theoretical ghettoization of women's issues.

Indeed, feminists working with a political economy framework have made significant contributions to knowledge about women in Canada and about the overall organization and dynamics of Canadian society.[2] In this process they have argued that if political economy is to fulfil its promise as a holistic theory, on the one hand, and as a framework for radical action, on the other, it must take up challenges posed by feminists to integrate the dimensions of gender and, more recently, "race" into its analysis. For just as activists in NAC have had difficulty in breaking the mould which narrowly defined women's issues, so too the transformative implications of feminist analyses of gender and racialization have scarcely been acknowledged by mainstream political economy.[3]

Since the 1970s, a major concern of left-wing feminists has been to understand the relation between sex and class. Central to this project has been an engagement with Marxist political economy.[4] Marxism already offered a critical theory of class and some analysis of women's subordination, while its practical orientation to struggle made a place for women's liberation. Engels's classic formulation offered a starting point:

According to the materialist conception, the determining factor in history is, in the final instance, the production and reproduction of immediate life. This, again, is of a twofold character: on the one side, the production of the means of existence, of food, clothing and shelter and the tools necessary for that production; on the other side, the production of human beings themselves, the propagation of the species. The social organization under which the people of a particular historical epoch and a particular country live is determined by both kinds of production: by the stage of development of labour on the one hand and of the family on the other.[5]

In that vein, a Marxist-influenced approach, now usually called socialist feminism, set out to develop integrated theory capable of analysing societies, starting from "the production and reproduction of immediate life" – that is, human beings and the goods and services necessary to sustain them.

Some feminists argued that Marxist political economy is too sex-blind, too focused on "malestream" concepts of class, to be useful in analysing either women or gender relations.[6] Others suggested that two theories are necessary: feminism for sex and Marxism for class.[7] Too often, their scepticism has been reinforced by mainstream political economy's reluctance to incorporate anything more than "a limited analysis of the interaction of class and gender inequalities."[8] Dorothy Smith argues that such resistance is not accidental. Rather, the institutional organization of Canadian political economy as a discipline – that is, its core theories and judgments about what constitutes evidence, its departments, journals, and social networks – actually resists the kind of changes necessary to take account of women's lives. "The central relevancies, assumptions, methods and conceptual practices of political economic discourse remain largely unchanged by attempts to embed feminist topics in the discourse."[9]

Nevertheless, Bakker and Smith, among others, insist that the engagement of feminism and political economy is both possible and necessary. For example, in our *Feminism and Political Economy*, we argued that the requisite new theory needed to transform both Marxism and feminism. Political economy could not just add women on. It would have to allow for dual causation – that is, not just for the determination of family, household, and gender by the exigencies of production, but also for the possibility that these areas of social life could advance, inhibit, or in some way shape developments in "the economy." For Canada, it would also have to take account of the historical intersection of gender, class, race/ethnicity, colonialism, state, politics, ideology, sexuality, and identity.[10] Politically, such theory would also be related to a struggle "for the liberation of women as part of the liberation of all human beings."[11]

Despite conceptual uncertainties, feminist political economy has been fruitful in examining "women" and, more widely, gender relations and politics in several areas. First, there have been extensive studies of women at work in the labour force and in the household, especially their bearing of and caring for children. Second, other investigations, focused on the state and women's movements, have, along with work on sexuality and class formation, raised questions of agency, subjectivity, and political identity.

However, in the 1980s, academic political economy, particularly its feminist current, was criticized for ignoring the way in which "race" entered into and distorted its work. Indeed, the problematic of "sex and class" is itself blind to the primary importance of race, ethnicity, and nation in the experience of many women. Moreover, the development of capitalism as an international social and political force posed a new set of issues with regard to its mode of development, its global class and state forms, and evolving strategies of resistance.[12]

Thus, by the beginning of the 1990s, two further analytical preoccupations emerged. The first was historical: how to understand the changes referred to as globalization, restructuring, or post-fordism. The second was conceptual and political: a challenge to political economic theory and analysis to take into account the ways in which race/ethnic or national relations intersect with those of gender and class.

GENDER AND THE MODE OF PRODUCTION

Emphasizing the two-sided character of production, whether thought of as life and subsistence, people and goods, or in the household and the formal economy, has implications for sociological and economic categories at all levels from macrosocial to microsocial. It also poses question about the scope of each and its relation to the other. How is that relation best thought of: as two aspects of one system or as separate, dual systems? The concepts of mode of production, family, and class would all have to be rethought if we are to take seriously the production and reproduction of life. We note some contributions to this revision before turning to studies of the labour force.

First, at the level of mode of production, Wally Seccombe's two-volume study, *A Millennium of Family Change* and *Weathering the Storm*, is an outstanding contribution. It takes up one of the vexed questions of economic historiography: why did English capitalism develop early? While it is clear that there was a relation between property and family in the dominant classes, exploring this question for subordinate classes, whose lives are generally less well preserved in documents, is much more difficult. Still Seccombe traces the interconnection of the forces and relations of production and family forms in Europe over a thousand years from feudal agriculture to early-twentieth-century industrial capitalism. His expanded concept of mode of production, developed in the first volume takes into account relations of property, productive technology, labour force or population density, family formation, and male-female power relations among labourers, smallholders, and better-off peasants. Marriage, family, and household forms operated as "the conjugal valve" to control access to land, lifetime birth rates, and gender hierarchy within feudal society. Along with inheritance patterns, they also affected the rate of development of a pool of labourers necessary for capitalist production and the rate of capital accumulation. In other words, the social forms of "the production of life" had a causal effect on the "early" transition to capitalism in England. The second volume takes up the more familiar issues of changing family size and gender relations in the transition to industrial production. In both volumes, a convincing case is made that gender and economy are best thought of as aspects of an integrated social formation.

Jane Ursel's *Private Lives, Public Policy: 100 Years of State Intervention in the Family* theorizes mode of production starting with a different society, Canada, and with a dual-systems perspective. For her, "production and reproduction are distinct but interdependent imperatives that constitute the base of society."[13] She goes on to analyse the relation between the institution structured by patriarchy (the family) and the institution that has become the terrain of struggle over patriarchy (the state). Since her main interest is political rather than economic history, the work does not really contribute to conceptualizations of economic development. She directs attention instead to the state: is the state a power that women can invoke to dismantle patriarchy, or a tool of patriarchal interests? Given the variable outcome of women's struggles to date, is it possible that the state is a contested terrain on which struggles for and against patriarchy are waged? If the state is a contested terrain, how do women distinguish the issues on which state involvement would be helpful from those in which it would be harmful?

Several studies of the encounter between Native peoples and imperialism effectively deploy a sense of mode of production expanded by colonialism, as well as by gender and class. For Huron society, colonization undermined a more communal organization of production. Colonizers imposed new legal forms for the holding of property; fragmented kin-based patterns of work and ownership, with the result that gender differences were sharpened, to women's disadvantage; and promoted puritanical control over women's sexuality and freedom to engage in and leave marriage.[14] Later, in western Metis society, Aboriginal women's subordination became central to the colonial project of capitalist expansion in what was to become Canada.[15] In recent years, Native migration from reserves into the urban heart of capitalist society has given rise to a new poor, single-parent, mostly female-headed family, which has become the "primary mechanism" for perpetuating Native disadvantage. According to Falconer, mainstream research and policy have failed to take the nature of this family form, gender, race, or class seriously, while the demands put forward by movements for Native rights led by men passed over the needs of such families.[16] Perhaps because they study processes where colonizers displaced existing social formations and modes of production, these studies tend to place greater causal weight on the economy and politics than on family and household.

It is the use of revised or unrevised concepts of family and household and the ghettoized or general integration of the analysis of the production of "immediate life" into political economic analysis that best illustrate the contradictory way theoretical innovations of feminist political economy have been taken up or neglected. In the 1970s and early 1980s, women's unpaid work, its importance to capital accumulation, households as workplaces, the role of "housework" in the daily and generational reproduction of workers with a capacity, desire, and need to work, and the ideological covering over of all this by the blanket term "family" were the main foci of the "domestic labour

debate."[17] Though one of its main theoretical issues – how to conceptualize economic "value" of housework in Marxist terms – has faded
from view unresolved, understandings of housework developed in
these debates are now basic throughout sociology and economics. In
spreading this concept, feminist political economy has had its greatest
success. For example, most studies of women's paid employment take
into account the ways in which domestic responsibilities and labour-
force participation interact, as do family law and liberal feminist policy
analysis.[18]

However, John Hofley warns against a "serious omission." "Almost
all studies from a political-economy perspective neglect families and
households in their analysis" or do little to analyse the race/ethnic and
class differences among families.[19] Racial ideologies, global economic
disparities, and Canadian labour law certainly lie behind the policies
and practices that recruit women for paid employment as domestic
workers, ensure their exploitation, and reproduce one form of class
relations between women.[20] In conceptualising family, then, it is important to understand not only how family/household relations are
structured by the larger political economy but also "family" as a site of
practices that organize gender, race/ethnic, or class relations and so
shape macro-level political and economic organization.

With some exceptions, feminist political economy since the mid-
1980s seems to have turned from the production of life itself: "begetting babies and raising children."[21] Socialist-feminist legal scholars
seem to be most engaged in paradigm debate with liberal or radical
feminist analyses of family.[22] Compulsory heterosexuality and ho-
mophobia powerfully shape mother-child relations and the work of
mothering for mothers who are lesbians[23] – as well as indirectly those
who are not. Jane Jensen and Heather Jon Maroney have offered non-
functionalist analyses of why governments in France and Quebec,
respectively, turned to pronatalist policies to solve political, demographic, and population problems.[24] It is not only at the abstract level
of mode of production but also with regard to feminist and social-
democratic or socialist policy that a great deal of this discussion
occurs.

Finally, concepts of class come under scrutiny. "When the mode of
production is understood to include relations of reproduction as well
as production, then the conceptualization of class must change.
Household and gender relations must be taken into account."[25] Beginning from a concept of capital/labour as a relation (rather than a
structure), Roxanna Ng, Dorothy Smith, and Himmani Bannerji all
argue that capitalism is best understood as a relations among gender,
race, and class.[26]

Granted this now-accepted understanding that class is gendered and gender is classed, what are the implications for reconceptualizing class? One possibility is to look at the effect of household and gender relations on class consciousness and class political action. Is it still useful to think of "class" as belonging to an individual, as resulting from an occupation in the sphere of "production," strictly defined? Or do we need to stress instead the dynamic and collective aspects of households as sources of class consciousness and class-based activism? According to MacDonald and Connelly, static and individualized concepts of class do not adequately explain the kind of consciousness involved in political actions in Canada's east-coast fishing communities. Instead, in order to understand how individuals engage in struggle one needs to take account not just of the usual indicators of class (that is, current and past participation in paid employment) but also their place in a gendered division of labour (that is, their situation in a family or household, family work patterns, and family strategies). "Both will affect a person's current class identification. This is crucial for understanding class struggle."[27] Lest one think that the effect of gendered households and family strategies on class consciousness and action is peculiar to fisheries, the same connections exist in the heart of industrial production – steel making.[28]

Another possibility is to focus more narrowly on the workplace. Is what happens there also affected by gender relations or just as an effect of capitalist relations of production? Considering this question in their analysis of comparative data on class, Wallace Clement and John Myles strongly concur that workplace authority relations are not gender neutral: "[W]hat we have been calling class relations are not just class relations and what we have been calling a class structure is more than a class structure. ... Relations of power and authority in the modern work place exist to regulate relations between capital and labour but also to reproduce a particular way of organising relations between men and women."[29]

On the whole, then, feminist analyses of the various ways that class and gender intersect have convincingly displaced gender-neutral concepts of class. And though paying attention to both sides of production – subsistence and life itself – they generally support integrated, rather than dual-systems, analysis.

WOMEN AT WORK IN THE LABOUR FORCE AND HOUSEHOLD

Studies of women and work, the area where integration of political economy and feminism is strongest, offer excellent examples of what the best of feminist political economy can do. Most now recognize a complex interplay of capital accumulation, labour markets, state policies (especially regarding public-service funding and employment legislation), reproduction of labour power in daily and generational cycles, family household demographics, forms of organization and divisions of labour, and workplace, trade-union, and political organizing by workers. Such studies also investigate the fundamental contradiction between the demands of the way paid employment is organized and the requirements of domestic/household life, the brunt of which is borne by women, who mediate the contradictions between the two production processes and locations. Gendered relationships and subjectivities are produced in the labour force as well as through "socialization" in families or educational institutions.[30]

Too many studies of the operation of gender and class in the labour force now exist to permit their examination in any detail here. Some examine branches of industry: garment trades, fast food, health care, steel manufacturing, and the fisheries.[31] There are also numerous local studies of the sex/gender division of labour and of the complexity of relations between households and paid workplaces.[32] Along with macro-level statistical analysis, these case studies deepen our understanding of women's paid and unpaid (mostly household) labour.

Overall, most women are in paid employment for most of their adult lives, despite heavy domestic and community responsibilities. Compared to men, women are also still typically in fewer occupations (clerical, sales, and service) and more likely to have low-paid, often part-time or irregular jobs. In 1994, women employed full time earned 70 per cent of what men earned.[33] However, that general figure masks the significant differences among women. For some social groups income differences are sharper: women of colour earn only 59 per cent of what men of colour earn and only 51 per cent of white men's incomes. While entry-level wages for all jobs are down, among employed recent university graduates, especially those in social sciences and humanities, male-female income differences continue to be significant.[34]

Most labour-force research focuses either on general trends or, like the case studies of occupations or economic sectors noted above, on working-class women. Political economy has not paid much attention to women as members of the capitalist or business class and little to women professionals.[35] The domestic labour of "middle-class" housewives, including the way they organize relations with schools and other public institutions, certainly contributes to creating "middle-classness" and passing it on to their children.[36] In Hamilton Ontario, there are differences for working, middle, and upper classes in household divisions of labour, married women's employment, and social attitudes. However, in all classes women's having paid employment increases their relative power inside their households.[37]

Race/ethnicity and/or national origin have historically shaped women's and men's work, family life, and patterns of political involvement.[38] More important, Statistics Canada found inequalities based on race/ethnicity to be persistent and resistant to change. "Racial minority women and aboriginal women continue to be virtually excluded from [much of] the work force, face discrimination both at entry level and promotion and experience scandalous unemployment rates. The only women that are experiencing any advancement are white women, and it is at a glacial pace."[39] Lack of advance can be partly explained by labour and immigration law. Here, regulations fit immigrants to the specifications of working-class jobs or discriminate against some immigrant women (and men), particularly foreign domestic and agricultural workers, by depriving them of the protection won by the majority of workers.[40] In this context, immigrant women's strong support for reformed gender relations contrasts with immigrant men's conservatism and points to "strained domestic relations."[41]

RESTRUCTURING: ECONOMY, GOVERNMENT, AND STRUGGLE

During the 1980s, Canada's economy, like other Western developed market economies, underwent dramatic changes with the spread of microtechnology, the growth of global markets, and signing of the North American Free Trade Agreement. There were also signs of stagnation: the decline of manufacturing, high levels of unemployment, and "jobless growth." In response to fiscal pressures, governments sought solutions in cutbacks, privatization, and deregulation.[42] At the same time, capital penetrated formerly unwaged and informal activities, such as meal preparation, child care, and care of the aged, creating a highly fragmented and competitive service sector. Jobs in capital-intensive heavy industry, which typically were full time and unionized, had relatively good wages and benefits, were held mostly by men, and accounted for much of the male-female wage differential, disappeared.[43] Instead, what the Economic Council of Canada called "bad jobs" or "non standard" forms of paid work have increased in quantity and as a proportion of all jobs. Part-time and temporary employment also increased. For example, between 1990 and 1992 Canada lost 458,000 full-time jobs and gained 126,000 part-time positions. In 1992 125,000 full-time women's jobs disappeared, while there was an increase of 69,000 part-time posts for women.[44]

Overall, restructuring of capital has "femininized the workforce," as men's former patterns of labour-force involvement have been eroded and their work histories and rates of earnings have come to resemble the patterns formerly associated with women. Though this flattening is far from complete, as we noted above, the directions and extent of these developments need to be monitored.

As Martha Macdonald notes, however, little attention has been paid to gender differences in analysing all these labour-market changes, including those affecting the "middle sector," where women previously held good jobs.[45] Instead, it has been left to feminist researchers to draw attention to the particular effects for women in paid and household activities, which can be seen at two levels. First, while the decline in "good jobs," high levels of unemployment, and cuts in benefits and available services have eroded the standard of living for most Canadians – even for those working in the public sector, where women were most likely to find secure, unionized, adequately paid employment – wage cuts, cutbacks, and privatization have had a greater impact on women. In the private service and sales sector, where job growth has occurred, a high ratio of labour to capital means that profits are made by control of the total wage bill, through low pay rates or a flexible workforce. Largely as a result of employers' opposition, these jobs have lower rates of unionization and, even if unionized, tend to have poorer wages and fewer benefits. Women and immigrant and racial-minority workers of both sexes are disproportionately represented in the worst-paid and most insecure job sectors.[46]

Where in 1970 it took 45 hours a week to earn sufficient income to support a typical family of two adults and two children, it now takes 65–80 hours. In other words, because the cost of living has almost doubled, and is increasing, one income can no longer support a household.[47] People have responded by working more hours. Where possible, family households have increased the numbers of members in paid employment. As a result, the number of women withdrawing from the labour market to work full time in their homes, particularly to care for young children, continues to decline.

Despite having life-long labour-force patterns that more and more closely resemble those of men, women retained primary responsibility for work in the home.[48] As a result, women work a double day, putting in one day's work at their paid workplace and a second at home. Despite publicity about more flexible work or, as business publications put it, the "mummy [or sometimes parent] track," most workplaces do not accommodate competing demands on workers' lives.[49]

One way that women have historically tried to balance needs for income and child care in the face of public unconcern has been through accepting subcontracted manufacturing or home work. Both activist and academic researchers have documented an alarming growth in these activities – forms of employment that increase exploitation.[50] In part because of linguistic and cultural isolation, immigrant women today, like female immigrants in the past, take work in which basic health and safety regulations do not apply and where stress is intense.[51] Its location in the "home" and its immigrant female workforce have tended to construct home work as something apart from "real" work and union concerns. Today, however, public- and private-sector employers are promoting "teleworking" – a new form of home work made possible by low-cost computers, faxes, and electronic mail – for office workers and professionals. As a result, trade unions, workers, and feminist activists have cooperated with each other to investigate the effects of the new forms and to campaign for improved working conditions and union rights.[52]

Second, public-sector restructuring has meant that Canadian federal, provincial, and municipal governments have all tried to cut spending on social services, in part by privatizing delivery. As noted above, such cuts have undermined women's labour-force security and earning power. But as public services erode, women in general have picked up as unpaid labour many of the services previously provided by hospitals, child care centres and other state agencies. In short, both aspects of women's labour – paid and unpaid – have intensified in response to the competitiveness and austerity of post-fordist transformation.[53]

For workers who remained in the public sector, cutbacks have resulted in heavier workloads, intensified supervision, and more stress. In the Ontario health-care system, for example, spending cuts, job reorganisation, and social-contract legislation undermined the amount and quality of care actually received by patients, despite extraordinary increases in workloads.[54] Management strategies put in place in the interests of cost cutting sharpened class differences among nurses; some moved up into management positions, while others had their work subjected to the sort of close supervision more typical of proletarianized labour processes than of the helping (semi-)professions.[55] Responses were of two sorts: "fight" and "flight." Health-care unions struggled for good-quality care, decent working conditions, and pay equity. At the same time, feeling betrayed and resisting new working conditions, about 30 per cent of Ontario's nurses voluntarily left the profession, with the incidental result that public investment in their education would not be realized. Political economy, Jerry White concludes, must pay attention to the complexities of "the relationship between gender, class, labour process, and militancy" if it is to understand these individual and collective responses.[56]

Since 1980 economic restructuring has profoundly affected the context in which the issues and politics of the women's and labour movements have unfolded. Assessing the outcomes of reforms or movements over the last fifteen years is far from easy. On the one hand, formal, or contract gains in employment rights were made; on the other, working conditions worsened. The situation for the women's movement, including its organised working-class component, seems equally ambiguous. Trade-union feminism seems firmly entrenched in the labour centrals, and working-class Québécois and Canadians support feminist views and demands.[57] But the power of the women's movement may well have been damaged as public-sector and some private-sector unions, which provided a powerful base for advancing women's demands, risk running out of money and members.[58]

At the heart of women's- and labour-movement campaigns, as well as of feminist debate in the 1980s, was pay equity. Its strategic utility lay in its ability to increase the wages of women in the female-dominated occupations where most women work. Some analysts worried that a scheme for "equal wages" based on the value of a job to the employer would increase employers' control or freeze women's wages at too low a level while giving an appearance of justice. Though pay-equity strategies may have temporarily displaced other forms of wage struggle, the educational process about "equal value for equal work" seems to have strengthened feminist trade-union activism.[59]

The need for critical policy analysis and policy alternatives by the activist side of feminist political economy described by Judy Rebick at the beginning of this chapter seems to have placed a wide range of equity issues, to do with class, region, race, ethnicity or national status, and gender, in the framework of restructuring. For example, Majorie Cohen's work on free trade was partly inspired by NAC's need to develop policy in "response to the government's lack of concern about what free trade will mean for women."[60] Aptly named, Bakker's *Strategic Silence: Gender and Economic Policy* aims at "systematically linking a gender-relations analysis to an economic-policy framework" (page 3).

WOMEN'S MOVEMENTS, STATE, AND POLITICS

Here the core questions are: how is a gender order, including its sexual dimension, organized through the state, and how can women organize against their subordination? In one dimension, these questions consider the form of the state: is it male, masculinist, patriarchal, fraternal, or heterosexual, and how does its gendering relate to class and other forms of domination? In another, they look to action. How can activists best organize – by seeking to build alternate, women-centred spaces and organizations, or by seeking reform in and through existing state and social institutions? While classical Marxism stresses human agency – summed up in the notion that "[wo]man makes history, but not under conditions of [her] own choosing" – postmodernist views problematizing the "integral subject" have increasing influenced more recent reflections on politics and activism.[61]

In the late 1980s, discussion of these analytical and strategic issues was influenced by both Canadian and international political developments. In addition to facing an increasingly hostile government in the Mulroney years, this already-thorny set of questions was further complicated, as the editors of *Social Movements/Social Change* point out, by apparent weaknesses in social-democratic, socialist, and Soviet regimes, by the collapse of an influential far left in Canada, and by the challenges of new social-movement theory.[62] Under a "new right attack," feminists and gay, lesbian, and youth movements lost ground in defining a sex-positive, critical family and gender politics as central to public discussion.[63]

Still, assessments by activists and academics alike point out that a kind of socialist or social-democratic feminism, particular to Canada's political culture, became institutionalized as a central current in the activist women's movement.[64] It was a strong influence in NAC, the abortion-rights movement, the day-care movement, trade unions, and the NDP.[65] Facing right-wing opposition and challenged by increasingly complicated definitions of "women," it also participated in wider campaigns against, for example, free trade or constitutional proposals, in alliance with trade unions or other feminist currents.[66] In these circumstances, socialist-feminist organizers had a working answer to the intricacies of the gender/race/class question: because the class structure of capitalism "maintains and perpetuates" racism, sexism, and heterosexism, it must be "overturned before such problems can be entirely eradicated," by the means of coalition politics, in which all the partners' goals are "truly integrated" as part of the same struggle and also as part of a struggle for socialism.[67]

In general, theories of gender and state have developed separately in ways that restrict the scope of both. In the face of a certain wariness about the state, Judith Grant and Peta Tancred began "unpacking" the "black box" of the state to look at its layers as legislator, employer, and site of struggle.[68] Canadian analysis was strongly influenced by instrumental views of the state, whether Mary McIntosh's functionalism or Zillah Eisenstein's modified dual-systems theory.[69] Though differing sharply about dual-systems theory, Adamson, Briskin, and McPhail's *Feminist Organizing for Change* and Ursel's *Private Lives,*

Public Policy both see the state acting for capitalism and patriarchy. By the mid-1980s, however, instrumentalism was itself criticized – for example, for (like functionalism more generally) imputing systemic coherence or rationality to the state, for being overly deterministic, and for failing to take account of the multiplicity of actors, relations, and struggles on the political field or to explain clearly relations between them. Cross-national comparisons show that the British "breadwinner/housewife," family-wage solution was not a functional necessity of capitalism and that a quite-different political outcome – more equal wages and state support for childbirth and day care – obtained in France.[70] In the name of postmodernism and with a reference to women's movements, Magnusson and Walker urged "a reconceptualization of politics that would de-centre the state as the subject of political analysis, the object of political struggle, and the basic category of political understanding."[71]

At the same time, other forms of theory shed light on the ways "patriarchy" emerges through various forms of state practices. For example, a politically and culturally sensitive blend of neo-Gramscian and Foucauldian theory was applied to analysis of state formation.[72] In brief, for the state to work ideologically and programmatically it needs to create governable subjects – that is, individuals with the capacities and willingness to put into practice state programs. In this view, state practices create and regulate, rather than simply repress, subjects, sexualities, and non-state institutions.[73] In examining educational reform, Curtis also revealed – without actually problematizing the female side of gender or sexuality as such – how masculinity was embedded in the organization of educational reform or, conversely, how state formation in Canada West (Ontario) rested on the creation of masculine subjects and servants at its core. The scope of state regulation has been wide: policing prostitutes, rape and sexual violence, and homosexuality; responding to social-purity movements' versions of race, class, and women's issues; and attempting to prevent further rebellion in Quebec after the 1837 *Patriot* movement.[74]

Dorothy Smith's emphasis on examining the fine details of the content and handling of documents and texts in organizing state-society relations has also proved fruitful. The effects of government regulation and hearings on immigrant women's centres, development organizations, debates about family violence, parents' groups, policing the gay community, and rape legislation have been examined in this way.[75] Meeting government requirements partially circumscribes political independence, work practices, and feminists' capacity to define issues in their own terms. At the same time, despite government's ideological management of issues, at least in some cases some gains are made, the terrain of struggle shifts, and some practices change. State institutions thus are neither simply male nor wholly patriarchal, but a terrain where some gains can be made through struggle, or where hegemony can be shifted.[76]

Finally, a new concern with political identity appeared in two quite distinct ways. First, realization that political identity and indeed political interests are socially constructed extends debates about political "subjects" and (new) social movements. The dominion/federal Office (later Department) of the Secretary of State has been a crucial macro-political player in construction of such identities and interests for women's, official-language minorities', and ethnic groups through the very acts of organizing the Canadian state's relation with their representatives.[77] Retaining a political economy understanding of economic constraint to counter more radical, postmodern moves of decentring, Jenson argues that construction of political identities is constrained by the overall political field, which she dubs "the universe of political discourse."[78] Second, there have emerged new groups of activists operating from a proliferating salience of political "identities." Aiming at balancing cross-class political solidarity for anti-capitalist struggles, while also supporting claims for autonomous organizing on the part of, for example, Québécoises, women with disabilities, sexual and race/ethnic/national minority groups, creates real theoretical and practical tensions. NAC's experiments at finding balance once more point to the way in which theoretical aims take shape in concrete, organizational practices.[79]

CHALLENGING THE PARADIGM — RECOGNIZING RACE/ETHNICITY

Just as mainstream political economy can be accused of "adding women on" without transforming its concepts, so feminist political economy itself can often be charged with just "adding race on." " 'Racism' and 'race' as well as non-white women as producers of theory or politics, are generally absent from the textual world of 'marxist/socialist feminism'." Bannerji goes on to suggest that often "gender, race and class" has become a litany, in response to "protest and analysis by non-white women,"[80] noted rather than developed centrally in the analysis. Linda Carty was "forced to reassess the relevance of marxist feminism which, although it has gone much further than any previous theoretical paradigm in analyzing class and gender, has also failed to theorize race."[81] There is a worrying tendency among other writers to introduce "race" while reducing class to an empty category.[82] Indeed, according to Tania das Gupta, most theoretical and empirical work concentrates on one or possibly two areas; very little integrates all three.[83]

Linda Carty and Dionne Brand make a related critique of policy: federal and provincial governments have been instrumental in initiating organizations that reduce differences among women from a variety of racial backgrounds, collapsing them into categories such as "immigrant women" and "visible-minority women." Such labels lump together women from diverse backgrounds – European or Chinese immigrants, Black or African Canadians whose ancesters have lived in Canada for seven generations, and First Nations women – while glossing over class differences within race/ethnic groups.[84] This terminological short hand can too easily lead to sloppy formulations in political discussion or the analysis of racism. Overgeneralization not only misrepresents the experiences of particular women but means that feminism is deprived of understandings produced by individuals and organizations from the standpoint of different immigrant and race/ethnic and national groups.

The efforts necessary for Native, Black, immigrant, women of colour, and other "minority women" to win a space for themselves and their issues in feminist organizations and in feminist historiography are now being documented.[85] Where such work has been done, attention to race/ethnic as well as gender relations shows their mutual self-construction and that the state is implicated in their organization.[86] The challenge for feminism and political economy separately and together is to continue to develop theory and practice informed by the critiques of the past decade. As Nandita Sharma argues, the contemporary political and economic climate "depends on our ability to transcend past barriers to cooperative organization, barriers such as the historical construction and perpetuation of sexism and racism (to mention but two)."[87]

What next? Theoretically, feminism has reshaped the core issues of traditional political economy; production now must be understood as both of goods and of people. Of course, history does not stand still, and ongoing economic developments need to be monitored with an eye to their effect on women's economic and social position and their political capacity to shape history. Will greater gender equality between women and men inside classes emerge at the cost of greater polarization between women and men in different classes? Of what use will a weakened post-fordist state be for feminist reform? Work on gender, "race," and class is an impressive start, though much more remains to be done. Demographic changes inside the pan-Canadian state underline this need. At all levels, the changing race/ethnic composition of women's organizations, trade unions, and university graduates – those people most likely to take up feminist political economy as a political or professional practice – means that there are new intellectual resources available for this work.

Elsewhere feminist political economy is in a bind. As long as mainstream political economy maintains the indifference and resistance noted by feminist political economists, empirical and theoretical development will be limited. Without new feminist work, the mainstream is likely to remain unimpressed. As a consequence, left-wing feminists will be less and less likely to address political economy as a body of theory or as a discipline and will simply get on with their own work. If this happens, an opportunity will have been lost.

NOTES

Preparation of this paper was supported by a grant from Carleton University. Thanks to Mathew Deline for critical comments on the draft.

1 Rebick, "Interview," 58–9. NAC is a coalition of over 550 women's organizations. Founded in 1972, it works to defend, protect, and advance the status of women, especially by lobbying the federal government.

2 Connelly and Armstrong, "Introduction."

3 In this chapter, we use the terms "racialization" and "race/ethnic and national" to identify the processes by which racial and ethnic and national relations are socially constructed; see Anthias and Yuval-Davis, "Conceptualising Feminism." See Sharma "Restructuring Society," note 2: "The term 'race' is not ... acceptable ... as it reifies the racist notion that there are indeed separate and discrete 'races' of humanity. The term also ignores the historical process of 'racialization' which shapes the realities of groups of people based upon their skin colour, their nationality, their ethnicity, and, ultimately, their incorporation into capitalist social relations. Instead it focuses on the physical characteristics of people as somehow accounting for their different treatment." See Stasiulis, chapter 7, below, for further discussion.

4 Geutell, *Marxism*; D. Smith, "Women." We focus on this stream rather than on radical-feminist (such as Firestone, *Dialectic*) or other analyses of the intersection of politics and economics in the organization of gender; see Peters, Grashman, and Lauring, *Changing Directions*.

5 Engels, *Origin*.

6 Brodribb, *Nothing*.

7 Hamilton, *Liberation*.

8 Bakker, "Political Economy," 90. Though Laxer, *Open*, tips a marginal hat to feminists in anti–free trade mobilizations, the body of the work lacks any consideration of the ways in which women, their work, and their organizing might have shaped the polity or economy. While it is not clear how the analysis would have been changed by taking gender into account, other

European and Canadian investigations of comparable developments show that women contributed to capital accumulation, owned and operated farms, and were mobile and cheap labour in Upper and Lower Canada. See Tilly and Scott, *Women*, and Cohen, *Women's Work*. In contrast, Drache and Glasbeek, *Changing*, integrates gender into its analytical and political framework.

9 Smith, "Feminist," 37–59.

10 Maroney and Luxton, "Introduction" and chap.1, in their *Feminism*. See Armstrong and Armstrong "Limited"; Bannerji, "But Who?," "Introducing," "Returning," and "Turning."

11 Rowbotham, *Women*, 11.

12 Marchak, *Integrated*.

13 Ursell, *Private*, 19.

14 Anderson, *Chain*.

15 Bourgeault, "The Indian," "Development," "Indigenous Women," and "Race"; St-Onge, "Race"; and Poelzer, "Metis."

16 Falconer, "Overlooked."

17 Luxton, *More*. This debate concerned the capacity of classical Marxist theory to understand family and household forms, sexual divisions of labour, and gender inequality. See Fox, *Hidden*.

18 Duffy et al., *Few Choices*; Proulx, *Women*.

19 Hofley, "Long," 171.

20 Arat-Koc, "Importing"; Silvera, *Silenced*; Calliste, "Canada's."

21 Luxton and Maroney, "Begetting"; Fox, "Reproducing." Hamilton, "Feminism."

22 See Morton, "Cost"; Boyd, "Some"; Gavigan, "Paradise"; and chapter 13, below, by Bakker and Scott.

23 Arnup, "In."

24 Jenson "Gender"; Maroney, "Who?" Folbre, *Who?*, does not include Canada in her comparison of northwestern Europe, the United States, Latin America, and the Caribbean.

25 MacDonald and Connelly, "Class," 62.

26 D. Smith, "Women"; Ng, "Sexism"; Bannerji, *Returning*; Muszynski, "What?" draws on their work.

27 MacDonald and Connelly, "Class," 62.

28 Livingstone and Mangan "Class."

29 Clement and Myles, *Relations*, 140, provides comparative data for Canada (1982), the United States, and Nordic countries, collected as part of a study of class structure.

30 On subjectivity, men, and masculinity, especially in the paid workplace, see Dunk, *It's*; Livingstone and Luxton, *Gender*.

31 Reiter, *Making*; Campbell, "Management"; Armstrong, Choinière, and Day, *Vital*; Corman et al., *Recasting*; Gagnon, "Reflections"; Lipsig-Mumme, "Future conditional."

Johnson and Johnson, *Seam.*

The fishery is of particular interest for feminists studying substantive relations and developing critical political economic theory. As well as Macdonald and Connelly, see Muszynski, "Class" and "Race"; Binkley, *Voices*; Martha MacDonald, "Restructuring"; and Neis, "Flexible."

32 Parr's comparative study of furniture and textile manufacturing towns, *Gender*, is a sterling example of historical work. See Armstrong and Armstrong, *Theorizing*, for an extensive bibliography of English-Canadian work, and *Double*, for a summary to 1993.

33 Statistics Canada, *Review*, 15; for Quebec, see Meintel et al., "New."

34 Myles, Picot, and Wannell, *Good Jobs.* Following decades of steady increases in women's paid labour, in 1992 there was a small, as-yet-not-analysed reduction in labour-force participation among young women.

35 There is a rich historical literature on teachers, doctors, and lawyers, but little recent material works with a political economy perspective; see Khayatt, "Lesbian." There is also a booming practical literature on women in management.

36 D. Smith, "Women's"; Griffith and Smith, "Constructing." The maternal-feminist activism of middle-class female reformers in nineteenth-century social-purity movements, construed as a kind of expanded, moralized housewifery, helped organize class and race as components of Canadian society; Valverde, *Age.*

37 Corman et al., *Recasting.*

38 Frager, *Sweatshop*; Brand, *No Burden*; Iacovetta, *Such.*

39 Statistics Canada, *Review*, 6.

40 Arat-Koc, "Importing"; Silvera, *Silenced*; Ng, *State.*

41 Clement and Myles, *Relations*, 226.

42 This is a bare-bones sketch. Measures to deregulate the labour market include failing to enforce existing regulations, casualization, privatization, and contracting out. On technological innovation see Menzies, *Fast*, and Marchack, *Integrated.*

43 For a discussion of the components of wage discrimination and new service industries, see Phillips and Phillips, *Women*, 50–74, 143–4. A related issue is how skill is defined in a gendered way; for a recent contribution see Tillotson, "We"; Reiter, *Fast.*

44 Economic Council of Canada, *Good Jobs*; Armstrong, "Feminization"; Armstrong and Armstrong, *Theorizing.*

45 MacDonald, "Restructuring"; Myles, Picot, and Wannell, *Good Jobs*; Economic Council of Canada, *Good Jobs* and *Employment.*

46 Warskett, "Bank"; Phillips and Phillips, *Women*, 143; Bakker, "Pay"; Sharma, "Restructuring."

47 Statistics Canada, *Labour Force*; Gunderson, Muszynski, and Keck, *Women.*

48 Michelson, "Divergent"; Corman et al., *Recasting*; Luxton, "Taking."

49 De Wolff, *Strategies.*

50 Arnopoulous, *Problems*; Leach, "Flexible"; The Conference Handbook Committee, *From.*

51 Giles and Arat-Koc, eds., *Maid.*

52 Borowoy, Gordon, and Lebans, "Are?".

53 Jessop, "Toward," identified the hollowed-out post-fordist state but ignored this gender dimension. Contrast the attention to women's work in Bullock, "Community."

54 Armstrong, Choinière, and Day, *Vital.*

55 Campbell, "Management."

56 Jerry White, *Hospital.*

57 Julie White, *Sisters*, 103–34; Clement and Myles, *Relations.*

58 Julie White, *Sisters*; Luxton and Reiter, "Double."

59 See the essays in Fudge and McDermott, *Just*; Warskett, "Wage."

60 Cohen, *Free*, 16.

61 Macdonald, "Trouble"; Stavro-Pierce, "Towards."

62 Cunningham et al., *Social.*

63 Rayside, "Gay"; Luxton and Maroney, "Begetting"; Helvacloglu, "The God–Market"; Whitworth, "Planned."

64 Vickers, "Intellectual"; Egan, Gardener, and Persad, "Politics."

65 Vickers, Rankin, and Oppelle, *Politics*; Briskin, "Socialist"; Reinart, "Three"; Adamson, Briskin, and McPhail, *Feminist*; Weir, "Social"; Colley, "Day."

66 Razak, *Canadian*, 74–81; Cohen, *Free.*

67 Egan, Gardener, and Persad, "Politics."

68 Mahon, "From," and Randall, "Feminism," provide overviews. See also Lamoureux, "De la quete"; d'Augerot-Arend, "Feministes"; and Findlay, "Feminist." Grant and Tancred begin "unpacking" the "black box" of the state in relation to women, "Un point."

69 McIntosh, "The State"; Eisenstein, *Radical.*

70 Seccombe, "Patriarchy"; Jenson, "Gender."

71 Magnusson and Walker, "De-centring." For a critique see Jenson and Keyman, "Must we?"; Helvacoglu, "Thrills."

72 This approach rests on Foucault, "Govermentalities." It is developed in part by Corrigan and Sayers, *The Great Arch*, and is laid out concisely by Curtis, *True Government inspection, education and state formation in Canada* and developed further in his "Class."

73 De la Cour, Morgan, and Valverde, "Gender"; Valverde, Weir, "Struggles."

74 Greer, "Birth"; Kinsman, "Regulation"; Dubinski, *Improper*; Young, "Positive Law"; Backhouse, *Petticoats.*

75 Smith, "Women's Work"; Ng, "Sexism"; Ng, "State"; De Wolff, "Resources"; Khosla, "1993"; Walker, *Family*; Walker, "Conceptual"; Dehli, "Women"; Smith, George, "Policing."

76 Schreader. Alicia 1990 "State-funded"; Warskett, "Wage" and "Democratiz-ing"; Walker, "Reproducing"; Findlay, "Feminist"; Maroney, "Using." At the

same time, despite changes in governing parties, it is clear that Canadian economic and social policies (such as taxation, training programs, and unemployment insurance) are consistently gendered in that they treat men and women differently or if formally gender neutral still affect the sexes differently, usually to women's disadvantage, if not detriment. See Woolley, Marshall, and Vermaeten, "Ending."

77 Pal, *Interests.*
78 Jenson, "Gender" and "Naming."
79 Gottlieb, "What about Us?"
80 Bannerji, "But Who?" and "Turning."
81 Carty, "Black."
82 Gavigan "Paradise"; Maroney and Luxton, "Feminism."
83 Das Gupta, "Introduction."
84 Carty and Brand, "Visible."
85 Egan, Gardener, and Persad, "Politics"; das Gupta, "Introduction"; Pierson, "Mainstream"; Abdo, "Race."
86 See, for example, Ng, "Sexism"; Bourgeault "Race"; Monture-Oksanee, "Violence"; Calliste, "Canada's."
87 Sharma, "Restructuring," 29.

REFERENCES

Abdo, Nahla. "Race, Gender and Politics: The Struggle of Arab Women in Canada." In Linda Carty, ed., *And Still we Rise: Feminist Political Mobilizing in Contemporary Canada*, 73–98. Toronto: Women's Press, 1993.

Adamson, Nancy, Briskin, Linda, and McPhail, Margaret. *Feminist Organizing for Change: The Contemprary Women's Movement* Toronto: Oxford University Press, 1988.

Anderson, Karen. *Chain Her by One Foot: The Subjugation of Women in Seventheenth Century New France.* London: Routledge, 1991.

Anthias, Floya, and Yuval-Davis, Nira. "Conceptualising Feminism: Gender, Ethnic and Class Divisions." *Feminist Review*, 15 (1983), 62–75.

Antonyshuyn, Patricia, Lee, B., and Merill, Alex. "Marching for Women's Lives: The Campaign for Free-Standing Abortion Clinics in Ontario." In Frank Cunningham et al. eds., *Social Movements/Social Change: The Politics and Practice of Organising.* Toronto and Winnipeg: Between the Lines and Society for Socialist Studies/Société d'études socialistes, 1988.

Arat-Koc, Sedef. "Importing Housewives: Non-Citizen Domestic Workers and the Crisis of the Domestic Sphere in Canada." *Studies in Political Economy*, 28 (1989), 33–58. Armstrong, Pat. "The Feminization of the Labour Force: Harmonizing down in a Global Economy." In K. Messing et al., eds., *Invisible Workers: Issues in Women's Occupational Health*, 368–92. Charlottetown: Gynergy, 1995.

Armstrong, Pat and Armstrong, Hugh. *The Double Ghetto: Canadan Women and Their Segregated Work.* 3rd ed. Toronto: McClelland and Stewart, 1994.

– "Limited Possibilities and Possible Limits for Pay Equity." In Judy Fudge and Patricia McDermott, eds., *Just Wages: A Feminist Assessment of Pay Equity* Toronto: University of Toronto Press, 1991.

– *Theorizing Women's Work.* Toronto: Garamond, 1990.

Armstrong, Pat, Choinière, Jacqueline, and Day, Elaine. *Vital Signs: Nursing in Transition.* Toronto: Garamond Press, 1993.

Arnopoulous, Sheila. *Problems of Immigrant Women in the Canadian Labour Force.* Ottawa: Canadian Advisory Council on the Status of Women, 1979.

Arnup, Katherine. "Finding Fathers: Artificial Insemination, Lesbians, and the Law." *Canadian Journal of Women and the Law,* 7 no. 1 (1994), 97–115.

– "In the Way of the Family: Lesbian Mothers in Canada." In Meg Luxton, ed., *Family Politics: Policy Issues and Critical Practices.* Halifax: Fernwood Press, forthcoming.

Asner, Elizabeth. "Class, Gender and Generation: A Life Course Approach to Married Women's Employment Choices and Feminist Consciousness." PhD, thesis, Department of Education, University of Toronto, 1993.

Backhouse, Constance. *Petticoats and Prejudice: Women and Law in Nineteenth Century Canada.* Toronto: Women's Press, 1991.

Backhouse, Constance, and Flaherty, David, eds. *Challenging Times: The Women's Movement in Canada and the United States.* Montreal: McGill-Queen's University Press, 1992.

Bakker, Isabella. "Pay Equity and Economic Restructuring: The Polarization of Policy?" In Judy Fudge and Patricia McDermott, eds., *Just Wages: A Feminist Assessment of Pay Equity,* 254–80. Toronto: University of Toronto Press, 1991.

– "The Political Economy of Gender." In Glen Williams and Wallace Clement, eds., *New Canadian Political Economy,* 99–115. Montreal: McGill-Queen's University Press, 1989.

– *Strategic Silence Gender and Economic Policy.* London: Zed Books, 1994.

Bannerji, Himani. "But Who Speaks for Us? Experience and Agency in Conventional Feminist Paradigms." In Himani Bannerji et al., eds., *Unsettling Relations The University as a Site of Feminist Struggles,* 67–107. Toronto: Women's Press, 1991.

– "Introducing Racism: Notes towards an Anti-Racist Feminism." *Resources for Feminist Research,* 16 no. 1 (1987), 5–9.

– *Returning the Gaze: Essays on Racism, Feminism and Politics.* Toronto: Sister Vision, 1993.

– "Turning the Gaze." *Resources for Feminist Research,* 20 nos. 3–4 (1991), 5–11.

Barrett, Michele, and Hamilton, Roberta, eds. *The Politics of Diversity: Feminism, Marxism and Canadian Society.* London: Verso, 1987.

Binkley, Marian. *Voices from Off Shore: Narratives of Risk and Danger in the Nova Scotia Deep-Sea Fishery.* St John's, Nfld.: ISER, 1993.

Borowoy, Jan, Gordon, Shelly, and Lebans, Gayle. "Are These Clothes Clean? The Campaign for Fair wages and Working Conditions for Homeworkers." In Linda Carty, ed., *And Still We Rise: Feminist Political Mobilizing in Contemporary Canada*, 299–330. Toronto: Women's Press, 1993.

Bourgeault, Ron. "The Development of Capitalism and the Subjugation of Native Women in Northern Canada. *Alternative Routes*, 6 (1983), 109–40.

– "The Indian, the Metis and the Fur Trade: Class, Sexism, and Racism in the Transition from 'Communism' to Capitalism." *Studies in Political Economy*, 12 (fall 1983), 45–80.

– "Indigenous Women and Capitalist Exploitation: Ron Bourgeault Replies to Jesse Russell." *Alternative Routes*, 8 (1988), 144–152.

"Race, Class and Gender: Colonial Domination of Indian Women." In Jesse Vorst et al. *Race, Class, Gender: Bonds and Barriers*, 87–115. Toronto: Between the Lines and Winnipeg: Society for Socialist Studies/Société d'études socialistes, 1989.

Boyd, Monica. "Immigrant Women: Language, Socioeconomic Inequalities and Policy Issues." In Shiva Halli, Frank Trovato, and Leo Driedger, eds., *Ethnic Demography: Canadian Immigrant Racial and Cultural Variations*, 275–93. Ottawa: Carleton University Press, 1990.

Boyd, Susan. "Some Postmodern Challenges to Feminist Analysis of Law, Family and State: Ideology and Discourse in Child Custory Law." *Canadian Journal of Family Law*, 10 (1991), 79–113.

Brand, Dione. *No Burden to Carry: Narratives of Black Working Women in Ontario, 1920s to 1950s*. Toronto: Women's Press, 1991.

Briskin, Linda. "Socialist Feminism: From the Standpoint of Practice." *Studies in Political Economy*, 30 (autumn 1989), 87–114.

Briskin, Linda, and McDermott, Pat, eds. *Women Challenging Unions: Feminism, Democracy, and Militancy*. Toronto: University of Toronto Press, 1993.

Brodribb, Somer. *Nothing Mat(t)ers: A Feminist Critique of Postmodernism*. Toronto: Lorimer and Co., 1992.

Bullock, Anne. "Community Care: Ideology and Lived Experience." In Roxanna Ng, Gillian Walker, and Jacob Muller, eds., *Community Organization and the Canadian State*, 65–82. Toronto: Garamond Press, 1990.

Calliste, Agnes. "Canada's Immigration Policy and Domestics from the Carribean: The Second Domestic Scheme." In Jesse Vorst et al. eds. *Race, Class, Gender: Bonds and Barriers*, 133–64. Toronto: Between the Lines and Winnipeg: Society for Socialist Studies/Société d'études socialistes, 1989.

Campbell, Marie. "Management as Ruling: A Class Phenomenon in Nursing." *Studies in Political Economy*, 27 (autumn 1988), 29–51.

Carty, Linda. "Black Women in Academia: A Statement from the Periphery." In Himani Bannerji et al., eds., *Unsettling Relations: The University as a Site of Feminist Struggles*, 13–44. Toronto: Women's Press, 1991.

Carty, Linda, and Brand, Dionne. " 'Visible Minority' Women – a Creation of the Canadian State." *Resources for Feminist research/Documentation sur la recherche féministe*, 17 no. 3 (Sept. 1988), 39–42.

Clement, Wallace, and Myles, John. *Relations of Ruling: Class and Gender in Postindustrial Societies.* Montreal: McGill-Queen's University Press, 1994.

Cohen, Marjorie. "British Columbia: Playing Safe Is a Dangerous Game." *Studies in Political Economy*, 43 (spring 1994), 149–59.

– *Free Trade and the Future of Women's Work: Manufacturing and Service Industries.* Toronto: Garamond Press, 1987.

– "Social Democracy – Illusion or Vision?" *Studies in Political Economy*, 37 (spring 1992), 151–60.

– *Women's Work, Markets, and Economic Development in Nineteenth-Century Ontario.* Toronto: University of Toronto Press, 1988.

Colley, Sue. "Day Care Organising." Paper presented at CSAA/CCS conference, Victoria, BC, 1990.

Conference Handbook Committee. *From the Double Day to the Endless Day: Proceedings from the Conference on Homeworking*. Toronto: Canadian Centre for Policy Alternatives, 1992.

Connelly, Patricia, and Armstrong, Pat, eds. "Introduction." In *Feminism in Action Studies in Political Economy*, ix–xix. Toronto: Canadian Scholars Press, 1992.

Corman, June, Livingstone, David, Luxton, Meg, and Seccombe, Wally. *Recasting Steel Labour: The Stelco Story* Halifax: Fernwood, 1993.

Corrigan, Philip, and Sayer, Derek. *The Great Arch: English State Formation as Cultural Revolution.* Oxford: Basil Blackwell, 1985.

Cunningham, Frank, Findlay, Sue, Kadar, Marlene, Lennon, Alan, and Silva, Ed, eds. *Social Movements/Social Change: The Politics and Practice of Organising.* Toronto: Between the Lines and Winnepeg: Society for Socialist Studies/ Société d'études socialistes, 1988.

Curtis, Bruce. "Class Culture and Administration: Educational Inspection in Canada West." In Alan Greer and Ian Radforth, eds., *Colonial Leviathan: State Formation in Mid-Nineteenth-Century Canada*, 103–31. Toronto: University of Toronto Press, 1992.

– *True Government by Choice: Men, Inspection, Education and State Formation in Canada.* Toronto: University of Toronto Press, 1992.

d'Augerot-Arend, Sylvie. "Féministes et l'état canadien: Tensions théoriques et divergences pratiques." *Resources for Feminist Research/Documentation sur la recherche féministe*, 17 no. 3 (1988), 22–5.

das Gupta, Tanya. "Introduction." In Jesse Vorst et al. eds., *Race, Class, Gender: Bonds and Barriers*, 1–9. Toronto: Between the Lines and Winnipeg: Society for Socialist Studies/Société d'études socialistes, 1989.

Dehli, Kari. "For Intellegent Motherhood and National Efficiency: The Toronto Home and School Council, 1916–1930." In Ruby Heap and Alison Prentice, eds., *Gender and Education in Ontario: An Historical Reader*, 000–00. Toronto: Canadian Scholars Press, 1991.

- "Women in the Community: Reform of Scooling and Motherhood in Toronto." In Roxanna Ng, Gillian Walker, and Jacob Muller, eds., *Community Organization and the Canadian State*, 47–64. Toronto: Garamond Press, 1990.

de la Cour, Lykke, Morgan, Celia, and Valverde, M. "Gender Regulation and State Formation in Nineteenth Century Canada." In Alan Greer and Ian Radforth, eds., *Colonial Leviathan: State Formation in Mid-Nineteenth-Century Canada*, 163–91. Toronto: University of Toronto Press, 1992.

De Wolff, Alice. "Managing Charitable Donations: Gender in the Income Tax Act." *Resources for Feminist Research/Documentation sur la recherche féminine*, 17 no. 3 (Sept. 1988), 78–82.

- *1992 Review of the Situation of Women in Canada*. Toronto: National Action Committee on the Status of Women, 1992.

- *Strategies for Working Families*. Toronto: Ontario Coalition for Better Child Care, 1994.

Drache, Daniel, and Glasbeek, Harold. *The Changing Workplace: Reshaping Canada's Industrial Relations System*. Toronto: J. Lorimer, 1992.

Dubinski, Karen. *Improper Advances: Rape and Heterosexual Conflict in Ontario, 1880–1929*. Chicago: University of Chicago Press, 1993.

Duffy, Ann, Mandell, Nancy, and Pupo, Noreen. *Few Choices: Women, Work, and Family*. Toronto: Garamond Press, 1989.

Dunk, Thomas. *It's a Working Man's Town: Male Working-Class Culture in Northwestern Ontario*. Montreal: McGill-Queen's University Press, 1991.

Economic Council of Canada. *Employment in a Service Economy*. Ottawa: Supply and Services Canada, 1991.

- *Good Jobs, Bad Jobs: Employment in the Service Economy*. Ottawa: Supply and Services Canada, 1990.

Egan, Carolyn, Gardener, Linda Lee, and Persad, Judy Vashti. "The Politics of Transformation: Struggles with Race, Class and Sexuality in the March 8th Coalition." In Frank Cunningham et al., eds., *Social Movements/Social Change: The Politics and Practice of Organizing*, 20–47. Toronto: Between the Lines and Winnipeg: Society for Socialist Studies/Société d'études socialistes, 1988.

Eisenstein, Zillah. *The Radical Future of Liberal Feminism*. New York: Longman, 1981.

Engels, Fredrick. *Origin of the Family, Private Property and the State*. New York: Pathfinder Press, 1972.

Firestone, Shulamith. *The Dialectic of Sex: The Case for Feminist Revolution*. New York: Bantam Books, 1970.

Falconer, Patrick. "The Overlooked of the Neglected: Native Single Mothers in Major Cities on the Prairies." In James Silver and Jeremy Hull, eds., *The Political Economy of Manitoba*, 368–92. Regina, Sask.: Canadian Plains Research Centre, University of Regina, 1990.

Findlay, Sue. "Democratizing the Local State: Issues for Feminist Practice and the Representation of Women." In Leo Panitch, Gregory Albo, and

D. Langille, eds., *A Different Kind of State: Popular Power and Democratic Administration*, 155–64. Toronto: Oxford University Press, 1993.

– "Feminist Struggles with the Canadian State: 1966–1988." *Resources for Feminist Research*, 17 no. 3 (Sept. 1988), 5–9.

– "Making Sense of Pay Equity: Issues for a Feminist Political Practice." In Judy Fudge and Patricia McDermott, eds., *Just Wages: A Feminist Assessment of Pay Equity*, 81–109. Toronto: University of Toronto Press, 1991.

Folbre, Nancy. *Who Pays for the Kids? Gender and the Structures of Constraint.* London: Routledge, 1994.

Foucault, Michel. "Governmentality." *Ideology and Consciousness*, (1979), 5–12.

Fox, Bonnie. "Reproducing Difference: Parenthood and Gender Inequality." In Meg Luxton, ed., *Family Politics: Policy Issues and Critical Practices.* Halifax: Fernwood Press, forthcoming.

– ed. *Hidden in the Household: Women's Domestic Labour Under Capitalism.* Toronto: Women's Press, 1980.

Frager, Ruth. *Sweatshop Strife: Class, Ethnicity, and Gender in the Jewish Labour Movement of Toronto, 1900–1939.* Toronto: University of Toronto Press, 1992.

Fudge, Judy, and McDermott, Patricia. *Just Wages: A Feminist Assessment of Pay Equity.* Toronto: University of Toronto Press, 1991.

Gagnon, Mona-Josée. "Reflections on the Quebec Public Sector Negotiations." *Studies in Political Economy*, 31 (1990), 169–80.

Gavigan, Shelly A. M. "Paradise Lost, Paradox Revisted: The Implications of Familial Ideology for Feminist, Lesbian, and Gay Engagement to Law," *Osgoode Hall Law Journal*, 31 no. 3 (1994), 1–35.

Geutell, Charnie. *Marxism and Feminism* Toronto: Women's Press, 1974.

Giles, Wenona, and Arat-Koc, Sedef, eds. *Maid in the Market: Women's Paid Domestic Labour.* Halifax: Fernwood Publishing, 1994.

Globe and Mail. "Male-Female Income Gap Widens." 20 Dec. 1995, A 10.

Gottlieb, Amy. "What about Us? Organizing Inclusively in the National Action Committee on the Status of Women." In Linda Carty, ed., *And Still We Rise: Feminist Political Mobilizing in Contemporary Canada*, 371–85. Toronto: Women's Press, 1993.

Grant, Judith. "Women's Issues and the State: Representation, Reform and Control." *Resources for Feminist Research/Documentation sur la recherche féministe*, 17 no. 3 (1988), 87–9.

Grant, Judith, and Peta, E. Tancred. "Un point de vue féministe sur la bureaucratie étatique." *Sociologie et Société*, 23 no. 1 (1991), 201–14.

Greer, Alan. "The Birth of the Police in Canada." In Alan Greer and Ian Radforth, eds., *Colonial Leviathan: State Formation in Mid-Nineteenth-Century Canada*, 17–49. Toronto: University of Toronto Press, 1992.

Greer, Alan, and Radforth, Ian, eds. *Colonial Leviathan: State Formation in Mid-Nineteenth-Century Canada.* Toronto: University of Toronto Press, 1992.

Griffith, Alison, and Smith, Dorothy. "Constructing Cultural Knowledge: Mothering as Discourse." In Jane Gaskell and Arlee McLaren, eds. *Women and Education: A Canadian Perspective*, 87–103. Calgary: Detselig, 1987.

Gunderson, Muszynski, L., and Keck, J. *Women and Labour Market Poverty*. Ottawa: Canadian Advisroy Council on the Status of Women, 1990.

Hamilton, Roberta. "Feminism and Motherhood, 1970–1990: Reinventing the Wheel?" *Resources for Feminist Research/Documentation sur la recherche féministe*, 19 nos. 3–4 (1990), 23–32.

Hamilton, Roberta *The Liberation of Women* London: George Allen and Unwin, 1978.

Helvacloglu, Banu. "The God–Market Alliance in Defence of Family and Community." *Studies in Political Economy*, 35 (summer 1991), 103–34.

– "The Thrills and Chills of Postmodernism: The Western Intellectual Vertigo." *Studies in Political Economy*, 38 (summer 1992), 7–34.

Hofley, John. "The Long Revolution in Canadian Families." In James Silver and Jeremy Hull, eds., *The Political Economy of Manitoba*, 171–87. Regina, Sask.: Canadian Plains Research Centre, University of Regina, 1990.

Iacovetta, Franca. *Such Hardworking People: Italisn Immigrants in Postwar Toronto*. Montreal: McGill-Queen's University Press, 1992.

Jenson, Jane. "Gender and Reproduction, or Babies and the State." *Studies in Political Economy*, 20 (summer 1986), 9–46.

– "Naming Nations: Making Nationalist Claims in Canadian Public Discourse." *Canadian Review of Sociology and Anthropology*, 30 no. 3 (1993), 335–58.

Jenson, Jane, and Keyman, Fuat. "Must We All Be Post-Modern?" *Studies in Political Economy*, 31 (spring 1990), 141–57.

Jessop, Bob. "Toward a Schumpeterian Workfare State? Preliminary Remarks on Post-Fordist Political Economy," *Studies in Political Economy*, 40 (1993), 7–39.

Jiwani, Yasmin. 1994. "Feminism and Poverty." *Kinesis* (Feb. 1994).

Johnson, Laura C., and Johnson, Robert E. *The Seam Allowance*. Toronto: Women's Press, 1982.

Khayatt, Didi M. "Lesbian Teachers: An Invisible Difference." In Frieci Fornan, ed., *Feminism and Education: A Canadian Perspective*, Toronto: Centre for Women's Studies in Education, Ontario Institute for Studies in Education, 1990.

Kinsman, Gary. *The Regulation of Desire*. Montreal: Black Rose, 1987.

Khosla, Punam. *1993 Review of the Situation of Women in Canada*. Toronto: National Action Committee for the Status of Women, 1993.

Lamoureux, Dianne. "De la quête de l'argent de poche au renforcement de l'état-providence." *Resources for Feminist Research/Documentation sur la recherche féministe*, 17 no. 3 (1988), 72–4.

Laxer, Gordon. *Open for Business: The Roots of Foreign Ownership in Canada*. Don Mills, Ont.: Oxford University Press, 1989.

Leach, Belinda. "Flexible Work, Precarious Future: Some Lessons for the Canadian Clothing Industry." *Canadian Review of Sociology and Anthropology*, 30 no. 1 (1993), 64–82.

Leah, Ronnie. "Linking the Struggles: Racism, Feminism and the Union Movement." In Jesse Vorst et al., *Race, Class, Gender: Bonds and Barriers*, 166–95. Toronto: Between the Lines and Winnipeg: Society for Socialist Studies/Société d'études socialistes, 1989.

Lipsig-Mumme, Carla. "Future Conditional: War of Position in the Quebec Labour Movement." *Studies in Political Economy*, 36 (1991), 73–107.

Livingstone, David, and Luxton, Meg. "Gender Consciousness at Work: Modification of the Male Breadwinner Norm among Steelworkers and Their Spouses." *Canadian Review of Sociology and Anthropology*, 26 no. 2 (May), 240–75.

Livingstone, David, and Mangan, Marshall. "Class, Gender, and Expanded Class Consciousness in Steeltown." *Research in Social Movements, Conflicts and Change*, 15 (1993), 55–82.

Luxton, Meg. *More Than a Labour of Love: Three Generations of Women's Work in the Home*. Toronto: Women's Press, 1980.

– "Taking on the Double Day: Housewives as a Reserve Army of Labour." *Atlantis*, 7 no. 1 (fall 1981), 12–22.

Luxton, Meg, and Maroney, Heather, Jon. "Begetting Babies, Raising Children: The Politics of Parenting" in *The Crisis in Socialist Theory, Strategy and Practice*, vol. 7, 161–98. Winnipeg: Society for Socialist Studies, 1992.

Luxton, Meg, and Reiter, Ester. "Double, Double, Toil and Trouble … Canadian Women's Experience of Work and Family, 1980–1993." In Sheila Shaver, ed., *Gender, Citizenship and the Labour Market: The Australian and Canadian Welfare States*, Social Policy Research Centre, *Reports and Proceedings*, no. 109 (Aug. 1993), 71–92.

MacDonald, Eleanor. "The Trouble with Subjects: Feminism, Marxism, and the Questions of Poststructuralism." *Studies in Political Economy*, 35 (summer 1991), 43–71.

MacDonald, Martha. "Restructuring in the Fishing Industry in Atlantic Canada." In Isabella Bakker, *Strategic Silence: Gender and Economic Policy*. London: Zed Books, 1994.

MacDonald, Martha, and Connelly, Pat. "Class and Gender in Fishing Communities in Nova Scotia." *Studies in Political Economy*, 30 (autumn 1989), 61–85.

McIntosh, Mary. "The State and the Oppression of Women." In A. Kuhn and A. Wolpe, eds., *Feminism and Materialism: Women and Modes of Production* 254–89. London: Routledge and Kegan Paul, 1978.

Magnusson, Warren, and Walker, Rob. "De-centring the State: Political Theory and Canadian Political Economy." *Studies in Political Economy*, 26 (summer 1988), 37–71.

Mahon, Rianne. "From 'Bringing to Putting': The State in Late Twentieth-Century Social Theory." *Canadian Journal of Sociology*, 16 no. 2 (1991), 119–44.

Marchak, Patricia. *The Integrated Arais: The New Right and the Restructuring of Global Markets.* Montreal: McGill-Queen's University Press, 1991.

Maroney, Heather Jon. "Challenging the Paradigm: Feminism and Political Economy." Paper presented at the CSAA/CSS meeting, Calgary, 1994.

– "Using Gramsci for Women: Feminism and the Quebec State, 1960–1980." *Resources for Feminist Research/Documentation sur la recherche féministe*, 17 no. 3 (1988), 26–30.

– " 'Who Has the Baby?' Nationalism, Pronatalism and the Construction of a 'Demographic Crisis' in Quebec, 1960–1988." *Studies in Political Economy*, 39 (autumn 1992), 7–36.

Maroney, Heather Jon, and Luxton, Meg. *Feminism and Political Economy: Women's Work, Women's Struggles.* Toronto: Methuen, 1987.

– "Feminism and Political Economy: Challenging the Paradigms." Paper presented at the Canadian Sociology and Anthropology Association and the Socialist Studies Society Meetings, 1994.

Meintel, Diedre, Labelle, M., Tourcotte, G., and Kemeneers, M. "The New Double Workday of Immigrant Women Workers in Quebec" *Women's Studies*, 13 no. 3 (1987), 273–93.

Menzies, Heather. *Fast Forward and Out of Control: How Technology Is Changing Your Life.* Toronto: Macmillan of Canada, 1989.

Michaud, Jacinthe. "The Welfare State and the Problem of Counter Hegemonic Responses within the Women's Movement." In William K. Carroll, ed., *Organizing Dissent: Contemporary Social Movements in Theory and Practice*, 200–14. [Toronto]: Garamond, 1992.

Michelson, William. "Divergent Convergence: The Daily Routines of Employed Spouses as a Public Affairs Agenda." In Caroline Andrew and Beth Moore Milroy, eds., *Life Spaces.* Vancouver: University of British Columbia Press. 1988.

Monture-Okanee, Patricia. "The Violence We Women Do: A First Nations View." In Constance Backhouse and David Flaherty, eds., *Challenging Times The Women's Movement in Canada and the United States.* 193–200. Montreal: McGill-Queens University Press, 1992.

Morton, Mary. "The Cost of Sharing, the Price of Caring: Problems in the Determiniation of 'Equity' in Family Maintenance and Support," In Joan Brockman and Dorothy Chiunn, eds., *Investigating Gender Bias: Law, Courts, and the Legal Profession*, 191–211. Toronto: Thompson, 1993.

Muszynski, Alicja. "Class Formation and Class Consciousness: The Making of Shoreworkers in the BC Fishing Industry." *Studies in Political Economy*, 20 (summer 1986), 85–116.

– "Race and Gender: Structural Determinants in the Formation of British Columbia's Salmon Cannery Labour Force." *Canadian Journal of Sociology*, 13 nos. 1–2 (1988), 103–20.

– "What Is Patriarchy?" In Jesse Vorst et al., eds., *Race, Class, Gender: Bonds and Barriers*, 65–86. Toronto: Between the Lines and Winnipeg: Society for Socialist Studies/Société d'études socialistes, 1989.

Myles, John. "Decline or Impasse? The Current State of the Welfare State." *Studies in Political Economy*, 26 (summer 1988), 73–107.

Myles, John, Picot, G., and Wannell, T. *Good Jobs, Bad Jobs and the declining middle*. Statistics Canada Research Paper No. 28. Ottawa, 1990.

Neis, Barbara. "Flexible Specialization: What's That Got to do with the Price of Fish?" *Studies in Political Economy*, 36 (autumn 1991), 145–75.

Ng, Roxanna. "Sexism, Racism, and Canadian Nationalism." In Jesse Vorst et al., *Race, Class, Gender: Bonds and Barriers*, 10–25. Toronto: Between the Lines and Winnipeg: Society for Socialist Studies/Société d'études socialistes, 1989.

– "State Funding to a Community Employment Centre: Implications for Working with Immigrant Women." In Roxanna Ng, Gillian Walker, and Jacob Muller, eds., *Community Organization and the Canadian State*, 165–83. Toronto: Garamond Press, 1990.

Pal, Leslie. *Interests of State: The Politics of Language, Multiculturalism and Feminism in Canada*. Montreal: McGill-Queen's University Press, 1993.

Parr, Joy. *The Gender of Breadwinners: Women, Men, and Change in Two Industrial Towns*. Toronto: University of Toronto Press, 1990.

Peters, Suzanne, Grashman, R., and Lauring, C., *Changing Directions in Public Policy: Debates and Choices, Carts and Horses*. Toronto: Peters Research Associates, 1993.

Phillips, Paul, and Phillips, Erin. *Women and Work: Equality in the Canadian Labour Market*. Rev. ed. Toronto: Lorimer, 1993.

Pierson, Ruth. "Gender and Unemployment Insurance debates in Canada, 1934–1940." *Labour/Le travail*, 25 (spring 1990), 77–103.

– "The Mainstream Women's Movement and the Politics of Difference." In Ruth Pierson, Marjorie Cohen, Paula Bourne, and Philinda Masters, eds., *Canadian Women's Issues, Vol. 1, Strong Voices*, 186–214. Toronto: Lorimer, 1993.

Poelzer, Irene. "Metis Women and the Economy of Northern Saskatchewan." In Jesse Vorst et al., *Race, Class, Gender: Bonds and Barriers*, 196–216. Toronto: Between the Lines and Winnipeg: Society for Socialist Studies/Société d'études socialistes, 1989.

Prentice, Susan. "Kids Are Not for Profit: The Politics of Childcare." In Frank Cunningham et al., eds., *Social Movements/Social Change: The Politics and Practice of Organising*, 98–128. Toronto: Between the Lines; Winnepeg; Society for Socialist Studies/Société d'études socialistes, 1988.

- "The 'Mainstreaming' of Daycare." *Resources for Feminist Research/Documentation sur la recherche féministe*, 17 no. 3 (1988), 59–63.
- "Workers, Mothers, Reds: Toronto's Postwar Daycare Fight." *Studies in Political Economy*, 30 (autumn 1989), 115–41.
Proulx, Monique. *Women and Work: Five Million Women, a Study of the Canadian Housewife.* Ottawa: Canadian Advisory Council on the Status of Women, 1978.
Randall, Melanie. "Feminism and the State: Questions for Theory and Practice." *Resources for Feminist Research/Documentation sur la recherche féministe*, 17 no. 3 (1988), 10–16.
Rayside, David. "Gay Rights and Family Values." *Studies in Political Economy*, 26 (summer 1988), 109–47.
Razak, Sherene. *Canadian Feminism and the Law: The Women's Legal Education and Action Fund and the Pursuit of Equality.* Toronto: Second Story Press, 1991.
Rebick, Judy. "An Interview." *Studies in Political Economy*, 44 (1994), 58–9.
Reinart, Ustun. "Three Major Strands of the Women's Movement in Manitoba, 1965–1985." In J. Silver and J. Hull, eds., *The Political Economy of Manitoba*, 151–68. Regina, Sask.: Canadian Plains Research Centre, University of Regina, 1990.
Reiter, Ester. *Making Fast Food: From the Frying Pan into the Fryer.* Montreal: McGill-Queen's University Press, 1991.
Rowbotham, Sheila. *Women, Resistance and Revolution.* First published 1972. Harmondsworth: Penguin, 1975.
St-Onge, Nicole. "Race, Class and Marginality in a Manitoba Interlake Settlement." in Jesse Vorst et al., *Race, Class, Gender: Bonds and Barriers*, 116–32. Toronto: Between the Lines and Winnipeg: Society for Socialist Studies/Société d'études socialistes, 1989.
Schreader. Alicia. "The State-Funded Women's Movement: A Case of Two Political Agendas." In Roxanna Ng, Gillian Walker, and Jacob Muller, eds., *Community Organization and the Canadian State*, 184–99. Toronto: Garamond Press, 1990.
Seccombe, Wally. *A Millennium of Family Change: Feudalism to Capitalism in Northwestern Europe.* London: Verso, 1992.
- "Patriarchy Stabilized: The Construction of the Male Breadwinner Wage Norm in Nineteenth-Century Britain." *Social History*, 11 (1986), 43–76.
- *Weathering the Storm: Working Class Families from the Industrial Revolution to the Fertility Decline.* London: Verso, 1993.
Sharma, Nandita. "Restructuring Society, Restructuring Lives: The Global Restructuring of Capital and Women's Paid Employment in Canada." *Socialist Studies Bulletin/Bulletin d'études socialistes*, 37 (1994), 18–46.
Silvera, Makeda. *Silenced.* 2nd ed. Toronto: Sister Vision Press, 1989.
Smith, Dorothy. "Women, Class and Family." In Dorothy Smith and Varda Burstyn, *Women, Class, Family and the State*, 1–44. Toronto: Garamond, 1985.

– "Feminist Reflections on Political Economy." *Studies in Political Economy*,
  30 (autumn 1989), 37–59.
– "Women's Work as Mothers: A New Look at the Relation of Class, Family
  and School Achievement." In Frieda Forman, ed., *Feminism and Education:
  A Canadian Perspective*, 241–64. Toronto: Centre for Women's Studies in
  Education, Ontario Institute for Studies in Education, 1990.
Smith, George. "Policing the Gay Community." In Roxanna Ng, Gillian Walker,
  and Jacob Muller, eds., *Community Organization and the Canadian State*,
  259–85. Toronto: Garamond Press, 1990.
– *Review of the Situation of Women in Canada*. Ottawa: Minister of Supply and
  Services, 1992.
Statistics Canada. *Labour Force*. Cat. No. 71001. Ottawa: Minister of Supply and
  Services, 1992.
Stavro-Pierce, Ellen. "Towards a Posthumanist Feminism." *Economy and Society*,
  23 no. 2, (1994), 217–45.
Strong-Boag, Veronica, and Fellman, Anita Clair, eds. *Rethinking Canada: The
  Promise of Women's History*. 2nd ed. Toronto: Copp Clark Pitman Ltd, 1991.
Tillotson, Shirley. "We May All Soon Be 'First-Class Men': Gender and Skill in
  Canadian Early Twenthieth Century telegraph Industry." *Labour/Le travail*,
  27 (spring 1991), 97–125.
Tilly, Louise, and Scott, Joan. *Women, Work and Family*. New York: Holt, 1978.
Ursell, Jane. *Private Lives, Public Policy: 100 Years of State Intervention in the Family*.
  Toronto: Women's Press, 1992.
Valverde, Mariana. *The Age of Light Soap and Water: Moral Reform in English
  Canada* Toronto: McCelland and Stewart, 1991.
Valverde, Mariana, and Weir, Lorna. "The Struggles of The Immoral: Prelimi-
  nary Remarks on Moral Regulation." *Resources for Feminist Research/Docu-
  mentation sur la recherche féministe*, 17 no. 3 (1988), 31–4.
Vickers, Jill. "The Intellectual Origins of the Women's Movement in Canada."
  In Constance Backhouse and David Flaherty, ed., *Challenging Times:
  The Women's Movement in Canada and the United States*, 39–60. Montreal:
  McGill-Queen's University Press, 1992.
Vickers, Jill, Rankin, Pauline, and Appelle, Christine. *Politics as if Women
  Mattered: A Political Analysis of the National Action Committee on the Status of
  Women*. Toronto: University of Toronto Press, 1993.
Walker, Gillian. "The Conceptual Politics of Struggle: Wife Battery, the Women's
  Movement and the State." *Studies in Political Economy*, 33 (autumn 1990),
  63–90.
– *Family Violence and the Women's Movement*. Toronto: University of Toronto
  Press, 1990.
– "Reproducing Community: The Historical Development of Local and Extra-
  Local Relations." In Roxanna Ng, Gillian Walker, and Jacob Muller, eds.,

Community Organization and the Canadian State, 31–47. Toronto: Garamond Press, 1990.

Warskett, Rosemary. "Bank Worker Unionization and the Law." *Studies in Political Economy*, 25 (spring 1988), 41–73.

– "Democratizing the State: Challenges from Public Sector Unions." *Studies in Political Economy*, 42 (autumn 1993), 129–40.

– "Wage Solidarity and Equal Value: Or Gender and Class in the Structuring of Workplace Hierarchies." *Studies in Political Economy*, 32 (summer 1990), 55–83.

Weir, Lorna. "Social Movement Activism in the Formation of Ontario New Democratic Party Policy on Abortion, 1982–1984." *Labour/Le travail* (forthcoming).

White, Jerry. "Changing Labour Process and the Nursing Crisis in Canadian Hospitals." *Studies in Political Economy*, 40 (spring 1993), 103–34.

– *Hospital Strike: Women, Unions, and Public Sector Conflict.* Toronto: Thompson Educational Publishing, 1990.

White, Julie. *Mail and Female: Women and the Canadian Union of Postal Workers.* Toronto: Thompson Educational Publishing, 1990.

– *Sisters and Solidarity: Women and Unions in Canada.* Toronto: Thompson Educational Publishing, 1993.

Whitworth, Sandra. "Planned Parenthood and the New Right: Onslaught or Opportunity." *Studies in Political Economy*, 35 (summer 1991), 73–101.

Woolley, Frances, Marshall, Judith, and Vermaeten, Arndt. "Ending Universality: The Case of Child Benefits." In Meg Luxton, ed., *Family Politics: Policy Issues and Critical Practices.* Halifax: Fernwood Press, forthcoming.

Young, Brian. "Positive Law, Positive State: Class Realignment and the Transformation of Lower Canada, 1815–1866." In Alan Greer and Ian Radforth, eds., *Colonial Leviathan: State Formation in Mid-Nineteenth-Century Canada*, 163–91. Toronto: University of Toronto Press, 1992.

6 Understanding What Happened Here: The Political Economy of Indigenous Peoples

FRANCES ABELE

Shopping centres, streets, warships, community colleges, automobiles, hair styles, sports teams,[1] and neighbourhoods – all have been given the names of the Indigenous nations[2] of North America by the settlers who came from other continents, and by the settlers' children. Like migrants everywhere, the newcomers to North America tended to rename their "New World" with the familiar placenames of home. Frequently, however, they also adopted Indigenous toponyms: from Miramichi to Iqaluit, from Aklavik to Osoyoos, the original names survive,[3] often more visible than the nations that coined them. *Why is this so?*

On ceremonial occasions – international sporting events, receptions for visiting heads of state, solemn commemorations of various kinds – Indigenous people are almost invariably invited to participate, as individuals and importantly, as representatives and as symbols.[4] *But symbols of what?*

These are not simple questions, and there are no simple answers. In this chapter I argue that the best way to approach these matters is to raise another, even more fundamental question. This is perhaps the great, complex question of Canadian history, shared by descendants of the Indigenous nations and by descendants of the settlers, by people of mixed heritage and by recent immigrants, by anglophones, francophones, and allophones. How did the northern part of North America pass from the control of Indigenous nations possessing several languages, that farmed, fished, hunted, and gathered in relative environmental balance, that were allied, federated, and sometimes at war, and that were internally organized in a variety of ways, to become a modern nation-state, in which a majority population, dominated by the languages and traditions of Europe, farmed and built factories, highways, and huge cities while they entirely reorganized the political map of the continent – literally as well as ideologically pushing the original land-holders to the margins? *What happened here?*

That we all need and want to know is evident everywhere. There are the aforementioned acknowledgments in placenames and ceremonies of the importance of Indigenous peoples to "Canadian identity" – despite their small numbers. There are the many friendships and family relationships among Indigenous and non-Indigenous people – as well as incidents of racism and violence.[5] There is the prominence afforded Aboriginal leaders and representatives in specific aspects of Canadian public life. There is the remarkable population distribution of Canada, in which virtually all of the non-Indigenous people live within 700 kilometres of the Canada–United States border, while in the northern two-thirds of the country, Aboriginal people form the majority or a large minority (though they are fewer than 4 per cent of the Canadian population overall).[6] There are, finally, the conflicts over land and resources that persist and fester between outbreaks of media attention. These conflicts, as well as the treaties[7] and modern comprehensive claims agreements,[8] all indicate unfinished business between the Indigenous peoples and the newcomers, as well as a shared history and an important story to tell.

Several years ago, Daiva Stasiulis and I argued that, with some significant exceptions, the Canadian political economy tradition ignored the centrality of Indigenous–non-Indigenous relations to many of the key questions of Canadian development, hampering understanding and weakening the prospect for progressive change.[9] Here I explore similar questions from a different perspective. Drawing on writings chosen for their potential usefulness to political economists rather than for their status as works of political economy, classically defined,[10] I highlight the connections among historical understanding, political struggles, and economic transformation and identify some analytical tasks that lie immediately ahead.

WHO ARE THE INDIGENOUS PEOPLES?

The Canadian constitution identifies "Indians, Inuit and Metis" as the Aboriginal peoples of Canada.[11] "Indians" are Indigenous people who are members of the nations of peoples that have lived in northern North America, generally south of the treeline, from time immemorial.[12] Frequently, Indians are spoken of as First Nations, as they refer to themselves in the name of the national federation that represents most of them – the Assembly of First Nations. Some members of First Nations are descendants of Indigenous people who signed treaties, but treaties have not been negotiated yet for large portions of Canada, particularly in the north and west.

Despite their ability to formulate and work towards common objectives, the Indian First Nations are outstandingly heterogeneous – culturally, linguistically, economically, and politically, as they have been since the times before Europeans arrived. It is as difficult to generalize about First Nations as it is to generalize about the diverse nations of the United Kingdom and Europe. Historically, their societies range from the caribou-hunting Innu of Labrador and northern Quebec to the settled fishing societies, like that of the Haida, on the west coast. Today, members of First Nations live in small, fly-in communities (as do the Dene of northern Manitoba, Saskatchewan, Alberta, British Columbia, Northwest Territories, and Yukon), on reserves near cities (as do the Mohawks of Kahnewake), and, increasingly, intermingled with other residents of Canada in cities and towns.

Another distinct people are Inuit, who live in Canada's Arctic north of the treeline.[13] For thousands of years, most Inuit have made their living in seasonal harvests of ocean and coastal lands; now, though (in Canada) they have been living in small communities for about two generations, most still depend heavily on the fruits of the land for their livelihood. Inuit are a circumpolar people, with relatives in Alaska, Canada, Greenland, and Russia. Their national organization is the Inuit Tapirisat of Canada, representing Inuit of Labrador, Nunavik (northern Quebec), and Northwest Territories; internationally, they have formed the Inuit Circumpolar Conference, to protect the Arctic basin and to support each other in political development.

"Metis" is the term generally adopted by two quite distinct groups of people. The people sometimes referred to as the "Red River Metis" are the descendants of the historical Metis Nation, whose rebellion, led by Louis Riel and Gabriel Dumont, led to the foundation of the province of Manitoba. The Red River Metis are the culturally distinct descendants of early unions of French and Scottish fur traders and Indigenous women.[14] They now live all over Canada, represented politically by the Metis Nation. Other people of mixed Indigenous and non-Indigenous heritage also identify themselves as Metis, though they do not share the particular cultural tradition or the lineage of the Metis Nation. Many of the non–Red River Metis are represented by the Council of Aboriginal Peoples (formerly the Native Council of Canada).

THE POLITICS OF HISTORY:
SYMBOLS OF WHAT?

"... the sincerity of the guilt felt for the mistreatment of the Aborigine in the past does not allow the Aborigine to be other than of the past. The Aborigines are a base for Australian culture, not a part of its developing fabric."[15] Terry Goldie's comment about a particular genre of Australian literature applies equally well to the serious intellectual and political difficulties facing those who seek to accept the implications of the shared histories of Indigenous and non-Indigenous peoples in North America. Goldie's remark might be extended to provide one answer to the first question raised at the beginning of this chapter, concerning what the participation of Indigenous peoples in major ceremonies is meant to symbolize. On Goldie's analysis, the settlers' regret over their ancestors' actions leads them to denial, to cast living Indigenous people as symbols of past events, even as those same people participate in the everyday and public life of their countries.

It is likely, however, that to some observers and to the Aboriginal participants themselves, the ceremonies have quite another significance. Indigenous people who take public office and who participate in ceremonies could also be seen as asserting the importance of offering continued endorsement from Aboriginal people to Canadian institutions. Some may, as well, mean to indicate the openness of the Indigenous nations to respectful diplomatic and other relationships. Certainly by their active presence they contradict the tendency of some to relegate Indigenous people to the past and the margins.

These different meanings and their diverging implications appear able to coexist, in dynamic contradiction. Different understandings of Canadian history, and different assessments of the current political balance, create the gap between the two interpretations of the symbolism of Aboriginal participation.[16] Though their progress may not have been remarked on by all, Canadian historians have confronted and largely surmounted a number of challenges in developing a less polarized story of Canada.

The first and most obvious of the challenges has been that of inclusion – the project of writing histories of Canada that provide a realistic sense of the role of Indigenous peoples. Historians of Canada have produced a major body of work, which, while far from complete and certainly not without controversies, analyses the history of Indigenous nations and peoples and their relations with the newcomers.[17]

Part of the challenge has been simply to find material to apply to particular problems of historical reconstruction. Explorers, missionaries, and colonizers usually take a purposeful interest in the nations they encounter, but only rarely are they motivated to assist in the preservation of those nations' own historical records. Sometimes they have wanted to obliterate them;[18] other times, newcomers came with keen ethnographic purpose and have helped to preserve knowledge that might otherwise have been lost.[19] For those nations whose history relies primarily on oral preservation and communication, a great deal was lost in the mass deaths that came with the spread of the new diseases that accompanied the settlers from other continents.[20]

Despite these difficulties, during the last twenty years there has been a wonderful explosion of published historical research about Indigenous peoples and their relations with their neighbours, from both Indigenous and non-Indigenous writers.[21] One of the most striking sources of insight about the period of contact between Aboriginal and non-Aboriginal peoples is a growing – if still rather lopsided – collection of first-person accounts. Indigenous people's early impressions of the newcomers are not as scarce as they once seemed. Some Indigenous historical knowledge was recorded, and more has been passed from generation to generation in the traditional way.

First, there are some early writings in English and French by Indigenous peoples.[22] Editor Penny Petrone collected hundreds of texts (letters, speeches, essays, petitions, essays, and sermons), aiming "to show the beginnings and development in Canada of an Indian literary tradition in English." She found that from this work "a good deal can be learned about the Indian view of Canadian history."[23]

An example of the power of such work is the following testimony from Mistahimaskwa (Big Bear), the great Cree leader who was tried for treason after he refused the terms of the treaties offered by the dominion government and fought in the 1885 rebellion. He told the court:

I have ruled my country for long. Now I am in chains and will be sent to prison … Now I am as dead to my people. Many of them are hiding in the woods, paralyzed with fear. Can this court not send them a pardon? My own children may be starving and afraid to come out of hiding. I plead to you Chiefs of the white man's laws for pity and help for the people of my band.

I have only a little more to say. The country belonged to me. I may not live to see it again. … I am old and ugly but I have tried to do good. Have pity for the children of my tribe. Because Big Bear has always been a friend of the white man, you should send a pardon to my people and give them help.[24]

Even in translation, this is a speech of a temper and tone rarely found in Canadian political writing, more democratic and more reasoned than can be found in most of the recorded negotiations among political and economic elites that led to Confederation. As Reg Whitaker has soberly noted:

The constitution of Canada has been, from 1867 onward, an arrangement between elites, particularly between political elites. Constitutions are normally arrangements between people and their governments. ...

The British North America Act ignored individual Canadians, except as they qualified through membership in a church or a language group. The BNA Act was itself never submitted to a popular referendum for ratification, except when Newfoundland was asked if it wanted *in*, and when Quebec was asked if it wanted *out*. But to make matters worse, almost all the commentary – whether political, judicial or academic – on the nature and reform of the constitution has tended to ignore the question of the relation of people to government, or of people to each other, in favour of persistent attention to the relation of government to government, or of Crown to Parliament, or of Canada to the British Parliament.[25]

Mistahimaskwa's speech, and several others retrieved by Petrone,[26] suggest that not all residents of the young dominion ignored the relationships of governments to people. They do suggest that the political elites that sought Confederation may have had a major incentive to ignore those who raised such questions, at least during the period when control over dominion territory was still being consolidated.

A view of the early times from the other side of the cultural divide is also available. Many of the non-Aboriginal explorers, missionaries, and traders kept journals, often as part of their responsibilities to their commercial or religious sponsors. These are as coloured by their times and the preoccupations of their authors as any historical documents, but they can reveal much about the Indigenous nations as they were as long as four hundred years ago, and much as well about the purposes, fears, and imaginings of the explorers themselves.[27] Kerry Abel's *Drum Songs*[28] makes extensive use of explorers' journals, as well as oral testimony, archaeological findings, folk traditions, and linguistic studies, to reconstruct primarily the last two hundred years of Dene history. The general emphasis in this richly detailed book is (almost by default) on the facets of Dene history that involved contact with explorers and missionaries, providing, as Abel acknowledges, "glimpses" into the rest. Part of Abel's purpose in writing Dene history is explicitly practical and political: "A better understanding of Canadian history should help other Canadians to recognize both the narrowness of old, ethnocentric interpretations of Canadian history and the failure of government policy based on the assumptions of those old interpretations. Small but dynamic aboriginal societies continue to exist among us; we need to recognize that fact and attempt to understand the aspirations of those who want to safeguard a future of continuing choices for their children. Only then can we choose appropriate government policies and constitutional structures."[29]

A DEEPER EPISTEMOLOGICAL CHALLENGE

Fascinating insights about the recent past of Indigenous people may be found in the "life stories" or "life histories" collected by a new generation of anthropologists. Because many Indigenous people tell their own life stories as an aspect of other social and cultural events, and in light of the historical and mythological themes that they have been taught, much more than a life is told. As Julie Cruikshank has explained:

In 1974 I began recording life histories of several Yukon Native women born just before or shortly after the Klondike gold rush (1896–98). As our work progressed, it became clear that these women were approaching our task with a different narrative model of "life history" from my own. My expectation had been that our discussions would document the social impact of the Klondike gold rush at the turn of the century, the construction of the Alaska Highway during the Second World War, and other disruptive events. From the beginning, several of the eldest women responded to my questions about secular events by telling traditional stories. The more I persisted with my agenda, the more insistent each was about the direction our work should take. Each explained that these narratives were important to record *as part of* her life story.

Their accounts, then, included not only personal reminiscences of the kind we normally associate with autobiography, but detailed narratives elaborating on mythological themes. Also embedded in the chronicles were songs ... Their life stories were framed by genealogies and by long lists of personal names and place names that appear to have both metaphoric and mnemonic value. In addition to biographical material, we recorded more than one hundred stories about the origins and transformations of the world and the beings who inhabit it.[30]

Cruikshank's comments bring a deeper challenge, created by the reality that history itself, as an enterprise, is conceived differently by historians of at least some Indigenous nations.[31] Integrating the historical knowledge and analysis of Cruikshank's Tagish, Tlingit, and Southern Tutchone collaborators is not simply a matter of including the information they provide; it is a matter of understanding history in a different way and of finding some means to include a quite different view of the individual in society, and in history, from that now common.[32] Appreciating the practical implications of this circumstance is difficult enough in the context of adequate cross-cultural communication; when Indigenous historical approaches encounter law and politics, outcomes can be most uncertain.

This is evident in the jurisprudence of the last twenty-five years. On the whole the drift of recent Canadian jurisprudence has been to expand legal notions of the degree of sovereignty and the rights of Indigenous peoples, but this has occurred in an uneven and contradictory fashion. A landmark example of the problems raised by Indigenous historical knowledge for Canadian jurisprudence is testimony by the Gitskan and Wet'suwet'en nations in a suit to establish their sovereignty in British Columbia.[33] Gitskan and Wet'suwet'en historical knowledge was offered in court at great length and in the style of its preservation, but it was not accepted as evidence that the form of government described was in essential respects identical with what existed before European settlement of their lands.

UNDERSTANDING THE CHANGING POLITICAL BALANCE: *WHAT HAPPENED HERE?*

The political participation of Indigenous people in Canadian political institutions has been rewarded in recent years by a steady advance to the centres of political power. Today there are three Aboriginal members of Parliament, two Aboriginal senators, and one Aboriginal premier of a territory whose legislature has had a majority of Indigenous members for nearly twenty years. Each major group of Indigenous peoples is represented by a national organization; each as well is part of provincial and regional bodies formed for general political representation and also to provide particular social and economic services. There are also national political and professional organizations formed by Indigenous women.[34]

Various forms of limited self-government are being practised across Canada.[35] Perhaps most strikingly, not only have Inuit succeeded in negotiating comprehensive claims agreements in almost all their territories,[36] but they have had considerable success in negotiating self-government. In 1999 Nunavut Territory will be established as a jurisdiction in northeastern Canada in which Inuit will form at least 80 per cent of the electorate; at the same moment, a new western territory will be created, home to a much more heterogeneous population of Dene, Metis, Inuvialuit, and non-Indigenous people.[37] In Nunavik (northern Quebec) a significant degree of regional self-government has been negotiated by Inuit with the province of Quebec, building on the terms of the James Bay and Northern Quebec Agreement.

In light of these achievements, it is startling to realize that for most of the twentieth century the frank assessment of most of those in power was that the Indigenous cultures and societies would inevitably disappear; the stated goal of public policy was to hasten this development, so that Indigenous people would be sooner assimilated into full citizenship.[38] From the beginnings of dominion adminstration of Indians until quite recently, Indigenous peoples' forms of political organization and related traditions were discouraged and often repressed vigorously.[39] As recently as 1953, it was illegal for Indians to raise money for the purpose of forming political organizations.[40] "Registered" Indians were not allowed the federal franchise until 1960.[41]

The increased political integration of Indigenous people is the fruit of three decades of community organizing, mobilization, internal debate about strategy and constitutional and governance matters, and development of solidarity networks.[42] In this period there have been two major reversals in federal policy, each a response to "pressure from below," and each in turn responsible for a radical reshaping of the political movement of Indigenous peoples in Canada. The first reversal was the extension of the franchise to status Indians and the concurrent initiatives by the federal Department of Indian Affairs to promote the political self-organization of Indians on reserves.[43] The reasons for this major shift in official thinking appear to be a compound of the inspiration of the civil disturbances and mass mobilizations that were part of the u.s. civil rights movement and worldwide liberation movements and recognition that such forces were stirring in Canada and needed a safe channel.[44] Whatever the motivations within the state, for Indians and later for other Aboriginal peoples this shift in policy made available new means for political action. Aboriginal peoples' political mobilization had produced reasonable levels of federal funding, both for general institutional support of advocacy and for representative organizations. A tradition of federal funding for special projects – such as research on key policy questions – was established.

A second major shift in federal policy took place between 1969 and 1982. This change involved gradual recognition of the importance of treaties already negotiated and the need to negotiation new, treaty-like arrangements with those Indigenous nations and peoples that had not yet consented to share their territories. In 1969, the new Trudeau government issued a *Statement on Indian Policy*, the infamous White Paper, which denied the modern relevance of treaties and stated as an ultimate goal of public policy extension of equal rights to all Indians as individuals. This announcement encountered enormous and vigorous resistance from Indians across Canada. By 1973, the government publicly drew back from the principles of the White Paper and proclaimed its willingness to negotiate comprehensive land claim agreements – sometimes called modern treaties – with those peoples whose ancestors had not signed treaties.

To date, nine comprehensive claims agreements have been concluded, while several others are in active negotiation. Critics of the process are numerous,[45] but there is no question that it has provided many Aboriginal peoples with a legal framework to protect at least some of their resources and a significant pool of capital for internal development.

A high-water mark was reached in 1982, when the "existing Aboriginal and treaty rights" of Indians, Inuit, and Metis were entrenched in the newly patriated Canadian constitution. Further efforts to define these rights constitutionally, and to entrench other advances, have failed,[46] but the principle that all Aboriginal peoples share certain collective rights has been established. Many provincial governments as well as the federal minister of Indian affairs have recognized formally Aboriginal peoples' inherent right of self-government, though the practical consequences of this step are not yet fully apparent.[47]

In 1996, the Royal Commission on Aboriginal Peoples will submit a final report to the federal government. The royal commission was announced in the fall of 1990, in the aftermath of the crisis at Kanesetake (Oka), in which an attempt by the Mohawk to stop a municipal golf course from being constructed on land they believed to be theirs led to an armed stand-off and one death.[48] The sixteen-point mandate of the royal commission was drafted by former Supreme Court Chief Justice Brian Dickson, after wide consultations with Aboriginal peoples and others across Canada; it encompasses virtually every feature of the institutional relationships between Aboriginal and non-Aboriginal Canadians. The release of the commission's report is expected to reopen public discussion of these matters, which, despite the existence of the constitutional amendment, are still largely unresolved – especially with regard to landownership and the powers of Aboriginal governments.[49]

Clearly the first questions confronting political economy in light of the remarkable transformation in Indigenous-state relations since 1960 arise from the speed with which Indigenous representative organizations have been created and accommodated within state and governing institutions. Indigenous people as a group form only a small proportion of the general population; as peoples and nations, they are much smaller and presumably much less influential than Canada's other significant cultural collectivity, comprised of francophones in and outside Quebec. Though certainly the processes of transformation have been documented, and some of their implications pondered, the task of understanding the implications of these events for our analysis of state power and political community remains.[50]

It is possible that this analytical task will lead past the standing institutions of Canadian liberal democracy, towards the struggles that attended their formation, up to and including the forms of political organization and representation that had been developed by Indigenous nations and peoples. In the literature to date, there is not much discussion of these matters, and less that connects Indigenous governing traditions to the political and military struggles that led to the formation of Canada. The degree of their influence remains an open question.

THE STATE AND ECONOMIC DEVELOPMENT

Everywhere in the world, the role of the state in economic development is being changed. State capitalist endeavours and public social-welfare spending are being curtailed and reviled; initiatives to moderate the effects of capitalism, such as labour legislation and environmental regulatory regimes, are being dismantled. Yet states continue to interact with and to serve capitalist development, as they continue to be the focus of the economic aspirations of their citizens. It has never been more important to understand the role of the state in capitalist development and in the integration of local and national economies into the institutions of global capitalism.

For Indigenous peoples, these matters are particularly sharply defined. Where they do not live disproportionately in poverty, Indigenous people often rely on a natural-resource base that can be protected and husbanded for their use only by an active state. Peter Usher and other scholars have documented the dynamics of what is now referred to as the "mixed" or "domestic" economy of the predominantly Aboriginal communities of the north.[51] In the mixed economy, income-in-kind from the land, and cash income from wages and social transfers, are shared within households. The mixed economy has proved viable and relatively stable over several decades, valued for its ability to make the best use of all available economic opportunities in areas where wage employment is scarce and unreliable and also for its reliance on traditional Indigenous knowledge and skills for success. In this last capacity it strengthens Aboriginal communities as well as feeds them.

The continued survival of the mixed economy depends on two policy measures that only a legitimate public authority – a state – can provide. The first is steady access to the fruits of the land, assured by regulated land use. The second is small infusions of cash, in the form of income from commodity sales, wages, or social transfers. While commodity sales and wages depend on private enterprise, their availability to the residents of the small communities where the mixed economy flourishes almost always requires regulatory and other initiatives of the public authority.

The current period, of declining state powers and weakening commitment to intervention and regulation, does raise serious questions about the availability of the mixed economy to those Aboriginal peoples who depend on it for their livelihood. There is a growing body of literature, primarily from political economists, geographers, and anthropologists, that addresses the question of future public policies and state institutions that will protect and develop the mixed economy.[52]

Other features of economic policies and economic-development initiatives, for those Aboriginal communities not well placed to participate in the mixed economy as well as for those who are, have also begun to be analysed.[53] The work highlights the difficulties faced by "external" states (such as federal and provincial governments) in organizing the development of Indigenous communities, while clearly showing that external resources will certainly be required. Nor is it clear that transferring fiscal control and the public expenditure budget to Aboriginal communities will provide a full solution: there are unresolved issues of internal structure, community control, effective decision making, and the necessary maintenance of relations with external organizations such as banks, corporations, and labour and commodity markets. Autarky is an option for very few communities today. The task for political economists therefore is to understand closely and well the means by which relations with external economic agents may be maintained, without total cession of local control and initiatives.

One dimension of this analysis will certainly require research on the ways in which the major economic institutions of Canada, in their domestic and international connections, shape and limit economic and social development in Aboriginal territories. Another, however, must be internal. The social relations of production in Indigenous communities today grew from the traditional pre-contact societies, were elaborated over the centuries of "contact" with the evolving institutions of capitalism, and finally have been organized by various forms of specialized state policies, especially since 1945. It is no simple matter to understand the class structure of various nations and peoples, but it is important to do so before designing both economic and political institutions for self-determination. Much of this work will be done by Indigenous people themselves, but all of it will be of deep interest to political economy.

CONCLUSIONS

As Kerry Abel noted, the work undertaken by writers inside and outside the universities to rewrite Canadian history in a way that includes Indigenous peoples, and to understand the reality of differing perceptions, is basic to the development of healthy political institutions for resolving the problems of the present. Resolution is not, however, as simple as developing realistic solutions in light of an accurate understanding of the past, and then choosing them. Both political and economic forces are engaged by any such choices. There are certainly challenges for scholarship and for the imagination – but there are also challenges arising directly from power contested.

Today Indigenous peoples comprise less than 4 per cent of the Canadian population, but they live not as individuals but as members of collectivities. In those collectivities they are stronger than their proportion would suggest. Further, Indigenous people in Canada do not live today in isolation from their non-Indigenous co-residents. Our fates, our families, and our neighbourhoods are intermingled, a reality that is reflected in the institutions of political life. The sources and implications of the current structural resolution have yet to be fully understood.

Such an understanding is particularly important now, as state capacities all over the world are being eroded by major global economic transformations. For the small nations and peoples within Canada, as for the other communities, it is particularly urgent to understand how states may still be used to protect and to develop local social and economic capacities. Even the political capacities of Aboriginal governments may be affected. The existing Aboriginal organizations and governments in Canada are artifacts of a period in Canadian public spending that may have passed for ever. As not only federal budgets for social protection but also citizens' participation and advocacy organizations disappear, how will Indigenous people sustain a public voice? It remains to be seen whether the institutions they have entrenched in the constitution, the claims process, and self-government negotiations will be able to adapt to fill this role.

ACKNOWLEDGMENTS

This essay is heavily mortgaged in the currency of both professional and domestic life. I want to thank Wallace Clement for great editorial patience and tact, and my husband, George Kinloch, for inspiration, unstinting support, and abiding intellectual companionship. Peter Usher's comments remedied and provoked, as usual. More than they can know, my former colleagues at the Royal Commission on Aboriginal Peoples have enriched this analysis, though of course neither they nor the commission necessarily agree with anything that I have said.

NOTES

1 In professional sports, the Edmonton Eskimos, the Atlanta Braves, the Chicago Black Hawks, and their like still exist, but there has been a recent trend among university sports teams to retire names of Indigenous nations. For example, the Sea Hawks basketball team of the Memorial University of Newfoundland was formerly called the Beothuks, after a nation of Indigenous people whose long tenure in what is now Newfoundland was terminated by disease, displacement, and murder by the early European settlers to the island.

2 The terms used to refer to the descendants of the original inhabitants of North America are hardly neutral; I hope most would accept "Indigenous peoples" or "Aboriginal peoples" as suitable collective nouns. The terms refer to all the nations and peoples who have inhabited North America for thousands of years. Where possible, I follow the preferable practice of referring to Indigenous nations by their own proper names: Haida, Siksika, Cree, Miq'mac, and so on.

3 In Northwest Territories, where Aboriginal people form the majority and where the legislative assembly has been under Aboriginal control for nearly two decades, there has been a steady trend to move into common usage the Aboriginal names for communities and peoples. For example, Frobisher Bay is now called Iqaluit, as Inuit have always known it.

4 Canada's ambassador to the circumpolar countries is the distinguished Inuk leader Mary Simon. For many years, Aboriginal veterans have participated as Aboriginal people as well as veterans in commemorative celebrations. In a separate category, worthy of separate analysis, are the various "settler" celebrations, such as the Calgary Stampede, in which the cowboy culture of the newcomers is paraded along with an almost entirely visual presentation of the culture of Indigenous peoples.

5 The complexities of belonging and exclusion can often be read most plainly in autobiographies, such as Maria Campbell, *Half-Breed*; Charlie Snowshoe, "A Trapper's Life"; Dorothy Daniels, "Metis Identity"; and Minnie Freeman, *Life among the Qallunaat.*

6 Indigenous people are the majority of the population of Northwest Territories and northern Saskatchewan, while they comprise significant pluralities in Yukon and the northern halves of Quebec, Manitoba, and Alberta.

7 Treaties were negotiated by the first emissaries from Europe with the nations they encountered; these "pre-Confederation Treaties" usually establish a formal diplomatic relationship between the Indigenous nation and the newcomers. After Confederation, a series of "numbered" treaties (1 through 11) were negotiated with Indigenous nations in Ontario, Manitoba, Saskatchewan, Alberta, and Northwest Territories. In many cases the written versions diverge from the oral version remembered by the Indian signatories. See, for example, Fumoleau, *As Long.*

8 Comprehensive claims agreements are sometimes referred to as "modern treaties." They are negotiated between the government of Canada and Indigenous nations, especially but not exclusively nations not already parties to a treaty. The first comprehensive claims agreement is known as the James Bay and Northern Quebec Agreement, signed in 1975 by the Cree and Inuit of northern Quebec, the governments of Canada and Quebec, and Hydro-Québec.

9 Abele and Stasiulis, "Canada."

10 Ibid. discusses many works of classical political economy. The school has of course continued to grow since 1989, but in the present chapter I do not try to encompass all the new work. An excellent selection and overview appears in Satzewich and Wotherspoon, *First.*

11 Constitution Act [1982] s. 35.

12 For somewhat contrasting accounts of the origins and evolution of the Indigenous nations, see Sioui, *For*; and Dickason, *Canada's.*

13 The treeline marks the boundary between the subarctic boreal forest and the tundra of the Arctic. It runs approximately diagonally from the northern part of the Yukon–Alaska border in the northwest to the point where the Manitoba–Northwest Territories border touches Hudson Bay and from there across northern Quebec and Labrador at about the 55th parallel.

14 Slobodin, *Metis*; Sylvia Van Kirk, "*Many.*"

15 Goldie, *Fear.*

16 Here I step reluctantly past a now-substantial literature on these and related issues. See, for example, *Native Studies Review*, Special Issue; Pakes, "Seeing"; Goldie, *Fear*; and McMahon, *Arctic.* More generally, see Francis, *Imaginary*; Berkhofer, *White* and *Salvation.*

17 Besides the references in Abele and Stasiulis, "Canada," see, for example, Sioui, *For*; Dickason, *Canada's*; Trigger, *Indians* and *Natives*; Van Kirk, "*Many*"; Coates, *Best*; and Lange, "Changing."

18 Wright, *Stolen*.

19 Cruikshank with others, *Life*, 1–36; for example, see Boas, "Mythology."

20 Some entire peoples were annihilated by disease, displacement, and warfare; many others were reduced to perhaps one-tenth of their original population in a very few years. See Jennings, *Invasion*. Alaskan Yupik analyst Harold Napoleon has likened the impact of the loss of family members and sometimes entire communities, and the knowledge they carried, to post-traumatic stress syndrome identified in Vietnam war veterans. See Napoleon with Madsen, eds., *Yuuyaraq*.

21 Some useful reviews and bibliographies include (for documents published by Aboriginal and non-Aboriginal governments) Canada, Royal Commission, Report, vols. 1–4, and (for writings on Aboriginal economic and social development) Elias, *Development*.

22 Petrone, ed., *First* and *Northern*; Moody, ed., *Indigenous*.

23 Petrone, ed., *First*.

24 Quoted in ibid., 5.

25 Whitaker, "Democracy," 206 and 207.

26 See the quotations from Shinguaconse, Piapot, and Pitikwahanapiwtyin (Poundmaker) in Petrone, *First*, 59, 64, 65, respectively.

27 Hearne, *Journey*; Thompson, *David*; Mealing, *Jesuit*. Arguably, the genre of explorers' journals continues well into the twentieth century: Hugh Brody, *Maps* and *People's*; P.D. Downes, *Sleeping*; and Kevin McMahon, *Twilight*, are all superlative – and very different – "journals" that are essentially explanatory narratives addressed to the people at home.

28 Abel, *Drum*.

29 Ibid., 269.

30 Julie Cruikshank, with Sidney, Smith, and Ned, *Life*, 2. There are many now who take an approach similar to Cruikshank's, learning from what the living members of Indigenous nations have to say about the past. See for example, Crnkovich, "*Gossip*", and Eber, *When*. Further evidence of the vitality of the oral tradition may be found in recorded testimony to various public inquiries, such as the (Berger) Inquiry into the Construction of a Mackenzie Valley Pipeline (1974–77) and the Royal Commission on Aboriginal Peoples (1992–95), and in court actions.

31 Blondin, *When*, and Snowshoe, "Trapper's," wrote for somewhat different purposes, and their work does not share all the qualities of Sidney, Smith, and Ned, who worked with Cruikshank. Blondin and Snowshoe each offer another, somewhat different kind of history.

32 For another example, see Blondin, *When*. Blondin is a Dene elder and historian. I do not mean to suggest that Indigenous ways of conceiving and communicating historical knowledge are homogeneous, nor that they are totally different from any traditions of other civilizations, such as the European or Asian ones. There are many degrees of overlap and continuity among all these civilizations at different times in their development. But certainly the approach to history practised by Blondin and by Cruikshank's three collaborators is quite different from the work of most historians practising in Canada today.

33 *Delgamuukw v. the Queen*, in *Canadian Native Law Reporter*, 1991–1993. See Culhane, "Adding" and *Delgamuukw*; Elias, *Development*, 126–9; and Cassidy, ed., *Aboriginal*.

34 These are the Native Women's Association of Canada, a federation of provincial and territorial First Nations and Metis women, and Pauktuutit, the Inuit Women's Organization.

35 Cassidy, *Indian Government*.

36 Inuit live in Northwest Territories, northern Quebec, and Labrador. In Northwest Territories, all Inuit are beneficiaries of one of two comprehensive claims agreements (the Inuvialuit Final Agreement, 1984, and the Nunavut Final Agreement, 1992); in northern Quebec, in concert with the Cree, they negotiated the James Bay and Northern Quebec Final Agreement (1975). The Labrador Inuit Association is still in negotiations.

37 Residents of both Nunavut and the future new western territory have been at work for at least two decades in developing new political forms that will suit the demographic and geographic character of the the north. See Dacks, *Choice*; Jull, *Politics*; and Abele, "Canadian."

38 See, for example, Scott, *Administration*.

39 Practices integral to cultural continuity and social order, such as the potlach and the sundance, were prohibited. See Pettipas, *Severing*; Berger, *Fragile*; and Kulchyski, " 'Considerable'."

40 Berger, *Fragile*; Kulchyski, " 'Considerable'."

41 Registration meant that an individual was listed by the federal government as being an Indian and was thereby entitled to the benefits thereof. In order to have the right to vote, and to exercise certain other citizens' rights, registered Indians were required to renounce their status. In doing so, they became citizens like any others and no longer entitled to treaty rights.

42 Cf., for example, Cardinal, *Rebirth*; Dosman, *Indians*; Boldt and Long, *Quest*; Ponting and Gibbins, *Out*.

43 Weaver, *Making*.

44 For a discussion of the formative years of the national Aboriginal movements, see McFarlane, *Brotherhood*; Weaver, *Making*; Ponting and Gibbins, *Out*; Dosman, *Indians*; Ryan, *Wall*; Adams, *Prison*; Duffy, *Road*; Jull, *Nunvut*

and *Politics*; Cardinal, *Rebirth*; Manuel and Posluns, *Fourth*; and Lauritzen, *Oil*.

45 The process is time consuming and expensive – though perhaps not more so than any of the alternatives. Furthermore, despite the federal insistence that Aboriginal signatories cede all Aboriginal rights not mentioned specifically in the claims agreement, most groups have been able to use the process to entrench at least some collective political rights. For a fresh approach, see Canada, Royal Commission, *Treaty-Making*.

46 Banting and Simeon, eds., *And*; Schwartz, *First.*

47 Even in Quebec, where provincial policies are most advanced, it seems clear that Aboriginal governments will not be seen as "separate but equal" partners in the territory; the institutions of self-government for Aboriginal people in northern Quebec are established by provincial legislation.

48 Horn, "Beyond"; York and Pindera, *People.*

49 A list of the royal commission's main publications, available as this chapter went to press, appears in the bibliography.

50 Driben and Gummer, "Native." For some further thoughts, see Abele, "Various."

51 Usher, Tough, and Galois, "Reclaiming"; Usher, "North"; Myers, *Evaluation.*

52 There is an excellent beginning in Canada, *Report.* More recently, see Usher, Tough, and Galois, "Reclaiming"; and Young, *Third.*

53 Elias, *Development*; John Loxley, " 'Great'"; Dobbin, "Prairie"; Wein, *Rebuilding*.

REFERENCES

Abel, Kerry. *Drum Songs: Glimpses of Dene History*. Montreal and Kingston: McGill-Queen's University Press, 1993.

Abele, Frances. "Canadian Contradictions: Forty Years of Northern Political Development." *Arctic*, 40 no. 4 (1989), 310–20.

– "Various Matters of Nationhood: Aboriginal People and Canada outside Quebec." In Ken McRoberts, ed., *Beyond Quebec*, 297–312. Montreal: McGill-Queen's University Press, 1995.

Abele, Frances, and Stasiulis, Daiva. "Canada as a 'White Settler Colony': What about Natives and Immigrants?" In W. Clement and G. Williams, eds., *The New Canadian Political Economy*, 240–77. Montreal: McGill-Queen's University Press, 1989.

Adams, Howard. *Prison of Grass*. 2nd ed. Saskatoon: Fifth House Publishers, 1990.

Banting, Keith, and Simeon, Richard, eds. *And No One Cheered: Federalism, Democracy and the Constitution Act*. Toronto: Metheun, 1983.

Berger, Thomas R. *Fragile Freedoms: Human Rights and Dissent in Canada*. Toronto: Clark Irwin, 1981.

Blondin, George *When the World Was New.* Yellowknife: Outcrop, 1991.

Berkhofer, Robert F. *Salvation and the Savage: An Analysis of Protestant Missions and American Indian Responses, 1787–1862.* Lexington: University of Kentucky Press, 1965.

Berkhofer, Robert F. *White Man's Indian.* New York: Knopf, 1978.

Blondin, George. *When the World Was New: Stories of the Sahtu Dene.* Yellowknife: Outemp, 1990.

Boas, Franz. "Mythology and Folk Tales of the North American Indian." *Journal of American Folklore,* 27 (1914), 374–410.

Boldt, Menno, and Long, J. Anthony. *The Quest for Justice: Aboriginal Peoples and Aboriginal Rights.* Toronto: University of Toronto Press, 1985.

Brody, Hugh. *Maps and Dreams: A Journey into the Lives and Lands of the Beaver Indians in Northwest Canada.* Vancouver: Douglas and McIntyre, 1981.

– *The People's Land: Eskimos and Whites in the Canadian Arctic.* London: Penguin Books, 1975.

Campbell, Maria. *Half-Breed.* Toronto: McClelland and Stewart, 1973.

Canada. *Report of the Mackenzie Valley Pipeline Inquiry* (Berger Report). 2 vols. Ottawa: Ministry of Supply and Services, 1977.

Canada, Royal Commission on Aboriginal Peoples. *Aboriginal Self-Government: Legal and Constitutional Issues.* Ottawa: Ministry of Supply and Services, 1994.

– *Bridging the Cultural Divide: A Report on Aboriginal People and Criminal Justice in Canada.* Ottawa: Ministry of Supply and Services, 1996.

– *Canada's Fiduciary Obligation to Aboriginal Peoples in the Context of Accession to Sovereignty by Quebec.* Ottawa: Ministry of Supply and Services, 1995.

– *Choosing Life: Special Report on Suicide among Aboriginal People.* Ottawa: Ministry of Supply and Services, 1995.

– *High Arctic Relocation: A Report on the 1953–55 Relocation.* Ottawa: Ministry of Supply and Services, 1994.

– *Partners in Confederation: Aboriginal People, Self-Government, and the Constitution.* Ottawa: Ministry of Supply and Services, 1993.

– *Treaty-Making in the Spirit of Co-existence.* Ottawa: Ministry of Supply and Services, 1994.

Cardinal, Harold. *The Rebirth of Canada's Indians.* Edmonton: Hurtig Publishers, 1979.

– *The Unjust Society: The Tragedy of Canada's Indians.* Edmonton: Hurtig Publishers, 1969.

Cassidy, Frank, ed. *Aboriginal People in British Columbia: Delgamuukw v. the Queen.* Lantzville, BC: Oolichan Books, 1992.

– *Indian Government: Its Meaning in Practice.* Lantzville, BC: Oolichan Books, 1989.

Coates, Kenneth. *Best Left as Indians: Native-White Relations in the Yukon Territory, 1840–1973.* Montreal: McGill-Queen's University Press, 1991.

Coe, Michael D. *The Maya.* First published 1966. 5th ed. London: Thames and Hudson, 1993.

Crnkovich, Mary. *"Gossip": A Spoken History of Women in the North*. Ottawa: Canadian Arctic Resources Committee, 1990.

Cruikshank, Julie, with Sidney, Angela, Smith, Kitty, and Ned, Annie. *Life Lived Like a Story*. Vancouver: University of British Columbia Press, 1990.

Culhane, Dara. "Adding Insult to Injury: Her Majesty's Loyal Anthropologist." *B.C. Studies*, no. 92 (autumn 1992), 66–92.

– *"Delgamuukw* and the People without Culture: Anthropology and the Crown." PhD dissertation. Department of Sociology and Anthropology, Simon Fraser University, 1994.

Dacks, Gurston. *A Choice of Futures: Politics in the Canadian North*. Toronto: Methuen, 1981.

Daniels, Dorothy. "Metis Identity: A Personal Perspective." *Native Studies Review*, 3 no. 2 (1987), 7–16.

Dickason, Olive Patricia. *Canada's First Nations: A History of Founding Peoples from Earliest Times*. Toronto: McClelland and Stewart, 1992.

Dobbin, Murray. "Prairie Colonialism: The CCF in Northern Saskatchewan." *Studies in Political Economy*, 16 (spring 1985), 7–40.

Dosman, Edgar J. *Indians: The Urban Dilemma*. Toronto: McClelland and Stewart, 1972.

Downes, P.G. *Sleeping Island: The Story of One Man's Travels in the Great Barren Lands of the Canadian North*. First published 1943. Foreword, notes, and revised photo section by R.H. Cockburn. Saskatoon: Western Producer Prairie Books, 1988.

Driben, Paul, and Gummer, Burton. "The Native Interface: An Emerging Role in Government-Native Relations." *Native Studies Review*, 1 no. 2 (1985), 33–46.

Duffy, Richard. *The Road to Nunavut: The Progress of the Eastern Arctic Inuit since the Second World War*. Montreal: McGill-Queen's University Press, 1988.

Eagleton, Terry. *Ideology: An Introduction*. London: Verson, 1991.

Eber, Dorothy Harley. *When the Whalers Were up North: Inuit Memories from the Eastern Arctic*. Montreal: McGill-Queen's University Press, 1989.

Elias, Peter Douglas. *Development of Aboriginal People's Communities*. Lethbridge and North York: Centre for Aboriginal Management Education and Training and Captus Press, 1991.

Fleras, Augie, and Elliot, Jean Leonard. *The Nations Within: Aboriginal-State Relations in Canada, the United States and New Zealand*. Toronto: Oxford University Press, 1992.

Francis, Daniel. *The Imaginary Indian*. Vancouver: Arsenal Pulp Press, 1992.

Freeman, Minnie. *Life among the Qallunaat*. Edmonton: Hurtig, 1978.

Fumoleau, René. *As Long as This Land Shall Last: A History of Treaty 8 and Treaty 11, 1870–1939*. Toronto: McClelland and Stewart, 1973.

Gibson, James R. *Otter Skins, Boston Ships, and China Goods: The Maritime Fur Trade of the Northwest Coast, 1785–1841*. Montreal: McGill-Queen's University Press, 1992.

Goldie, Terry. *Fear and Temptation: The Image of the Indigene in Canadian, Australian and New Zealand Literature.* Montreal: McGill-Queen's University Press, 1989.

Gryger, Pat Sandford. *A Long Way from Home: The Tuberculosis Epidemic among the Inuit.* Montreal: McGill-Queen's University Press and Hannah Institute Studies in the History of Medicine, Health and Society, 1994.

Hearne, Samuel. *A Journey from Prince of Wale's Fort in Hudson's Bay to the Northern Ocean Uncertaken by Order of the Hudson's Bay Company for the Discovery of Copper Mines, a Northwest Passage, &c. in the Years 1769, 1770, 1771, & 1772.* Edmonton: Hurtig, 1971.

Horn, Kahn-Tineta, "Beyond Oka: Dimensions of Mohawk Sovereignty." Interview. *Studies in Political Economy,* 35 (summer 1991), 29–42.

Jennings, Francis. *The Invasion of America: Indians, Colonialism and the Cant of Conquest.* Chapel Hill: University of North Carolina Press, 1975.

Jull, Peter. *Nunvut: A History.* Yellowknife: Government of the Northwest Territories and Nunavut Constitutional Forum, 1983.

– *The Politics of Northern Frontiers.* Darwin: Northern Australia Reseach Unit, Australian National University, 1991.

Kulchyski, Peter. "'A Considerable Unrest': F.O. Loft and the League of Indians." *Native Studies Review,* 4 nos. 1 and 2 (1988), 95–118.

Lange, Lynda. "The Changing Situation of Dene Elders, and of Marriage, in the Context of Colonialism: The Experience of Fort Franklin, 1945–1985." In Gurston Dacks and Ken Coates, eds. *Northern Communities: The Prospects for Empowerment,* 61–72. Edmonton: Boreal Institute for Northern Studies, 1988.

Lauritzen, Philip. *Oil and Amulets.* Halifax: Breakwater Books, 1983.

Loxley, John. "The 'Great Northern Plan'." *Studies in Political Economy,* 6 (autumn 1981), 151–82.

McFarlane, Peter. *Brotherhood to Nationhood: George Manuel and the Making of the Modern Indian Movement.* Toronto: Between the Lines, 1993.

McMahon, Kevin. *Arctic Twilight: Reflections on the Destiny of Canada's Northern Land and People.* Toronto: James Lorimer and Company, 1988.

Manuel, George, and Posluns, Michael. *The Fourth World: An Indian Reality.* Toronto: Collier and Macmillan, 1974.

Mealing, Stanley A., ed. *The Jesuit Relations and Allied Documents: A Selection.* Toronto: McClelland and Stewart, 1963.

Moody, Roger, ed. *The Indigenous Voice: Visions and Realities.* 2 vols. London and Atlantic Highlands, NJ: Zed Books, 1988.

Myers, Heather. "An Evaluation of Renewable Resource Development Experience in the Northwest Territories, Canada." Doctoral dissertation, Scott Polar Research Institute, University of Cambridge, 1994.

Napoleon, Harold, with Madsen, Eric, eds. *Yuuyaraq: The Way of the Human Being.* Fairbanks: Centre for Cross Cultural Studies, University of Alaska, 1991.

Native Studies Review. Special Issue on Native Peoples, Museums, and Heritage Resource Management. Vol. 3 no. 2 (1987).

Pakes, Fraser J. "Seeing with the Stereotypical Eye: The Visual Image of the Plains Indians." *Native Studies Review,* 1 no. 2 (1985), 1–32.

Petrone, Penny, ed. *First People, First Voices.* Toronto: University of Toronto Press, 1984.

– *Northern Voices: Inuit Writing in English.* Toronto: University of Toronto Press, 1988.

Pettipas, Katherine. *Severing the Ties that Bind: Government Repression of Indigenous Religious Ceremonies on the Prairies.* Winnipeg: University of Manitoba Press, 1994.

Ponting, J. Rick, and Gibbins, Roger. *Out of Irrelevance.* Toronto: Butterworths, 1980.

Raunet, Daniel. *Without Surrender, without Consent: A History of the Nishga Land Claims.* Vancouver: Douglas and McIntyre, 1984.

Ryan, Joan. *Wall of Words: The Betrayal of the Urban Indian.* Toronto: Peter Martin Associates, 1978.

Satzewich, Vic, and Wotherspoon, Terry. *First Nations: Race, Class and Gender Relations.* Scarborough, Ont.: Nelson, 1993.

Schwartz, Bryan. *First Principles, Second Thoughts: Aboriginal Peoples, Constitutional Reform, and Canadian Statecraft.* Montreal: Institute of Research on Public Policy, 1986.

Scott, Duncan Campbell. *The Administration of Indian Affairs in Canada.* N.p.: Canadian Institute of International Affairs, 1931.

Sioui, George. *For an Amerindian Autohistory: An Essay on the Foundations of a Social Ethic.* Montreal: McGill-Queen's University Press, 1989.

Slobodin, Richard. *Metis of the Mackenzie District.* Ottawa: St Paul University Press, 1966.

Snowshoe, Charlie. "A Trapper's Life" in Mel Watkins, ed., *Dene Nation: The Colony Within,* 28–31. Toronto: University of Toronto Press, 1977.

Thompson, David. *David Thompson's Narrative of His Explorations in Western America 1784–1812.* J.B. Tyrell, ed. Toronto: Champlain Society, 1916.

Tobias, J. "Protection, Civilization, Assimilation: An Outline of Canada's Indian Policy." *Western Canadian Journal of Anthropology,* 6 no. 2 (1976), 13–30.

Trigger, Bruce. *Indians in the Heroic Age of New France.* Ottawa: Canadian Historical Association, 1977.

– *Natives and Newcomers: Canada's "Heroic Age" Reconsidered.* Montreal: McGill-Queen's University Press, 1985.

Usher, Peter. "The North: One Land, Two Ways of Life." In L.D. McCann, ed., *Heartland and Hinterland: A Geography of Canada,* 231–47. Scarborough, Ont.: Prentice-Hall, 1982.

Usher, Peter, Tough, Frank, and Galois, Robert. "Reclaiming the Land: Aboriginal Title, Treaty Rights, and Land Claims in Canada." *Applied Geography,* 12 no. 2 (April 1992), 109–32.

Van Kirk, Sylvia. *"Many Tender Ties": Women in the Fur Trade Society in Western Canada, 1670–1870.* Winnipeg: Watson and Dwyer, 1980.

Weaver, Sally. *Making Canadian Indian Policy: The Hidden Agenda 1968–70.*
    Toronto: University of Toronto Press, 1981.

Wein, Fred. *Rebuilding the Economic Base of Indian Communities: The Micmac in
    Nova Scotia.* Montreal: Institute for Research in Public Policy, 1976.

Whitaker, Reg. "Democracy and the Canadian Constitution." In Keith Banting
    and Richard Simeon, eds., *And No One Cheered: Federalism, Democracy and the
    Constitution Act,* 240–60. Toronto: Methuen, 1983. Reprinted in Whitaker, *A
    Sovereign Idea: Essays on Canada as a Democratic Community,* 205–30. Montreal:
    McGill-Queen's University Press, 1992.

Wright, Ronald. *Stolen Continents: The New World through Indian Eyes since 1492.*
    Markham, Ont.: Viking, 1993.

York, Geoffrey, and Pindero, Lorene. *The People of the Pines: The Warriors and the
    Legacy of Oka.* Boston: Little Brown, 1991.

Young, Elspeth. *The Third World in the First.* London: Routledge, 1994.

7 The Political Economy of Race, Ethnicity, and Migration

DAIVA STASIULIS

International migration and race and ethnic relations have shaped Canadian development and society since European settlement in the seventeenth century. The Aboriginal peoples who had inhabited North America "since time immemorial" had levels of ethnic and linguistic diversity that surpassed Europe,[1] but it was the European newcomers who invested race and ethnicity with an immense power to exclude, rank, order, and subjugate the cultures and institutions of different populations. Race and ethnicity became constituent features of a complex set of social relations, including class and gender, which structured free and unfree labour markets, the constitution of the Canadian state and liberal democracy, the official and popular discourses of belonging, and entitlement to the rights of an imaginary Canadian (and Québécois) community.

At the eve of the third millennium, questions about immigration and racial and ethnic diversity have attained heightened importance in debates regarding Canada's future and its place in a dramatically changed world order. Canada is one of the few advanced capitalist societies (along with the United States, Australia, New Zealand, Germany, and Israel) to have large-scale immigration at a time when heightened North–South inequities, debt crises, civil wars, and ecological deterioration put pressure on citizens of poorer countries to migrate.

Perhaps more significant than the continued high volume of immigration are the major transformations that have occurred during the past twenty-five years in Canada's ethnic/racial and religious composition. The notions of white European Christian supremacy woven into

Canada's immigration policy and practices throughout most of its history have been dramatically confronted by recent trends in regional and national sources of immigrants. Since the early 1970s, non-European regions such as the Caribbean, South and Central America, Africa, the Middle East, the Pacific, and especially Asia have overtaken Europe as sources for Canadian immigration.[2] Thus, while European-born immigrants represented 90 per cent of those who arrived before 1961, they accounted for only 25 per cent of those arriving between 1981 and 1991.[3]

For the 1.24 million immigrants who came to Canada between 1981 and 1991, six of the ten top source countries were Asian. Hong Kong and China are in the top three reported countries by place of birth.[4] Approximately 90 per cent of these immigrants have settled in Canada's eight largest metropolitan areas.[5] The dominant discourses on Canada's racial/ethnic constitution ("two founding nations," and indeed the now beleaguered "multiculturalism") are inadequate in reconciling this diversity with Canada's history of "racial/ethnic formation."[6]

The class and occupational character of contemporary immigration is also changing in response to the reorganization of the world economy and its effects on both Canada and countries that are major senders of immigrants to Canada. Those entering with "family class" status, many of whom provide the labour for precarious, low-wage service and manufacturing jobs in declining sectors of the urban economies, remain the largest component of newcomers. Guided by a right-wing discourse that views immigrants solely in terms of their market utility, recent policy has reduced the proportion of family-class immigrants, while the proportion with job-ready skills in the "independent class" has been increased.[7] In addition, there have been more business immigrants; while they represented only 3.6 per cent of all immigrants in 1980, by 1992 they comprised 11.1 per cent.[8] For some critics, this increase, particularly in the category of affluent "investor immigrants," reflects the fact that wealth has its privileges, including "the purchase of immigration and [First World] citizenship status."[9]

The majority of these much-sought-after members of transnational capitalist elites are Chinese from Hong Kong, who have been met with novel racial stereotypes and historically based racial animosity towards Asians among Euro-Canadians. Such contemporary immigration patterns reveal the complex reconfigurations of power based on relations of race, ethnicity, and class posed by immigration in a country historically constructed as a "white settler society." While this notion and derivative constructs such as "two founding nations" are hegemonic, taken for granted by many (particularly Canadians of British and

French origins), they have inscribed much of the otherwise-critical Canadian political economy tradition.[10] The basic assumptions of the settler-society model of Canadian development, with its implicit foundations of given racial/ethnic, class, and gender hierarchies, are dramatically challenged by new constellations of power based on these axes.

The purpose of this chapter is to illuminate some key debates about the formative and dynamic roles played by international migration, race, and ethnicity in the increasingly challenging project of nation building in Canada. Given the potentially enormous scope of any discussion pertaining to immigration and racial/ethnic diversity, treatment of these issues here is necessarily selective. This chapter accordingly explores two themes: first, the role of Canadian immigration in nation building and the cultural, economic, and political forces historically shaping the character and differential rights of immigrants; and, second, modern Canadian discourses of race/ethnicity and racism. As the history of immigration to Canada is indelibly linked to racism, the two themes are intimately interrelated.[11] The chapter concludes with a discussion of contemporary patterns of international migration to Canada, the dynamics underlying this migration, and the emergence of new and hybrid racial/ethnic and national identities.

CANADIAN IMMIGRATION AND NATION BUILDING — GENERAL HISTORY

Much of the radical work on the political economy of migration and racism in the 1970s and 1980s produced in Canada, Europe, the United States, and Australia was informed by structuralist neo-Marxism. Such an approach viewed immigration as the means by which ruling classes in advanced capitalist economies procure cheap and exploitable foreign labour forces – reserve armies of labour "freed" by the uneven internationalization of capitalism from land and subsistence production in peripheral or Third World economies. Structuralist Marxism views racism as the ideological means by which ruling classes have divided the proletariat and justified colonialism and superexploitation of immigrants and non-white minorities.[12]

While building on the important insights into the structural bases of migration and racism, recent critical work has treated these phenomena in a less economistic, class-reductionist, and functionalist manner. The dynamics of class conflict in Canada, and capital accumulation on a global and national scale, help explain immigration and racism. None the less, they are not nearly the whole and often not even a fundamental part in any accounting of the diversity and sources of migration flows and the content and shifts in racialized expression. More recent work has accordingly focused on the often-contradictory economic and cultural imperatives shaping immigration policy, the multiple, overlapping determinations of racial/ethnic discourses, and the mutual conditioning of relations of race with gender and class.[13]

A major development in recent theorizing on racism has been a move away from identification of race with class. Such identification, contends David Leo Goldberg, leaves "unexplained those *cultural* relations race so often expresses, or it wrongly reduces these cultural relations to more or less veiled [manifestations] of class formation."[14] By extension, a political economy of migration, race/ethnicity, and racism in Canada would be impoverished if it failed centrally to consider the cultural, ideological, and moral implications of Canada's construction as a "white settler society."[15]

The history of colonization of North America and Canada's privileged position as a self-governing settlement within the British Empire have shaped international migration to Canada and immigration policy.[16] "Nation building" required more than construction of transportation systems, development of successive staples for export, and industrialization through import substitution. Nor was it a matter of simply recruiting and assembling the social classes necessary to provide the capital and/or labour for these industries. It also entailed planned development of a morally and physically healthy settler population and later a citizenry based on "love and loyalty to Canada and the British Empire."[17] Colonial and Canadian state elites, as well as influential groups in civil society, accordingly drew from British imperial philosophies ideas about the appropriate character, physical stock, and behaviour of settler women and men. Such nation-building discourses were imbued with Eurocentric, gendered, and class standards about what constituted "civilization," against which every potential group of immigrants was measured and ranked.

As a settler colonial society, Canada was peculiarly endowed with the settler projects of two competing colonizing powers – France until the mid-eighteenth century, and Britain thereafter. Efforts of British and British-Canadian elites to swamp and assimilate the French-Canadian population with imported anglophones from the United States and Britain not only failed but fuelled a sense of national oppression. So successful were the consequences of French settler colonization of North America that a "common-sense" assumption held widely among Canadian political economists is that in so far as ethnicity or race is concerned, "French-English dualism has been the central element in Canadian historical development."[18] Until recently, however, the accommodation by British-Canadian elites of the "French fact" occurred more through the bicultural discourse and organization of Canadian state institutions and constitutional arrangements, protecting religious, educational, and language rights of French minorities than through immigration policy.[19]

The settler colony replication project meant a "White Canada" immigration policy that aggressively recruited the "best classes" of British men and women and excluded non-Europeans (or less desirable Europeans) or granted them only limited access to settlers' and citizens' rights if their cheap labour was desired. Importation of Asian, Caribbean, and continental European immigrants, often as migrant, indentured, and superexploited labour, was an intrinsic element in sustaining development of Canada's famed "high wage" proletariat. In fact, the latter group constituted at best a minority of mostly male, white, and British skilled craft workers.[20] Indeed, as in other advanced capitalist formations typified by "free" and impersonal labour relations, it is striking how common racialized, unfree, and personal labour systems have been in Canada.[21] Thus exclusion, subordination, and unfreedom based on race/ethnicity (in articulation with gender) have been prominent features of the formation of Canadian capitalism, its class structure, and its segmented labour markets, as well as of state policies and social movements structuring and shaping immigration.

Throughout most of Canada's history of settler colonization, recruitment of British immigrants was actively pursued by private interests on both sides of the Atlantic – land and railway companies, wealthy philanthropists, and upper-class women, as well as British-centric state officials. Though many of these immigrants to the Canadas and Maritimes crossed into the United States, there is little doubt of the success of British colonization efforts. By 1867, the year of Confederation, an estimated two-thirds of British North America's population was British in origin.[22] Irish immigration between 1846 and 1854, provoked by the devastating potato famine, brought approximately 400,000 persons to Upper Canada/Canada West. As government land-granting and settlement policies placed land beyond the reach of these impoverished newcomes, the Irish found work in lumbering, shipping, and shipbuilding and in construction of the massive Welland and St Lawrence canal systems.

Clare Pentland argued in his classic study, *Labour and Capital in Canada 1650–1860*, that migration of this group of plentiful and highly mobile workers provided a reserve army of labour and marked the transition from precapitalist, unfree (indentured, slave, convict, personal) labour systems to a capitalist labour market.[23] The new Canadian political economy of immigration and racism has debunked the notion that free-wage labour and market exchange were for workers the definitive social relations under Canadian capitalist development.[24] Depending on their position in the racial/ethnic pecking order, foreign-born workers were differentially incorporated into production relations as unfree temporary/migrant labour, unfree immigrant/settler labour, or free immigrant/settler labour.[25]

The labour needs of key eras of expansion complicated the process of building an ethnically pure British settler colony in Canada. This dilemma was most apparent from 1880 to 1920, a period of unprecedented agricultural and industrial expansion. Led by Clifford Sifton, Wilfrid Laurier's minister of the interior, who was convinced that massive agricultural immigration was the key to Canadian prosperity, aggressive recruitment efforts were undertaken not only to induce British and white American but also central and eastern European immigration. In courting agriculturalists from continental Europe, Sifton relied on a vivid stereotype of "a stalwart peasant in a sheepskin coat, born to the soil, whose forefathers have been farmers for ten generations, with a stout wife and a half-dozen children."[26] British–Canadians and white American immigrants were less sanguine about the peasant ways of new Ukrainian and Russian agriculturalists, whom they viewed as ruled by violence, pagan excess, and idleness.[27] A number of social-reform movements – the social gospel, prohibition, and women's rights – shared the view that non-British immigrants posed a threat to their common ideal of a homogeneous social order based on Protestantism and British democratic institutions. Opposition to the arrival of non-British immigrants was fuelled by an incendiary mix of race-sex fears (the sexual threat to white women posed by racial-minority men), anti-semitism, anti-radicalism, eugenics, and nativism.[28]

Despite such opposition, the years from 1880 to 1920 saw the first large-scale recruitment of immigrants who, in varying degrees, departed from the model of the ideal settler. Many had travelled from peasant villages in eastern, central, and southern Europe, China, Japan, and India. While immigration policy gave preference to farmers to develop the western wheat economy, many immigrants ended up working in mines, laying railway track, or drifting into the urban working class.

The options and fates of these immigrants were regulated by a highly profitable commerce of migration. As in other lucrative ventures in Canada's development, private-sector corporate actors shared state power by being "deputized" by the dominion government to take on the public functions of immigration and settlement.[29] Private corporations such as the Canadian Pacific Railway held a "franchise" of state power in these matters and in turn subcontracted through a pyramid structure to fiercely competing steamship companies in Canada and Europe and thousands of recruiting subagents.[30] Many immigrants were ruthlessly exploited by agents for the railway companies, who shared their ethnicity, in a padrone system, analogous in its coercive character to indentured bondage.[31] The polarized class conditions of many of these workers in newly opened staples-producing regions and in sweated industries "often produced more violent and class conscious responses ... than was prevalent among established workers."[32]

Next to the British, white Protestant Americans and northern Europeans were regarded as the most culturally appropriate and assimilable of settlers. Eastern and central Europeans, including Jews, were viewed by Canadians of Anglo-Celtic origins with contempt and suspicion. Deemed "enemy aliens" because of their labour radicalism and socialist traditions during the First World War, many were deported.[33] The most virulent and institutionalized forms of racism, however, were reserved for non-white migrants and Aboriginal peoples.[34]

A "dialectic of political, economic and ideological relations" structured the manner of incorporation of Asians and Blacks into the labour market and the Canadian nation-building project.[35] Labour shortages – specifically, the demand for cheap and malleable (often contract and seasonal) labour in perilous, back-breaking, or servile occupations – was virtually the only imperative leading to recruitment or acceptance into the country of these otherwise-despised peoples.[36] Racist fear of the "yellow peril" pervaded all classes of the British-Canadian population but was most emphatically organized within the white, male, working class in British Columbia, where the low wages and perceived docility of Asian workers provoked fear of undercutting and strike-breaking.[37] In the context of near-hysterical opposition in western Canada from all classes of British Canadians to settlement by Asian communities, migration of Chinese, South Asians, and Japanese was designed, through a web of immigration regulations and provincial legislation, to be extensively policed and temporary.

A chief objective of anti-Asian immigration regulations was to prevent entry of wives and children of Asian migrants, thus stemming the growth of Asian populations in Canada through natural increase. This was clearly the intention of such measures as the progressively stiffer head taxes culminating in an outright ban imposed on the entry of Chinese and the quotas fixed on Japanese immigration in the 1908 "Gentleman's Agreement" with Japan. Not content to destroy the family lives of Chinese male migrants, provincial governments such as those in British Columbia, Saskatchewan, and Ontario acted on Orientalist fears of the depraved nature of Chinese men by passing legislation designed to "protect" white women from the alleged danger of working for "oriental" male employers.[38]

A "sex-race panic" also prevented the influx into Alberta in 1910 of a small group of Black Oklahoma farmers fleeing persecution and murder by the Ku Klux Klan. Chiefly spurred by the image of helpless white women homesteaders endangered by the presence of Black men, perniciously portrayed as "over-sexed" and potential rapists,[39] "the first racial exclusion ordinance in the Western Hemisphere" was drafted, though never implemented.[40] Henceforth the immigration department compiled lists distinguishing between "preferred" and "non-preferred" or "prohibited" countries and made racist administrative decisions based on sociobiological arguments. Officials repeatedly made reference to the biological incapacity of Caribbean and other Blacks ("persons from tropical and sub-tropical countries") to adapt to the "temperate" Canadian climate, a competitive economy, and democratic institutions.[41] The exclusion of prospective female Caribbean domestic workers was also informed by invidious myths of the promiscuous nature and proneness to single parenthood of Black women.[42]

The effectiveness of the racial selectiveness of Canadian immigration policy is reflected in the fact that between 1947 and 1962 less than 10 per cent of "people admitted to Canada as permanent settlers were from outside of Western Europe, the United States and Australia."[43] In spite of the history of emigration in some Caribbean nations, resulting from creation of a reserve army of labour through uneven development associated with European colonialism, Caribbean immigrants to Canada constituted less than 1 per cent of the flow of settler immigration.[44]

UNFREE/FREE AND MIGRANT/IMMIGRANT: FARM AND DOMESTIC LABOUR

The political economy approach to migration has been significantly enriched by the exploration of the role of racialized (and gendered) discourses in shaping the "mode of incorporation"[45] of migrants and immigrants into the Canadian labour market and within the boundaries of the Canadian nation/state. The articulation between types of labour migration and racial/ethnic state and popular discourses has most fully been explored in two areas of employment shunned by established, citizen workers – seasonal agricultural work and private domestic service. The evolution of the racial/ethnic profile of labour within these two occupations has been constructed, as predominantly male and "naturally" female domains of employment, respectively.

In his meticulous historical research on foreign labour on south-western Ontario farms from 1945 to the early 1970s, Satzewich demonstrates the correspondence between the racial/ethnic valorization by immigration officials of different groups of foreign-born workers and their manner of incorporation into production relations and into the Canadian nation-building project. The undesirable conditions characterizing farm-labouring jobs have meant that farmers in the fruit and vegetable industries traditionally face problems in recruiting and retaining suitable supplies of wage labour for the harvest. Given the inadequacy of spontaneous migrations from underdeveloped regions within the country to fill the unabating demand for farm labourers, the postwar Canadian state facilitated fruit and vegetable production through recruitment and control of foreign labour.

Polish war veterans who had fought alongside the Allies, and Baltic and other eastern European "displaced persons" (DPs), were the first groups recruited after the Second World War to work in Ontario's fruit and vegetable industry.[46] Some 4,500 Polish veterans were offered the chance to apply for Canadian citizenship after fulfilling a labour contract binding them to two years of agricultural employment. Similarly, Latvian, Estonian, and Lithuanian DPs who had been temporarily housed in Allied-run camps in Germany, and from whom the young and able-bodied were selected as contract labourers (tied to domestic service, mining, forestry, construction, and agricultural work), were expected to settle permanently in Canada. None the less, both groups were incorporated into production relations as unfree immigrant labour – immigrant, in the sense that they were defined as potential future settlers and citizens, some of whom were permitted to bring in family members immediately,[47] yet unfree in so far as their free movement in the Canadian labour market was curtailed by their indentured-labour status.[48]

Ambiguous ideological conditions provided the framework for the ambiguous legal status of eastern Europeans from wartorn Europe. "Balts" were generally regarded favourably in comparison with alternative groups of Europeans, and their acceptance as immigrants met Canada's international obligation to settle at least a token number of displaced persons.[49] In the cultural context of Anglo-conformity[50] and the reality in which British Canadians were a clear demographic majority, however, some Canadian officials thought that "the new 'Central Europeans' [should] be balanced by an equal number of Anglo-Saxon immigrants."[51] It is ironic that the unfree, coercive, labour relations in which DP workers were inserted were justified through the discourse of "opportunity" and "freedom" provided by the immigration/labour contracts to refugees lacking the option of repatriation – "unfortunate people who are now in Displaced Person Camps to come to *free* Canada."[52]

Another group recruited as farm labour in southwestern Ontario's produce industry was comprised of Dutch farmers and their families, brought in through an agreement reached in 1947 between the Canadian and Dutch governments. In contrast to foreign DP and Polish veteran farm labour, the Dutch were incorporated into the state and labour market as free immigrant labour. "Those recruited by the Dutch government for emigration were defined by Canadian authorities as permanent settlers. They qualified for citizenship after five years of residence. Furthermore, once they entered Canada they could circulate freely in the labour market."[53]

Positive stereotypes of the Dutch as appropriate settler material constructed by Dutch officials and Canadian immigration gatekeepers facilitated and rationalized their specific mode of incorporation. Canadian immigration officials contended that the Dutch immigrants were a "naturally 'free' group of people" whose "well known responsibility, ... free initiative, ... close family ties and ... spiritual and moral characteristics" made them "naturally" suited to be Canadian settlers and immigrants, rather than part of an unfree, bulk movement to meet labour shortages.[54]

Beginning in 1966, an increasingly common source region for labour on Ontario farms was the Caribbean – specifically, in descending order of numbers, Jamaica, Barbados, Trinidad and Tobago, Grenada, Montserrat, and Dominica. In stark contrast to the status conferred on European farm labourers, all of whom were provided with the right to settle and become citizens, male Caribbean workers were brought in as unfree migrant labour – temporary workers afforded no possibility of permanent settlement. Relations of "unfreedom" characterizing this labour force were constituted by the Canadian state, which threatened, and sometimes carried out, repatriation of such workers for breach of their contract.[55] Unlike European "guestworkers" who were permitted at least to apply for permanent residence in labour-importing states such as the Netherlands and Switzerland after five to ten years of residence, the option of applying for permanent settlement was denied to temporary Caribbean farm workers in Canada.[56]

The regulation of entry and access to Canadian settler and citizenship rights of different racial/ethnic groups has also been intrinsic to historic shifts in construction of the labour market in private domestic service. Several scholars have addressed foreign domestic work, including Sedef Arat-Koc, Sheila Arnopoulos, Abigail Bakan and Daiva Stasiulis, Marilyn Barber, Agnes Calliste, Patricia Daenzer, Milda Danys,

Franca Iacovetta, Varpu Lindstrom-Best, and Makeda Silvera. Their studies have produced detailed historical and analytical portraits of the contributions of various structural and ideological processes to the character of this superexploited domain for female foreign labour. These processes include internationalization of production, (neo-)colonialism, nation-to-nation relations, devaluation of domestic labour, and, often-contradictory demands for cheap, malleable labour and racial/cultural concerns arising out of the white settler nation-building project. As in seasonal agricultural labour, the manner of incorporation of foreign domestic labour as free or unfree, immigrant or migrant, reflected the group's position within a racial/ethnic pecking order that was also gendered and shaped by class interests.

In Canada and worldwide, domestic labour has been female-dominated. Domestic labour (housework, child care) has been feminized – viewed as "naturally" linked to distinct female biological roles (having babies), and such largely "invisible" work, "hidden in the household," carries low status and little or no remuneration. While recruitment of domestic servants from abroad has existed since the inception of the French and British settler projects, the foreign component of paid domestic labour increased as employment opportunities outside family households in factories, schools, offices, and shops expanded in the early twentieth century for Canadian-born women, particularly those of hegemonic ethnic origins.

Prior to the 1960s, the major sources of foreign domestics were the United Kingdom and continental Europe. "Unmarried young women of comely appearance ... thoroughly trained in domestic ... service"[57] from England and Scotland were recruited with an eye to a racially identified nation-building project. The anticipation was that these women of "good stock" would become wives of white Canadian men and mothers of white Canadian children. Encouraged by such schemes for British female emigration as the Empire Settlement Act of 1923, middle-class British-Canadian women's organizations were deputized by the Canadian government to recruit suitable British "girls."[58] Once again, however, commercial interests subverted British-Canadian ethnic preferences, as Ottawa authorized the Canadian Pacific Railway and Canadian National Railways, through the Railways Agreement of 1925, to recruit and place domestics and agriculturalists from "non-preferred" countries such as Hungary, Poland, Romania, and Russia.[59]

Following the Second World War, Canadian authorities capitalized on the vulnerability of eastern European refugees and accepted their entry into Canadian domestic service as unfree immigrants. Like their male counterparts who accepted one-year contracts for heavy labour in primary resource industries, female DPs were similarly indentured as domestics to Canadian families for a period of one year.[60] In light of the temporary nature of DP immigration, the Canadian government in the early 1950s was prompted to establish "bulk order" movements (permitted by order-in-council) of German, and then Italian and Greek, domestics, who were, in contrast to British domestics, subjected to unusual scrutiny and the suspicion of immigration authorities.[61] Both of these postwar immigration schemes for "non-preferred" European domestics, however, permitted these newcomers to choose to reside permanently in Canada and become "naturalized" citizens.

As the availability of European women for this type of work declined, new sources for servant labour were opened up through the effects of colonial policies in dislocating millions of non-white women from agricultural subsistence production in Asia, the Caribbean, and Latin America. The African slave trade and the expansion of plantation societies in the Caribbean and the southern United States had been similarly central in globally linking racism with exploitation of female domestic labour. Black women, as slaves and servants, were commoditized as the labourers and sexual objects of their white masters. Out of these historical conditions of slavery and colonialism, and of an increasingly international labour market, various racialized and gendered images of domestic workers grew, some of which still persist. Thus the servile image of "Aunt Jemima," the Black "mammy," who was expected to care for the children of white ladies in the slave conditions of the plantation, has been the most persistent media, celluloid, and mass-marketed image of African-American women in popular North American culture.[62] The caricature of the debased Black domestic slave contrasts sharply with that of Mary Poppins, the firm but loving white governess for white, upper-class children.[63]

In Canada, where settler immigration of Caribbean Blacks was virtually prohibited by the "White Canada" policy, Caribbean domestic workers were brought in as unfree migrant labourers. Some of the small group of domestics who were taken in "experimentally" from Guadeloupe and the British Caribbean were subsequently deported during the 1913–15 recession when a reserve army of unemployed Canadian women was willing to undertake domestic service.[64] A secular decline in rights and freedoms available to foreign domestic workers coincided with a transition in the racial/ethnic sources of this form of female migration from Europe to Third World regions of the Caribbean and, latterly, the Philippines.[65]

The increased restrictions on foreign domestics rights are most apparent in the introduction by the Canadian federal government in 1973 of the Temporary Employment Authorization Program. This scheme gave domestic workers short-term, renewable work permits and allowed them to stay in Canada conditional on performance of domestic work for a designated employer. Earlier groups of domestics had entered Canada with permanent-resident status, and so it is evident that the 1973 program institutionalized the transition from free or unfree immigrant labour to unfree migrant labour.[66] Subsequent reforms to the program in 1981 and 1992, arising in part out of the vigorous protest and lobbying efforts of grassroots domestic advocacy groups, reinforced its most repressive aspects. The temporary-migrant or "visitor" status of foreign domestics, and the requirement that workers "live in" the homes of their employers, are only the most blatant of conditions viewed by critics as violations of basic worker and human rights.[67]

In superexploited areas of employment that have traditionally recruited foreign workers to fill chronic labour shortages, such as agricultural seasonal work and domestic service, the migration process and specific mode of incorporation of migrant labour are negotiated within a framework of uneven global relations. Specific ties between nations, such as investment and trade, existing between labour-exporting and -importing countries also play a critical role. Thus Agnes Calliste points out that the inception of the Second Caribbean Domestic Labour Scheme in 1955 was negotiated by Ottawa as a "gesture of goodwill" in order to maintain a preferential trade and investment position in the British Caribbean.[68]

The links between sending and receiving countries have not, however, been limited to economic relations. Migration processes are not structured solely by economic considerations stemming from the exigencies of capital accumulation.[69] As a critical reading of Canada's development as a "white settler society" reveals, the influence of Canada's privileged position within the British Empire in shaping the racialized content of its immigration policies has reflected a dialectic of economic, cultural/moral, political, diplomatic, military, and ideological concerns. In late-twentieth-century Canada, immigration and racism share a number of general traits with earlier eras. But they are also predicated on specific and changed conditions arising out of the reorganization of the global economy and forces such as ethnic nationalist strife, ecological destruction, and other sources of population displacement.

GLOBALIZATION, IMMIGRATION, AND DISCOURSES OF RACE AND PLURALISM

Several general observations are pertinent to an assessment of contemporary immigration policy, migration trends, and racial/ethnic diversity in Canada. First, the growing heterogeneity of international migration, even within the category of "labour migration," that passes through or takes up residence in Canada must be acknowledged. The restructuring of the global economy has produced a variety of structures that generate international migration. These include internationalization of production, global debt crises, links between "former colonialist powers and former colonies, international trade and tourism, study abroad, and transnational business practices."[70] The revolutions in mass transportation and telecommunications have facilitated this migration. Migration patterns have become vastly more complicated as the global economic system, once centred in Europe and the United States, has become multicentred, to include the interlinked economies of Japan and the newly industrializing nations of Southeast Asia.[71] The legal-juridical status, duration in the country, and mode of incorporation in the labour market and within the Canadian state of the diverse waves of migrants vary immensely. No current theory of international migration deals with all the diversity and dynamism of today's international population movements.[72]

Second, the transformations in populations, cultures, and communities conditioned by recent migration have been most apparent in Canada's "global cities" – Toronto, Vancouver, and Montreal. As "control centres of the global economic system," such centres "serve as a magnet for immigrants ranging from itinerant capitalist investors and managers of multinational corporations, through transilient professionals, educators, and technicians, to temporary and permanent migrants who provide the less well-paid services necessary to sustain the system."[73] For many parts of the country, issues surrounding immigration, racism, and multiculturalism do not have the same resonance. For example, the Maritimes currently receive only about 2 per cent of Canadian immigrants,[74] and Saskatchewan, the north, and much of rural Canada receive virtually none. Outside metropolitan centres, one finds communities descended from the old settler populations that were predominantly of British, French, and other European origins or from First Nations.

Third, the popular image of Canada as a "country of immigration" or peopled primarily with permanent or settler immigrants persists. This image must be qualified. It does not consider how very porous the Canada-u.s. border has been for many migrants, such that Canada has served as a "sieve for immigrants to the United States."[75] As well, in recent years the number of employment authorizations, for people working in Canada on temporary work visas, matches or exceeds the number of incoming landed applicants.[76]

The heterogeneity of people in Canada on employment authorizations (ranging from domestic servants and seasonal agricultural labour to business managers and performing artists[77]) makes it difficult to generalize about the significance of the striking increase in then numbers. None the less, the increasing resort to temporary workers is one aspect of structural change in global and Canadian capitalism, marking what many observers have observed to be a new "post-fordist" regime of accumulation.[78] The many components associated with post-fordism include the ubiquity of advanced technologies and "fourth-generation" computerization, deindustrialization, growth in the tertiary sector of employment and in internationalized, "just-in-time" production systems, and dismantling of the Keynesian welfare state. The augmenting reliance on labour, across levels of income, skills, and job security, that temporarily sojourns rather than permanently settles in Canada fits well with the analysis of labour-market restructuring as representing a shift to "flexible accumulation."[79]

For the growing "peripheral" group of workers, the new accumulation regime and the associated system of political regulation offer geographical mobility accompanied by few benefits as workers or citizens, routine and deskilled work, job insecurity, and lives filled with uncertainty and instability on many levels (spatial, financial, familial, and so on).[80] Home workers, who tend to be non-anglophone immigrant women, and who endure precarious, unhealthy, below-minimum wage conditions, "are the ultimate in 'just-in-time' or 'flexible' workers."[81]

Fourth, Western states increasingly police access of migrants to the fruits of First World citizenship. For example, in response to strong migratory pressures from the former Soviet bloc and Third World countries, western European countries have introduced stronger controls on refugees. California, where whole sectors of the economy have relied on the cheap labour of undocumented workers, has recently voted to remove access to all medical, educational, and other social services for illegal migrants. The harmonization by the most prosperous countries of immigration and refugee policies in restrictive directions has been described as "a form of 'global apartheid' designed to protect their privileged status in the face of overwhelming demographic and political pressures from less affluent societies" in Africa, Asia, and Latin America.[82] Such harmonization has been facilitated by a rise in movements, parties, and popular sentiment that reflect inward-looking, protectionist, xenophobic, and even neo-fascist sentiments.[83]

In Canada, increasing preoccupation with policing of borders and access to citizenship rights was reflected in the administrative grouping by the federal Tory government in 1993 of immigration with Canada's spy agency CSIS, the RCMP, and prisons in a new Ministry of Public Security. Responding to Reform party pressure and the prevailing anti-immigrant climate, in July 1994 Sergio Marchi, the new Liberal immigration minister, proposed a series of "law-and-order" changes to immigration and deportation regulations that gave further popular purchase to the fearful linking of race, crime, and immigration.[84] The new Immigration Act, legislated by Mulroney's Conservatives in 1992, introduced a whole series of measures – such as fingerprinting asylum seekers, "indenturing" immigrants to particular places for two years after arrival, and screening out applicants connected with "subversive" organizations – which reflected the Canadian state's preoccupation in immigration policy with issues of security and border control. Racial preferences, long apparent in Canada's refugee policy,[85] were obvious in the delayed reaction of Canada "to the prolonged plight of refugees in Somalia and other regions of Africa, compared with the response to those in former Yugoslavia."[86] Finally, the narrow commodification of immigrants as vehicles for transfer of capital and economic skills is also apparent in the ten-year immigration plan proposed by the Liberal government in November 1994. This plan dropped overall immigration targets, slashed refugee-intake targets, decreased the proportion of family-class immigrants, toughened enforcement of sponsorship obligations to preclude access to welfare benefits, and broadened the intake of business and investor immigrants.[87] The February 1995 federal budget substantially increased processing fees for immigrants and refugees and was labelled a new form of "head tax" by critics.[88]

These broad trends in capitalist restructuring, migration, and immigration policies evident in the global and Canadian economies intersect with, and draw upon, historical inequities based on colonialism and imperialism, race/ethnicity, gender, and class. Thus migratory movements from Third to First World countries, as Robert Cox states, have "combined with the downgrading of job opportunities in advanced capitalist countries (the McDonaldization of the workforce) [to] constitute what has been called the 'peripheralization' of the core."[89] Within the growing sector of low-wage, unprotected jobs, the class division that defines a capitalist labour force is further segmented by gender, race, and ethnicity. These divisions are overlaid by hierarchies in citizenship status, which, in turn, has governed access to a whole range of political, civil, and social rights, including the protection offered by labour legislation and entitlement to social welfare benefits.[90]

Yet the trends in Canadian immigration over the past quarter-century suggest that the ways in which these global and national relations of gender, race/ethnicity, class, and citizenship intersect are producing novel and more complex configurations of power. Indeed, the growing racial and ethnic diversity in immigration, and the multiple forms of identity and politics flowing from this diversity, offer a lesson in how settler societies, and the legitimacy of assumed racial/ethnic hierarchies, eventually come undone. Aided by the proliferation of capitalist centres in formerly colonized countries, the "Empire has struck back"[91] not only in former imperial centres such as Britain but within its "white dominions" as well. Since the 1970s, immigration trends in Canada have bolstered the population that is ethnically neither of the two (British or French) settler groups – particularly the previously feared, despised, and colonized Asians – thus contravening the intentions of a century and a half of immigration policy.

Unlike in the past, when immigration officials saw cheap and expendable labour as the only rationale for Asian entry into Canada, the class character and entry statuses of Asian migration to Canada have become extremely diverse. Between 1975 and 1981, some 77,000 Indochinese refugees entered the country. While Canada accepted these refugees in order to honour international (United Nations) obligations and humanitarian objectives, the majority of these newcomers have joined the ranks of the reserve army of labour and the most exploited sections of the working class. Indicative of their ghettoization in cheap-labour and worker-repressive sectors, while only 7 per cent of all employed Canadian women in 1986 worked in product-fabricating or processing/machining occupations, as many as 41 per cent of Indo-Chinese women were found in these low-grade jobs.[92]

In sharp contrast, since the mid-1980s, extremely wealthy Chinese immigrants from Hong Kong have topped the list of sources for business immigrants, especially "investor immigrants" who are required to make a business investment of between $250,000 and $350,000 in Canada to be eligible for the program.[93] Up to 80 per cent of business immigration has gravitated to Toronto, Vancouver, and Montreal.[94] The major incentives for the heightened interest in attracting Hong Kong capitalists to Canada are the substantial and increased flow of capital that such migration brings and the bi-directional investment links between Asia and Canada that such migration helps foster.[95] This novel Asian migration reflects emergent trends in the globalization and regional integration of the Canadian economy – in Vancouver's case, its growth, fuelled by trade with the Pacific rim, necessary for its establishment under the North American Free Trade Agreement (NAFTA) as the primary commodity gateway for the u.s. market.[96] Despite the advantaged class position of these immigrants they share similarities with Chinese labourers who migrated to Canada in the nineteenth century. Both waves of migration are characterized by gender bias (favouring male principal applicants),[97] and both have received a hostile reception from white Canadians.

As Peter Li argues, there were many sources for the housing crisis that emerged in the mid-1980s in Vancouver, "characterized by high real estate prices, overbuilt neighborhoods and rapid urbanization that destroyed traditional residential communities and the [white, British] heritage they represented."[98] The conspicuous presence of Chinese immigrants, however, in British "old-money" neighbourhoods led to the major share of blame for this crisis being placed on the shoulders of the newcomers. A racialized discourse emerged, centred on "monster houses" and "unneighbourly houses" – terms that are not used to refer to equally large homes in neighbourhoods where non-Chinese predominate. Reworked Orientalist discourses expressed the racial resentment of white, middle-class Canadians towards a despised group that was faring considerably better than they.[99]

The class-variegated character of current Chinese and more broadly Asian migration illustrates how complicated articulations of race/ethnicity with class and gender have become in Canadian political economy. Wealthy Hong Kong and Taiwanese Chinese immigrants to Canada, like other transnational elites, have constructed an "astronaut's" life-style that straddles two or more continents.[100] They identify themselves as "global citizens," speak several languages, feel comfortable in many cultures, and have the means to set their own terms for integration into Canada. Residing in a province with a historical, cultural scaffolding of virulent anti-Asian hostility, Chinese immigrants have been met with tart resentment for their visibility and conspicuous affluence.

The class position of the business immigrants, however, has for the most part shielded them from the extensive and institutionalized racism experienced by the Indochinese refugees and the Black and South and East Asian populations of major cities, particularly those funnelled into the most precarious and low-wage jobs.[101] Systemic racism and sexism in immigration, job, and language-training policies have forced many non-anglophone and Third World women into "McJobs" in the service sectors and declining industries such as the garment trades and health sectors, where employment is threatened by NAFTA.[102] Globalization of the Canadian economy and migration have thus not undermined the importance of race/ethnicity and gender for shaping the social structure. They have simply meant that the threads of the social order have been pulled apart and rewoven in new and more complicated patterns.

CONCLUSION: EMERGENT SUBJECTIVITIES AND DISCOURSES IN THE NEW CANADIAN POLITICAL ECONOMY

In their obsession with economic rationalism and the fiscal debt that has marked recent immigration-policy reforms, Canadian policy makers have given little thought to the impact of altered immigration patterns on the changing and dynamic roles played by race and ethnicity in Canadian nation building. What rights and benefits regulated by the state should be made accessible to groups of migrants and immigrants who take up residence for varying lengths of time and who experience varying degrees of loyalty and sense of belonging to the Canadian nation and/or state? Indeed, the absence of attention given to the integration of the multitude of racialized and ethnic "Others" into the new and changing pecking orders embodied in immigration reforms is reflected in the brief but telling discussion about a new Citizenship Act in a recent Citizenship and Immigration document. Here discussion of citizenship is restricted to mention of widening "the conditions under which granting citizenship will be *prohibited*."[103]

From its establishment as official federal policy in 1971, multiculturalism was supposed to be the policy that made palatable for ethnic minorities their exclusion from the settler-society construct of a "bilingual and bicultural" Canada. As dub poet and journalist Joseph Clifton evocatively questions, "Why would, and yeah, why should the non-French and non-English communities who have contributed valiantly to the development of Canada ultimately settle for the subordinate position under some fabled jive of the two '(lost/&) found(ing) races'?" Distancing himself from the major tenor of assaults on multiculturalism policy that has been a recurrent theme in popular and elite opinion since the mid-1980s, Clifton argues that the architects of "official" multiculturalism failed to "*really*, and equitably, redefine the country, taking all of its cultures into *full* consideration."[104] The need for bold, innovative, and inclusive approaches to challenge the antiquated white, Christian definitions of the country that hide behind official discourses on Canadian identity is suggested by the growth of emergent sensibilities about race, nation, and belonging.

Thus the consciousness of members of the transnational Chinese-Canadian elites, who "work in several global sites … [and] negotiate the new spaces of late capitalism to their supreme advantage,"[105] is quite distinctive for "global citizens" who may identify *wu ming di* ("a place with no name") as their home town.[106] This disjunctive sense of identity needs to be distinguished from the alarming reality of homelessness and even statelessness experienced by the growing millions of internally displaced persons, refugees, and asylum seekers. These populations find the doors to safety increasingly closing in advanced industrialized countries or, if allowed in, discover "less understanding and awareness, and more reactionary responses on the part of the host countries."[107]

In addition to these two extremes, the growing circularity in population movements that pass through Canada, and the ubiquity of satellite communications, have increased a sense of hybridity in identity among many, particularly urban, Canadians. Some cultural anthropologists, for instance, now view most cultures as "creolized." Creolization is also intrinsic to the identities of the growing number of Canadians who are products of mixed parentage of First World/Third World ethnic origins. Major metropolitan centres in the West are connected to other world societies, and thus decreasingly "Western."[108] Many "local" identities within polyethnic, cosmopolitan urban centres are in fact based on membership in international (Muslim, Jewish, Hindu, Buddhist, and so on) communities of faith, which have in turn been shaped in complex ways by various national/ethnic cultures.

Through global restructuring and growth in the density of Canada's capital, population, and cultural ties with the Asia-Pacific region and other non-Western regions, multiple subjectivities have replaced the white, European subject assumed by much of the Canadian political economy tradition. A grid of "scattered hegemonies" has replaced the simpler racial/ethnic hierarchical model of white settler societies such as Canada.[109] As the Economic Council of Canada's *Good Jobs, Bad Jobs* revealed, a stark polarization in the labour market has emerged in Canada;[110] however, this polarization is the product of a variety of power relations which include North–South, race/ethnic, and gender relations and cannot be comprehended through the prism of class-reductionist frameworks.

The growing volume of insightful work on race and ethnicity in Canada reveals the centrality of these social, cultural, and economic relations in shaping the nature of the Canadian social formation and its incorporation into the international political economy. Unfortunately, the observation made by Frances Abele and me in 1989 in *The New Canadian Political Economy* – that "the Canadian political economy tradition has only unevenly absorbed an adequate analysis of race and ethnicity and ... [has largely set] aside these issues as irrelevant" – holds equally true today.[111] In order for political economy to be useful in resisting inequality, it must analytically address these complex categories of identity and affiliation, which are the effects as well as the determinants of ever more intricate configurations of power and inequality in Canada and globally.

NOTES

I gratefully acknowledge the helpful comments on this chapter provided by Yasmeen Abu-Laban, Wallace Clement, and Radha Jhappan.

1 Olive Dickason, *Canada's*, 66.

2 Canada, Citizenship and Immigration, *Facts*, 5.

3 Badets, "Canada's," 29.

4 Ibid.

5 Canada, Employment and Immigration Canada, "Immigration to Canada: A Statistical Overview," 8.

6 As defined by Michael Omi and Howard Winant, "racial formation" refers to "the sociohistorical process by which racial categories are created, inhabited, transformed, and destroyed." Further, "[f]rom a racial formation perspective, race is a matter of both social structure and cultural representation." Omi and Winant, *Racial*, 55–6. I have extended this term to include consideration of the social construction and transformation of ethnic categories on the assumptions that both race and ethnicity are socially constructed and that the boundary between the two is historically muted.

7 Canada, Citizenship and Immigration Canada, "Speaking," 3.

8 Harrison, "Class," 8, 9 (Table 1).

9 Ibid., 1.

10 For an elaboration of this argument, see Abele and Stasiulis, "Canada," 240–77; and Stasiulis and Jhappan, "Canada."

11 Collins and Henry, "Racism," 547.

12 Important works in the political economy of migration and racism informed by this approach have included: Castles and Kosack, *Immigrant*; Bolaria and Li, eds., *Racial*; Phizacklea and Miles, *Labour*; Miles, *Racism*; and Collins, *Migrants*.

13 For a critical discussion of selected Canadian and international literature on intersections among race/ethnicity, gender, and class, see Stasiulis, "Theorizing."

14 Goldberg, *Racist*, 70.

15 Laura Macdonald has similarly argued the utility of examining Canada's development as a "white settler colony" in understanding its foreign policies towards the Third World. Macdonald, "Unequal."

16 Much of the following discussion on the role of Canada's cultural link to the British Empire in shaping immigration patterns and policy relies heavily on Stasiulis and Jhappan, "Canada."

17 Barbara Roberts, "Work," 186; see also Valverde, *Age*.

18 Laczko, "Canada's," 26.

19 In 1977, Quebec entered into a special agreement with the federal government, enabling it to set up its own immigration offices abroad and become directly involved in the selection process. Richmond, *Global*, 183.

20 Panitch, "Dependency," 16–17.

21 Satzewich, "Racism," 40. The prevalence of unfree labour systems in advanced capitalist formations is a theme of Miles, *Capitalism*. Personal labour relations are characterized by the imposition by employers of non–work-related bonds of attachment and are thus frequently influenced by paternalism. For a discussion of personal and unfree labour relations in the Ontario tomato industry today, see Wall, "Personal."

22 Knowles, *Strangers*, 30.

23 Pentland, *Labour*, 258.

24 This assumption is central in the writings of political economists such as Leo Panitch who argue that Canadian industrial workers constituted a "high-wage proletariat" for various reasons, "not least among them being Canada's roots as a white settler society carrying with it the level of civiliza-tion achieved by Western Europe and increasingly dependent on the attrac-tion of skilled labour from Europe by the mid to late nineteenth century. Panitch, "Dependency," 17.

25 Satzewich, "Racism," 9; see also Miles, *Capitalism*; and Calliste, "Women."

26 Quoted in Knowles, *Strangers*, 64.

27 Swyripa, *Wedded*, 34–5.

28 McLaren, *Our Own*, 48. See also Valverde, *Age*, 107–8, and Palmer, *Patterns*.

29 Laczko, "Canada's," 34.

30 Harney and Troper, *Immigrants*, 4–6.

31 Harney, "Montreal's," 63; Avery, "*Dangerous*."

32 Ehrensaft and Armstrong, "Formation," 142.

33 Avery, "*Dangerous*."

34 Woodsworth, *Strangers*, 279. For a classic study of the racial/ethnic pecking order in Canadian immigration policy, see Palmer, "Reluctant."

35 Satzewich, *Racism*, 43; see also Calliste, "Women," 87.

36 Bolaria and Li, *Racial*.

37 Creese, "Exclusion"; Li, "Unneighbourly," 17–18.

38 Li, *Chinese*, 29.

39 Valverde, *Age*, 13.

40 Knowles, *Strangers*, 86.

41 Calliste, "Women," 88–9.

42 Calliste, "Canada's," 142; Satzewich, "Racism," 92.

43 Satzewich, "Racism," 79.

44 Ibid., 79.

45 Satzewich, *Racism*, 35.

46 Ibid., 82.

47 Danys, *DP*, 166.

48 Satzewich, *Racism*, 85–98.

49 Danys, *DP*, 69, 76.

50 The racism and anti-semitism characteristic of this era of Anglo-conformity
   are reflected in one official from the Pacific region – F.W. Smelts's advice
   "against taking the 'Mongol type of Jew from Poland and Russia' who, in
   his opinion would not assimilate well"; Ibid., 76.

51 Ibid., 76.

52 Arthur MacNamara, minister of labour in 1949, largely responsible for the
   DP scheme. Quoted in Satzewich, *Racism*, 95, italics added, 120.

53 Satzewich, *Racism*, 99.

54 Ibid., 119–20.

55 Ibid., 114.

56 Ibid., 115.

57 Quoted from "Pretty Scotch Lassies Ready to Come to Western Canada,"
   Manitoba Free Press, 23 March 1907, reproduced in Barber, "Servant," 104.

58 Ibid., 107.

59 Ibid., 108–9.

60 Danys, *DP*, 128–60.

61 Daenzer, "Ideology," 123–6; Iacovetta, *Such*, 29.

62 Jewell, *From*; Turner, *Ceramic*, 49–61.

63 Bakan and Stasiulis, "Making."

64 Calliste, "Canada's," 142.

65 For a discussion of the restrictions, such as threat of deportation, inherent
   in the 1955 Second Caribbean Domestic Scheme, see ibid. and Daenzer,
   Regulating.

66 See Daenzer, *Regulating*; Macklin, "Foreign."

67 Arat-Koc and Villasin, Report.

68 Calliste, "Canada's," 143–5.

69 Satzewich, *Racism*, 32.

70 Borowski, et al., "International," 47.

71 Ibid., 61.

72 Ibid., 51.

73 Richmond, *Global*, 108–9. Richmond has coined the term *transilience* to
   refer to the constant exchanges of skilled and highly qualified migrants
   between advanced economies. Ibid., 31, 51.

74 Canada, Citizenship and Immigration Canada, *Facts*, 4.

75 Krotki and Reid, "Demography," 25.

76 Canada, Citizenship and Immigration Canada, *Facts*, 2, 56; Borowski et al.,
   "International," 53.

77 The low value of the Canadian dollar and lower wage rates in Canada compared with the United States have attracted much of the American film industry to Canada, which has consequently been dubbed "Hollywood North."

78 See Harvey, *Condition*; Murray, "State." Political economists disagree about
   whether we can talk about a clearly defined "post-fordist" regime of accumulation. More consensus exists in the view that "recent attempts for

restructuring present a divergence from classical fordism." Koc, "Global-ization," 14.

79 Harvey, *Condition*, 147–53.

80 Ibid.

81 Borowy, Gordon, and Lebans, "Are These?" 305.

82 Borowski et al., "International," 61.

83 Ibid.

84 Noorani and Wright, "They," 32.

85 Racism in Canada's refugee-determination system is extensively docu-mented in Matas with Simon, *Closing*; and Malarek, *Haven's*.

86 Richmond, *Global*, 214.

87 Canada, Citizenship and Immigration Canada, *Into*; Winsor and Greenspan, "Canada," A1, A3.

88 Canadian Press, "After," A4.

89 Cox, "The Global Political Economy and Social Choice", 340.

90 Bakan and Stasiulis, "Foreign," 9.

91 Centre for Contemporary Cultural Studies, *Empire*.

92 White, "Indo-Chinese," 44.

93 Canada, Citizenship and Immigration Canada, *Into*, 30.

94 Borowski and Nash, "Business," 243.

95 While "in the mid-1980s, direct investment from Hong Kong was only about $170 million per year," by 1990, such investment rose to $1.3 billion. Li, "Chinese," 225. "Between 1983 and 1990, investments from Pacific Rim countries quadrupled," those from Japan tripled, while those from Hong Kong increased by nine times. Sixty-three per cent of the capital flow of $3.5 billion from Hong Kong to Canada was transferred by the business-migration component. Mitchell, "Multiculturalism," 267.

96 Mitchell, "Multiculturalism," 266.

97 Borowski and Nash, "Business," 243. Unlike the early Chinese migrants, however, business immigrants are able to bring in immediate members of their family.

98 Li, "Unneighbourly," 20.

99 Ibid., 23, 25.

100 Ibid.

101 Stasiulis, "Minority."

102 Immigrant women from Asia, Africa, the Caribbean, Central and South America, and Oceania are heavily concentrated in clothing industries (accounting in 1989 for 23.5 per cent of employees in this sector), textiles (12.3 per cent), and leather-product industries (10.8 per cent). They make up 6.3 per cent of the female labour force. Seward and Tremblay, "Immigrants." Asian women lacking official-language skills are heavily concentrated in service occupations and in the food and accommodation industries. Fincher et al., "Gender," 183.

103 Canada, Citizenship and Immigration Canada, "Into," 59, emphasis added.
104 Ibid. For a recent popular, but muddled critique of multiculturalism,
    see Bissoondath, *Selling*. An analysis of the ideological diversity of
    arguments against multiculturalism is found in Abu-Laban and Stasiulis,
    "Ethnic."
105 Mitchell, "Multiculturalism," 268.
106 Joyce Li, "Living," 34.
107 Helvacioglu, "Thrills," 22. By 1991, the number of officially (United
    Nations) recognized refugees globally totalled 16 million. If one added to
    this number persons in "refugee-like situations" and internally displaced
    persons, the total exceeds 40 million. Rogers, "Future," 1112.
108 Grewal and Kaplan, "Introduction," 14.
109 Ibid., 7.
110 Economic Council of Canada, *Good*; Abele and Stasiulis, "Canada," 268.

REFERENCES

Abele, Frances, and Stasiulis, Daiva. "Canada as a 'White Settler Society':
    What about Natives and Immigrants?" In W. Clement and G. Williams,
    eds., *The New Canadian Political Economy*, 240–77. Montreal: McGill-
    Queen's University Press, 1989.
Abu-Laban, Yasmeen, and Stasiulis, Daiva. "Ethnic Pluralism under Siege:
    Popular and Partisan Opposition to Multiculturalism." *Canadian Public
    Policy*, 18 (Dec. 1992), 365–86.
Arat-Koc, Sedef. "Immigration Policies, Migrant Domestic Workers and the
    Definition of Citizenship in Canada." In *Deconstructing A Nation: Immigration,
    Multiculturalism and Racism in '90s Canada*, 229–42. Halifax: Fernwood
    Publishing, 1992.
– "In the Privacy of Our Own Home: Foreign Domestic Workers as Solution to
    the Crisis of the Domestic Sphere in Canada." *Studies in Political Economy*,
    28 (spring 1989), 33–58.
Arat-Koc, Sedef, and Villasin, Fely. Report and Recommendations on the
    Foreign Domestic Movement Program. Report prepared for INTERCEDE to
    be submitted to the Ministry of Employment and Immigration, 1990.
Arnopoulous, Sheila McLeod. *Problems of Immigrant Women in the Canadian
    Labour Force*. Ottawa: Ministry of Supply and Services, 1979.
Avery, Donald. *"Dangerous Foreigners": European Immigrant Workers and Labour
    Radicalism in Canada, 1896–1932*. Toronto: McClelland and Stewart, 1979.
Badets, Jane. "Canada's Immigrants: Recent Trends." In *Canadian Social Trends*,
    vol. 2, 27–30. Toronto: Thompson Educational Publishing, 1994.
Bakan, Abigail B., and Stasiulis, Daiva K. "Foreign Domestic Worker Policy in
    Canada and the Social Boundaries of Modern Citizenship." *Science and
    Society*, 58 no. 1 (1994), 7–33.

- "Making the Match: Domestic Placement Agencies and the Racialization of Women's Household Work." *Signs: Journal of Women in Culture and Society*, 20 no. 2 (1995), 303–35.

Barber, Marilyn. "The Servant Problem in Manitoba, 1896–1930." In M. Kinnear, ed., *First Days, Fighting Days: Women in Manitoba History*, 102–19. Regina: Canadian Plains Research Centre, 1987.

- "Sunny Ontario for British Girls, 1900–30." In J. Burnet, ed., *Looking into My Sister's Eyes*, 55–73. Toronto: Multicultural History Society of Ontario, 1986.

Bissoondath, Neil. *Selling Illusions: The Cult of Multiculturalism in Canada*. Toronto: Penguin Books, 1994.

Bolaria, B. Singh, and Li, Peter S., eds. *Racial Oppression in Canada*. 2nd ed. Toronto: Garamond Press, 1988.

Borowski, Allan, and Nash, Alan. "Business Migration." In H. Adelman et al., *Immigration and Refugee Policy: Australia and Canada Compared*, vol. 1. Toronto: University of Toronto Press, 1994.

Borowski, Allan, Richmond, Anthony, Shu, Jing, and Simmons, Alan. "The International Movements of People." In H. Adelman et al., *Immigration and Refugee Policy: Australia and Canada Compared*, vol. 1. Toronto: University of Toronto Press, 1994.

Borowy, Jan, Gordon, Shelley, and Lebans, Gayle. "Are These Clothes Clean? The Campaign for Fair Wages and Working Conditions for Homeworkers." In L. Carty, ed., *And Still We Rise: Feminist Political Mobilizing in Contemporary Canada*, 299–330. Toronto: Women's Press, 1993.

Boyd, Monica. "Immigrant Women in Canada." In R.J. Simon and C. Bretell, eds., *International Migration: The Female Experience*. Totowa, NJ: Rowman and Allenheld, 1986.

Boyd, Monica, DeVries, John, and Simkin, Keith. "Language, Economic Status and Integration." In H. Adelman et al., eds., *Immigration and Refugee Policy: Australia and Canada Compared*, vol. 2. Toronto: University of Toronto Press, 1994.

Calliste, Agnes. "Canada's Immigration Policy and Domestics from the Caribbean: The Second Domestic Scheme." *Socialist Studies* 5 (1989), 136–68.

- "Women of 'Exceptional Merit': Immigration of Caribbean Nurses to Canada." *Canadian Journal of Women and the Law*, 6 (1993), 85–102.

Canada, Citizenship and Immigration Canada. *Facts and Figures: Overview of Immigration*. Strategic Research, Analysis and Information Branch, Policy Sector, November 1994.

- *Into the 21st Century: A Strategy for Immigration and Citizenship*. Ottawa: Minister of Supply and Services, 1994.

- "Speaking Notes for the Honourable Sergio Marchi, P.C., M.P., Minister of Citizenship and Immigration: Tabling of the Strategy and the Immigration and Citizenship Plan." 1 Nov. 1994.

Canada, Employment and Immigration. "Immigration to Canada: A Statistical Overview." Ottawa: Ministry of Supply and Services, 1995.

Canadian Press. "Alter Immigration Fee, Liberals Urge." *Globe and Mail*, 3 March 1995, A4.

Castles, Stephen, and Kosack, Godula. *Immigrant Workers and Class Structure in Western Europe.* 2nd ed. London: Oxford University Press, 1985.

Centre for Contemporary Cultural Studies. *The Empire Strikes Back: Race and Racism in 70s Britain.* London: Hutchinson, 1982.

Collins, Jock. *Migrant Hands in a Distant Land.* Sydney: Pluto Press, 1988.

Collins, Jock, and Henry, Frances. "Racism, Ethnicity and Immigration." In H. Adelman et al., eds., *Immigration and Refugee Policy: Australia and Canada Compared*, vol. 2. Toronto: University of Toronto Press, 1994.

Cox, Robert. "The Global Political Economy and Social Choice." In D. Drache, ed., *The New Era of Global Competition: State Policy and Market Power*, 335–50. Montreal: McGill-Queen's University Press, 1991.

Creese, Gillian. "Exclusion or Solidarity? Vancouver Workers Confront the 'Oriental Problem'." *B.C. Studies*, 80 (1988–89), 24–51.

Daenzer, Patricia. "Ideology and the Formation of Migration Policy: The Case of Immigrant Domestic Workers, 1940–1990." PhD dissertation, School of Social Work, University of Toronto, 1991.

– *Regulating Class Privilege: Immigrant Servants in Canada, 1940s–1990s.* Toronto: Canadian Scholars Press, 1993.

Danys, Milda. *DP: Lithuanian Immigration to Canada after the Second World War.* Toronto: Multicultural History Society of Ontario, 1986.

Das Gupta, Tania. "Political Economy of Gender, Race and Class: Looking at South Asian Immigrant Women in Canada." *Canadian Ethnic Studies*, 26 no. 1, (1994), 59–73.

Dickason, Olive P. *Canada's First Nations: A History of Founding Peoples from Earliest Times.* Toronto: McClelland and Stewart, 1992.

Economic Council of Canada. *Good Jobs, Bad Jobs.* Ottawa: Supply and Services Canada, 1990.

Ehrensaft, Philip, and Armstrong, Warwick. "The Formation of Dominion Capitalism: Economic Truncation and Class Structure." In A. Moscovitch and G. Drover, eds., *Inequality: Essays on the Political Economy of Social Welfare.* Toronto: University of Toronto Press, 1981.

Fincher, Ruth, Foster, Lois, Giles, Wenona, and Preston, Valerie. "Gender and Migration Policy." In H. Adelman et al., eds., *Immigration and Refugee Policy: Australia and Canada Compared*, vol. 2. Toronto: University of Toronto Press, 1994.

Goldberg, David Theo. *Racist Culture: Philosophy and the Politics of Meaning.* Oxford: Blackwell Publishers, 1993.

Grewal, Inderpal, and Kaplan, Caren. "Introduction: Transnational Feminist Practices and Questions of Modernity." In *Scattered Hegemonies: Postmodernity and Transnational Feminist Practices*, 1–33. Minneapolis, Minn.: University of Minneapolis Press, 1994.

Harney, Robert. "Montreal's King of Labour: A Case Study of Padronism." *Labour/Le travailleur*, 4 (1979), 57–84.

Harney, Robert, and Troper, Harold. *Immigrants: A Portrait of the Urban Experience, 1890–1930*. Toronto: Van Nostrand Reinhold, 1975.

Harrison, Trevor W. "Class, Citizenship and Global Migration: The Case of the Canadian Business Immigration Program." Paper presented at the Annual Meeting of the Canadian Sociology and Anthropology Association, Calgary, June 1994.

Harvey, David. *The Condition of Postmodernity: An Enquiry into the Origins of Cultural Change*. Cambridge, Mass.: Blackwell Publishers, 1989.

Helvacioglu, Banu. "The Thrills and Chills of Postmodernism: The Western Intellectual Vertigo." *Studies in Political Economy*, 38 (summer 1992), 7–34.

Iacovetta, Franca. *Such Hardworking People: Italian Immigrants in Postwar Toronto*. Montreal: McGill-Queen's University Press, 1992.

Inglis, Christine, Birch, Anthony, and Sherrington, Geoffrey. "An Overview of Australian and Canadian Migration Patterns and Policies." In H. Adelman et al., *Immigration and Refugee Policy: Australia and Canada Compared*. Toronto: University of Toronto Press, 1994.

Jewell, K. Sue. *From Mammy to Miss America and Beyond: Cultural Images and the Shaping of US Social Policy*. London: Routledge, 1993.

Joseph, Clifton. "On Your Mark! Get Set! Go Multi-culti." *This Magazine*, 28 no. 5 (Jan.–Feb. 1995), 24–8.

Khan, Shahnaz. "Canadian Muslim Women and Shari'a Law: A Feminist Response to 'Oh! Canada!'" *Canadian Journal of Women and the Law*, 6 (1993), 52–65.

Knowles, Valerie. *Strangers at Our Gates: Canadian Immigration and Immigration Policy, 1540–1990*. Toronto: Dundurn Press, 1992.

Koc, Mustafa. "Globalization As a Discourse." Paper presented to the Canadian Sociology and Anthropology Meetings, Calgary, 1993.

Krotki, Karol J., and Reid, Colin. "Demography of Canadian Population by Ethnic Group." In J.W. Berry and J.A. Laponce, eds., *Ethnicity and Culture in Canada: The Research Landscape*, 17–59. Toronto: University of Toronto Press, 1994.

Laczko, Leslie. "Canada's Pluralism in Comparative Perspective." *Ethnic and Racial Studies*, 17 no. 1 (Jan. 1994), 20–41.

Li, Joyce. "Living between Two Worlds." *Maclean's*, 108 no. 5 (30 Jan. 1995), 32–4.

Li, Peter S. *The Chinese in Canada*. Toronto: Oxford University Press, 1988.

– "Chinese Investment and Business in Canada: Ethnic Entrepreneurship Reconsidered." *Pacific Affairs*, 66 no. 2 (summer 1993), 219–43.

- "Unneighbourly Houses or Unwelcome Chinese: The Social Construction of Race in the Battle over 'Monster Homes' in Vancouver, Canada." *International Journal of Comparative Race and Ethnic Studies*, 1 no. 1 (1994), 14–33.

Lindstrom-Best, Varpu. *Defiant Sisters: A Social History of Finnish Immigrant Women in Canada*. Toronto: Multicultural History Society of Ontario, 1988.

Macdonald, Laura. "Unequal Partnerships: Politics and Discourse in Canada's Relations with the Third World." *Studies in Political Economy*, 47 (summer 1995), 111–41.

Macklin, Audrey. "Foreign Domestic Worker: Surrogate Housewife or Mail Order Servant?" *McGill Law Journal*, 37 no. 3 (1992) 681–760.

McLaren, Angus. *Our Own Master Race: Eugenics in Canada, 1885–1945*. Toronto: McClelland and Stewart, 1990.

McLellan, Janet, and Richmond, Anthony H. "Multiculturalism in Crisis: A Postmodern Perspective in Canada." *Ethnic and Racial Studies*, 17 no. 4 (Oct. 1994), 662–83.

Malarek, Victor. *Haven's Gate: Canada's Immigration Fiasco*. Toronto: Macmillan, 1987.

Matas, David, with Simon, Ilana. *Closing the Doors: The Failure of Refugee Protection*. Toronto: Summerhill Press, 1989.

Miles, Robert. *Capitalism and Unfree Labour: Anomaly or Necessity?* London: Tavistock, 1987.

- *Racism and Migrant Labour*. Boston: Routledge & Kegan Paul, 1982.

Mitchell, Katharyne "Multiculturalism, or the United Colors Of Capitalism." *Antipode*, 25 no. 4 (1992), 263–94.

Murray, Robin. "The State after Henry." *Marxism Today* (May 1991).

Ng, Roxana. "The Social Construction of Immigrant Women in Canada." In R. Hamilton and M. Barrett, eds., *The Politics of Diversity*, 269–86. London: Verso, 1986.

Noorani, Arif, and Wright, Cynthia. "They Believed the Hype." *This Magazine*, 28 no. 5 (Jan.–Feb. 1995), 29–32.

Omi, Howard, and Winant, Howard. *Racial Formation in the United States: From the 1960s to the 1990s*. New York: Routledge, 1994.

Palmer, Howard. *Patterns of Prejudice: A History of Nativism in Alberta*. Toronto: McClelland and Stewart, 1982.

- "Reluctant Hosts: Anglo-Canadian Views of Multiculturalism in the Twentieth Century." In *Multiculturalism as State Policy: Conference Report*, 81–118. Ottawa: Canadian Consultative Council on Multiculturalism, 1976.

Parr, Joy. *Labouring Children: British Immigrant Appretices to Canada, 1869–1924*. Montreal: McGill-Queen's University Press, 1980.

Panitch, Leo. "Dependency or Class in Canadian Political Economy." *Studies in Political Economy*, 6 (1981), 7–34.

Pentland, Clare. *Labour and Capital in Canada, 1650–1860*. Toronto: James Lorimer.

Phizacklea, Annie, and Miles, Robert. *Labour and Racism.* London: Routledge & Kegan Paul, 1980.

Richmond, Anthony H. *Global Apartheid: Refugees, Racism, and the New World Order.* Toronto: Oxford University Press, 1994.

Roberts, Barbara. " 'A Work of Empire': Canadian Reformers and British Female Immigration." In L. Kealy, ed., *A Not Unreasonable Claim: Women and Reform in Canada, 1880s–1920s,* 185–201. Toronto: Women's Press, 1979.

Rogers, Rosemarie. "The Future of Refugee Flows and Policies." *International Migration Review,* 26 no. 4 (1993), 1112–43.

Sassen, Saskia. *The Mobility of Labor and Capital: A Study of International Investment and Labor Flow.* Cambridge: Cambridge University Press, 1988.

Satzewich, Vic. "Racism and Canadian Immigration Policy: The Government's View of Caribbean Migration, 1926–66." *Canadian Ethnic Studies,* 21 no. 1 (1988), 282–304.

– *Racism and the Incorporation of Foreign Labour: Farm Labour Migration to Canada since 1945.* London: Routledge, 1991.

Seward, Shirley, and Tremblay, Marc. "Immigrants in the Canadian Labour Force: Their Role in Structural Change." *Studies in Social Policy* (1989).

Silvera, Makeda. *Silenced: Talks with Working Class Caribbean Women about Their Lives and Struggles as Domestic Workers in Canada.* 2nd ed. Toronto: Sister Vision Press.

Stasiulis, Daiva. "Minority Resistance in the Local State: Toronto in the 1970s and 1980s." *Ethnic and Racial Studies,* 12 no. 1 (1988), 63–83.

– "Theorizing Connections: Gender, Race, Ethnicity, and Class." In Peter S. Li, ed., *Race and Ethnic Relations in Canada,* 269–305. Toronto: Oxford University Press, 1990.

Stasiulis, Daiva, and Jhappan, Radha. "Canada: The Fractious Politics of a Settler Society." In D. Stasiulis and N. Yuval-Davis, eds., *Unsettling Settler Societies: Articulations of Gender, Race, Ethnicity and Class,* 95–131. Sage: London, 1995.

Swyripa, Frances. *Wedded to the Cause: Ukrainian-Canadian Women and Ethnic Identity, 1891–1991.* Toronto: University of Toronto Press, 1993.

Turner, Patricia A. *Ceramic Uncles and Celluloid Mammies: Black Images and Their Influence on Culture.* New York: Anchor Books, 1994.

Ujimoto, K. Victor. "Racism, Discrimination and Internment: Japanese in Canada." In B. Singh Bolaria and Peter S. Li, eds., *Racial Oppression in Canada,* 2nd ed., 209–30. Toronto: Garamond Press, 1988.

Valverde, Mariana. *The Age of Light, Soap and Water: Moral Reform in English Canada, 1885–1925.* Toronto: McClelland and Stewart, 1991.

Wall, Ellen. "Personal Labour Relations and Ethnicity in Ontario Agriculture." In Vic Satzewich, ed., *Deconstructing a Nation: Immigration, Multiculturalism and Racism in '90s Canada,* 261–75. Halifax: Fernwood Publishing, 1992.

Ward, W. Peter. *White Canada Forever: Popular Attitudes and Public Policy towards Orientals in British Columbia*. Montreal: McGill-Queen's University Press, 1978.

Wardhaugh, Ronald. *Language and Nationhood: The Canadian Experience*. Vancouver: New Star Books, 1983.

White, Pamela M. "The Indo-Chinese in Canada." In *Canadian Social Trends: A Canadian Studies Reader*, vol. 2, 41–4. Toronto: Thompson Educational Publishing Inc., 1994.

Winsor, Hugh, and Greenspon, Edward. "Canada to Cut Immigration in 1995." *Globe and Mail*, 29 Oct. 1994, A1, A4.

Woodsworth, J.S. *Strangers within Our Gates or Coming Canadians*. First pub. 1909. Reprint. Toronto: University of Toronto Press, 1972.

8 Going Global: The Politics of Canada's Foreign Economic Relations

LAURA MACDONALD

Dramatic changes have occurred in the global economy over the last twenty years: the decline of u.s. hegemony; the rise of new economic competitors in Europe and Asia; changes in the General Agreement on Tariffs and Trade (GATT) and, particularly, the Canada–United States Fre Trade Agreement (FTA) and its expansion through the North American Free Trade Agreement (NAFTA). As a result of this turbulence in the international economy, Canadians are faced with unprecedented uncertainties about their economic prospects. This situation is compounded by some dire predictions of the inevitability of the country's economic and political decline as a result of current trends. Writers from different ideological persuasions disagree on the sources of the dangers and offer opposite solutions.

Influential business writer and editor of the *Financial Post* Diane Francis, for example, warns:

Canada is unwittingly at a crossroads. If we are to pass the baton of high living standards onto the next generation, we must realize that economic competition is ferocious. We must understand how the world evolves. We must streamline governments to save money by dismantling our provinces and welfare state. If we do not take such proactive steps, the debt crisis will force us to act anyway, and we will probably end up as Americans.

... There is no point in railing against the Americans and the globalization of the economy, or in erecting tariff barriers, opting out of trade agreements or wishing things were like the good old days when the United States and Canada were virtually the only industrialized economies around. No one owes Canada a living.[1]

On the left, James Laxer argues in *False God: How the Globalization Myth Has Impoverished Canada* that

... the Conservative government has carried out a wilful assault on Canada's institutions, traditions, and society. Further, this assault has been made in the name of globalization, which is a false god that has done vast destruction in many parts of the world. While Canadians did not invent globalization, they may well be the first people to preside over the dissolution of their country as a direct result of obeying its commandments.

The very survival of Canada has never been more in doubt than it is now. To a great degree, this is because the Conservative government has embraced the idea of globalization and all its consequences.[2]

Despite the obvious differences between them, both authors agree that Canadians need to understand the nature of changes in the global economy in order to formulate viable alternatives. In an era of global economic restructuring and the consolidation of regional economic trading blocs, the connections between international economic changes and domestic political and economic options are clearer than ever.

This chapter examines the dilemmas confronting Canada in its foreign economic relations.[3] The first section provides a historical overview of Canada's position in the international economy. In the contemporary period, Canadians' perceptions of their role in the international economy are heavily shaped by Canada's implementation of the FTA from January 1989 and of NAFTA since January 1994. However, this process of "regionalization" within the North American economy operates hand in hand with broader processes of "globalization". The second section looks to the tradition of the new Canadian political economy to find guidance in interpreting the meaning of globalization and regionalization. The new Canadian political economy provides the basis for a useful critique of neo-liberal prescriptions by interpreting the structural weaknesses of the Canadian economy. Until recently, however, Canadian political economists have failed to move beyond the nationalist positions formulated in the 1960s and 1970s. In the third and final section, I present an alternative perspective on Canadian political options in the NAFTA era. I argue that in a time of globalization of capital, political economy also must "go global." In particular, the left-nationalist stance that characterizes

Canadian political economy must be revised to develop new political strategies capable of confronting the new global economy.

CANADA IN THE CHANGING WORLD ECONOMY

As James Laxer and Diane Francis's statements indicate, our times are frequently seen as shaped by the forces of "globalization." This concept is commonly defined as the outcome of the interaction of several simultaneous processes: the expansion of multinational corporations seeking larger markets and cheaper production sites; the increased mobility of financial capital resulting from deregulation of financial markets; and the reduction in states' barriers to the mobility of capital.[4] Most accounts (both enthusiastic and critical) emphasize the revolutionary changes in the relationships among individuals, states, and firms arising because of multinational corporations' expanding scope of operation.

Kenichi Ohmae argues that "more informed and demanding customers" are driving multinationals to "operate, develop, make and sell in many countries at once and ... in the process are helping to create a borderless economy where trade statistics are meaningless."[5] According to liberal optimists such as Ohmae, the logic of the increasingly integrated international marketplace operating through changes in currency and wage rates means that no nation will emerge as an absolute loser or winner in this process. Globalization means, however, that traditional Keynesian policies based on macroeconomic statistics no longer work: integration of the world's major economic powers "has made obsolete the traditional instruments of central bankers – interest rate and money supply."[6]

This thesis about the inevitable "disarming" of the nation-state[7] by the irresistible forces of globalization, if true, clearly has profound implications for any progressive political project. Writers and activists on the left have always viewed state intervention as necessary to shield vulnerable actors (workers, women, minorities, the poor, and so on) from the logic of the marketplace, which is viewed (contrary to Ohmae's benevolent vision) as harsh and unforgiving.

A glance at Canada's economic history shows that much of the emphasis in the globalization literature on the novelty of current trends towards economic integration and the pressures on the state from international economic forces is misplaced. Canada has always been shaped by its relationships with other states because of its heavy dependence on foreign trade and investment. Canada's economic prosperity, despite its low indigenous industrial-technological base, is to a large extent a result of its special ties with the two hegemonic powers of the last two centuries, first Britain and then the United States.[8] As a "white settler colony," Canada, along with Australia, New Zealand, Rhodesia, and South Africa, was afforded privileges denied to colonial possessions in other parts of Africa, Asia, and the Caribbean. According to Glen Williams, "Canada and the other white Dominions ... were developed as overseas extensions, miniature replicas, of British society, complete with a large measure of local political autonomy."[9]

Canadian governments worked for increased autonomy within the British Empire until full independence was achieved during the Second World War. The struggle was waged, however, on behalf of the white dominions only, not the non-white colonies. Moreover, during the early years of the Depression, the Canadian government strongly promoted increased economic links within the empire, in the form of an imperial preference that was resisted by British free traders. No general system of preference was adopted, but in 1932 Britain and the dominions agreed to a series of bilateral agreements, with limited economic impact.[10] Canada further expanded concessions to the entry of British and Australian goods in 1937.

Despite the links with Britain, Canada's history is, to a large extent, the story of successive attempts to manage economic integration with the United States while maintaining some degree of independence. Canadian policy makers tried to reap economic advantages from a special relationship with Canada's hegemonic allies while using the nation-state as a tool to carve out a distinct political community within the North American economy. From before Confederation, successive generations of policy makers carried out a long flirtation with the notion of continental integration until economic integration with the United States was formally consummated with the FTA of 1988.[11]

Based on earlier work by Vernon Fowke and Donald Smiley, Janine Brodie conceptualizes Canadian economic history as shaped by a series of "national policies" in which the state formulated general developmental strategies in response to both internal political pressures and demands of the international political economy (see her chapter, no. 11, below).[12] None of these policies was purely nationalist or inward-looking; instead they involved a complex balance between economic integration and independence. Brodie also notes: "The shadow of free trade has always lurked in the wings when the logic of the prevailing national development strategy has eroded in the face of changing international conditions."[13]

The first National Policy, enacted by Sir John A. Macdonald in 1879, attempted to build a nation in the northern part of the continent through high tariff walls, promotion of immigration to the west, and construction of a railway from coast to coast. The second National Policy, formulated after the Second World War, was based on the Keynesian economic policies that were adopted throughout the West in response to fears of repetition of the Depression. The federal government undertook a series of social welfare measures, including unemployment insurance, family allowances, health-care reforms, and a limited commitment to full employment. It also launched a series of macroeconomic demand-management policies, using fiscal and monetary tools.[14] During the postwar period, increased state intervention in the domestic economy occurred in tandem with progressive liberalization of the international economy under U.S. leadership. The U.S. dollar became the dominant currency (originally supported by the gold standard) and a series of GATT rounds gradually dismantled tariff borders. These measures paved the way for rapid expansion of international trade and of multinational corporations. John Gerald Ruggie has referred to this combination of international liberalization and state intervention as "embedded liberalism," a compromise between alternative visions of capitalism.[15]

Canada, because of its heavy reliance on trade and close ties with the United States, actively supported these changes. Part of Canada's commitment to middle-power diplomacy and multilateralism included strong advocacy for creation and maintenance of such economic institutions as the International Monetary Fund (which provided short-term loans and regulated a system of fixed exchange rates tied until 1971 to the U.S. dollar). Emerging from the war in a position of relative economic strength, Canada played a role in the deliberations of the great powers about the postwar monetary system. A Canadian participant, A.W.F. Plumptre, described Canadian motivations in this way:

It is true, and it was true at the time, that the new international institutions, largely fashioned in Washington, were designed to serve the international interests of the United States. The charge that they could in many respects be considered as the creatures of American 'capitalist imperialism' can in a sense be accepted. It does not follow, however, that their establishment and operation were contrary to Canadian interests as perceived at the time or subsequently by Canadian governments or Canadians generally. The kind of postwar world the Americans, in collaboration with the British, were attempting to build was one that was in large measure well adapted to Canadian requirements, and as a result of Canadian efforts the adaptation was improved.[16]

At the Bretton Woods discussions of 1944, only Canada, in addition to the United States and Britain, put forward a detailed proposal on the shape of the new monetary system. Though intellectually attracted to British representative Lord Keynes's more ambitious design, Canadian officials advanced ideas closer to those of the United States, reflecting in part recognition of Washington's power in the system.[17] Canada also strongly supported liberalization of international trade under GATT, which was signed in 1947. The GATT treaty committed signatories to meet on a regular basis to dismantle trade barriers gradually. Canada's tariffs adopted after Confederation remained in place, however, until they were significantly reduced as a result of the 1970s Tokyo Round of GATT.[18]

At the same time as it supported multilateral institutions to liberalize the world economy, the Canadian state also pursued measures to increase economic links with the United States.[19] Economic cooperation had increased dramatically during the war because of the halt in trade with Europe and the need to coordinate production for the war effort. Continental integration was reinforced after the war. A key measure was the 1965 Canada-U.S. Auto Pact, which rationalized automobile production on a continental basis, thereby protecting Canada's share of the industry. From the 1940s to the 1970s, Canada relied on its "special relationship" with Washington, based on geographical proximity, cultural and ideological similarity, and shared perception of the need for cooperation in response to the Soviet threat. Canada gained privileged access to strategic intelligence information and defence contracts and exemption from protectionist measures. In return, Canada acted as a loyal foreign-policy ally, reserving any dissension for backroom "quiet diplomacy."[20]

Despite some nationalist measures and the maintenance of tariff barriers, Canadian economic policy between 1945 and the 1970s was essentially continentalist, resulting in increasing domination of the economy by branch plants of U.S.-based corporations. The "special relationship" was shaken in 1971, however, when President Nixon tried to reverse the U.S. economic decline by withdrawing suddenly from the gold standard which was draining U.S. reserves, placing a surcharge of 10 per cent on all imports, and offering tax incentives for American corporations to export from the United States rather than from their branch plants abroad. Canada was neither exempted nor privately informed in advance of these unilateral changes.

Nixon's actions resulted from new challenges to U.S. dominance in the international economy that emerged in the late 1960s and early 1970s. The success of earlier policies designed to stimulate world trade and promote relocation of multinationals abroad helped bring about the relative decline of U.S. economic power relative to Japan and western Europe; the emergence of low-waged, newly industrializing countries in Southeast Asia, which attracted production away from former manufacturing centres; imbalances in the international monetary system; and the rapid rise in energy prices after the formation of the Organization of Petroleum Exporting Countries (OPEC).

After 1973, Canada suffered slow growth and high rates of both inflation and unemployment. Inflation rates dropped in the early 1980s, producing the worst economic recession since the 1930s. Disillusionment with Keynesian demand-management techniques spread, as did criticism of the costs of social welfare programs.[21] Concerns increased about the extent of U.S. ownership of the Canadian economy, since the United States was declining relative to other Western powers. As well, U.S.-based multinationals were responding to changing opportunities in the international political economy by closing Canadian operations and moving them to low-wage areas such as Southeast Asia. The Liberal government of Pierre Trudeau attempted to respond in a limited nationalist way by setting up a Canadian Development Corporation to promote Canadian entrepreneurs; Petro-Canada, a state-owned oil company; the Foreign Investment Review Agency (FIRA) to review foreign investment based on the criterion of whether it was of "significant benefit to Canada"; and the National Energy Programme (NEP) of 1980, designed to Canadianize the industry and increase the power of the central government.[22]

In order to seek out alternative markets in the light of the changing relationship between Canada and its major trading partner, in 1972 Secretary of State for External Affairs Mitchell Sharp published a paper in which he advocated a "Third Option" – expansion of relations with other countries, particularly Europe and Japan. However, Canada's trading relations failed to diversify as a result of this initiative, which was withdrawn in 1983.

None of these attempts to carve out a more independent economic policy reduced Canada's economic dependence on the United States or increased its international competitiveness, and Trudeau's nationalism awakened substantial opposition from the western provinces and the private sector and from the United States. The demise of the special relationship with the United States became clear after the election of Ronald Reagan as president in 1980 on a neo-conservative economic platform. He did not grant Canada exemptions from the standards applied to the rest of the world; Stephen Clarkson argues: "On the contrary, Canada became a showcase for Reaganism's international economic policy, a test to show the world that the new administration was going to be tough with its partners and insist that they play by the formal rules as established by such bodies as the General Agreement on Tariffs and Trade."[23]

Washington targeted such practices as the NEP and FIRA as unacceptable and threatened retaliation unless they were withdrawn. As a response, the nationalist wing of the Liberal party was sidelined, and former protectionist measures were weakened or abandoned. Having failed to articulate a new national policy, in 1982 the Liberals appointed Donald Macdonald to head the Royal Commission on the Economic Union and Development Prospects for Canada. The commission did not issue its report until the fall of 1985, after the election of the Progressive Conservatives under Brian Mulroney. The new government was much closer ideologically and temperamentally to Reagan's. It was the Liberal-appointed Macdonald Commission that recommended adoption of a free-trade agreement with the United States, combined with market-driven economic strategies at home.

At the same time as it protested state intervention in Canada in the free operation of the market, the United States increased its own protectionist measures through non-tariff barriers to trade. This marked a new phase in Canadian-U.S. relations. In an effort to reverse its economic decline, the United States focused on consolidating its remaining economic dominance within the Americas. Moves towards greater continental integration emerged not as an alternative to multilateral forums, however, but as a way of forcing U.S. goals on recalcitrant allies outside the western hemisphere.

Within Canada, free trade with the United States was increasingly embraced by formerly protectionist actors within the private sector and by economic analysts as the only solution to Canada's economic woes. Continental rationalization of industry was promoted as a means to develop exports from both the traditional resource sector and a technologically advanced manufacturing sector. Efficiency gains were to be made through cheaper domestic and imported inputs and the spin-offs of a dynamic export sector.[24] The main rationale, however, was defensive. In the context of increasing economic competition at the global level and the failure of earlier efforts to diversify markets, the FTA promised to preserve Canada's stable and secure access to the U.S. market, which was under threat from protectionist forces in Washington.

Even though the agreement did not deliver on this promise, the decision to accede to NAFTA was also primarily defensive. Given that Mexico and the United States were pursuing a free-trade agreement, Canadian decision makers did not want to be left out of the negotiations nor risk erosion of the FTA gains. A former Liberal minister of international trade, Gerald Regan, explained how Canadian manufacturers would be disadvantaged by the establishment of the United

States as a "hub" connected through separate bilateral trade deals to subordinate "spokes" – Canada and Mexico: "The point is if a company in Germany were intending to service the entire North American market from a plant on this continent, and the United States had free access for a product manufactured in that country, but Canada had it only with the United States, it would be one more argument in favour of siting your plant in the u.s. rather than in Canada."[25] Incorporation of Mexico also was seen as increasing the competitiveness of Canadian companies by creating the option of relocating labour-intensive processes to that low-wage area.

Because of the high public profile of these two trade agreements, Canadians tend to interpret the country's external economic relations primarily or even exclusively in terms of them. In fact, however, as it has been argued, economic integration in North America cannot be separated from global economic restructuring. We return below to the question of how these diverse aspects of economic change are interrelated.

INTERPRETING CANADA'S FOREIGN ECONOMIC POLICIES

There is little dialogue between opponents and proponents of economic liberalization. Academic supporters of free trade and globalization are located primarily in departments of economics and business and base their arguments on neo-classical trade theory. Like Kenichi Ohmae, most economists argue that because of the gains from trade through increased efficiency and productivity and economies of scale, liberalization of markets automatically delivers benefits to all participating countries. The Macdonald Commission drew on these arguments, as well as highly abstract statistical models designed to calculate the macroeconomic effects of free trade. The predictions derived from these models seem absurdly optimistic in the light of the economic crisis that Canada has experienced since the launching of the FTA. Supporters argue that however bad the situation, it would have been worse without an FTA. Some claim that improvements in Canada's trade balance with the United States show that the FTA is working.[26]

These arguments, and the evidence used to support them, have come under heavy attack by political economists. Ricardo Grinspun argues that an overvalued Canadian dollar and declining competitiveness of Canadian industry since 1985 have seriously affected firms' ability to restructure in response to the demands of continental integration. The FTA also restricts the state's capacity to increase productivity through programs in areas such as education, regional development, job training, research and development, and social and health programs. Under the terms of the FTA, the United States can challenge many Canadian programs targeted to a specific sector or region as "unfair" trade practices.[27] Neo-classical economic arguments also neglect to incorporate intrafirm trade – trade among affiliates of transnational corporations (TNCs) – which accounts for much of the commerce among Canada, the United States, and Mexico.[28]

To political economists, the assumptions of neo-conservative thought appear not as the basic common sense which its advocates purport but as a revolutionary doctrine that rips apart the social contract that held nations together in an earlier era.[29] Stephen Clarkson views neo-conservative economic doctrine as an ideology ("a body of ideas with the power to move adherents to political action") masquerading as an objective science of society. The literature written by economists about free trade is characterized by a "missionary aura" and a "proselytizing zeal."[30] "The radically simplified assumptions about human behaviour, the biases against politics, and the ahistorical perspectives" of the literature take on more than purely academic implications because of the increased political power of economic analysis.[31] Neo-conservatism in the academy and in the corridors of power is mutually reinforcing. The fact that economic analysts overlook important aspects of the debate on free trade – distributional implications, social dimensions, human costs – justifies and legitimizes the absence of mechanisms to attend to these concerns in the free-trade agreements.

Apart from its critique of neo-conservatism, how does the tradition of the new Canadian political economy help us interpret the implications of changes in the North American and global economies? One of its major concerns has been Canada's relationship with the United States and Canada's role in the international economy. Considerable debate has occurred over the implications of Canada's international position for its domestic development. Early approaches to the issue drew on dependency theory – a radical critique of the global capitalist system that emerged in the 1960s as an explanation of Latin American "underdevelopment." Dependency theorists argued that the failure of independent economic development in the countries of the periphery was not primarily the result of internal factors; rather their dependence on the industrialized countries of the centre locked them into production of primary export commodities and drained them of their surplus. Canadians such as Kari Levitt and Daniel Drache compared Canada's plight to that of the Latin American economies because of similarities in levels of foreign investment, trade in resources, and relatively low levels of technological development and manufacturing capacity.

As Glen Williams points out, this perspective was open to attack because of its failure to explain the obvious differences between Canada and Third World countries, such as high wage levels and standards of living and the strength of liberal democracy and social programs, in contrast to highly exclusionary, authoritarian political systems, which are common in the South. Dependency theory itself has come under attack for its economic determinism, excessive focus on international forces, and insufficient attention to class structures.[32] Williams categorizes subsequent views of Canada as an "intermediary," an "advanced imperialist" nation, or, his own view, "as region within the centre."[33] Williams summarizes this final position as follows: "Indeed, when investment, production, and trade are considered, the Canadian economy may now be usefully conceptualized as a geographically large zone within the US economy. While itself regionally divided, this zone has until now maintained the capacity to reproduce its own unique social and political formations rooted in various popular and elite conceptions of a distinct Canadian nationality and culture."[34]

In this view, growing constraints on Canadian policy makers' capacity to define a nationalist alternative to continental economic integration result not only from economic ties with the United States but also "from the continentalist definitions of the Canadian national interest found both generally within civil society and especially among state elites."[35] The "Canada as region within the centre" position focuses on important factors such as politics, ideology, region, and class more than did the early dependency approach. Moreover, in the light of the growing gap between rich and poor in the world economy, it is clearly important to recognize the position of privilege that most Canadians enjoy.

How do the various theoretical approaches outlined above help us to interpret recent events in Canada? Because the FTA and NAFTA are based on neo-liberal economic principles and favour the interests of multinational corporations, they run directly against the logic of the new Canadian political economy. Nevertheless, political economists differ among themselves in their approaches to these agreements. In particular, various authors provide different pictures of the importance of free-trade agreements: are they a bang or a whimper in the process of national self-destruction?

Some political economists, particularly those who were active in the struggle against free trade, are vehement in their characterization of the FTA and NAFTA as watersheds in the history of the country. This position recalls the dependency perspective outlined above, which emphasizes the inevitability of economic stagnation for the weaker partner when it increases its integration with a stronger economic power. Mel Watkins points out the contradiction in the fact that Canada is told to follow free trade both when the United States follows free trade and when it ceases to do so; the contradiction, he says, "inheres in dependency and impotence." He continues: "If the point of the present scenario is to secure trade, what is the likelihood that it will also secure – that is, entrench – the nature of that trade, namely, Canada's status as a staple producer or resource hinterland. Our five-century history indicates that it is extremely difficult for Canada to break out of this pattern."[36]

In contrast, the "Canada as a region of the centre" perspective portrays the FTA and NAFTA in less dramatic terms. It underlines the evolution of domestic political forces in favour of continental integration and their interaction with political and economic leaders in the United States. Since Williams emphasizes the degree to which the Canadian economy had become integrated with the American as a result of the Auto Pact and GATT, he argues that the FTA did not play a decisive role in continental restructuring of North American production: "Rather than being the cataclysmic economic event of popular lore, it was little more than a marker on a much longer road."[37] Leo Panitch also rejects a dependency-style approach to NAFTA: "*This is not something imposed on the Canadian and Mexican states by American capital and state as external to the latter; rather it reflects the role adopted by the Mexican and Canadian states in representing the interests of their bourgeoisies and bureaucracies as these are already penetrated by American capital and administration.*"[38] Panitch thus depicts the FTA not as a new chapter but as "the punctuation mark on a very long historical sentence of economic and cultural integration with American capitalism."[39]

The real importance of the FTA and NAFTA relative to broader processes of globalization lies not so much in their economic impact on levels of trade and investment but in their political implications. Both the Mulroney and Salinas regimes were already committed to economic liberalization and continental integration, so trade and investment barriers would have come down with or without the FTA and NAFTA. Signing trade agreements, however, entrenched these reforms and made it very difficult for future governments to backtrack on them. Ricardo Grinspun and Robert Kreklewich thus argue that free-trade agreements "serve as 'conditioning frameworks' to promote and consolidate neoliberal restructuring. Both the negotiation and the implementation of an FTA modify the conditions under which economic and social decision making is conducted domestically. The FTA may come before or after the process of restructuring – depending on whether its main role is to promote (as in Canada), or consolidate (as in Mexico) the neoliberal transformation. The disturbing implication of these FTAs is that they preclude progressive alternatives."[40]

The FTA and NAFTA were also important as symbols of the political right's possession of a concrete and apparently pragmatic economic program. In contrast, the opposition to the agreements seemed committed to economic nationalist measures widely seen as unviable in an age of large government deficits and globalization. It appeared to lack a forward-looking, alternative project.

This emphasis on the politics of trade reflects the major point of difference between political economists and neo-classical economists – namely, the degree to which globalization and regionalization and the decline of the nation-state are inevitable. Political economists insist that social choice is still possible. In her study of national investment policies in the three major countries of North America, Barbara Jenkins insists that the current economic restructuring is indeed highly political. It is bound to lead to serious political disputes unless appropriate adjustment measures are put into place: "despite the current emphasis on market forces and globalization, the need for effective national and subnational state policies is greater than ever."[41] While important new institutional barriers exist for new policies to regulate capital, these can be overcome as long as there is political will: "Thus, Canada's ability to intervene in this area is as much a reflection of the balance of political and institutional forces as it is of Canada's constrained position as a continental partner of the United States."[42]

Laxer similarly insists that "the most profound error we can make is to believe that we are going to live in a borderless world, with the state put into retirement. The state remains central to how things will turn out."[43] Though some weapons available to states are now obsolete, new ones are being developed. The Conservative government made a fatal mistake in forming a regional pact with the United States – a declining economy – especially since the terms of the FTA prevent Canada from adopting an industrial policy that would permit it to compete with the Americans. In his view, abrogation is the only viable way of avoiding this trap and adopting an alternative strategy that would truly make Canadian industry internationally competitive. This strategy would involve screening of foreign investment, performance standards for multinationals in strategic industries, heavy investment in education, social programs and infrastructure, and a more fair and progressive system of taxation.[44]

These arguments for an industrial strategy do not differ significantly from social democrats' traditional commitment to economic nationalism. From a Marxist perspective, Panitch denounces such attempts at "grabbing hold of the bourgeoisie's hand and trying to run faster and faster to match the pace of changes set by contemporary capitalism." Instead, he argues, the left should be concerned less about adapting to capitalist change than about "developing the capacity to mobilise more broadly and effectively *against* the logic of competitiveness and profit in order eventually *to get somewhere else*, that is, to an egalitarian, cooperative and democratic social order beyond capitalism."[45] Panitch attacks not only attempts to create a more competitive form of capitalism in Canada but also recent proposals by authors such as Perry Anderson and David Held that the left too must become globalized and compete with capital on the terrain of "global civil society," since capital has become internationally mobile. According to Panitch, this position suffers from two problems. It both overestimates the extent to which nation-states were capable of controlling capital in an earlier era and ignores the role of states as authors of the process of globalization, which is primarily about reorganizing, rather than by-passing states: "It promotes, in this sense, a false dichotomy between national and international struggles and diverts attention from the Left's need to develop its own strategies for transforming the state, even as a means of developing an appropriate international strategy."[46] For Panitch, the prime locus of socialist struggle remains the nation-state, though opposition to contemporary forms of capitalism will not succeed unless it occurs in more than one country.

GLOBALIZING POLITICAL ECONOMY – ALTERNATIVE PERSPECTIVES

As reviewed above, the political economy tradition helps us understand current changes in Canada's foreign economic policies. The concerns that have until recently dominated its treatment of Canada's role in the international political economy, however, tend to foreclose a number of issues that are now becoming more important. The typically Canadian preoccupation with "placing" ourselves within a given hierarchy of world power (near the top, the middle, or the bottom) has led to a rather static and parochial line of analysis. The analyst's glance has rapidly shifted away from the global system towards Canada's position within that system and its effects on levels of industrialization, the nature of the indigenous capitalist class, Canadian culture, and so on. Instead of providing a detailed examination of the nature of power in the international economy and its changing shape, writers were primarily concerned with describing Canada's relationship with the United States.

This emphasis was understandable in the 1960s, when U.S. hegemony appeared uncontested. In an era of multiple challenges to the economic power of the United States and its capacity or willingness to set the rules of the game, this singular focus on the bilateral relationship is unsatisfactory (even if Canada's own integration with the United States is increasing).[47] For example, U.S. motivations in pursuing free-trade agreements with both Canada and Mexico cannot be understood outside the broader economic context. Nor can the future directions of the regional trading bloc – whether towards a closed, protectionist "Fortress North America" or greater liberalization of the world economy and trade and investment among the three major trading blocs (Europe, North America, and Asia).

While the left is still licking wounds suffered in the struggles against the FTA and NAFTA, the Canadian state's international economic program continues apace. Moves are afoot to include other states in Latin America – Chile is the next candidate – within an expanded NAFTA, based on its accession clause. The Uruguay Round of GATT incorporated many areas – such as trade in services and intellectual property rights – that were part of NAFTA. It also put in place a new World Trade Organization (WTO) to replace GATT. The WTO will create a stronger institutional apparatus than GATT and will attempt to build bridges with the regional agreements such as the European Union and NAFTA.[48] A narrow focus on Canada's bilateral relationship with the United States and on the need for abrogation of the FTA and NAFTA ignores the extent to which the commitments undertaken in those agreements are increasingly incorporated within other multilateral forums.

Moreover, in an era of globalization, typical Canadian political economy concerns about integration and calls for greater independence seem at the same time less unique and to a certain extent outmoded. Canada may well have special vulnerabilities in the new global economy because of its low levels of technological innovation and the continued dominance of staples in its trading profile. As we have seen, the increased concentration and mobility of capital have created real challenges to all countries. In particular, globalization calls into question traditional conceptions about the role of the nation-state and the importance of state sovereignty.

As Rianne Mahon puts it, despite debates within the new Canadian political economy about the nature of the Canadian state ("instrumentalist" versus "structuralist"), both sides "shared a sense that the struggle for change was a struggle that would take place within *national* boundaries – with greater or lesser room for provincially-based strategies."[49] This left-nationalist posture included the following assumptions: "the importance of industrial or technological 'sovereignty' to the struggle for independence and socialism; the centrality of class or class alliances forged on the basis of a common national interest to explanations of, and efforts to transform, Canada's position within the global economy; and the critical role played by the national (and/or provincial) state in reproducing or challenging the status quo."[50] This sense of space was derived from assumptions inherited from nineteenth-century European conceptions of the bounded nature of nation-states.

Though Panitch criticizes social democratic solutions, he shares the perspective that the nation-state is still the prime actor in the international system and that oppositional strategies must be located primarily at this level: "[G]lobal class interpenetrations and contradictions needed to be understood in the context of specificities of the nation state's continuing central role in organising, sanctioning and legitimising class domination within capitalism." Instead of a global civil society, Panitch advocates a series of nationally based movements, which may influence each other and which, he hopes, "will as far as possible be solidarisitic with one another, even though international solidarity movements cannot be taken for alternatives, rather than as critical supplements, to the struggles that must take place on the terrain of each state." Panitch identifies the role of nation-states in implementing globalizing reforms and the rather romantic nature of calls for a global civil society.[51] By insisting on the primacy of domestic class relations and the role of nation-states, however, he forecloses on alternative lines of thought and action. While reforms are necessarily undertaken by individual states, their simultaneous enactment on a global level has a cumulative and synergistic effect. The whole thus becomes more than the sum of its parts. Panitch does recognize a role for international solidarity but poses it as secondary in significance to purely domestic strategies, and it is unclear in what ways distinct national struggles may influence each other.

Both social democratic and Marxist solutions thus remain fixed on the idea of the nation-state as prime location for democratic struggle. More recent economic, cultural, and environmental trends have opened up debate over these assumptions, leading to different positions on the part that the nation-state can and should play and on its continued identification as the main agent of progressive transformation of society. In place of old attachments to crumbling categories such as state sovereignty, Rianne Mahon adopts the postmodern approach suggested by Edward Soja, who defines space as "a configuration of differentiated and hierarchically organized locales" in which centres of power at the local, national, and supranational level interact in a complex and dynamic way. According to Mahon, this perspective "helps open up new strategic horizons by rendering visible the multiplicity of sites of action that have simultaneously to be considered."[52] Such an approach retains a theoretical openness about the source of the problems and the level at which opposition to corporate strategies may be deployed at any given moment.

The need to think about space in a new way has become particularly urgent since Mexico's inclusion within NAFTA. The incorporation of an underdeveloped country within the continental trading agreement raises difficult new issues for Canadians not adequately addressed within the political economy tradition. Canadian opponents of NAFTA have responded to Mexico's inclusion in two ways. There is a protectionist instinct to denounce the loss of Canadian jobs to Mexicans willing (or forced) to work for much lower wages. Another tendency is to argue that the agreement is a pure expression of corporate interests, equally damaging to the popular classes in both Canada and Mexico. This perspective reflects a dependency-theory approach that equates Canada's economic problems with those of Third World countries. While there are good reasons to believe that economic liberalization will not improve the lot of most Mexicans, this position ignores Canada's ranking towards the top of the global hierarchy of wealth and power.[53] As a result, it cannot be assumed that the interests of working people in Canada and Mexico entirely coincide.

The trinational coalition composed of labour unions, environmentalists, women's groups, farmers' unions, and so on that fought against NAFTA is an example of the possibilities as well as the limitations of transnational responses to economic restructuring. Social movements from all three countries felt the need to join forces just as corporate elites did in promoting the continental accord. Both the Canadian and Mexican political systems permitted little effective domestic opposition once the governments had decided to pursue a trade agreement. The U.S. congressional system, however, provided greater opportunities for lobbying and publicity. Participants were disappointed with the results (the ineffective "side deals" on the environment and labour rights), but shifting the terrain of struggle did permit more influence than was available without joint action. Trinational links also allowed participants from Canada and the United States to learn about the distinct concerns of activists in Mexico.

Mexicans were worried that opposition to NAFTA might provoke racist reactions in the United States.[54] One Canadian participant, Sandra Sorenson, admits that during their initial contacts with Mexicans, Canadians were very strident in calling for Canada's abrogation of the FTA, while the Mexicans were looking for political space within the

NAFTA process. According to Sorenson, "At times, Canadians have been quick to talk, slow to listen, partly because of the urgency with which people wanted to tell their story. At first, we wanted Mexicans to learn the lessons we had learned through the FTA. Well, gradually we came to understand that Mexico had already been through it, and were sort of welcoming us to reality."[55]

While Mexican activists and academics have many reservations about the hyper-liberal nature of NAFTA, the abject failure of the earlier nationalist economic model has made this type of solution politically unviable. Mexicans thus tend to promote more egalitarian forms of trading agreements rather than retreat to inward-looking development strategies.[56] Canadian left-nationalist solutions fail to respond to demands from Mexico and other Third World countries for renegotiation of the rules of the current international economic system, which favours countries in the North.

In addition to being criticized for its limitations in defining relevant spaces and strategic actors, the political economy tradition has come under attack for paying insufficient attention to non-class identities such as gender, race, and ethnicity and how they interact with class. To date, these concerns have been directed largely at the analysis of domestic political relations, rather than of Canada's foreign economic policies. Globalization, however, is not a gender-neutral process. Marjorie Cohen's path-breaking study predicted that the FTA would have a disproportionate impact on women, who tended to work in low-wage, labour-intensive "declining industries" such as textiles, which were threatened by the agreement. In contrast, Pat Armstrong argues that globalization and "flexibilization" of the workforce have made women's and men's work more similar, not because of an improvement in women's position, but "because fewer people of both sexes have a choice about the kinds of paid work they take and because more of the jobs are 'bad jobs'. Job insecurity, less union representation, less opportunity for promotion or skill development, lower wages, more unemployment and underemployment [have] come with globalization."[57]

As I argue elsewhere along with Christina Gabriel, there are many similarities in the effects of economic integration on the lives of women in both Canada and Mexico. In both countries, for example, women have unequal access to resources, their participation in economic activities is largely governed by the sexual division of labour within the household, their work in reproduction and production is undervalued, and gender underpins definitions of skill.[58] In each country, however, gender differences also interact with differences of class, race, and ethnicity. Mexican women's views of NAFTA are affected both by their position within the international political economy, which is very different from that of Canadian women, and by their relationship with a semi-authoritarian state. As Chandra Mohanty suggests, shared interests between women in the North and South cannot be assumed but must be developed on the basis of long-term dialogue and negotiation.[59]

CONCLUSION

It has become impossible for Canadians to ignore the changes occurring in the international economy. For example, the Purple Book released by Liberal Finance Minister Paul Martin in October 1994, titled "A New Framework for Economic Policy," argues that all economies are being shaped by three fundamental economic trends: "(1) rapid evolution toward a globally integrated economy based on market principles; (2) the emergence of highly dynamic economies in what used to be called the Third World, and (3) a revolution in technology, based on the microchip and related innovations, that has put knowledge and information at the cutting edge of economic progress."[60] All domestic policy issues, such as employment policy and social policy, are subordinated to the seemingly ineluctable demands of the international market.

Political economists have raised fundamental questions about the inevitability of this process and the implications of further embrace of economic liberalization for the Canadian economy. The world, however, has changed, and political economy must also adapt. The parochial elements of Canadian political economy must be replaced by greater internationalism. In particular, the assumptions that the nation-state is necessarily the major tool for progressive change, and that democratic struggles must centre on the state, must be re-evaluated. As well, in an era of globalization, Canadian political economists must take into account both in their analyses and in their strategies Canada's privileged position vis-à-vis other countries. The appropriate level of resistance to the globalization of capital (whether local, national, regional, or global) cannot be decided by theoretical fiat but must be approached flexibly. Any rethinking of strategy must incorporate attention to the intersections of race, ethnicity, and gender. As well, criticisms of the impact of economic integration inside must be balanced by attention to the fate of the large proportion of the world's population located outside the islands of privilege in North America, Europe, and Asia, which are increasingly cut off from foreign investment and aid.

NOTES

1 Francis, *A Matter of Survival*, 8–10.
2 Laxer, *False God*, 3.
3 I do not deal specifically with Canada's development policies. For a critical perspective on Canada's relations with the Third World, see Macdonald, "Unequal Partnerships," 111–41.
4 Drache and Gertler, "Preface," xi.
5 Ohmae, *The Borderless World*, x.
6 Ibid., x.
7 Bienefeld, "Financial Deregulation," 347–70.
8 For different perspectives on hegemony, see Keohane, *Neorealism and Its Critics*; Kennedy, *The Rise and Fall of the Great Powers*; and Cox, *Power, Production and World Order.*
9 Williams, "Canada," 30.
10 Stacey, *Canada and the Age of Conflict*, 135–45. See also Sara Jeanette Duncan's 1904 novel *The Imperialist* for a contemporary account of the idealist fervour of the imperialist cause in early twentieth century small-town Ontario.
11 Granatstein, "Free Trade," 11–55.
12 Brodie, "The Political Economy of Regionalism," 149–50.
13 Brodie, *The Political Economy of Canadian Regionalism*, 216.
14 Ibid., 149–51.
15 Ruggie, "International Regimes, Transactions, and Change." See also Black and Sjolander, "Canada in the Transition."
16 Plumptre, *Three Decades of Decision*, 31. See also Granatstein, *The Ottawa Men*, 139–53.
17 Ibid, 29.
18 Williams, *Not for Export*, 143–6.
19 Cutler and Zacher provide a useful critique of approaches that exaggerate Canada's commitment to multilateral forums and mechanisms in the introduction to their edited collection, *Canadian Foreign Policy and International Economic Regimes*, 3–16.
20 Clarkson, *Canada and the Reagan Challenge*, 6–7.
21 Brodie, *Regionalism*, 182–7.
22 Ibid., 187–8.
23 Clarkson, *Canada*, 29.
24 Grinspun, "The Economics of Free Trade in Canada," 105.
25 Quoted in Williams, *Not for Export*, 179.
26 Campbell, "Restructuring the Economy," 89.
27 Grinspun, "The Economics of Free Trade in Canada."
28 Grinspun and Cameron, "The Political Economy of North American Integration," 9.

29 See Polanyi, *The Great Transformation*.

30 Clarkson, "Economics," 62.

31 Ibid., 63.

32 Panitch, "Dependency and Class in Canadian Political Economy." As Williams also notes, Canadian political economists primarily drew upon the cruder versions of dependency theory which became popularized in English by writers such as Andre Gunder Frank, rather than more sophisticated versions that drew attention to the interaction between international and domestic structures, and left open the possibility of a form of "dependent development." For an example of the latter, see Cardoso and Faletto, *Dependency and Development in Latin America*.

33 Williams, "Canada in the International Political Economy," 126–33.

34 Ibid., 132. Williams also classifies the following authors under this position: Panitch, "Dependency and Class"; Laxer, "Foreign Ownership and Myths about Canadian Development" and "Class, Nationality and the Roots of the Branch Plant Economy"; and Clark-Jones, *A Staple State*.

35 Williams, "Canada," 132. See also *Not for Export*.

36 Watkins, *Madness and Ruin*, 79.

37 Williams, *Not for Export*, 162.

38 Panitch, "Globalisation and the State," 75.

39 Ibid., 77.

40 Grinspun and Kreklewich, "Consolidating Neoliberal Reforms," 34. For a similar approach, see Clarkson, "Constitutionalizing the Canadian American Relationship," 3–20.

41 Jenkins, *The Paradox of Continental Production*, x.

42 Ibid., 154.

43 Laxer, *False God*, 35.

44 Ibid., 130–2.

45 Panitch, "Globalisation and the State," 61.

46 Ibid., 63.

47 A major exception to this lack of attention to other dimensions of the global economy was the subschool of Canadian political economy concerned with describing Canada's relations with the Third World. However, the insights of its writers were rarely integrated into the mainstream of the new Canadian political economy.

48 Hart, *What's Next*, 44–5.

49 Mahon, "The 'New' Canadian Political Economy Revisited," 5.

50 Ibid., 9–10.

51 See Macdonald, "Globalising Civil Society?"

52 Mahon, "New Canadian Political Economy Revisited," 14.

53 Macdonald, "Canada and the New World Order," 40–54.

54 Foster, "The Canadian Case," 30.

55 Interview, Ottawa, March 1994.
56 For one proposal, see Castañeda and Heredia, "Another NAFTA," 78–91.
57 Armstrong, "The Feminization of the Labour Force."
58 Gabriel and Macdonald, "NAFTA, Women and Organizing in Canada and Mexico."
59 Mohanty, "Under Western Eyes."
60 *CCPA Monitor,* special issue, 3.

REFERENCES

Armstrong, Pat. "The Feminization of the Labour Force: Harmonizing Down in a Global Economy." In Isabella Bakker, ed., *Rethinking Restructuring: Gender and Change in Canada.* Toronto: University of Toronto Press, 1996.

Bienefeld, Manfred. "Financial Deregulation: Disarming the Nation State." In Jenson, Mahon, and Bienefeld, eds., *Production, Space, Identity,* 347–70.

Black, David, and Sjolander, Claire Turenne. "Canada in the Transition: Prospects for a Re-constituted Multilateralism." Paper prepared for Canadian Political Science Association, Ottawa, 6–8 June 1993.

Brodie, Janine. *The Political Economy of Canadian Regionalism.* Toronto: Harcourt Brace Jovanovich, 1990.

– "The Political Economy of Regionalism." In Wallace Clement and Glen Williams, eds., *The New Canadian Political Economy,* 138–59. Montreal: McGill-Queen's University Press, 1989.

Campbell, Bruce. "Restructuring the Economy: Canada into the Free Trade Era." In Grinspun and Cameron, eds., *Political Economy.*

Cardoso, Fernando Henrique, and Faletto, Enzo. *Dependency and Development in Latin America.* Berkeley: University of California Press, 1979.

Castañeda, Jorge G., and Heredia, Carlos. "Another NAFTA: What a Good Agreement Should Offer." In Ralph Nader et al., *The Case against NAFTA,* 78–91. San Francisco: Earth Island Press, 1993.

CCPA Monitor. Special Issue. Ottawa: Canadian Centre for Policy Alternatives, October 1994.

Clark-Jones, Melissa. *A Staple State: Canadian Industrial Resources in Cold War.* Toronto: University of Toronto Press, 1987.

Clarkson, Stephen. *Canada and the Reagan Challenge.* Toronto: James Lorimer & Company, 1982.

– "Constitutionalizing the Canadian-American Relationship." In Duncan Cameron and Mel Watkins, eds., *Canada under Free Trade,* 3–20. Toronto: James Lorimer & Co., 1993.

– "Economics: The New Hemispheric Fundamentalism." In Grinspun and Cameron, eds., *Political Economy.*

Cox, Robert W. *Power, Production and World Order: Social Forces in the Making of History*. New York: Columbia University Press, 1987.

Cutler, A. Claire, and Zacher, Mark W. "Introduction." *Canadian Foreign Policy and International Economic Regimes*. Vancouver: UBC Press, 1992.

Drache, Daniel, and Gertler, Meric S. "Preface." Drache and Gertler, eds., *The New Era of Global Competition: State Policy and Market Power*. Montreal and Kingston: McGill-Queen's University Press, 1991.

Foster, John. "The Canadian Case: A Participant's Reflections." Draft paper presented to the research seminar "Redefining Governance: The Transnationalization of Civic Participation in North America." Center for U.S.-Mexican Studies, University of California, San Diego, 17 March 1993.

Francis, Diane. *A Matter of Survival: Canada in the 21st Century*. Toronto: Key Porter Books, 1993.

Gabriel, Christina, and Macdonald, Laura. "NAFTA, Women and Organising in Canada and Mexico: Forging a 'Feminist Internationality.' " *Millennium*, 23, no. 3 (winter 1994), 535–62.

Granatstein, J.L. "Free Trade between Canada and the United States: The Issue that Won't Go Away." In D. Stairs and G. Winham, eds., *The Politics of Canada's Economic Relationship with the United States*, 11–55. Toronto: University of Toronto Press, 1985.

– *The Ottawa Men: The Civil Service Mandarins, 1935–1957*. Toronto: Oxford University Press, 1982.

Grinspun, Ricardo. "The Economics of Free Trade in Canada." In Grinspun and Cameron, eds., *Political Economy*, 105–21.

Grinspun, Ricardo, and Cameron, Maxwell A., eds. "The Political Economy of North American Integration: Diverse Perspectives, Converging Criticisms." In Grinspun and Cameron, eds., *Political Economy*, 3–23.

– eds. *The Political Economy of North American Free Trade*. New York: St Martin's Press, 1993.

Grinspun, Ricardo, and Kreklewich, Robert. "Consolidating Neoliberal Reforms: 'Free Trade' as a Conditioning Framework." *Studies in Political Economy*, 43 (spring 1994), 33–61.

Hart, Michael. *What's Next: Canada, the Global Economy and the New Trade Policy*. Ottawa: Centre for Trade Policy and Law, 1994.

Jenkins, Barbara. *The Paradox of Continental Production: National Investment Policies in North America*. Ithaca, NY: Cornell University Press, 1992.

Jenson, Jane, Mahon, Rianne, and Bienefeld, Manfred, eds. *Production, Space, and Identity: Political Economy Faces the 21st Century*. Toronto: Canadian Scholars' Press Inc. 1993.

Kennedy, Paul. *The Rise and Fall of the Great Powers: Economic Change and Military Conflict from 1500 to 2000*. New York: Random House, 1987.

Keohane, Robert. *Neorealism and Its Critics*. New York: Columbia University Press, 1986.

Laxer, Gordon. "Class, Nationality and the Roots of the Branch Plant Economy." *Studies in Political Economy*, 21 (autumn 1986), 7–56.

– "Foreign Ownership and Myths about Canadian Development." *Canadian Review of Sociology and Anthropology*, 22 no. 3 (Aug. 1985), 311–45.

Laxer, James. *False God: How the Globalization Myth Has Impoverished Canada*. Toronto: Lester, 1993.

Macdonald, Laura. "Canada and the New World Order." In Whittington and Williams, eds., *Canadian Politics in the 1990s*, 40–54.

– "Globalising Civil Society?: Interpreting International NGOs in Central America." *Millennium*, 23 no. 2 (summer 1994), 267–85.

– "Unequal Partnerships: The Politics of Canadian Relations with the Third World." *Studies in Political Economy*, 47 (summer 1995), 111–41.

Mahon, Rianne. "The 'New' Canadian Political Economy Revisited: Production, Space, Identity." In Jenson, Mahon, and Bienefeld, eds., *Production, Space, and Identity*, 1–21.

Mohanty, Chandra Talpade. "Under Western Eyes: Feminist Scholarship and Colonial Discourses." In Mohanty et al., eds. *Third World Women and the Politics of Feminism* 51–80. Bloomington: Indiana University Press, 1991.

Ohmae, Kenichi. *The Borderless World: Power and Strategy in the Interlinked Economy*. New York: Harper Business, 1990.

Panitch, Leo. "Dependency and Class in Canadian Political Economy." *Studies in Political Economy*, 6 (1981), 7–34.

– "Globalisation and the State." In Ralph Miliband and Leo Panitch, eds., *Socialist Register 1994*, 60–93. London: Merlin Books, 1994.

Plumptre, A.F.W. *Three Decades of Decision: Canada and the World Monetary System, 1944–75*. Toronto: McClelland and Stewart, 1975.

Polanyi, Karl. *The Great Transformation*. Boston: Beacon Press, 1957.

Ruggie, John. "International Regimes, Transactions, and Change: Embedded Liberalism in the Post-War Economic Order." *International Organization*, 36 (spring 1982), 379–415.

Stacey, C.P. *Canada and the Age of Conflict: A History of Canadian External Policies*. Vol. 2. Toronto: University of Toronto Press, 1981.

Watkins, Mel. *Madness and Ruin: Politics and the Economy in the Neoconservative Age*. Toronto: Between the Lines, 1992.

Whittington, Michael, and Williams, Glen, eds. *Canadian Politics in the 1990s*. 4th ed. Toronto: Nelson Canada, 1995.

Williams, Glen. "Canada in the International Political Economy." In Wallace Clement and Glen Williams, eds., *The New Canadian Political Economy* 116–37. Montreal: McGill-Queen's University Press, 1989.

– "Canada – the Case of the Wealthiest Colony." *This Magazine* (Feb.-March, 1976), 28–32.
– *Not for Export: Towards a Political Economy of Canada's Arrested Industrialization.* 3rd ed. Toronto: McClelland & Stewart, 1994.

9 Imag(in)ing Canadian Foreign Policy

MARK NEUFELD AND
SANDRA WHITWORTH

Canadian foreign policy encompasses a wide range of issues, from peacekeeping to testing of cruise missiles, from free-trade initiatives to Canadian participation in the G-7's efforts to coordinate the global capitalist economy. Consideration of even one of these issues in depth is beyond the limits of this chapter. Accordingly, we focus on the more general and fundamental question of what kind of overall vision has informed – and should inform – Canadian foreign policy.

Before turning to Canadian foreign policy, however, we should note the distinctiveness of the notion of political economy that informs our analysis. In its most general sense, what characterizes the approach of political economy is the insistence that the interrelationship of politics and economics is central to understanding the social realm. However, as a lens through which to view social and political phenomena, political economy can be understood in different ways. One may see its holistic emphasis as the best strategy for achieving an accurate representation of the world around us, thus conceiving it as the same in its goals – if not its methodology – as traditional social science.[1] Alternately, one can view it as a self-consciously critical discourse distinguished not by the quest for more "accurate representation" but by its orientation to political and social life, which differs qualitatively from that of traditional social science. The adequacy of its interpretations then becomes a function of their ability to inform radical practice oriented to changing the world in a way consistent with the goal of human emancipation – not just to study the world, but to change it.

It is this second understanding that informs the present discussion of Canadian foreign policy. And the contribution of one of Canada's pre-eminent critical political economists – Harold Innis – can serve here as a resource and inspiration, in at least three specific senses. First, in his work, Innis stressed the holistic nature of the approach of political economy, understood not only as the interrelationship of economics and politics but also as the interconnection of the various levels of human social interaction, from local, through national, to global. Second, Innis recognized the importance and role of ideas and ideologies in their interplay with material circumstances, allowing us to appreciate the active and non-reductive role played by ideas/ideologies in determining the course of public life,[2] and the fact that dominant ideas and ideologies are not neutral, but regularly serve the interest of power and privilege. Third, there is Innis's conception of the role to be played by engaged intellectuals, particularly visible in his admonition to those working in the academy that to them belongs the task of "questioning the pretensions of organized power."[3]

With this view of political economy in mind, we examine the Canadian foreign policy record in two steps. First, we review it through the lens of the perhaps-still-dominant conceptualization of Canada as a middle power, in conformity with the general tenets of liberal internationalism and functionalism. Second, we conceptualize it in terms of three images – "loyal ally," "loyal opposition," and "extra-parliamentary opposition." "Imaging" Canadian foreign policy in this way can help to promote both a more nuanced understanding of the role that the Canadian state has played on the world stage and a critical "imagining" of progressive alternatives. Such an imagining, moreover, is appropriate today, for many of the material underpinnings of Canada's middle-power role (most specifically, American hegemony) are in flux.

LIBERAL INTERNATIONALISM AND CANADA AS MIDDLE POWER

Little has been written about Canadian foreign policy decisions or analyses prior to the Second World War. As a British dominion, Canada's early involvement in foreign and diplomatic affairs followed strictly the norms and policies dictated by the British government. Indeed, Canada established the Department of External Affairs only in 1909, some forty-two years after Confederation.[4] In general, the BNA Act of 1867 remained "silent," as Kim Richard Nossal writes, on matters of foreign policy, not even indicating whether foreign policy was a matter of provincial or federal jurisdiction. As Nossal notes, the reason for the silence was simple: Canada was not considered sovereign in the normal sense, and it was assumed that matters of foreign policy would be addressed by the British state.[5]

It was only with the Statute of Westminster of 1931 that the Canadian government could sign its own treaties and act independently of the British House of Lords in a variety of matters, including that of foreign affairs.[6] That "independence," however, was not acted upon quickly, and except for its continued calls to be recognized as an independent state separate from Great Britain,[7] the Canadian government tended to accept the leading role of the British, following them, as Kenneth McNaught writes, "to war in 1939, just as we had 25 years before, in defence of policies in whose formation we had refused to participate."[8]

Whether or not it simply followed Britain's lead into the Second World War, Canada's massive involvement and its subsequent engagement with the creation of Western-based international institutions signalled at least a marginally different role for Canada in world affairs. For more pessimistic and critical observers, that role changed only in so far as Canada would, from the Second World War onwards, accept the policy directives not of Britain but of the United States.[9] For more optimistic, and mainstream, observers, this shift marked the beginning of Canada's autonomy in foreign policy. This section focuses on the latter accounts of Canadian foreign policy and returns to critiques below.

The most common themes found in any mainstream description of Canadian foreign policy are those of liberal internationalism and Canada's status as a middle power.[10] According to these notions, Canada has, since 1945, pursued the liberal internationalist objective of creating and supporting multilateral organizations, designed to coordinate an open international trading order, while simultaneously defending that order from external threats (the Soviet bloc). Moreover, it has done so in its capacity of middle power, through which it exercised significant influence over great powers such as the United States.

James Eayrs reports that the term "middle power" was first hinted at by Prime Minister King in an August 1944 statement to Parliament. "The simple division of the world between great powers and the rest," said King, "is unreal and even dangerous."[11] As he noted, other states in the world possessed "varying degrees" of power, with some not far below the great powers and others possessing "almost zero."[12] For Eayrs, and numerous other commentators, King's statements were part of the general effort within the government to find and defend a post-war role for Canada "commensurate with wartime stature."[13]

The liberal internationalist undertones of this vision were clarified by Secretary of State for External Affairs Louis St Laurent in his 1947

Gray Lecture.[14] As the first full-time foreign minister, St Laurent argued that Canada should be helping to create new international institutions as part of a larger effort to encourage nation-states to pursue economic progress, global stability, and peace.[15] Canada, with its influence in both the United States and Great Britain, he argued, could facilitate the emergence and creation of such institutions.

The conceptual underpinnings of this doctrine were known as "functionalism." Functionalism was the assumption, as John Holmes wrote, "that each nation should have responsibility appropriate to its particular capacities."[16] Thus states possessing superior military and economic capabilities were the great powers, whose function it was to lead the new postwar international system, while lesser powers, with few or no military and economic resources, were not considered influential. Middle powers such as Canada, however, occupied an intermediate position between the "strongest" and the "weakest" and could, by this view, exert a certain amount of influence on great powers while organizing the lesser powers into coalitions around particular issues.

Commitments to liberal internationalism, functionalism, and middle-powermanship[17] were put into action through a number of policy measures. Lester Pearson, Prime Minister St Laurent's secretary of state for external affairs, became a central contributor to the workings of the United Nations and the establishment of NATO.[18] The Canadian government also supported creation of the International Monetary Fund and the International Bank for Reconstruction and Development (IBRD, or more popularly, the World Bank), as well as the General Agreement on Tariffs and Trade (GATT), and participated in the United Nations Educational, Scientific and Cultural Organization (UNESCO), the International Labour Organization (ILO), and many others. Canadian delegates and foreign policy pronouncements both supported the creation of these new institutions and worked to ensure that they would not be dominated by the great powers.[19]

Canada's support for the postwar order ranged from unobtrusive efforts "behind the scenes" to occasional, outspoken criticism of actions or policies considered inimical to the interests of the Western alliance as a whole. The Diefenbaker government serves as a good example in this regard. On the one hand, it was generally willing to play its part in the construction of the postwar global order. In 1957, for example, John Diefenbaker agreed to the North American Air Defense Agreement (NORAD), signalling initially a continued close relationship with the United States.

On the other hand, Diefenbaker was not unwilling to break with the Americans when larger issues made it necessary. For example, after

American surveillance planes discovered intercontinental ballistic missile (ICBM) silos being constructed in Cuba in October 1962, ten days of "brinkmanship" politics brought the world closer to a nuclear confrontation than had been seen before or since.[20] Diefenbaker differed with the U.S. administration over the handling of the crisis and at first refused in cabinet to put the Canadian component of NORAD on alert, despite the urging of both the minister of defence and the United States.[21] While the prime minister eventually agreed, the delays foreshadowed the government's growing concern over accepting nuclear warheads on Canadian interceptor aircraft. Diefenbaker announced that Canada would not accept nuclear weapons while disarmament discussions continued.[22]

The government was defeated by Lester B. Pearson's Liberals, who promised in their election campaign to honour Canada's NATO commitments and accept nuclear warheads on Canadian planes and on Canadian soil.[23] Pearson had launched a major theme of Canadian foreign policy a decade earlier, support for United Nations peacekeeping missions, as an architect of UNEF I – the first UN peacekeeping effort, which lasted some eleven years in the Suez.[24] The accomplishment had won him the Nobel Peace Prize. The peacekeeping innovation was prompted by a desire to regulate conflict among core members of the Western Alliance (Great Britain, France, and the United States) and was therefore quite consistent with middlepowermanship and liberal internationalism.

When he was prime minister, Canadian foreign policy was characterized by liberal, internationalist commitments, particularly "quiet diplomacy" – "behind-the-scenes" efforts to influence the Americans. In addition to making a commitment to accept nuclear warheads, the Liberals gave the United States full support in its Vietnam policy, from advocating the American view of fair negotiation conditions, through endorsing U.S. aims in Vietnam and selling the Americans military hardware, to providing the United States with intelligence on the situation in Vietnam.[25] This is not to say that the Pearson government was in full agreement with American activities in Southeast Asia; but, as Pearson wrote in response to anti–Vietnam war protestors: "Confidential and quiet arguments by a responsible government are usually more effective than public ones ... Too many public declarations and disclosures run the risk of complicating matters for those concerned ... The more complex and dangerous the problem, the greater is the need for calm and deliberate diplomacy."[26]

Ultimately, however, when quiet diplomacy failed to have the desired effect, Pearson adopted Diefenbaker's tactic of public criticism. In his April 1965 speech at Temple University, he suggested that a pause in the bombing of North Vietnam might solicit a more flexible response from Hanoi.[27] Pearson was both privately and publicly rebuked for the criticisms, considered especially inappropriate by President Lyndon Johnson because they were delivered when Pearson was a guest within the United States. Overall, however, the Liberals continued to be supportive of u.s. war aims.[28]

This mix of behind-the-scenes support and occasional public questioning – albeit, always within limits – is also recognizable in the Trudeau government. Like Pearson, Pierre Trudeau was willing to honour alliance "commitments" by supporting missile deployments in Europe and cruise missile testing at home. However, in the face of a nuclear build-up that exceeded any rational requirements, Trudeau used his final days in office to criticize nuclear-deterrence policy and to visit the heads of state of the nuclear club, urging them to supplement nuclear-force modernization with more effective arms control and arms reduction and to end the Cold War.[29]

The landslide victory of Brian Mulroney's Conservatives in 1984 initiated the reaffirmation of a close and supportive relationship with the United States. The new government welcomed American investment in Canada and free trade with the United States and publicly supported Ronald Reagan's Strategic Defence Initiative (more disparagingly known as "Star Wars").[30] It also pledged at the start to bring its defence priorities and spending more in line with u.s. expectations, though by 1993 it had closed Canada's NATO bases in Europe and shifted its NATO forward deployment forces into peacekeeping in the former Yugoslavia.[31]

The closing of bases and shift into peacekeeping were not simply a response to fiscal restraint. The end of the 1980s and the early 1990s saw some important changes within world politics – most dramatically, the collapse of the Soviet Union and the apparent end of the Cold War. Foreign and defence planners and analysts since then have been dealing with a new international landscape, in which the assumed tensions between East and West have been at least partly replaced by rising nationalistic tensions and the former bipolar balance between the United States and the Soviet Union has been replaced by an (again apparently) unipolar world, dominated by the United States. Janice Gross Stein observes, however, that no matter how much change has occurred already, Canadians are faced with an "international system that will in all likelihood continue to change at an even faster rate and in more complex ways than in the past."[32]

The Liberal government led by Jean Chrétien elected in 1993 responded to these changes by calling for a review of both foreign and defence policies. The resulting conclusions were mixed. On the one hand, one finds statements in support of Canada's traditional "selfless" foreign policy in the service of the "common interest." Recent government pronouncements note, for example, that while the end of the Cold War creates opportunities in global cooperation, it has simultaneously produced great uncertainty, which makes clear the need for prudent, multilateral management of the "new world order." Soviet-American conflict has given way to new sources of insecurity and concern, such as the vast movement of refugees, population pressures, and the rise of ethnic conflicts. This situation has led to an unprecedented demand for Canadian peacekeepers around the world. The image of Canada as peacekeeper par excellence informs media accounts and government statements and suits the role of Canada as middle power – acting, in the case of peacekeeping, as an interposition force between conflicting parties.[33] The rising demand for peacekeeping also serves well the Canadian defence establishment, providing an opportune justification for continued allocation of resources to the Canadian military.[34]

On the other hand, the government now suggests that the appropriate standard by which to measure Canada's conduct in foreign affairs is in terms of its domestic impact. Specifically, the government has announced that the first objective in foreign policy decisions must be the extent to which they promote prosperity and employment within Canada.[35] This apparent shift in emphasis has led some to speculate that the liberal, internationalist-inspired role of middle power has now been abandoned by the Chrétien government in much the same way as it has abandoned the traditional Liberal commitment to the welfare state.

BEYOND "MIDDLEPOWERMANSHIP"

Its dominant status in the interpretation of Canadian foreign policy notwithstanding, the liberal internationalist-inspired notion of middle power suffers from serious limitations. By framing the interpretation of Canadian policy in terms of the fixed nature of Canada's status (too small to be a great power, too big to be marginal) and the "objective" demands imposed by the global order (a "free world" requiring defence against communist aggression and expansion; a Liberal International Economic Order (LIEO) requiring multilateral management), middlepowermanship has too often appeared to be the only possible (read "rational") course of action. This in turn has had two negative consequences.

First, insufficient attention has been paid to the range of strategies encompassed by the practice of middlepowermanship. A more subtle account of Canadian foreign policy must be able to explain both quiet diplomacy and outspoken criticism. Even more critically, middle-power thinking has often served to render "out of bounds" any notion of Canada's playing a more progressive role on the global stage, not grounded in liberal-internationalist commitments.[36]

In order to explore alternative conceptualizations of Canadian foreign policy, we should first note the extent to which a revised notion of middlepowermanship can reveal important features of postwar Canadian conduct in world affairs. We must move beyond simple descriptive accounts of Canada's place in the world to its political practice, framed in terms of more analytical views of the global political economy. In this way, we can understand Canada's promotion of international institutions and its efforts to serve as interlocutor in conflicts, filling a role congruent with postwar maintenance of American hegemony.[37]

By "hegemony" we mean not simply dominance but rather the Gramscian notion of a major power's institutionalizing its dominance, rather than enforcing it. As Robert Cox writes: "The rules and practices and ideologies of a hegemonic order conform to the interests of the dominant power while having the appearance of a universal order of things which gives at least a certain measure of satisfaction and security to lesser powers. Such a hegemonic order rests ultimately upon superior force, but this force can most often remain in the background. The order does not usually need to be enforced by direct violence or threat of violence on the part of the founding power. Middle powers may play a supporting role in such a hegemonic order."[38]

The current changes faced by Canada and its new array of alternatives do not derive, by this view, strictly from the collapse of confrontation between East and West. Instead, this analysis looks to more fundamental shifts within the global political economy that have been taking place for more than two decades, and of which the collapse of the Soviet Union is only part. These developments include the disarray of the international monetary system from the early 1970s, oil shocks, inflation, reorganization of production and investment, labour segmentation and unemployment, declining faith in the "universalism" of American values, and debt crises.[39] Within this context of declining American hegemony, the role of middle powers is, at the very least, in flux.

This is an opportune moment to reassess the role of Canada in world affairs, in order both to provide a more nuanced picture of past practices and to present normative alternatives for future ones. We suggest reconceptualization of Canadian foreign policy within a tri-partite framework – of Canada as loyal ally, as loyal opposition, and as extra-parliamentary opposition.

Image I: Canada as Loyal Ally

The first image to be considered is that of "loyal ally." The geopoliti-cal reference point for this image is that of the Western Alliance – in the simplest terms, NATO and the Organization for Economic Cooper-ation and Development (OECD). In terms of this image, NATO was established in 1949, in the face of a military-political threat from the Soviet bloc, to defend Western freedom and democracy, understood to involve not only traditional political freedoms but economic ones as well ("free enterprise," free-market economies).

"Loyal ally" can best be understood by analogy with the position of a cabinet minister. In the British-style parliamentary system, the behav-iour of a minister is strictly regulated by the principle of cabinet soli-darity: a member may express disagreement with government policy only in private. In public, a minister must defend that policy, so as to present a united front to the opposition. A loyal minister is one who is loyal to the party and, above all, to its leader, who, as prime minister, holds the final word.

Extending this analogy to postwar Canadian foreign policy, Can-ada as a loyal ally is a cabinet minister serving in a government (the Western Alliance) led by a prime minster who holds the final word on government policy (the United States). Canada is free to express dis-agreement with alliance policy, but only behind closed doors. It is, above all, necessary to present a united front to the Opposition (the Soviet bloc).

The status of loyal ally need not entail being a "pushover," holding no independent views. On the contrary, disagreement is possible be-hind closed doors. Furthermore, in showing willingness vigorously to defend alliance policies once a decision has been taken, Canada, it can be argued, has established its reliability, enhancing its influence with regard to other alliance members and, most important, the U.S. gov-ernment. In this way, it is maintained, Canada can influence the global order in ways far out of proportion to its national capabilities.

The role of loyal ally can account for much of Canada's foreign pol-icy since 1945. There is considerable overlap between the image of Canada as loyal ally and the mainstream view of it as middle power. "Loyal ally" does not exhaust the notion of "middle power," however;

"middle power" defined exclusively as "loyal ally" cannot account for a small but important part of the historical record. It is, accordingly, necessary to supplement the two roles with that of loyal opposition.

Image II: Canada as Loyal Opposition

For some critics, the structuring of Canadian foreign policy in accordance with the role of loyal ally has resulted in serious liabilities. It is the result of conforming to the notion of loyal ally, they argue, that Canada has participated in and defended some rather ill-advised and even dangerous undertakings – for example, testing of the cruise missile.

Accordingly, these critics suggest that a second image guides Canada's foreign policy – loyal opposition.[40] Here the analogy is not to the cabinet but to the parliament as a whole, where the opposition is understood to be loyal directed not to the governing party but to the parliament as a whole (symbolized by the crown). Indeed, such loyalty demands that the opposition criticize the policies of the government of the day in as public a way as possible – forcing it to defend its policies in public – and that it vote against those policies if it concludes that they do not serve the public interest.

By analogy, the Western Alliance can be seen as the parliament, with the United States as the government of the day, and Canada as an opposition loyal not to the alliance leader (the United States) but to the alliance as a whole. Accordingly, Canada would publicly criticize u.s.-initiated policies and force the u.s. administration to defend and justify policies before they were adopted by the alliance as whole.

Would such an approach on the part of Canada undermine the alliance and its purpose? It can be countered that such an objection misunderstands the very purpose of the alliance. In the immediate postwar context, it was clear that only the United States could play the role of leader, provided that isolationist sentiments did not overwhelm its foreign policy, as they had after the First World War. There was, however, a concomitant fear that American policy makers might embark on a path of imprudent unilateralism. Accordingly, argue advocates, the Western Alliance was created as much to "control the Americans" as to "stop the Russians" – an insight that has been lost in many quarters. Thus for Canada to serve as loyal opposition would not undermine the alliance but revalorize the reason it was created in the first place.

As was noted above, a small but not insignificant fraction of the Canadian foreign policy record conforms to this image. One might list here the challenges to u.s. policies by Diefenbaker (on Cuba and

nuclear-weapons stockpiles on Canadian soil), Pearson (over unre-
mitting bombing of North Vietnam), and Trudeau (on nuclear-deterrence). Thus loyal opposition supplements the role of loyal ally.

From a critical perspective, this analysis remains inadequate. Oppositional behaviour remains dependent on – and supportive of – a hegemonic order that rests ultimately on willingness to employ technologies
of violence in the service of free-market economies (capitalism). It is
only to the extent that Canada remains usually loyal that it can have any
influence when it chooses to differ publicly from alliance policies. It
remains supportive of the hegemonic order even when it expresses
differences because its opposition does not challenge the fundamental
assumptions on which the pax Americana has been based. Indeed, Canada's willingness to criticize specific policies fulfills a legitimizing function, reinforcing the notion that the global order serves not the
parochial but the "universal interest." In sum, "loyal opposition" does
not go far enough in demarcating Canadian foreign policy from an
unjust and violence-prone status quo.

Thus the two images – loyal ally and loyal opposition – are in fact the
constitutive elements of the middlepowermanship. As two sides of the
same middle-power coin, however, they too narrowly restrict the role
that Canada could – and should – play. Accordingly, it is necessary to
extend our discussion to include a third image – Canada as extra-parliamentary opposition.

Image III: Canada as Extra-Parliamentary Opposition

Proponents of Canada as extra-parliamentary opposition (image III)
argue that the alternatives represented by the dominant players in the
"parliament" (Western Alliance) are too narrow to address the needs
of the marginalized majority. Accordingly, they urge Canada to align
itself with other actors in world politics – state and non-state – to
oppose the militarism and dependent development fostered by the
Western Alliance.

In parallel to the other two images, advocates argue that proper
understanding of the Western Alliance suggests the futility of working
for progressive change from within. NATO, they claim, was founded
not to stop the Russians or to control the Americans but to disem-
power progressive social forces. It was the fear of popularly elected
socialist governments in the late 1940s, particularly in Europe, where
conservatives and liberals had been tainted by their collaboration
with fascists, and the threat that such governments could pose to elite
business interests that led to creation of NATO and the OECD. The
Western Alliance has from the beginning thus been the cornerstone of

an American-led imperialist coalition, oriented to serving the interests of the rich and privileged.

The Canadian state, it is stressed, has actively participated in this project. It has sought and continues to seek to promote the interests of Canada's business elites. This fundamental determinant of Canadian foreign policy helps explain the seamier side of Canada's foreign-policy record – for example, its support for IMF "structural adjust-ment," despite its devastating consequences for the inhabitants of the South;[41] Canada's status as the seventh-largest arms supplier to Third World countries (many of which were engaged in a war or involved in human rights abuses);[42] and the reluctance of successive Canadian governments to criticize human-rights abuses – up to and including genocide – on the part of Third World governments with which Cana-dian business elites have strong economic ties.[43]

Like the other images, of course, this one can be criticized. Were it ever to guide policy it would probably lead even more than playing the role of loyal opposition, to retaliation from other members of the Western Alliance, as well as loss of influence with the United States. Undoubtedly the biggest obstacle facing adoption of this image in pol-icy circles, however, is the fact that Canada's foreign policy would change fundamentally only after a transformation of the structure of Canadian society as a whole. The image of extra-parliamentary opposi-tion runs counter not only to the interests of other members of the alliance but also to those of Canada's domestic economic and political elites.[44] In sum, Canada will take on that role on the world stage only when the extra-parliamentary opposition within Canada, born out of recent struggles around free trade, government cutbacks, and milita-rism,[45] effects fundamental change at home.

CONCLUSION

We have contrasted the traditional depiction of Canada as a middle power with images of Canada as loyal ally, loyal opposition, and extra-parliamentary opposition. The first two images can be used, in combi-nation to describe the historical record of Canadian foreign policy; the third remains a regulative ideal only. They all contain different norma-tive and political implications. Whereas the first two images prescribe very limited roles for the Canadian state in critiquing the existing international order, and indeed suggest that it is in Canada's interest to support an American-led "new world order," the third imagines the Canadian state using its influence not to maintain the system but to help to transform it.

This last image, of course, is the one that we prefer. How real are the possibilities that it will be actualized? There are reasons, as there always are, to be pessimistic. As noted above, only dramatic changes within Canadian society would allow the state to become an extra-parliamentary opposition within the international system. All evidence from the most recent foreign policy and defence reviews suggests exactly the opposite: the Department of National Defence has found new rationales for maintenance of a combat-ready Canadian Armed Forces (such as refugees, the rise of ethnic conflict, and the proliferation of nuclear weapons); and the Department of Foreign Affairs has argued that all foreign policy decisions must promote prosperity at home and competitiveness internationally. Neither of these principles lends itself to a transformative politics.

At the same time, the present context presents an opportunity to engage the wider public in serious consideration of this option. As noted above, the political elite's abandonment of even the modestly progressive dimensions associated with the notion of middle power parallels its accelerating abandonment of the commitment to the welfare state. It is easier now than it has been for some time to see connections between a domestic (and a global) society in which the interests of the few take precedence over those of the many and a state policy apparatus committed to maintaining the status quo in both contexts. Arguments in support of radical change in state policies – domestic and foreign – may thus appear more compelling.

In conclusion, the new political economy, from Innis forward, has made us aware of the degree to which material interests help explain political phenomena. A concern with the material, however, need not – indeed, should never – preclude paying attention to the role of ideas in political life.[46] Dominant ideas, which narrow the scope for political action and change, immunize established power and privilege from serious criticism. To the degree that we are unable to conceive of alternative ways of structuring our political-economic arrangements, to the degree that we are unable to *imagine* different ways of living, the given order is reinforced.

Nowhere is this more true than in Canadian foreign policy. Liberal-internationalist commitments and middle-power strategies have so monopolized thinking that fundamental questioning of Canada's role in the world has been made all but impossible. Accordingly, "imaging" Canada's foreign policy past and future in a more differentiated way is a crucial first step in the process of "imagining" possibilities for radical change in Canada's foreign and domestic political-economic arrangements.

NOTES

We wish to acknowledge the support of the Social Sciences and Humanities Research Council in the preparation of this chapter.

1 So conceived, political economy would qualify as a form of "traditional theory." See Max Horkheimer, "Traditional."

2 See Di Norcia, "Communications."

3 Innis, "The Canadian Situation," unpublished address (mimeo), 8–9, quoted in Neill, *Work*, 235–6.

4 Granatstein, "Introduction," 1–2.

5 Even the Constitution Act of 1982 remains silent on assigning authority for foreign affairs. This silence in 1982 was more complex; as Nossal notes, more important issues took precedence in constitutional deliberations, and the intervening history had set a number of precedents that could not be overruled easily. The result is that Canada is unusual in many respects, with subnational governments taking action on occasion in international affairs. Quebec has exercised this right more than most provinces and has seen that right closely linked to its special status within confederation and its aspirations towards nationhood. For a detailed account of the provincial role in foreign policy decisions and issues, see Nossal, *Politics*, chap. 9.

6 Granatstein, "Introduction," 2.

7 Nossal, *Politics*, 46.

8 McNaught, "Colony," 175.

9 Ibid., 175.

10 On the preoccupation with "place/location" in the Canadian foreign policy literature see Molot, "Where?" For a review of the literature that examines the decision-making process – a theme that is not our focus here – see Black and Smith, "Notable?"

11 Quoted in Eayrs, "Defining," 19.

12 Ibid.

13 Ibid.

14 Dewitt and Kirton, *Canada*, 48.

15 Ibid., 49. See also Dewitt and Brown, "Canada's," 6.

16 Holmes, *Better*, 7.

17 The term "middlepowermanship" was coined by John Holmes and was meant at least in part to be an ironic contrast with notions such as "brink-manship" and "one-upmanship" – forms of diplomacy practised by great powers. See Cox, "Middlepowermanship," 824, and Nossal, *Politics*, 50.

18 Ibid., 5.

19 Dewitt and Kirton, *Canada*, 51; Nossal, *Politics*, 48–9.

20 For a general account of the Cuban Missile Crisis, see Allison, *Essence*.

21 Granatstein, "Cooperation," 52.

22 Ibid., 56.

23 Ibid., 56–9.

24 Jockel, *Canada*, 12 and passim for a general introduction to Canada's involvement in peacekeeping operations.

25 Unlike its position on putting nuclear weapons on Canadian planes in Europe and on Canadian soil, in terms of Vietnam policy, the Liberals did not differ markedly from their Conservative predecessors. Taylor, *Snow*, 185 and passim; James Steele, "Canada's," 71–2 and passim; Holmes, "Canada," 184.

26 Cited from McNaught, "Colony," 177.

27 Granatstein, "Cooperation," 62.

28 As J.L. Granatstein writes: "[The Liberals] were willing to tweak tail-feathers, but not on vital questions. Pearson could complain about the Americans' Vietnam adventure in public and private, but he was still willing to act as an intermediary between Hanoi and Washington, conveying President Johnson's tough messages." Granatstein, "Introduction," 3.

29 His efforts became known as the "Trudeau Peace Initiative." See Dewitt and Brown, "Canada's," 8.

30 Michael K. Hawes, "Canada-u.s.," 195–6.

31 Ibid. 196; Dewitt and Brown, "Canada's," 9.

32 Janice Gross Stein, "Ideas," 40.

33 Jockel, *Canada*, chap. 1 and 2, passim.

34 For an excellent analysis of the "benefits" derived from peacekeeping by the Canadian military, see Dale, "Guns," passim. That the demand for peacekeeping serves as a convenient rationale for continued and increased military spending is illustrated well by Joseph Jockel's claim that the beating death of Somali teenager Shidane Arone by members of the Canadian Airborne Regiment happened because the army sent an unfit unit to Somalia, "squeezed [as it was] by its personnel shortage." By implication, properly trained soldiers would not commit such an act (Jockel, *Canada*, 33). Jockel's work is a thinly veiled lobbying piece, the publication of which was timed to coincide with the 1994 Defence Review.

35 Canada, *Canada and 1994*.

36 This is not to suggest that there have been no alternative accounts of Canadian foreign policy beyond that of Canada as middle power; rather, that the middle power notion has dominated. Though we do not follow this categorization (but use some of the literature found within it), analytical debates concerning Canada's foreign policy often focus on three views: Canada as middle power, as satellite, and as principal power. For a review of these approaches see Dewitt and Kirton, *Canada*, chap. 1; Nossal, *Politics*, chap. 3; and Hawes, *Principal*, passim.

37 See also Neufeld, "Hegemony."

38 Cox, "Middlepowermanship," 825–6.

39 Ibid., 829–33.

40 The fact that their work is suggestive of Canada as loyal opposition is not to say, of course, that these critics define themselves or their views in the exact terms used here. For examples of writings critical of Canadian foreign policy that, in our opinion, fit within that tradition, see the pieces in Regehr and Rosenblum, eds., *Canada*. See also Langille, *Changing*. Significantly, advocates of the loyal-opposition stance are referred to by some loyal-ally proponents as the "responsible wing" of the peace movement.

41 On this and other issues of Canada-South relations, see Swift and Tomlinson, eds., *Conflicts*.

42 David Todd, "Canada."

43 The case of Indonesia's genocidal policies in East Timor is perhaps the best example, though certainly not an isolated one.

44 For an analysis of the extent to which foreign and defence policy elites ignored "alternative" conceptualizations in the recent foreign and defence reviews, see Lawson, "Construction," and Whitworth, "Women."

45 See, for example, Pratt's notion of an emerging "counter-consensus" on foreign policy issues in his, "Dominant."

46 See, for example, Drache and Clement, "Introduction."

REFERENCES

Allison, Graham T. *Essence of Decision: Explaining the Cuban Missile Crisis.* Boston: Little Brown, 1971.

Black, David R., and Smith, Heather A. "Notable Exceptions? New and Arrested Directions in Canadian Foreign Policy Literature." *Canadian Journal of Political Science*, 26 no. 4 (Dec. 1993), 745–74.

Canada. *Canada in the World: Government Statement.* Ottawa: Government of Canada, 1995.

– *1994 Defence White Paper.* Ottawa: Government of Canada, 1994.

Cox, Robert W. "Middlepowermanship, Japan and Future World Order." *International Journal*, 44 (autumn 1989), 823–62.

Dale, Stephen. "Guns n' Poses: The Myths of Canadian Peacekeeping." *This Magazine*, 26 (March–April 1993), 11–16.

Dewitt, David B., and Brown, David Leyton. "Canada's International Security Policy." In David B. Dewitt and David Leyton Brown, eds., *Canada's International Security Policy*, 1–27. Scarborough: Prentice Hall Canada Inc., 1995.

Dewitt, David B., and Kirton, John J. *Canada as a Principal Power: A Study in Foreign Policy and International Relations.* Toronto: John Wiley and Sons, 1983.

Di Norcia, Vincent. "Communications, Time and Power: An Innisian View." *Canadian Journal of Political Science*, 23 no. 2 (June 1990), 335–57.

Drache, Daniel, and Clement, Wallace "Introduction: The Coming of Age of Canadian Political Economy." In D. Drache and W. Clement, eds., *The New Practical Guide to Canadian Political Economy*, ix–xxiv. Toronto: James Lorimer, 1985.

Eayrs, James. "Defining a New Place for Canada in the hierarchy of World Power." *International Perspectives* (May–June 1975).

Granatstein, J.L. "Cooperation and Conflict: The Course of Canadian-American Relations since 1945." In C.F. Doran, ed., *Forgotten Partnership: U.S.-Canada Relations Today*, 45–68. Baltimore: Johns Hopkins University Press, 1984.

– "Introduction." In J.L. Granatstein, ed., *Canadian Foreign Policy: Historical Readings*, 1–4. Toronto: Copp Clark Pitman, Ltd., 1993.

Hawes, Michael K. "Canada-U.S. Relations in the Mulroney Era: How Special the Relationship?" In Brian Tomlin and Maureen Appel Molot, eds., *Canada among Nations*, 189–253. Toronto: James Lorimer and Company, 1989.

– *Principal Power, Middle Power, or Satellite? Competing Perspectives in the Study of Canadian Foreign Policy.* North York, Ont.: Centre for International and Strategic Studies, York University, 1984.

Holmes, John. "Canada and the Vietnam War." In J.L. Granatstein and R.D. Cuff, eds., *War and Society in North America*, 184–99. Toronto: Thomas Nelson and Sons, 1971.

Holmes, John W. *The Better Part of Valour.* Toronto: McClelland and Stewart, 1970.

Horkheimer, Max. *Critical Theory: Selected Essays.* New York: Continuum, 1989.

Jockel, Joseph T. *Canada and International Peacekeeping.* Washington. DC: Center for Strategic and International Studies, 1994.

Langille, Howard Peter. *Changing the Guard: Canada's Defence in a World of Transition.* Toronto: University of Toronto Press, 1990.

Lawson, Bob. "Construction of Consensus: The 1994 Canadian Defence Review." In Maxwell Cameron and Maureen Appel Molot, eds., *Canada among Nations: Foreign Policy and Democracy*, 99–117. Ottawa: Carleton University Press, 1995.

McNaught, Kenneth. "From Colony to Satellite." In Stephen Clarkson, ed., *An Independent Foreign Policy for Canada?*, 173–83. Toronto: McClelland and Stewart, 1968.

Molot, Maureen Appel. "Where Do We, Should We, or Can We Sit? A Review of Canadian Foreign Policy Literature." *International Journal of Canadian Studies*, 1–2 (spring–fall 1990), 77–96.

Neill, Robert. "The Work of Harold Adams Innis: Content and Context." PhD thesis, Duke University, 1967.

Neufeld, Mark. "Hegemony and Foreign Policy Analysis: The Case of Canada as Middle Power." *Studies in Political Economy*, 48 (autumn 1995), 7–29.

Nossal, Kim Richard. *The Politics of Canadian Foreign Policy.* 2nd éd. Toronto: Prentice-Hall Canada, Inc., 1989.

Pratt, Cranford. "Dominant Class Theory and Canadian Foreign Policy: The Case of the Counter-Consensus." *International Journal*, 39 (winter 1983–84), 99–135.

Regehr, Ernie, and Rosenblum, Simon, eds. *Canada and the Nuclear Arms Race.* Toronto: James Lorimer, 1983.

Steele, James. "Canada's Vietnam Policy: The Diplomacy of Escalation." In Stephen Clarkson, ed., *An Independent Foreign Policy for Canada?*, 69–81. Toronto: McClelland and Stewart, 1968.

Stein, Janice Gross. "Ideas, Even Good Ideas, Are Not Enough: Changing Canada's Foreign and Defence Policies." *International Journal*, 50 (winter 1994–95), 40–70.

Swift, Jamie, and Tomlinson, Brian, eds. *Conflicts of Interest: Canada and the Third World.* Toronto: Between the Lines, 1991.

Taylor, Charles. *Snow Job: Canada, the United States and Vietnam (1954 to 1973).* Toronto: Anansi Press, 1974.

Todd, David. "Canada Sells Loads of Weapons to Warring Nations, Report Says." *Ottawa Citizen*, 29 May 1995, A4.

Whitworth, Sandra. "Women, and Gender, in the Foreign Policy Review Process." In Maxwell Cameron and Maureen Appel Molot, eds., *Canada among Nations: Foreign Policy and Democracy*, 83–98. Ottawa: Carleton University Press, 1995.

10 Remapping Canada: The State in the Era of Globalization

GREGORY ALBO AND JANE JENSON

The turbulence of the late twentieth century has wrought major alterations in the structure and policies of the Canadian state. The State's role in economic regulation has changed dramatically. Rather than promoting national markets, the federal government has pursued elimination of borders between the Canadian economy and the rest of the world and made the country's competitive position in global markets the privileged barometer of well-being. Attention to trade is, of course, not new. The Canadian state has long had a development strategy founded on the comparative trade advantage derived from abundant natural resources. It promoted mining, forestry, intensive agriculture, and gas and oil drilling, while also financing the railways, roads, and pipelines that sent the products to market. Now the ecological scars of overexploitation of the Atlantic fishery and Pacific forests are only the most striking signals that the traditional role of the Canadian state in promoting resource-based development is in jeopardy. Indeed, the opposition of a large number of Canadians – and non-Canadians – to resource-driven development means that debate about the state's ecological responsibilities will be as fierce in the future as they have been recently.

The long-sought alternative to reliance on resource exports was the hope of transforming Canada into a major manufacturing economy. Many political economists, including some located throughout the federal and provincial levels of the state, have advocated a state strategy to foster modern, technologically advanced manufacturing production that would transform Canada into a country of high value-added exports (beyond autos and resources). The establishment of a continental free-trade area and a division of labour in which Canada continues to be most prized as a source of primary resources could well mark the eclipse of that aspiration.

Along with the economic restructuring of the last two decades, there has been divisive political turbulence and change, which have moved Canadian politics far away from the familiar postwar patterns. There are ongoing conflicts over the legitimacy of a unitary "Canadian" state, with nationalist movements in Quebec and among Aboriginal peoples seeking to redefine the country's boundaries and remake several of its major institutions. But the recent period has also brought redefinition of the proper relationship between state and citizens. There has been fervent struggle over whether the state should even minimally promote social equality or whether everyone must accept "the discipline of the market," no matter the social costs. Social programs that often served, since the 1940s, to define the essence of Canadian distinctiveness within North America are seeing reduced expenditures and being redesigned to increase market-based incentives. The postwar promise of a "just society" seems an increasingly distant utopia amid widening social polarization and inequalities. The way in which the "re-engineering" of state policy is being done, as the federal government transfers responsibilities for social programs and other spending to the provinces, means that ties binding Canadians through country-wide institutions are being weakened if not completely severed. In effect, the Canadian state is dismantling itself, in terms of redistributive policies, while strengthening its capacity to regulate in favour of the priorities of the market.

The Canadian nation-state is not alone, of course, in confronting the strains and questions of its future under the conditions of "globalization." If few of the certainties that guided Canada's advance to capitalist modernity through the twentieth century remain intact, the same is true almost everywhere. The years from 1945 to 1974 are sometimes termed those of Fordism and described as a "golden age" for national production structures and the interstate system of the capitalist world. The combination of mass production for mass consumption that dominated the western European and North American economies after 1945 produced rapid growth, rising productivity, and higher wages for workers. The reconstruction of the interstate system after 1945 reinforced, albeit only modestly and somewhat contradictorily, the economic autonomy and sovereignty of nation-states. The postwar Keynesian welfare states presumed that national borders were also the primary boundaries for economic exchange and for political community.

The autonomous national regimes establishing social and economic rights of citizenship depended on states controlling access of persons to their national territory and to their social programs.

Since the mid-1970s, however, such assumptions have been difficult to sustain as the crisis of Fordism has unfolded. Canadian families seek live-in nannies from the Philippines so that mothers are able to fly to business meetings in Paris. Population flows have multiplied, and countries try to cope with more immigrants and temporary workers in labour markets, which are, paradoxically, both more spatially fluid and stagnant. Economic instability is endemic as the borders of all states become increasingly permeable. The New York bond market's assessment of the Canadian government's deficit has almost as much influence on budgetary policy as does the Toronto Stock Exchange. Economic crisis and the loss of national autonomy in directing the future have marked even the postwar miracle economies of (West) Germany, Japan, and Sweden. Indeed, the Europeans are voluntarily transferring sovereignty to the supranational European Union in the hope that a remapping of economic and political space will ward off the worst effects of globalization.

The current malaise about the role of the Canadian state is still a result, however, of the specific history of Canada's position within the advanced capitalist group of countries and its relationship with the international economy. As other countries moved towards full employment during the postwar "golden age," Canadian unemployment rates had already begun the climb that produced today's double-digit figures. As European and Japanese growth and productivity rates accelerated, they surpassed Canadian output levels. As recognition of the effects of globalization rose in the 1980s, Canada had the weakest and most foreign-dominated industrial structure among OECD countries, and this had long been the case.[1] The arrival of the "new world order" seems to offer only further decline. The first task of this chapter is to explain the social and political origins of Canada's trajectory towards decline, via an assessment of the economic development strategies of the Canadian state in earlier economic regimes.

In order to do so, we must assess the capacity of the state to act, both in the past and in this era of globalization. A steady process of trade liberalization, winding down of capital controls, and internationalizing of production has undermined the state's capacity to regulate the entire country as one economic unit. The decision to move towards free trade through the Canada United States. Free Trade Agreement (FTA) of 1989, for example, signalled that the state was willing to move its regulatory powers elsewhere – in this case, to an international treaty that set limits on state actions.

In recent years, too, regional and even local economies have forged new ties beyond national borders and begun to rely more on their local states, either provincial or municipal, to promote their own interests.[2] The restructuring of global economic relations and the transformation of Canada's production structures have only intensified the "spatial centrifugalism" already provoked by the uneven and disarticulated development of the national economy, which has always characterized Canada and profoundly shaped state institutions.[3]

Nor has this erosion of state autonomy simply evolved. Political actors, taking advantage of the restructuring of production and trade and of the interstate system, have pressed for decentralization, if not dismantling, of Canada's national institutions. This is partly because conflicts embedded in constitutional politics since Confederation provoked demands from Quebec for new state powers. Recognizing Aboriginal peoples' right to self-government also requires a certain devolutionist reordering of state institutions and constitutional power. Demands to alter the division of powers between levels of government continues, then, to be associated with economic restructuring, thereby creating the new spaces in which state action occurs.[4]

These are not the only efforts to shift the way the state regulates the national space, however. Within the federal government promoters of the new right agenda, who seek to reduce the role of the state in the economy and give free play to market forces, have undertaken a significant redistribution of responsibility for social programs and economic development. In tandem with severe program reductions, Ottawa has turned over responsibility to the provinces for providing those that remain. In this way, the federal level has effectively abrogated the responsibility that it assumed at the beginning of the "golden age" for overseeing country-wide social and labour-market institutions and for setting standards for equitable treatment of all Canadians. An analysis of these spatial shifts – and the economics, politics, and ideas that underpin them – is also a central task of this chapter.

CANADIAN DEVELOPMENT AND THE STATE

It is a commonplace that a unique element of Canadian history is the leading role played by the state in economic development since the nineteenth century. The history of railway building, of Ontario Hydro, and of public health care are frequently evoked to show that Canadians do not "fear" state intervention and that it has contributed to national well-being. Political economists, from both the staples and the Marxist traditions, share an interest in the formation of the Canadian state, even if they have not agreed on how to understand its relationship to civil society. Nor have such theoretical disputes lost their political urgency today. It is not simply of "academic" interest whether economic conditions in Canada are interpreted as only a temporary adjustment, as a cumulative process of economic failure specific to Canada, as a mere regional effect of a general crisis of capitalism, or a decline whose institutional origins need to be traced to earlier historical processes. Historical disputes about Canada's early formation shape individuals' positions within the field of political economy and within current political debates about the country's future in an era of globalization.

If there is disagreement about how to characterize the present, there is wider agreement among political economists that its roots reside in history.[5] An understanding of the forces shaping the current trajectory of the Canadian economy and the role of the state must seek their lineage in the legacies of the country's transition to capitalism in the mid-nineteenth century. Canada was both a late follower and a post-colonial state. Britain undertook a transition to capitalism and industrialization first; all other countries were "followers" of one sort or another, with Canada falling within the group of late followers, whose transition occurred in the second half of the nineteenth century. The Canadian colonies and the post-1867 dominion were, moreover, a "white-settler" extension of the British Empire, occupying a geographical space in competition with a powerful and expansionist southern neighbour. These political and spatial constraints gave a particular cast to Canada's transition to capitalism. Wedged between a dominant imperial power, which continued to maintain economic ties with its former colonies, and the rising industrial power of the United States, the Canadian colonies confronted an increasingly open and competitive international economy for their exports. The economic task of the late-follower transition to capitalism was either to "catch up" industrially or to be marginalized as a periphery of a larger, imperial power. Originating as a white-settler colony, Canada never had to break the grip of a feudal aristocracy, as so many European countries did. The political task of the transition was to consolidate the geographical space of Canada politically for European settlement and a national market. Canada's capitalist transition and initial industrialization emerged thus, in a social structure comprised of agrarian small property-holders, large mercantile and financial interests, and an Aboriginal population still occupying much of the territory.

This history has set the parameters of the new Canadian political economy's debates about models of development and state formation. Analyses seek the imprint left on the state from the transition to capitalism, and vice-versa. As well, they track the formation of capitalism's classes, particularly the industrial bourgeoisie and proletariat, in relation to other classes and to Aboriginal peoples living on the margins of the capitalist economy. Finally, political economists have tried to assess the effect of the balance between internal development and external dependence that characterizes Canada's insertion into the world economy.

The Canadian Transition: From One Staple to Another

The staples thesis of Canadian history provides perhaps the most common interpretation of Canada's economic development. Drawing on Adam Smith's *Wealth of Nations* (1776), it describes Canada's transition to capitalism as a successful extension across time and space of exchange relations and state building.[6] In the work that laid the foundation of Canadian political economy, Mackintosh and Innis present Canadian development as a continuing search for natural resources – that is, staples – to exploit. Fish, fur, timber, and minerals all propelled development forward in time and westward through space. Despite much historical debate and varying emphases in details, all adherents of the staples approach agree that the pace and form of development were determined by geographical possibilities and limitations, technological improvements, the division of labour, and, most crucially, the economic surplus generated by foreign demand for "resource-extensive exports."[7]

In Mackintosh's view, for example, industrialization passed through stages. Looking at Canada as an ex-colony of Britain, he said, "[R]apid progress in ... new countries ... [is] dependent upon the discovery of cheap supplies of raw materials by the export of which to the markets of the world the new country may purchase the products which it cannot produce economically at this stage of its development."[8] Innis had a darker vision of the exchange relationship between imperial centre and colonial periphery. He warned repeatedly of the rigidity of overhead costs and the instability of external demand, which could produce "disturbances incidental to dependence on staples," thereby cumulatively upsetting the development of the periphery.[9] None the less, both authors attributed a successful capitalist transition in mid-nineteenth-century Canada to an export staple that quickly propelled it, as a late industrializer, from the commercial-agriculture to the industrial stage of development.

Despite focusing on economic, technological, and geographical factors, staples theorists did not ignore the state. Indeed they produced two important and varying accounts of the economic and social relations that underpinned Canadian state building. At the centre of the dispute was the nature of the social projects, especially Confederation and the first National Policy of the 1870s, which generated regional tensions over the unequal terms of exchange of the newly formed national market. Writing from the perspective of central Canada, Creighton identified the commercial elite engaged in the staples trade, and concentrated in the commercial centres of Montreal and Toronto, with the national interest: "In the commercial group was concentrated a great proportion of economic power – the wealth, the energy and ability of the colony ... It was a re-enactment ... of the classic West-European struggle – the struggle between insurgent commercial capitalism and a desperately resisting feudal and absolutist state."[10] From the vantage point of the west, Fowke documented both that the links provided by its wheat exports were crucial to successful industrialization and that the National Policy exacerbated regional tensions. The unequal exchange relations that fuelled such tensions arose in large part because the Canadian state acted as – indeed was created to be – "an agent within the first national policy ... [of] its original principals, the commercial, financial, and manufacturing interests of the central provinces."[11]

When staples theorists analysed state actions they most often described them as direct responses to needs generated by the staples trade.[12] For some theorists, still writing from a Smithian perspective of trade as spur to development, the "entrepreneurial capacity" of the Canadian state in the National Policy set this country apart from both the British and the American market-led capitalist transitions. Aitken, for example, forcefully argued that the "defensive expansionism" of the Canadian state was a strategy for territorial integrity. It involved the state in "facilitating the production and export of staple products ... to forestall, counteract, or restrain the northward extension of American economic and political influence."[13] Thus the central responsibility of the state was management of exchange flows between Canada and the world economy.

An Exceptional Failure

The defensive-expansionism thesis, developed after 1945, was an optimistic reading of the way the Canadian state had managed trade relations and the contribution of resource exports to state building and economic progress. In later years, some political actors and academics became uneasy about the increasing ties between Canada and the United States. These ties were both economic – as continental trading relationships took precedence over the remnants of the post-colonial link with Britain – and political. In the Cold War interstate system Canada was not only clearly in the Western camp, in which the United

States had replaced Britain as the world hegemonic power. Its territorial integrity and sovereignty were also weakened by common North American defence systems and increasing integration of its international actions with those of its southern neighbour.[14] By the early 1960s concerns about economic as well as political sovereignty were emerging.[15]

This was the context in which the nationalist tendency within the new Canadian political economy first began to work. This position can be considered neo-Innisian, as it continued to share the focus of the staples thesis on resources and exchange relations. The traditional staples analysis was supplemented, however, with a dependency approach to the power relations that were formed by unequal exchange between a dominant manufacturing-based centre and a resource-exporting periphery. Where Innis saw constraints resulting from Canada's location on the margins of Western civilization, the neo-Innisians detected the blockages to development of a periphery.[16] Signs of dependence, which Canada shared with Latin America, were truncated industrial development in manufacturing branch plants that lacked export capacity, reliance on resource exports, and a state that lacked sufficient effective autonomy to direct the country's economy. As Levitt, one of the originators of this approach, summarized, the "new mercantilism of multinational corporations" prevented formation of a technologically advanced manufacturing sector, and this situation led to the "silent surrender" of sovereignty through the postwar period.[17]

These political economists sought the economic and social sources, internal as well as external, of Canada's failure to make a successful transition to an autonomous manufacturing economy. One root was clearly external, located in the pattern of trade relations between a resource periphery and manufacturing centre. "Canada was to be understood as an 'effect' of these ongoing and changing relationships with the two great imperial powers of modern capitalism."[18] The problem, however, was not just international trade patterns. Internal structures forged in a staples-dominated economy had a fundamental effect. The economic surplus earned in the staples trade opened a number of potential alternative paths to development: industrial diversification through import substitution, a switch to a new resource export staple, or a "staples trap" of continued reliance on a declining resource base. The choice of path depended on entrepreneurial capacity to convert the economic surplus generated by resource exports into economic linkages with other nationally controlled industries. Entrepreneurship, for the neo-Innisians, pivoted around the characteristics of Canada's capitalist class, which controlled the surplus and the staples trade. The new Canadian political economy revealed a Canadian capitalist class comprised of persistently strong mercantile and financial interests, dating back to a commercially based transition to capitalism. Industrial interests, moreover, were stunted, foreign owned, and technologically backward.[19] It was these interests and class alliances that had kept Canada in a "staples trap," predisposed to "development of inefficient non-innovative and backward industrial structures with a penchant for dependence on foreign technology, foreign capital and state assistance."[20]

In these formulations, mercantile capitalism had been replaced in the nineteenth century not by powerful industrialists but by a "financial-staples oligarchy," the precursor of the power of today's banks and multinational corporations, which themselves remain dependent on an imperialist centre within the world economy. In these histories the industrial development fostered by the National Policy brought stunted industrialization and loss of economic sovereignty, as American industrialists were induced to jump tariff walls or to buy Canadian firms to create branch plants to serve the Canadian market.

The state had a role to play in this story. It was, however, a different one from that recounted by the early staples theorists. Whereas for the latter the entrepreneurial capacity of the state had helped build the state and forge an autonomous economy, for the nationalist new political economists the Canadian state was foremost a subservient extension of Canada's commercial and financial capitalism.[21] The dominance of financial, commercial, and foreign manufacturing capital in Canadian society translated into a weak state, uninterested in fostering development or sustaining national sovereignty. In this formulation, the root of Canada's development impasse is social: the state was simply an instrument of the powerful elites in a truncated transition to capitalism. It was little wonder, then, that the state had failed to arrest dependence or to respond adequately to the signs of economic weakness and decline becoming visible in the 1970s. As Drache put it, Canada could not "transcend its commercial status as a supplier of resources and a market for manufactured goods ... [I]t could not acquire the capability to revolutionize its own mode of production."[22] The state was, in the vision of the new political economy, neither able nor willing to halt the reconfiguration of economic space in the direction of continentalism.

Less Exceptional than Different

For the new Canadian political economy heirs of Innis, Canada's capitalist transition was one of exceptional failure. Accordingly, Canada was "the world's richest underdeveloped country"[23] and had an economy that had failed to follow the normal development phases to an industrial society with an autonomous economy and state. Marxists and political economists influenced by class analysis provided a quite different reading of the same history.[24] Notably, they dismissed the idea that the country's development was stuck in a merchant capitalist phase or that Canada's major characteristic was its "exceptionalism."

These political economists argued instead that Canada had passed through the usual stages of capitalist development. Pentland, for instance, traced the transition from pre-capitalist "personal" and feudal relations of exploitation to capitalist social relations at mid-nineteenth century. Confederation and the National Policy signified a successful bourgeois revolution, reflecting the material interests of industrial capitalists facing monopolistic competition from the United States. Their state building and spatial extension yielded "an undivided protectionist voice."[25] In Ryerson's view, the "unequal union" of Confederation – of colonial Canada and imperial Britain, Quebec and Canada, Aboriginals and Europeans – reflected the growing strength of industrial capitalists, who required "a state of their own, under their control, capable of providing a favourable framework for the home market."[26] Labour historians, too, dissented from the picture of an exceptionalism in Canadian society. They focused on the growing strength of the working class and its institutions as industrial capitalism spread.[27]

Despite the similarities between Canada's history and the emergence of capitalism and state building in other countries, there were particularities to the Canadian story that received the attention they deserve only in later studies. As Panitch noted, political economists could not ignore the fact that Canada was "distinguished from other advanced capitalist societies in terms of its dependent industrialism."[28] Such observations call for a historicist method capable of exposing the ways abstract categories take on historical content as the result of the actions of social forces making their own history and thereby becoming the specific structures of Canadian capitalism.

The years of state building at the end of the nineteenth century and the first National Policy formed again the terrain worked over in three studies that sought to depict the origins and nature of the structural-institutional fusion between internal conservatism and external dependence that had perpetuated a model of development leading to "technological entropy." In Williams's view, the import-substitution strategy promoted by the National Policy had been a logical choice for state and business elites in a resource-endowed regional periphery. The process of "arrested industrialization" that took hold was increasingly difficult to overcome, because makers of state policy were "loath to disturb the investment climate" that recasting a non-innovative, branch-plant economy would entail.[29] It is with a similar sense of the failed "historical possibilities" that Laxer located Canada's "aborted industrialization." For him, in Canada, in contrast to all other late-follower countries, agrarian producers had not penetrated the power bloc and had never therefore forged the class alliances necessary "to take a leading role in creating the state and transforming the economy."[30] Without a national-popular movement to deter them, dominant elites maintained a crippling allegiance to the British (and then American) empire and state policies that sustained "foreign ownership and a truncated manufacturing sector."[31] For Mahon, the hegemony of the staples fraction of Canadian capital meant that "industrialization remained a secondary objective."[32] Even though it perceived the threat of deindustrialization, a marginalized nationalist manufacturing fraction and working class lacked enough power within an unequal structure of representation to force elaboration of an industrial policy.[33] In sum, for these authors, with their focus on either business elites or subordinate classes, the specificity of Canada's transition to industrial capitalism was the pattern of class power and the resulting alliances (or failed alliances) – weak national manufacturers (Williams), weak agrarians (Laxer), weak workers (Mahon).[34] The frail manufacturing class, in conjunction with other marginalized groups and classes, could never exercise sufficient political power to provoke normal development of an export manufacturing capacity. The institutional and policy legacies were the growing spectre of deindustrialization in an increasingly open and competitive world economy after 1945.

Building on such class-oriented and institutional studies, without ever ignoring the insight that Canada's dependent capitalism must be explained, it is possible to retell the story of these years of transition and spatial reconfiguration. We now see that the particular character of the Canadian transition lay in the combination of intensive and extensive forms of accumulation, which generated quite impressive productivity advances through the nineteenth century and moved Canada into the upper rank of capitalist countries.[35] Extensive accumulation was made possible by territorial expansion and absorption of new workers.[36] The state's territorial reach extended westward and northward. Territories that had been incorporated into the trading networks of imperialism were directly appropriated. Aboriginal lands were seized, and their pre-capitalist mode of production was liquidated.[37] As well, the labour supply was highly elastic for immigrants from Europe, who brought skills that Canada did not have to pay to develop, at the going wage.[38] Extensive accumulation did not prevent, and indeed encouraged, intensive accumulation by providing the surplus to pay for investment in capital goods (using foreign funds and technology) in both the agricultural and resource sectors. The growth of incomes also provided the inducement for mass-market industries – textiles, shoes, dry goods – to develop. The story told about Canada's economic transition is thus not one of merchant trade preserving pre-capitalist commercial and financial activities. Rather it is the creation of industrialism out of that combination of intensive and extensive accumulation that also implanted capitalist relations of production throughout the territory that became modern Canada.

This model of capitalist development also implied a certain specificity to the Canadian state structure.[39] The country created in 1867 was a liberal democracy, but one whose sovereignty was divided and parcelled. An ex-colony but still a "dominion" without recognition as a fully independent nation state, it was also internally divided by competing nationalist claims arising in French and English Canada and the unresolved history of the subjugation of Aboriginal nations. State structures were constructed in response to competing drives. Strong and centralized powers were sought by those whose goal was to create a single socio-economic space and to facilitate development of infrastructure to smooth the transition to industrialism. At the same time there were social forces that would accept only state structures sufficiently decentralized to accommodate the diversity of two nations in a single state and of regionally differentiated, unevenly developed economies. The result was the divided sovereignty of Canadian federalism and a "place-sensitive societal paradigm."[40]

These state structures would subsequently be forced to accept the consequences of divided sovereignty as well as the absence of a strong sense of pan-Canadian allegiance. At each moment of economic and political turbulence, the legitimacy of basic state institutions was called into question, so that Canadian history seemed to lurch from "constitutional crisis" to "constitutional crisis". The delicate elite negotiations that generated the new dominion underlined "the primacy attached to the preservation of property and the prerequisites of the accumulation process."[41] Popular democratic forces were weak, and the fact that institutions of federalism were privileged as the locale for conflict resolution between political and bureaucratic elites made it even more difficult for them to gain access. The unequal structures of representation of class-divided societies became even murkier in a situation in which the institutional routes to representation were varied and not always open.[42] Such a state did bring in a transition to capitalism based in both extensive and intensive forms of accumulation, but its limited capacity to sustain industrial or labour-market policies hindered Canada's emergence as a major industrial power in its own right.

Throughout this section we have seen that quite different readings of Canada's nineteenth-century exist. While everyone agrees that in the last decades of the century Canada set out on a trajectory that shaped the crisis of the late twentieth century, there is much less agreement about the parts played by the state, social actors, and institutions in these years. Some have seen the state as little more than the hand-maiden of large historical forces. For others the state was captured by the dominant class forces and did nothing to divert the country from a road of failure, directed towards a "staples trap" of dependence. For yet others, the pre-capitalist ruling class was displaced in the thorough-going capitalist project that was Confederation. This project, led by powerful social forces, created an influential state not simply in their own image but one that reflected and perpetuated the unequal struc-tures of representation and power in Canadian society.

These alternate explanations of Canada's capitalist transition are central to much more than theoretical academic disputes. Many politi-cal economists seek to understand the history of their present circum-stances as part of the effort to change them. Their attention turned therefore, even as they struggled to discern the role of the state in those crucial decades of the nineteenth century, to another matter: how can we comprehend Canada's current economic malaise, and what contri-bution has the state made to it?

POSTWAR CANADA AND THE LONG DECLINE

Just as the forces restructuring Europe and North America in the late nineteenth century provided foreign demand for Canada's primary commodity exports, the post-1945 golden age of Fordism similarly furnished buoyant foreign markets for Canada's primary commodities of hydro-electricity, oil and gas, and metals. The United States had dis-placed Britain as the undisputed economic centre of the world econ-omy during the war, and as a result Canada's "permeable Fordism" was profoundly shaped by American technology and manufacturing branch plants.[43]

There were, however, already disconcerting signs of a developing economic malaise during the postwar boom, despite impressive gains in productive capacity. Except in natural resources and a few manufac-turing sectors, domestic industry did not fare well when confronted by international competition. A number of trends stood out. The man-ufacturing sector ranked as one of the West's weakest in output and employment shares of the national economy. Levels of foreign direct investment were at new highs, bringing the expected liabilities for exports and innovation. Exports were concentrated in resources and

semi-processed goods, while imports were primarily high-end manufactured goods. Firms undertook only minimal research and development; there were shortages of skilled workers even though substantial
unemployment had appeared. All of this combined to produce Canadian productivity and growth rates chronically below the rest of the
Western economies, while much of the growth was simply the extensive
employment growth of an enlarging market.

The emerging picture was one of relative economic decline. While
the roots of this decline might be identified by the various approaches
to the new Canadian political economy in the formative processes
of the capitalist transition, it was still necessary to trace the history
from the nineteenth century to the present. Moreover, the contribution of the postwar state to the patterns of economic development and
state building had to be assessed. Here, again, different approaches
emerged.

The Smithian heirs of the original staples theory dominated postwar
economic thinking in Canada, within the state and among neo-classical
economists. They saw few problems with the patterns of trade and ownership. In their eyes, foreign investment helped address what they saw
as capital shortages; resource exports were Canada's natural comparative advantage.[44] None the less, there were some concerns about industrial production. Apprehensions began to mount as early as the Royal
Commission on Canada's Prospects (Gordon Commission) in 1957.
The Economic Council of Canada's reports of the 1970s picked up this
theme, and the Royal Commission on the Economic Union and Canada's Development Prospects (Macdonald Commission) in the mid-
1980s sounded an alarm as well. The underlying premise was that the
absence of economies of scale prevented full productivity increases and
stunted export trade in high value–added goods. This analysis gained
the support of both foreign and domestically controlled capital, which
also weighed in behind the solution proposed by these reports to
the state. This was to foster further continental integration through
creation of a common economic space. Indeed, the central recommendation of the Macdonald Report was that Canada seek a free-trade
arrangement with the United States. Such an accord would reconfigure economic space by expanding the single market and by harmonizing a broad range of economic policies. The federal government
pursued this recommendation, negotiating and then implementing
the Canada–United States Free Trade Agreement (FTA) of 1989. In effect, just as political institutions and state power had been crucial after
1867 in the creation of a single economic space from east to west, state
institutions in the mid-1980s led the move to redesign this economic
space by lifting the barriers that partly separated the two largest North

American economies. Extension of the trade pact by inclusion of Mexico within the North American Free Trade Agreement (NAFTA) of 1992 continued this remapping of economic space.

Not surprisingly, the neo-Innisian nationalist tendency within the new Canadian political economy was not enthusiastic about this prescription. Its diagnosis of the economic impasse since the 1970s had focused on political dependence and economic decline.[45] From within the state sector the alarm was sounded by the Science Council of Canada, which warned that Canada's branch-plant model of development was causing technological entropy through "truncated industries with a low technological capability becoming cumulatively dependent upon foreign industries."[46] The proposed corrective was a national industrial strategy that could foster "technological sovereignty" and generate an export-oriented manufacturing sector. This prescription received short shrift, however, as the state definitively moved towards the FTA. Indeed, anything resembling an industrial policy was ruled out of bounds by the prevailing laissez-faire policy, which characterized such activity as an inappropriate intervention by the state in the economy that would cause inefficiencies and as an unacceptable restraint on free trade.

Therefore the run-up to the FTA and the state's increasing enthusiasm for a continentalist strategy forced political economists to seek other strategies for reversing economic decline and to begin to treat the whole of North America as a potential space for political action. The particularities of Canadian economic decline had to be assessed relative to the restructuring occurring across the advanced capitalist countries. Because the internationalization of production was generalized, it was also necessary to reconsider the balance among national, continental, and international strategies as a potential space for political action. Niosi, Resnick, and Carroll, for example, examined the impact of the new conditions of the international economy on the characteristics of Canadian capital, including its ties to foreign capital. They contended that high levels of "foreign investment" characterized late capitalism as a whole: Canada was not exceptional. Carroll, for example, argued that foreign ownership and its consequences were simply part of a universal "world-wide process of capitalist internationalization."[47] Foreign investment in Canada had been declining since the early 1970s, so that the largest portion of assets remained under domestic control.[48] Such patterns belied any notion of a continuous regression to dependence. Canadian businesses were, moreover, investing abroad, while interlocking corporate ties had created a small monopoly of finance capitalists active in both manufacturing and financial sectors. For Resnick, such trends represented a maturing of

Canadian capitalism "over the postwar period, with Canadian banks and corporations increasingly in control of leading sectors of the Canadian economy and better able to project their influence abroad. The Canadian state has played a crucial role in furthering this process."[49] Bellon and Niosi argued too that the "continental and rentier nationalism" fostered by the state had "its logical outcome ... [in] growing integration into the North American market."[50]

In the view of these authors, "Canada simply presents the first case of a more *general* phenomenon" that has emerged in this age of globalization.[51] This rejection of Canada as an exceptional, failed late follower and its reclassification as one of several countries sharing a generalized experience of crisis and globalization elide the unique features of Canada's dependent capitalism. Observers of a more historicist position have sought not only economic but also political particularities of the "Canadian case," precisely because it is these specificities that set the constraints for action in the context of free trade and globalization.

In some cases their search led to development of new concepts. Indeed, the major theme of a recent collection is that the central concepts of the first generation of the new Canadian political economy – dependence, class, and state – have been supplanted by three others – production, space, and identity.[52]

A propos of the first concept, the implication is that the focus on the dependent status of Canada's production relations has given way to analyses that identify their specific historical forms, as well as their links to social classes. Such studies clarify the ways in which Canada's Fordism continued to depend on extensive accumulation. In postwar Canada, the "super-profits" that drive capital accumulation came in large part from economic rents from primary commodity production, employment rents generated by forgoing the training costs required for technologically leading production, and absolute growth in the market from immigration.[53] In addition, the pre-1940 politics of post-colonialism and the nascent manufacturing branch plants formed during the National Policy period sent Canada into the Fordist years highly permeable to foreign influences. Previous state policies as well as those promoted in the late 1940s meant that intensive accumulation relied on second-best technology adapted from the u.s. economy, whose capitalists were attracted to the vibrant Canadian economy. The result was a national system of innovation in which minimal research and development occurred, techniques were imported, and education and training structures remained underdeveloped. This industrial structure, with its adaptation of u.s. technology, became increasingly a barrier as the American technological edge in the formation of

Fordism declined relative to the later-formed flexible-production techniques of Japan and West Germany.

In other words, earlier state decisions, whether in the late nineteenth century or after 1945, set up the later economic weaknesses. They also shaped the constraints and choices for the 1980s and 1990s. Indeed, it is possible to see the move towards a continent-wide economic space as the most recent effort to build on Canada's strengths in primary products and to "cut the losses" of earlier hopes to advance a country-wide autonomous industrial economy. Thus NAFTA creates not only a new economic space but a particular division of labour. Canada provides resources, financial input, and some manufacturing, Mexico furnishes cheap labour, and the United States provides technology and representation of the regional bloc in the interstate system.

Second, recognition of the extent to which states as well as other institutions are crucial to the creation of economic and political space is the reason that political economists now pay attention to this concept. The break-up of Fordism has forced us to recognize that the correspondence between nation-states and the capitalist economy can take on new configurations. National states, for instance, are having greater difficulty in regulating their own economies at the same time as they are participating in the redrawing of borders. The free-trade agreements that the federal government signed are potent symbols that nation-states, and the powerful social classes represented in their structures, may choose to limit their own sovereignty.

This lesson is not lost on other social forces and political actors. It was noted above that the political practices of the Fordist period marginalized subordinate classes, particularly the labour movement. This marginalization allowed the state to enter into the free-trade agreements, despite the likely costs to manufacturing and other workers. Indeed, the job losses in the resulting restructuring have driven unemployment and welfare rates to postwar highs. Deregulation of national financial markets, moreover, repeats a historic pattern of capital mobility that is "dangerously unstable and ultimately economically inefficient."[54]

Political mobilization against the negative effects of free trade has been difficult to sustain. The political party traditionally associated with the labour movement – the New Democrats – structured much of its identity around the processes of national regulation of postwar Keynesianism, and it has not been able to abandon these commitments without consequences. The bourgeois parties have been less encumbered with the legacies of the past. Even the Liberal party, which constructed Canada's welfare state, has joined the Reform and Progressive Conservative parties in pursuit of the neo-conservative project of globalization. The provincial states controlled by the NDP have had little success in finding a "progressive competitiveness" option of empowering subordinate groups and protecting them from the adverse winds blowing through the global economy. The crisis has ripped apart the NDP and the labour movement, which now appear to support neither the old economic policies of national regulation nor a new economic project capable of accomplishing egalitarian or redistributive objectives.[55]

Nor have the disputes over regionalism and federalism that had characterized Canada's Fordism been overcome. Constitutional conflict both drove and was exacerbated by economic crisis. The Macdonald Commission itself was established in the early 1980s to inquire into both economic and constitutional restructuring. The existence of the Canadian state itself has been placed in question by the political fragmentation that has been encouraged by economic globalization and continentalism. There has in effect been a "double shift" away from the national state of the postwar years. The free-trade agreements, as well as the strengthening of the supervisory authority of the International Monetary Fund and the World Trade Organization, cede national sovereignty to opaque international institutions with few democratic credentials. The politics of Québécois and Aboriginal nationalisms seek not only a redefinition of state powers but also a reconfiguration of national political space. The sovereigntist movement in Quebec would redraw the formal borders of Canada, while both Québécois federalist nationalists and Aboriginal nationalists seek to realign the effective borders of political power via a process of devolution.[56]

Third, these movements have made it clear that the identity of Canadians is being altered in these years of crisis and change. The state has a central role to play here because it is the state that recognizes citizens, both those who have the right to call themselves citizens and the rights that citizens obtain. Both these aspects of inclusion are in dispute, and both are linked directly to current politics. Neither Québécois sovereigntists nor Aboriginal nationalists aspire to "Canadian" citizenship. The former want to realize their own national identities in an independent state, while Aboriginal peoples claim the collective rights of nations within Canada (as do many Québécois nationalists who wish to remain in Canada).

Many more Canadians than these are asking about the content of national identity. Immigrant flows around the globe are one important characteristic of globalization, and they are changing the racial, ethnic, and national composition of the country's population. These changes make any identity as an ex-colony of Britain – or France – very difficult to sustain. The ethnic and racial mix of the population means that Canadians have a multiplicity of links with a wide variety of countries and a political interest in seeing state policies in the realm of human rights, refugee policy, and international military action represent those links. It also means that anti-progressive politics must be combated by, for example, demonstration that an inclusive citizenship policy has been and continues to be central to the country's well-being, rather than contrary to it.

Citizenship is not simply about the borders between us and others, about the inside and outside. It is also about the rights of citizens within the country.[57] Here the Canadian state has been challenging and changing the postwar social identity of citizenship. The citizenship of Fordism was one that established and extended economic and social rights. There were two dimensions to this notion. First was the idea that the costs and consequences of life's hazards – unemployment, accident, sickness – as well as life's needs – education, and childbearing – should be shared, if not equally, with at least minimal standards of equity. Citizens were not considered to live as isolated individuals facing the risks and costs of everyday life alone. Social solidarity was a "public good" to be set against the insecurities of the capitalist market. Second, the Keynesian welfare state was organized around the idea that the state would extend and regulate national institutions such as labour markets, health care, and education to provide at least a minimal level of provision regardless of individuals' economic circumstance. Everyone had the right to unemployment insurance, to universal health care, and to access to educational institutions, no matter where she or he lived in the country. In a federal system such as Canada's, "portability" and "national standards" were crucial manifestations of the rights of national citizenship.

In the current political situation of post-Fordism, these citizenship rights have been called into question, and with them the political and social identities of Canadians. Citizens are being told that they alone, or with their families, have responsibility for their futures. The market and their own worthiness will determine not only whether they succeed or fail but whether they will live their lives with dignity or in fear of poverty and the other inherent risks of capitalist society. It is not by chance that one of the major fears of opponents of the FTA and NAFTA was that their citizenship right to universal health care would be threatened by the state's decision to break down trade borders. Indeed, in recent years we have been treated to a panoply of arguments emanating from the state and business elites to explain why the era of global competition has rendered the old programs outdated. The question for the future is whether the Canadian state will be forced, by democratic mobilization of its citizens, to find new versions of these programs that retain the same commitment to solidarity and equity or whether it will preside over the breaking of the ties that have bound the country together – and therefore over the dismantling of the country itself.

NOTES

1 On the economic crisis in Canada see J. Jenson, R. Mahon, and M. Bienefeld, eds., *Production, Space, Identity: Political Economy Faces the 21st Century* (Toronto: Canadian Scholars' Press, 1993); C. Gonick, *The Great Economic Debate* (Toronto: Lorimer, 1987); and S. McBride, *Not Working: State, Unemployment, and Neo-Conservatism in Canada* (Toronto: University of Toronto Press, 1992).

2 R. Cox, "Global Perestroika," in R. Miliband and L. Panitch, eds., *Socialist Register 1992: New World Order?* (London: Merlin 1992), 31; and J. Loxley, "Regional Trading Blocks," in J. Jenson, R. Mahon, and M. Bienefeld, eds., *Production, Space, Identity: Political Economy Faces the 21st Century* (Toronto: Canadian Scholars' Press, 1993), 305–26.

3 Jane Jenson, "Mapping, Naming and Remembering: Globalization at the end of the Twentieth century," *Review of International Political Economy*, 2 no. 1 (spring 1995), 96–116.

4 This has been a consistent theme of Canadian political science. See: J. Brodie, *The Political Economy of Canadian Regionalism* (Toronto: Harcourt Brace Jovanovich, 1990); G. Stevenson, *Unfulfilled Union* (Toronto: Macmillan, 1979); R. Whitaker, *A Sovereign Idea* (Montreal: McGill-Queen's University Press, 1992); and Jane Jenson, " 'Different' but not 'Exceptional': Canada's Permeable Fordism," *Canadian Review of Sociology and Anthropology*, 26 no. 1 (1989).

5 Neo-classical economists, in contrast, display a preference for ahistorical and monocausal explanations of the Canadian economic impasse. They identify either the "small size" of the national market or "over-governance" as producing market rigidities. These analyses do not adequately address the empirical situation, however. Extending exchange relations through continental free trade has compounded Canada's economic crisis. Reducing the public sector – already one of the most impoverished in the advanced capitalist zone – has resulted in further disintegration of the national state.

6 Another way of describing the process is as one of "nation building." We prefer to label it "state building" because it was a state and its institutions that were being built. The question of whether a "nation" was being forged continues to plague us today. Our term reminds us of Charles Tilly's obser-

vation that histories of the transition to capitalism and its development trajectories are closely linked to histories of state building. See C. Tilly, *Coercion, Capital and European States* (Oxford: Basil Blackwell, 1990).

7 M. Watkins, "A Staple Theory of Economic Growth," *Canadian Journal of Economics and Political Science*, 29 no. 2 (1963). For the relationship between Smith and Innis see W.T. Easterbrook, "Innis and Economics," *Canadian Journal of Economics and Political Science*, 19 no. 3 (1953). For a thorough neo-classical account of this period that discounts the role of staples industries, and much else, see I. Drummond, *Progress without Planning: Ontario's Economic Development, 1867–1941* (Toronto: University of Toronto Press, 1987).

8 W.A. Mackintosh, *The Economic Background of Dominion-Provincial Relations* (Toronto: McClelland and Stewart, 1964), 13. For essays surveying this theme see D. Cameron, ed., *Explorations in Canadian Economic History* (Ottawa: University of Ottawa Press, 1985); and D. Platt and G. di Tella, eds., *Argentina, Australia and Canada Compared: Studies in Comparative Development, 1870–1965* (New York: St Martin's Press, 1985).

9 H. Innis, *Essays in Canadian Economic History* (Toronto: University of Toronto Press, 1956), 381–2. The most important synthesis of this view of Innis is the insightful paper of D. Drache, "Harold Innis and Canadian Capitalist Development," *Canadian Journal of Political and Social Theory*, 6 nos. 1–2 (1982).

10 D. Creighton, *The Empire of the St. Lawrence* (Toronto: Macmillan, 1956), 40.

11 V.C. Fowke, *The National Policy and the Wheat Economy* (Toronto: University of Toronto Press, 1957), 276. See also K. Buckley, "The Role of Staple Industries in Canada's Economic Development," *Journal of Economic History*, 28 (1958).

12 For a detailed discussion of staples and the state see G. Albo and J. Jenson, "The Relative Autonomy of the State," in W. Clement and G. Williams, eds., *The New Canadian Political Economy* (Montreal: McGill-Queen's University Press, 1989), 183–7.

13 H. Aitken, "Defensive Expansionism: The State and Economic Growth in Canada," in W.T. Easterbrook and M. Watkins, eds., *Approaches to Canadian Economic History* (Toronto: McClelland and Stewart, 1967), 220–1. Easterbrook also noted with resignation that in Canada "centrally directed, 'induced' entrepreneurship established a pattern which remains largely intact." See his "Long-Period Comparative Study: Some Historical Cases," *Journal of Economic History*, 17 (1957), 576.

14 M. Clark-Jones, *A Staple State: Canadian Industrial Resources in Cold War* (Toronto: University of Toronto Press, 1987); and E. Regehr, *Arms Canada: The Deadly Business of Military Exports* (Toronto: Lorimer, 1987).

15 See H. Aitken, *American Capital and Canadian Resources* (Cambridge, Mass.: Harvard University Press, 1961); and W. Axline et al., eds., *Continental Community? Independence and Integration in North America* (Toronto: McClelland and Stewart, 1974).

16 G. Williams, "Canada in the International Political Economy," in W. Clement and G. Williams, eds., *The New Canadian Political Economy* (Montreal: McGill-Queen's University Press, 1989), 116–37.

17 K. Levitt, *Silent Surrender* (Toronto: Macmillan, 1970).

18 J. Myles, "Understanding Canada: Comparative Political Economy Perspectives," *Canadian Review of Sociology and Anthropology*, 26 no. 1 (1989), 1.

19 Levitt, *Silent Surrender*; T. Naylor, "Dominion of Capital: Canada and International Investment," in A. Kontos, ed., *Domination* (Toronto: University of Toronto Press, 1975); W. Clement, *Continental Corporate Power* (Toronto: McClelland and Stewart, 1977).

20 Naylor, "Dominion of Capital," 52.

21 For a more detailed presentation of state theory in this approach, see Albo and Jenson, "Relative Autonomy," 187–93.

22 D. Drache, "Harold Innis and Canadian Capitalist Development," *Canadian Journal of Political and Social Theory*, 6 nos. 1–2 (1982), 42.

23 Levitt, *Silent Surrender*, 24–5.

24 For a detailed consideration of class theorists' view of state power, see Albo and Jenson, "Relative Autonomy," 193–200.

25 H.C. Pentland, *Labour and Capital in Canada, 1650–1860* (Toronto: James Lorimer, 1981), 173. See also P. Phillips, "Unequal Exchange, Surplus Production and the Commercial-Industrial Question," in D. Cameron, ed., *Explorations in Canadian Political Economy* (Ottawa: University of Ottawa Press, 1984). Though Pentland was far from an orthodox Marxist, his study was influenced by the transition debate sparked by Dobb's *Development of Capitalism*.

26 S. Ryerson, *Unequal Union: Confederation and the Roots of the Conflict in the Canadas, 1815–1873* (Toronto: Progress Books, 1968), 310.

27 See especially G. Kealey, *Toronto Workers Respond to Industrial Capitalism, 1867–1892* (Toronto: University of Toronto Press, 1980); and M. Cohen, *Women's Work: Markets and Economic Development in Nineteenth Century Ontario* (Toronto: University of Toronto Press, 1988).

28 L. Panitch, "Dependency and Class in Canadian Political Economy," *Studies in Political Economy*, 6 (1981), 23. This more historicist Marxist theoretical tendency was associated with the formation of the journal *Studies in Political Economy*, which followed on the heels of L. Panitch, ed., *The Canadian State* (Toronto: University of Toronto Press, 1977).

29 G. Williams, *Not for Export* (Toronto: McClelland and Stewart, 1983), 130.

30 G. Laxer, *Open for Business* (Toronto: Oxford University Press, 1989), 151.

31 Ibid.

32 R. Mahon, *The Politics of Industrial Restructuring* (Toronto: University of Toronto Press, 1984), 14. This was a theme widely shared in Panitch, ed., *The Canadian State.*

33 Mahon, *Industrial Restructuring*, 3. This is a theme Mahon has reiterated: "The 'New' Canadian Political Economy Revisited," in J. Jenson, R. Mahon, and M. Bienefeld, eds., *Production, Space, Identity* (Toronto: Canadian Scholars' Press, 1993), 2–3.

34 On the continuing political blockages to a rearrangement of class power relations see J. Brodie and J. Jenson, *Crisis, Challenge and Change: Party and Class in Canada* (Toronto: Methuen, 1980).

35 On some of these issues see M. Abramovitz, "Catching Up, Forging Ahead, and Falling Behind," *Journal of Economic History*, 46 no. 2 (1986); A. Maddison, *Phases of Capitalist Development* (New York: Oxford University Press, 1982); and R. Pomfret, *The Economic Development of Canada* (Toronto: Methuen, 1981), chap. 4.

36 Extensive accumulation can be defined as capital accumulation via an extension of the scale of production, achieved without altering production techniques. This involves drawing on new sectors, workers, land, or a larger portion of the day, or using the same with greater intensity. Intensive accumulation applies science and technology, embodied in skills and machines, so that productivity advances rapidly. No regime of accumulation is exclusively intensive or extensive in its specific historical conditions or institutions. It is the mix of forms of accumulation that defines the specificity of a regime.

37 F. Abele and D. Stasiulus, "Canada as a 'White-Settler Colony': What about Natives and Immigrants?" in W. Clement and G. Williams, eds., *The New Canadian Political Economy* (Montreal: McGill-Queen's University Press, 1989). The poisonous dynamic of this internal colonialism remains imprinted in the Canadian state structure, just as extensive accumulation via geographical extension of the market remains part of Canada's development model. The westward territorial expansion of North America ran parallel to Europe's classic age of imperialism.

38 These wages were, moreover, relatively high, considering the productivity levels of North America, low living costs, and the possibility of independent commodity production. Panitch, "Dependency and Class."

39 For recent, creative efforts to rethink this process of state formation see G. Bernier and D. Salée, *The Shaping of Quebec Politics: Colonialism, Power and the Transition to Capitalism in the 19th Century* (Washington, DC: Crave Russak, 1992); and A. Greer and I. Radforth, eds., *Colonial Leviathan: State Formation in Mid-Nineteenth Century Canada* (Toronto: University of Toronto Press, 1992).

40 J. Jenson, "Representations in Crisis: The Roots of Canada's Permeable Fordism," *Canadian Journal of Political Science*, 23 no. 4 (1990), 672.

41 D. Wolfe, "The Canadian State in Comparative Perspective," *Canadian Review of Sociology and Anthropology*, 26 no. 1 (1989), 107; and P. Resnick, *The Masks of Proteus: Canadian Reflections of the State* (Montreal: McGill-Queen's University Press, 1990), 43–5.

42 On the unequal structures of representation of class-divided societies see R. Mahon, "Canadian Public Policy: The Unequal Structure of Representation," in L. Panitch, ed., *The Canadian State* (Toronto: University of Toronto Press, 1977), 165–98.

43 Jenson, " 'Different'."

44 This has been most forcefully stressed by Harry Johnson, *The Canadian Quandary* (Toronto: McClelland and Stewart, 1977).

45 See, for example, J. Laxer, "Canadian Manufacturing and u.s. Trade Policy," in R. Laxer, ed., *Canada, Ltd.: The Political Economy of Dependency* (Toronto: McClelland and Stewart, 1973), 127–52; D. Drache, "Re-discovering Canadian Political Economy," in W. Clement and D. Drache, eds., *A Practical Guide to Canadian Political Economy* (Toronto: Lorimer, 1978); and C. Gonick, *Inflation or Depression* (Toronto: Lorimer, 1975).

46 J. Britton and J. Gilmour, *The Weakest Link* (Ottawa: Supply and Services, 1978), 141.

47 Carroll, *Corporate Power*, 187.

48 J. Niosi, *Canadian Capitalism* (Toronto: James Lorimer, 1981) and *Canadian Multinationals* (Toronto: Garamond Press, 1985); Resnick, *Masks of Proteus*; W. Carroll, *Corporate Power and Canadian Capitalism*. (Vancouver: University of British Columbia Press, 1986) and "Neoliberalism and the Recomposition of Finance Capital in Canada," *Capital and Class*, 38 (1989), 81–112.

49 Resnick, *Masks of Proteus*, 187.

50 B. Bellon and J. Niosi, *The Decline of the American Economy* (Montreal: Black Rose, 1988), 153.

51 Carroll, *Corporate Power*, 200, emphasis added.

52 Mahon, "The 'New Canadian Political Economy' Revisited."

53 This interpretation can be gleaned from the data presented in M. Porter, *Canada at the Crossroads* (Ottawa: Supply and Services, 1991), chap. 2; and Royal Commission on the Economic Union and Development Prospects for Canada, *Report, Vol. 1* (Ottawa: Supply and Services, 1985), chap. 2.

54 M. Bienefeld, "Capitalism and the Nation State in the Dog Days of the Twentieth Century," in R. Miliband and L. Panitch, eds., *Socialist Register 1994: Between Globalism and Nationalism* (London: Merlin, 1994), 112.

55 G. Albo, "Competitive Austerity and the Impasse of Capitalist Employment Policy," in R. Miliband and L. Panitch, eds., *Socialist Register 1994: Between Globalism and Nationalism* (London: Merlin, 1994).

56 Jenson, "Mapping."

57 See J. Jenson, "Citizenship and Equity: Variations across Time and in Space," in J. Hiebert ed., *Political Ethics: A Canadian Perspective*, Vol. 12 of the Research Studies of the Royal Commission on Electoral Reform and Party Financing (Toronto: Dundurn Press, 1991); G. Albo, D. Langille, and L. Panitch, eds., *A Different Kind of State? Popular Power and Democratic Administration* (Toronto: Oxford University Press, 1993); and S. Phillips, ed., *How Ottawa Spends 1993–94: A More Democratic Canada?* (Ottawa: Carleton University Press, 1993).

11 The New Political Economy of Regions

JANINE BRODIE

Most observers of Canadian politics, both inside and outside the political economy tradition, agree that regionalism has been a "profound and fundamental feature" of Canadian life.[1] Canadian politics has revolved around persistent and often divisive conflicts about the "where" instead of the "who" or "what" of politics. Since Confederation, for example, prime ministers have discovered that their first political hurdle is to strike an acceptable balance of regional representation within cabinet. Similarly, voters' support for the major federal political parties has consistently displayed pronounced regional differences, while new parties have usually mounted their challenge to the old parties from a regional base.

Examples of regional influence on the content and course of Canadian politics are endless. Throughout much of the post–Second World War period, for example, Ottawa has made promotion of regional economic development one of its most important responsibilities. More recently, attempts at institutional reform have hinged on the claim that federal institutions would be improved by stronger guarantees for regional representation. The so-called Canada Round of constitutional reform is an obvious case and culminated in the Charlottetown Accord, which contained provisions for a "reformed" Senate on the grounds that it would better represent the people of the regions. In effect, questions of where people live and how economic development, state activity, and political power are distributed across geographical space often carry more weight in Canadian politics than other potentially loaded questions such as what people do or how well they live. In other words,

Canadians seem to be preoccupied more often with the "where?" of politics than with who gets what, when, and how.

Though Canadian politics has always been refracted through a geographical prism, there is little consensus among sociologists, economists, or geographers, let alone political scientists, about how best to interpret this regional dimension. In this chapter, I discuss some of the political meanings evoked by the concept of region, review some of the popular theoretical approaches, and trace the evolution of region within the Canadian political economy. I argue that Canadian regionalism is a dynamic historical force that can be best viewed through the lens of state development strategies, or "National Policies."[2]

THE PERPLEXITIES OF SPACE

In his last, insightful examination of Canadian federalism, the late Donald Smiley advised political scientists to "banish the term region from our vocabulary and speak instead of province."[3] Smiley was writing before implementation of the Canada–United States Free Trade Agreement (FTA) – the cornerstone of the "third national policy" (TNP) – and after over a decade of pronounced federal-provincial conflicts about power and jurisdiction, especially over control and development of natural resources. Nevertheless, his principal reason for questioning the continued utility and relevance of the term remains relevant today. He correctly argues that there is little agreement about what "region" actually means; more often than not the term is only "loosely" or "imprecisely" defined.[4] There has been a great deal of confusion and conceptual fuzziness associated with the term "region" in Canadian political discourse. The politics of space is so fundamental to Canadian politics that we often think about regional divisions as natural and inevitable without questioning what we mean when we evoke the terms "region" and "regionalism". In fact, the spatial dimension of Canadian politics conjures up a variety of meanings and a great deal of confusion, beginning with the term "spatial" itself. "Spatial" simply means pertaining to space – in this case, geographic space. Considerations of geographic space are fundamental to human thought and communication, because the identification of things is often tied to place. We suggest, for example, that a person is different because she came from the country, or Newfoundland, or Toronto. It is another matter, however, to suggest that these spatial designations are important politically. Why should considerations of where we grow up, work, or live colour our political identities?

The same can be said about "region." This term refers to some sort of spatial unit – a territorial entity having an organic unity or community of interests that is independent of political and administrative boundaries.[5] Constitutional arrangements such as federalism may set administrative boundaries on a map, but this does not make provinces the same as regions. The term "region" simply implies a sameness within a geographic space that separates or differentiates it from some other space.[6]

Regions can be defined in any number of ways – for example, in terms of topography, climate, land use, or demography. These distinctions are valuable tools for geographers but are quite irrelevant to understanding the politics of space.[7] The spatial dimension of Canadian politics involves much more than sterile, analytical distinctions, drawing lines on a map, and searching for regularities and dissimilarities in the location of things or types of behaviour. Regions in Canada have had concrete political and social dimensions that are deeply embedded in our collective historical experience. They are, in other words, much more than arbitrary intellectual constructs.[8]

The term "regionalism" is most often used to evoke these social, historical, and political considerations. Some authors suggest that it is a "state of mind," a way of seeing the world, that involves a strong identification with and commitment to territory. In turn, this sense of common identity and community informs how people assess political issues and objects. People might ask, for example, how will this policy affect our community? Other writers suggest that regionalism is inherently political, because economic, social, and cultural interests are defined and articulated in spatial terms. In this case, policies would be understood primarily as benefiting one region over another.

Regionalism is an interpretation of politics that gives greatest emphasis to the condition of the territorial entity rather than to relations among groups of people defined in non-territorial terms, such as gender, class, or race.[9] It structures political conflict around issues of territorial representation and the distribution of resources across geographical space. The imprint of regionalism runs throughout Canadian political history, but the recent struggle for Senate reform again provides an instructive example. The argument for reform centred on better representing the people of the regions rather than, for example, achieving a more equitable gender, class, or race balance in the upper chamber.

Regionalism leaves a distinctive mark on a political culture, forcing the complexities of politics through the prism of territory and territorial interest. It means that fundamental political disputes about allocation of power and resources among social groups often must pass the initial test of spatial distribution. From a definitional perspective, regionalism is simply a class of political expression and mobilization that emphasizes spatial inequalities. How regionalism is conceived or makes itself felt in national politics, however, differs substantially from one country to another and across time within the same country. The next section of this chapter briefly examines how social scientists have tried to make sense of this particularly Canadian phenomenon.

EXPLAINING CANADIAN REGIONALISM

Environmentalism

Perhaps the most familiar but least useful explanation of Canadian regionalism suggests that the vastness and diversity of Canadian geography necessarily produces profound spatial variations in culture and politics. We are often told, for example, that "nature" – the mountains, plains, and oceans – has carved Canadian geography into distinct and immutable regions that constitute an enduring and formidable obstacle to the achievement of a national identity and national unity. The Task Force on National Unity, for example, argued that "Canadian unity has always had to struggle against physical barriers which divide its territory."[10] It also has been suggested that geography is largely responsible for the great regional disparities in wealth in Canada. According to this perspective, regional variations can be explained by different and unequal endowments of natural resources, which in turn lead to differences in political culture and behaviour.

Explanations for Canadian regionalism that rely on environmental factors seem plausible, almost common sense at first blush, and are part of Canadian folklore. Nevertheless, they are deeply flawed on a number of counts. First, there is a strong element of geographical determinism in these arguments. They convey the unfounded notion that common environments give rise to similar political, social, and cultural characteristics and that human activity is ultimately explained by geography alone.[11] Second, environmental arguments suggest that regionalism is a universal political expression. But other countries that are similarly divided by geography and topography do not have regional political conflicts or, at least, not to the same degree as Canada. Why does "geography" produce "regionalism" in some countries and not in others?

As important, the environmental approach does not explain why regional identification and conflict change over time. It suggests that regionalism is as timeless and rigid as the geography to which it is tied, but, as Canadian history attests, both the sources and the content of regional conflicts have changed significantly since Confederation. All these criticisms point to one conclusion: regionalism, like all other forms of politics, is social and historical rather than natural and universal.[12] We can better understand it by looking at how people have lived out their histories on the Canadian landscape.

Institutionalism

Other political scientists have followed the route advocated by Smiley and prefer to equate regions with the provinces and the formal boundaries of federalism. They argue that regional differences, in order to become mobilized in politics, must have an institutional focus. They suggest that the provinces now provide this focus "around which parties, elections, and other political activities are organized."[13] Regionalism gives the provinces their strength, and the provinces in turn shape and reinforce this regionalism. From this perspective, provincial institutions have become the primary political institutions through which regional populations can organize and express themselves in Canadian politics.[14]

Even at the high point of Canadian provincialism in the late 1970s, this analytical conflation of region and province had problems. For one thing, by reducing regions to the institutional boundaries of federalism, researchers often saw regionalism as a simple matter of institutional conflicts and rivalries. Regions were depicted as "provincial societies" and thereby reduced to institutional actors with boundaries as rigid and permanent as constitutional jurisdictions.[15] Beyond this, the changing political economy of the late twentieth century has been the critical test for the provincial perspective. Provinces remain important actors in Canadian politics, but, unlike in the 1970s, they are no longer assertive and interventionist entities determined to shape an independent course for themselves. In the political economy of the late 1990s, they appear as only frail versions of their former selves. The provinces are now mired in deficits, starved of cash by repeated federal budget cuts to social welfare and regional development spending, weakened by declining resource prices and even the disappearance of key resources themselves, and constrained by the rules of the FTA and the North American Free Trade Agreement (NAFTA). In other words, these once powerful "regional" voices have been subdued. At the same time, new regional players have emerged in federal politics in the form of the Reform party and the Bloc Québécois.

The past decade has been marked by a profound change, commonly characterized as the "restructuring" of the economy and government programs. And these changes have influenced both the vehicles for and the content of spatial politics. Our recent experience suggests that regionalism is not the product of the "forces of nature" or of "institutional imperatives" but a malleable and fluctuating political force that is very much influenced by broader patterns in Canadian economic and political development. Put differently, Canadian history, including its regional underpinnings, was made not "by geographical forces of millions of years ago" but by the Canadian people and their politics.[16]

LINKING THE OLD AND NEW POLITICAL ECONOMIES OF REGIONALISM

Staples and National Policies

Canadian political economy has a long tradition of explaining regionalism from the perspective of the organization of human relations, particularly economic relations. Harold Innis, for example, a pioneer of Canadian political economy, argued that Canadian development could be understood only in relation to its own history. Innis argued that North America's experience was unique because it came into contact with Europe after capitalism had been firmly established as the dominant form of social organization there. Innis suggested that the key to understanding the pattern of Canadian development, including regional differences, was to trace how the invasion of European culture and the price system left their imprint on a geography that previously corresponded to the non-capitalist forms of social organization of the Aboriginal peoples.[17]

According to Innis, the new white-settler colonies of North America were forced to engage in a staples trade – unprocessed natural resources and agricultural commodities – with a series of imperial centres (first France and then Britain and the United States) in order to pay for the material and technological goods they needed for development. The type and location of economic activity within these colonies were thus determined by the imperial centre's demand for particular commodities. The exploitation of a series of staples – fish, fur, timber, wheat, and minerals – meant that different areas of the country developed at different times and in different ways as the demands of the centre changed. In general, new countries develop in relation to old countries, which, Innis stressed, has had lasting implications for Canada's economic, political, and social structure. "Each staple left its stamp, and the shift to a new staple invariably produced periods of crises."[18]

Innis argued that regional differences in social organization were attributable to political relationships, particularly the unequal relationship between the imperial centre and its colonies. This centre-periphery theme was, in turn, elaborated by the "hinterlanders school," which advanced the metropolitan-hinterland thesis of Canadian regionalism.[19]

This school argued that western Canada was created as an internal colony of central Canada. This subordinate and dependent relationship was enforced by the metropolitan-inspired policies of the federal government. These policies confined westerners to staples production and, at the same time, forced them to buy manufactured goods from the centre. Moreover, development in the hinterland was controlled and constrained by banking, business, and political actors all centred in the metropole and acting in the interests of the centre. As a result, the development of hinterland economies was thwarted and left vulnerable to the "boom and bust" of the international commodities markets, while central Canada and its economic elites reaped the benefits. Regional grievances about economic development and political representation became central themes in Canadian politics.

The metropolitan-hinterland thesis is largely concerned with explaining regional relationships during the height of the wheat boom in western Canada at the turn of the century. It has limited utility, however, for explaining the complexity and diversity of Canadian regionalism. It is unable, for example, to account for changes in centre-periphery relationships. The possibility that the dominance of the centre may be stopped or reversed by factors unrelated to the centre-periphery relationship (such as shifts in the international political economy) are ignored. Moreover, the thesis assumes that the periphery has no autonomous capacity for change.[20] While the hinterlander school is important because it emphasizes the role of social classes and state policy in the creation of Canadian regionalism, this perspective must be broadened to help us understand the many changes in the contours and content of regionalism since Confederation.

The work of Vernon Fowke, perhaps more than any other early political economist, is instructive for its focus on the role of state policy in the creation of regionalism. Fowke explicitly rejected environmental explanations for regional development patterns, emphasizing instead the central role of state policies. For Fowke, the state is a vulnerable political entity encumbered with the task of promoting national economic development and political stability within the context of unpredictable and sometimes predatory international conditions. Fowke argued that governmental policies could be ranked according to their impact on national economic development. Some policies had only minor or temporary effects, while others were pronounced and long-lasting, leaving a distinctive mark on the place and nature of economic development and pattern of politics. These "national policies" tended to be adopted in periods of crisis and were formulated in response to internal political pressures and to the demands of a changing international political economy.[21]

The concept of a "national policy" both directs our attention to the uncertainties of politics and provides a useful way of thinking about Canada's economic and political development. It underlines how state officials are mandated to promote economic development in a world of constraints and incalculables. National policies are framed within the context of shifting international circumstances, the political power of influential actors, the organization and mobilization of social forces, and the uncertainties of electoral politics. Generally, the prelude to a new national policy is deepening economic crisis and a sustained period of political instability during which state officials search for a new logic of development – another way to get the economy going again. As such, national policies represent state responses to historical change – external and internal to the state and domestic and international in origin. They comprise a logic for development which, if successful, has enduring consequences for a national political economy, structuring immediate and future patterns of investment and politics. Just important, they inform the changing fortunes and configuration of Canada's regions and the very content of spatial politics.

Radical Geography and Regulation

For many years, the new political economy tradition largely ignored spatial politics, focusing instead on creating a theory of the Canadian state. Elsewhere, however, radical geographers and economists were attempting to link national development strategies to regionalism and to historical packages of political relations. Without realizing it, they were elaborating on a perspective that informed the work of Innis and, especially, Fowke. The work of Massey, a British radical geographer, is an instructive example. Her approach to regionalism is relational, historical, and cumulative. She argues that regional differentiation is an explicitly historical process – "a series of rounds of new investment, in each of which a new form of spatial division of labour is evolved."[22] Massey, like Fowke, views regions as the consequence of historical patterns of investment, which, we might add, are structured by the prevailing national policy. And, similar to Innis, she considers regional boundaries to be relational and cumulative where packages of investment effects are layered one on top of the other in geographical space.

In many ways, Innis's encompassing vision of the multiple layers and manifestations of staples production is similar to contemporary thinking within regulation theory about the historical fit among capitalist accumulation strategies and dominant political institutions and patterns of politics. The regulation theorists employ a different language, but they, like Innis and Fowke, suggest that we should attempt to conceptualize regionalism as an integral part of historical packages of economic and political relations.

I can represent the work of the regulation theorists only very schematically here. According to these theorists, after the Second World War the economies and politics of Western liberal democracies were organized around what they term a "Fordist mode of regulation." Fordism was a whole package of relations, institutions, and arrangements that linked a particular logic of economic development during a specific historical period (the regime of accumulation) with an equally particular and complementary set of norms, habits, laws, regulations, and representations of reality (the mode of regulation).[23] The postwar years brought new understandings about, among other things, state intervention in the economy, an elaboration of bureaucratic institutions, especially in social welfare, and an expansion of the meaning of citizenship itself. At the same time, however, these theorists argue that Western democracies have now entered a new, uncertain age, which some call "post-Fordism." What this terminology is meant to convey is that we are embedded in a process of fundamental change entailing a paradigm shift in governing practices – a historic shift in state form that enacts simultaneous changes in cultural assumptions, political identities, and the terrain of political struggle, including spatial politics.

Both the old and new political economies tie periods of stability and change to historical packages of political and economic relations. Developing Fowke's perspective, I have argued that Canada's economic and political history can be roughly categorized under three national policies. Each had its separate logic of development, and each was separated from the other by a period of political and economic crisis during which politics revolved around struggles to construct a new formula for economic growth. In these periods of restructuring old logics of growth are abandoned, and there is a shift towards a significantly different order and configuration of social, economic, and political life.[24] It is widely recognized, as our politicians seem fond of reminding us, that Canada is currently undergoing a painful restructuring, which is undermining most of the familiar assumptions that have governed Canadian politics since the Second World War. What is less often recalled, however, is that Canada has undergone similar, abrupt reorientations twice before and that each period has brought different patterns of regional growth and political conflict.

But how does the idea of a national policy help us to understand spatial difference and regionalism? First, economic growth never occurs evenly in geographical space. Regional economic differentiation is inherent in capitalist development and the cumulative product of countless investment decisions. As well, national policies set out the conditions under which economic growth will take place – conditions such as the size of the market, the amount of competition from international competitors, and the degree of state intervention. National policies are a package of policies, some of which are spatially specific by design: they direct economic growth towards particular places, or they attempt to change particular environments.[25] Policies promoting western settlement or industrial-location grants, for example, would fall into this category. Other policies may have spatial effects even though they were not intended to do so. High tariffs on technological goods, for example, protect domestic manufacturers, but they also may discourage diversification of undeveloped local economies because they make new technologies too costly. Whether by intention or not, state development strategies cumulatively imprint patterns of economic development and political conflict on geographical space. Canada's history has been marked by waves of crisis, restructuring, and consolidation in the form of state development strategies or national policies.

In the remainder of this chapter, I briefly outline the major components of Canada's three national policies and their impact on regional development and politics. In particular, however, I want to outline the implications of Canada's third national policy for Canada's regions. This section cannot provide a comprehensive discussion of the rise and evolution of Canadian regionalism. Instead, it is intended to demonstrate the links between Canadian regionalism and historical shifts in the national and international political economy.

NATIONAL POLICIES AND REGIONALISM

The First National Policy

Canada's first national policy was a combination of policy initiatives – some spatial in design and others not – that took shape in the period between 1867 and 1885. The so-called first National Policy (FNP) of the Fathers of Confederation was devised on the premise that a new transcontinental economy, paralleling that of the United States, could be imposed on the landscape of the northern half of the continent by:

- integrating the former British colonies into a new federal state with sufficient legislative powers to underwrite and direct development;
- subsuming and developing the vast western territories under the auspices of the federal state;

- constructing transcontinental transportation and communication links;
- implementing a protective tariff to encourage trade between the various units of the new federation and stimulate domestic manufacturing.

Though Canada's first development strategy was called a "national policy," it was in fact a series of regional policies which invited each of the former colonies into the union in different ways and with different long-term political and economic consequences. Perhaps nowhere was this more obvious than in the west, where the Aboriginal lands and the property of the Hudson's Bay Company had to be transformed into a frontier for central Canadian investment, a market for eastern manufacturers and a source of supply for commodity traders.[26] The FNP had a westward bias in development opportunities, and its success depended on the rapid settlement and exploitation of the western hinterland. To this end, the dominion government moved quickly to establish the power of the Canadian state over the territory by creating the North West Mounted Police. It removed the Native population from valuable land through coercion and treaty making, actively sought producers and consumers through white-settler immigration, and underwrote construction of transportation links.[27]

These actions were designed to transform and integrate the western region into the new east-west economy, but from the beginning those occupying the west were placed in a subordinate relationship with the rest of the country. For one thing, the prairie region was slow to be granted provincial status and then was denied the same constitutional power over natural resources enjoyed by the other provinces. The west also was forced to pay higher freight rates than the east, even though it was totally dependent on the railways to transport wheat to eastern markets. So-called "fair discrimination" meant that the same bushel of wheat cost more to ship the same distance if it started its journey in the west. Later, western wheat producers were charged more to ship processed than unprocessed wheat, a disincentive to the growth of milling industry there.

The western settlement and freight rate policies were spatially specific – intentionally imposing different treatments on different parts of the new country. In contrast, the protective tariff, implemented in 1885, applied equally to all parts of Canada. Its impact, nevertheless, was decidedly spatial. In principle, the high-tariff policy was meant to protect Canada's infant industries from foreign competition through import-substitution industrialization (ISI). The idea was to put high duties on things for which there already was an established market, such as clothing and farm implements, so that imports would be more costly than domestic products. Internal demand in turn would help domestic industries expand, diversify, and eventually export their products.

Canada's high-tariff policy had pronounced and lasting consequences for the spatial distribution of industry and for the content of regional political conflict. It was, for example, a major source of tension between west and east. Western farmers resented it because it pushed up the cost of farm equipment, reduced profits, and delayed mechanization of farming. At the same time, it appeared to protect inefficient eastern industry. Meanwhile in central Canada, the tariff encouraged establishment of a branch-plant manufacturing sector. Locked out of the Canadian market, American industry simply set up subsidiary facilities largely in Ontario to gain access to Canadian consumers. Ontario industry was secure so long as the rest of Canada remained its captive market, while the west in particular had to endure the uncertainties of the international commodities market for its income. It is hardly surprising, then, that Ontario came to be known as the "fat cat" of Confederation and the tariff as a direct subsidy from the west to the east. These were central themes in the politics of regionalism during this period, leading to, among other things, the western farmers' revolt, the 1911 free-trade election, which pitted west against east; the meteoric rise of the Progressive party in the national party system; and the election of farmers' governments throughout the prairie provinces.

The case of the Maritimes vividly illustrates how a new logic of development – a change in the rules of the game – can effectively shift the spatial distribution of economic activity within a national territory and alter the future of its component parts. Prior to the development of the west, the Maritime provinces were favourably poised for industrialization. In fact, pro-Confederation forces there argued that the Maritimes ultimately would become the industrial heartland of the new dominion. They already had a growing manufacturing sector and boasted the country's only viable known coal and iron deposits. And in the beginning, industry grew faster in the Maritimes than anywhere else in Canada.

By the turn of the century, however, a number of factors converged to deindustrialize the Maritimes. These included the merger movement, during which larger, central Canadian enterprises swallowed up their Maritime competitors; freight-rate increases, which made it more costly for Maritime producers to compete on the western market-, and the investment decisions of Maritime industrialists. Not surprisingly, many successful Maritime companies shifted their investments westward in order to participate in the boom. By the 1920s, the region had been drained of much of its industry and population and had lost a good measure of political power. Central themes in its regional politics were demands for measures to reverse the downward spiral and return the region to its former role in Confederation. During the 1920s, the region also saw the rise of the Maritime Rights Movement, a separatist organization convinced that the region would be better off outside Confederation.

Maritime supporters of Confederation had envisioned increased prosperity and industrialization because it promised to provide transportation links to a larger market, new investment opportunities on the western frontier, and tariff protection from American competitors. As current-day opponents of free trade are quick to point out, however, the effects of economic integration are not unidirectional. Economic integration does give the smaller unit access to the larger market, but the larger market also invades the smaller unit. In the process, the smaller unit can become vulnerable to competition and concentration as capitalists in the newly integrated market rationalize production in relation to that market. Just as important, competitive producers in the smaller unit adapt to the logic of the new market. The links established by Confederation and the FNP did not merely establish a new external frame of reference, they recast the entire internal economic structure of the Maritime provinces.[28]

In sum, then, the FNP forged an east-west economy, leaving in its wake an industrializing and diversified centre, a deindustrialized east, and a primary-exporting western hinterland. By the 1920s, however, the conditions that had structured its logic and dynamic were quickly passing. The west had been settled, prairie farms were equipped with eastern products, and most of the good land was in production. As well, demand for resources was rapidly changing as the discovery of electrical power and the invention of the internal combustion engine stimulated production of electrical appliances and automobiles. The new industrialism strengthened the manufacturing sector at the centre and shifted the sites of resource extraction to the northern frontiers of Ontario, Quebec, and British Columbia.

The Great Depression of the 1930s, which saw the close of international markets for Canadian resources, dealt the final blow to the FNP. As the decade went on, it became clear that the old logics would no longer provide for growth or stability. Lost for solutions, the dominion government appointed the Rowell-Sirois Commission to devise a new national policy. In the meantime, prairie electorates experimented with new economic visions advanced primarily by Social Credit and the Co-operative Commonwealth Confederation. It would take a decade of economic and political crisis and a world war, however, before the many threads of the second national policy (SNP) were set in place.

The Second National Policy

Again, space does not allow for a detailed discussion of the SNP. Suffice it to say that it, like its predecessor, was an amalgam of several distinct policy initiatives, which together comprised a new model for economic growth and development. It also prescribed a central but different role for the national state. The Depression had underscored the fact that the old tools of economic management were no longer adequate to ensure economic stability and growth in mature capitalist economies. Unveiled in the last months of the war, the new growth plan contained three fundamental strands:

- development of social welfare programs;
- implementation of Keynesian-inspired, demand-management fiscal and monetary policies;
- a commitment to a liberalized international trading regime, especially with the United States.

The reign of the SNP was relatively short, but it supported an unprecedented period of economic growth, with a few brief interruptions, throughout the 1950s and 1960s. It was based on the assumption that economic prosperity could be achieved by liberalizing trade and ensuring that Canada had a healthy investment climate. Within the context of the immediate postwar period, however, this strategy effectively meant closer ties with American corporations and the continental market.

The SNP had a number of spatial and political effects that both built on and distinguished it from its predecessor. It established a new set of economic and political links that served to change the pattern of regional definition and integration. The Atlantic region remained depressed. It was neither rich in the relevant resources nor a significant manufacturing sector and thus was largely excluded from the new logic of development. Meanwhile, the invasion of American branch plants and direct investment in the resource sector entrenched Ontario's position as the dominant partner in Confederation. Equally important, the east-west logic of the Canadian economy gradually began to erode as different regional spaces were drawn into a north-south links with the American economy. Areas of the prairies, for example, that had been tied into a metropolitan-hinterland relationship with central Canada under the FNP gradually were transformed into a resource hinterland of the United States under the SNP.

This process, however, was selective in so far as some areas were prospering as a component of the new transnational market while others were irrelevant to it.[29] Economic growth and prosperity became increasingly uneven, with Ontario gaining the lion's share of the benefits of the new growth model. It was not long therefore before there was a revolt of the regions that had not benefited from the economic boom. During the late 1950s, the peripheries mobilized behind John Diefenbaker's Conservative party, which promised a new economic strategy based on northern and peripheral development. In the end, this coalition of outsiders could not match the political power of the continentalist forces, and Diefenbaker was driven from office. The regional revolt, however, did force successive federal governments to adopt a series of regional development initiatives throughout the 1960s and 1970s in an ill-fated attempt to reduce regional disparities and disarm political tensions. Paradoxically, the very success of the SNP, complete with its spatial biases, enabled Ottawa to finance its regional development policies.

The SNP brought a quarter-century of unprecedented growth and expansion of an increasingly continentalized, recourse-based and branch-plant economy. Redistribution was achieved through social-welfare policies, but social tensions could not be contained without also redistributing wealth across space. Postwar development had been highly uneven, giving most of the benefits to Ontario and the resource-rich provinces. Equalization and regional-development programs served to legitimate this growth model because, in combination with social welfare, they did boost per-capita income and underwrite provision of reasonable services in the have-not regions. These policies, however, never closed the gap between the rich and the poor regions. Spatial redistribution was necessary to cushion the disparities and contradictions inherent in the developmental strategy and to contain political protest.

The Third National Policy

By the 1970s, the logic of the SNP began to unravel as each of its strands was challenged by a rapidly changing economic environment. Increasingly these changes rendered the assumptions of the postwar economic order obsolete and altered relations between countries and within them. For example, the United States lost its hegemonic position in the world economy, while previous manufacturing centres such as Ontario and Quebec watched countless jobs move to low-wage countries. The federal government's initial response to these changes was to resort to the tried and true instruments of the SNP such as economic stimulation, including regional-development strategies, to get the economy back on its feet. But the economy proved increasingly

resistant to these tools as both unemployment and inflation (stagflation) remained high. By 1980, the economy fell into the deepest recession since the Depression, and nothing Ottawa did appeared to help.

The economy was in trouble, and the postwar consensus about Canada's national development strategy gradually but surely broke down.
These years were marked by economic crisis and conflict over alternative futures. Throughout the 1980s, however, the increasingly
ascendant view was that government spending, particularly on social-
welfare programs, and misguided Keynesianism were at the root of the
crisis. This neo-conservative critique, which embraced the tenets of classic laissez-faire liberalism, attacked two of the central tenets of the SNP.
It rejected the utility of Keynesian demand-management techniques,
advocating instead a supply-side and market-driven approach. It also
attacked government spending, especially on social welfare, as market
distorting and as luxuries that the economy could no longer afford.

By 1982, the federal government tacitly admitted that it was at a loss
as to how to chart the economic future and that the SNP had run its
course. It appointed the Royal Commission on the Economic Union
and Development Prospects for Canada and requested that it recom-
mend the "appropriate national goals and policies for economic development."[30] After three years of public consultation, compilation of
briefs from the private sector, and the commissioning of hundreds
of academic studies, the Macdonald Commission concluded that a
market-driven approach and free trade with the United States were the
only alternatives left to Canadian decision makers. There was no guarantee that this strategy would restore Canada to its previous prosperity.
Canadians would simply have to take a "leap of faith" because there
was nowhere else to turn.

Though the TNP is still in the process of negotiation and refine-
ment, its key elements are readily discernible. These include:

- hemispheric economic integration;
- market-driven development;
- reducing the role of the state, especially in the provision of social
  welfare;
- privatization.

The FTA and NAFTA are central to each of these elements of the TNP.
They define a new role for the federal state and the provinces. For
most of this century, nation-states acted to promote domestic welfare
and to protect national economies from disruptive international
forces.[31] Indeed, this was a fundamental motivation underlying both
the FNP and the SNP. The new logic of the TNP is that nation-states
must now abandon their role as buffer and force national economies

to adjust to the stark realities of the market and global competition. This vision gives priority to the market in the determination of alternative futures and thus requires the shrinking or "hollowing out" of the Keynesian welfare state.[32]

The FTA specifically limits the terrain of the political by prohibiting governments from either favouring domestic producers or subsidizing domestic industries. These strategies were an integral part of both the FNP and the SNP as well as regional-development policies during the 1960s and 1970s. NAFTA goes even further by effectively restricting the domain of the state. It refers to the public sector as "nonconforming" measures, limits use of public corporations, and requires that those remaining must operate according to proper commercial considerations. Again, public corporations have been key actors in promoting regional development in Canada. And, indeed, in recent years we have witnessed the virtual drying up of federal regional-development initiatives and regional-development funds.

The TNP is guided by the logic of classic laissez-faire economics and the perceived imperatives of globalization and free trade. The new consensus is that Canada has to change the rules of the economic union in order to survive in the new global order. These rules would ideally give priority to market forces in the determination and location of economic activity, promote regional specialization and competitiveness, and enable states to compete for highly fluid international capital. In more tangible terms, this means reducing fiscal and regulatory burdens on industry and lowering expectations about the role of the state, particularly in social welfare, employment, labour standards, and regional development.

While the provisions of the FTA and NAFTA go a long way towards realizing these ends, the Mulroney government attempted to constitutionalize these rules during the "Canada Round." A master of the politics of stealth, the Mulroney government attempted to achieve a new regulatory regime under the guise of constitutional renewal. Its "Proposals for a Stronger Economic Union" included a common-market provision that would forbid both the federal and the provincial governments from preventing the free movement of persons, goods, services, or capital within Canada. It also sought to empower the federal government to "exclusively make laws in relation to any matter that it declares to be for the efficient functioning of the economic union."[33] And, finally, it sought to harmonize provincial budgets with an anti-inflationary federal monetary policy.

Opposition from both the provinces and equality-seeking groups ensured that these proposals would not be part of the Charlottetown Accord, which itself failed. Nevertheless, many of these outcomes are being enforced through fiat. Throughout the 1980s and early 1990s, the Mulroney government's overriding agenda was tied to the dismantling of the state envisioned and constructed by the SNP. And the election of a Liberal government in 1993 has not slowed or reversed this process. This demolition project has largely been supported by the arguments that state activism stifles private-sector initiatives and that the economy is being strangled by a government-deficit crisis. This crisis has demanded, among other things, privatization of crown corporations, abandonment of regional-development policies, deregulation of industry, government cost cutting, and the complete redesign of unemployment-insurance and social-welfare policies.

Rhetoric aside, the federal government's greatest successes in deficit reduction during the 1980s and early 1990s were achieved by "downloading." It simply shifted larger and larger portions of social-welfare costs to the provinces. Ottawa historically has committed itself to paying 50 per cent of welfare costs, but during the 1990s it has progressively reduced its share.[34] In fact, with the introduction of the Canada Health and Social Transfer in the 1995 federal budget, the government signalled the end to cost-sharing in social welfare. Many provinces have an insufficient tax base to support existing services and thus have been forced to increase taxes, reduce the size of their public sector, and cut back on fundamental services. Similar to the pre-SNP period, provincial disparities in the provision of basic public services are quickly becoming the norm. The question of location is becoming central to both the availability and the quality of health care, education, and social welfare in Canada.

It is too early to appreciate fully how the TNP will reconfigure Canada's regions and regional politics, but some trends are discernible. First, the relative fortunes of the regions increasingly depend on how they integrate into the continental and global markets rather than the national market. British Columbia has been very successful in this regard, linking its economy both to the Pacific Rim countries and to the northwest American states. Indeed, there are some who now argue that this province should break with Confederation and form a new political unit called "Cascadia" with its adjoining American counterparts. Second, the massive deindustrialization of Ontario after the implementation of the FTA means that the Canadian economy has very much lost its centre. More than this, it means that there is much less room to redistribute income across the regions. When manufacturing jobs and profits flow from the centre to outside the country, there are neither the resources nor the political rationale to continue equalization and regional-development programs. Finally, we are also witnessing changes in the administration of space. The Maritime provinces, for example, are increasingly rationalizing their health and education systems as well as their procurement policies on a regional rather than a provincial basis. From west to east we are witnessing changing regional forms and increasing spatial differentiation in institutions, living standards, and government services. All these factors will lay the groundwork for the spatial politics of the TNP.

CONCLUSION

This chapter has argued that the shift from one national policy to another has profound implications for the spatial distribution of development and for the content of regional politics. The current round of restructuring is no exception. The TNP was the culmination of decades of ever-deepening continental economic integration with the United States and has irreversibly shifted the spatial logic of the economy from an east–west axis to north–south and global axes.

When Brian Mulroney tried to sell the FTA to the Canadian public, he argued that it would enable all of Canada's regions to "trade their way to prosperity."[35] It is readily apparent that the transition to a new development strategy has been more complex, changing the role of governments and the relative prosperity of regions. Similar to Confederation, the FTA and NAFTA represent a new external frame of reference that recasts the entire internal structure of the Canadian economy. The first years of the FTA have witnessed abrupt reversals in the fortunes of some of Canada's regions and the further marginalization of others. And as Canadian history demonstrates, such fluctuations are fuel for regionalism and regional politics. This time, however, the new rules of the game effectively prevent the federal government both from acting as a buffer between the domestic and international economies and from affecting the spatial distribution of growth within Canada. The future of Canada's regions will very much hinge on how successfully they can carve a unique position for themselves in the new economic order.

NOTES

1 Elkins and Simeon, *Small*, vii.
2 Brodie, *Political*, chap. 4.
3 Smiley, *Federal*, 22–3.
4 Ibid., 156–8.
5 Brodie, *Political*, chap. 1.
6 Matthews, *Creation*.

7 Brodie, *Political*, chap. 1.
8 Brodie, *Political*, 35–6.
9 Breton, "Regionalism," 59.
10 Canada, *Future*, 28.
11 Brym, *Regionalism*, 4.
12 Brodie, *Political*, 15.
13 Simeon and Elkins, *Small*, xi–xii.
14 Canada, *Future*, 27.
15 Cairns, "Governments."
16 Laxer, "Class," 336.
17 Innis, *Fur.*
18 Ibid., 385; see Berger, *Writing*, 91.
19 Works in this genre include Macpherson, *Democracy*; Mallory, *Social*; *Power in Canada* and Morton, *Progressive*.
20 Gore, *Regions*, 191.
21 Fowke, "National."
22 Massey, "Regionalism," 115.
23 Harvey, *Postmodern*, 121–3.
24 Soja, *Postmodern*, 159.
25 Gore, *Regions*, 212.
26 Phillips, *Regional*, 51.
27 Leadbeater, *Essays.*
28 Frost et al., *Industrialization and Underdevelopment.*
29 Stevenson, "Canadian."
30 Canada, *Report*, xii.
31 Cox, "Global."
32 Jessop, "Schumpeterian," 22.
33 Canada, *Shaping.*
34 *Toronto Star*, 22 Sept., 1993, A28.
35 Quoted in Brodie, *Political*, 1.

REFERENCES

Berger, Carl. *The Writing of Canadian History*. Toronto: Oxford University Press, 1976.

Breton, R. "Regionalism in Canada." In David Cameron, ed., *Regionalism and Supranationalism*, 57–82. Montreal: Institute for Research in Public Policy, 1981.

Brodie, Janine. *The Political Economy of Canadian Regionalism*. Toronto: Harcourt, Brace, Jovanovich, 1990.

– "Politics on the Boundaries: Restructuring and the Canadian Women's Movement." Eighth Annual Robarts Lecture. Robarts Centre for Canadian Studies, York University, 1994.

- "Regions and Regionalism." In James Bickerton and Alain-G. Gagnon, eds., *Canadian Politics*, 2nd ed., 409–25. Peterborough, Ont.: Broadview Press, 1994.

Brym, Robert. *Regionalism in Canada*. Toronto: Irwin, 1986.

Cairns, Alan., "The Governments and Societies of Canadian Federalism." *Canadian Journal of Political Science* (Dec. 1977), 695–726.

Canada. *Report of the Royal Commission on the Economic Union and Development Prospects for Canada*. Ottawa: Supply and Services, 1985.

- *Shaping Canada's Future Together: Proposals*. Ottawa: Supply and Services, 1991.

- Task Force on Canadian Unity Report. *A Future Together*. Ottawa: Supply and Services, 1979.

Cox, Robert. "The Global Political Economy and Social Choice." In Daniel Drache and Meric Gertler, eds., *The New Era of Global Competition: State Policy and Market Power*, 335–49. Montreal: McGill-Queen's University Press.

Elkins, David. and Simeon, Richard, eds. *Small Worlds: Provinces and Parties in Canadian Political Life*. Toronto: Methuen, 1980.

Fowke, Vernon. "The National Policy – Old and New." *Canadian Journal of Economics and Political Science*, 18 no. 3 (Aug. 1952), 271–86.

Frost, J., et al. *Industrialization and Underdevelopment in the Maritimes*. Toronto: Garamond Press, 1985.

Gore, Charles. *Regions in Question*. London: Methuen, 1984.

Harvey, David. *The Postmodern Condition*. London: Basil Blackwell, 1989.

Innis, Harold. *The Fur Trade in Canada*. Toronto: University of Toronto Press, 1956.

Jessop, Bob. "The Schumpeterian Workfare State." *Studies in Political Economy* (spring 1993), 7–40.

Laxer, Gordon. "Class, Nationality, and the Roots of the Branch Plant Economy." In Gordon Laxer, ed., *Perspectives on Canadian Economic Development*, 228–66. Toronto: Oxford University Press, 1991.

Leadbeater, David. *Essays on the Political Economy of Alberta*. Toronto: New Hogtown Press, 1984.

Lipietz, Alain. *Mirages and Miracles*. London: Verso, 1987.

Macpherson, C.B. *Democracy in Alberta: Social Credit and the Party System*. Toronto: University of Toronto Press, 1955.

Mallory, James. *Social Credit and the Federal Power in Canada*. Toronto: University of Toronto Press, 1954.

Massey, Doreen. "Regionalism: Some Issues." *Capital and Class*, 6 (1978), 56–77.

Matthews, Ralph. *The Creation of Regional Dependency*. Toronto: University of Toronto Press, 1983.

Phillips, Paul. *Regional Disparities*. 2nd ed. Toronto: Lorimer, 1984.

Schwartz, Mildred. *Politics and Territory*. Montreal: McGill-Queen's University Press, 1974.

Smiley, Donald. *The Federal Condition in Canada*. Toronto: McGraw-Hill Ryerson, 1986.

Soja, Edward. *Postmodern Geographies*. London: Verso, 1989.

Stevenson, Garth. "Canadian Regionalism in Continental Perspective." *Journal of Canadian Studies* (summer 1980), 48–72.

12 The Challenges of the Quebec Question: Paradigm, Counter-paradigm, and … ?

DANIEL SALÉE AND
WILLIAM D. COLEMAN

Perhaps more than any province, indeed perhaps more than Canada itself, Quebec offers a unique perspective on the major contemporary themes and issues of political economy. The particular turns of Quebec's history over the last three decades provide a range of societal experiences, processes, and realities that highlight the complexity of the dynamics of late modern capitalist societies.

In many ways, Quebec stands as a laboratory from which to explore, and take stock of, the changes that have marked Western social formations since the Second World War. Going from a rather defensive, inward-looking social perspective to one of political and economic emancipation and a concomitant, active openness to the world, French-speaking Quebecers transformed their outlook in the 1960s. In a bid to affirm themselves – to become "masters in our own home" – and to redress the socio-political imbalance they had historically suffered in spite of their being a cultural and linguistic majority in a territory they had come to call their own, they democratized their political, social, and educational institutions. In the process, they virtually erected a nation-state as they sought to take control of the province's economy. They created state institutions to support the development of a viable, indigenous, francophone capitalist class, and they imposed a French-dominated modus operandi for the conduct of public affairs within the province. The evolution of Quebec provides, in a microcosmic way, insights into patterns of global societal change that are marking advanced capitalist societies.

This chapter begins with a traditional political economy overview of the major processes at play in the shaping of Quebec's society over time. It then assesses critically more recent political economy thinking that raises questions about the traditional approach, and it concludes with an appraisal of the prospects and challenges confronting the analysis of Quebec's economy and society.

QUEBEC AND THE EMERGENCE OF A COUNTER-PARADIGM

During the nineteenth century, Quebec's political and economic elites were persuaded to join into a broader political union, the Canadian Confederation, that served the interests of an expanding capitalist class. Its history in this regard is similar to other regional or national communities of the world with a distinct society and a particular self-identity: Flanders in Belgium, Catalonia in Spain, Lombardy in Italy, Scotland in the United Kingdom, and Corsica in France were all invited or coerced to belong to a broader "country" – that is, to a political creation expected to further the domestic and foreign interests of a rising bourgeoisie.

Quebec was no exception. By 1867, the dominant anglo-Canadian capitalist class had built Montreal to be its financial and commercial capital. There was little question that the francophone hinterland for this class would accompany it into the new Canadian federation. Anglo-Canadian, British, and later American capital was to dominate the Quebec economy over the next century. As the territory of British North America was gradually absorbed into the Canadian federation, the French-speaking periphery in Quebec was joined by new areas rich in natural resources to the west and the north in particular. Under the import-substitution industrialization strategy, the anglo-Canadian capitalist class gradually extended capitalist market relations throughout most of the Canadian territory. Until the end of the Second World War, Quebec remained one cog among several in the domestic growth and expansion of the largely English-speaking Canadian and u.s. capitalist classes.

The integration of francophone Quebec and of other regions into the Canadian political union reflected the interest of big capital in constructing, developing, and protecting a large market base. The eventual, albeit reticent erection of a welfare state in the decades following the Second World War[1] was expected to cushion some of the unfortunate side effects of the business cycle in this large market. This welfare state was premised on Keynesian postulates: the Canadian economy must remain relatively closed and can be "managed" by the manipulation of fiscal and monetary policies. By the 1960s, Canada represented the realization of the nineteenth-century dream of Canadian capitalists: a stable, continent-wide economy where capitalist relations dominated in most economic exchanges. The inclusion of the distinct Quebec society in this country-wide market was consistent with this dream.

By the early 1970s, however, the liberalization pressures unleashed in the international system with successive agreements under the General Agreement on Tariffs and Trade (GATT) brought into question the continued viability of protected, country-wide markets. The growth of international banking, bond, and equities markets, coupled to liberalization of capital controls, undermined the efficacy of the policy levers that were key to the Keynesian welfare state. Faced with pressures from domestic capitalists forced to compete in broader world markets, governments were summoned to reduce the amount of revenues collected from capitalists. Reluctant to cut expenditures to match the decline of revenues, these same governments increased the public debt and the payments they owed to large domestic and foreign creditors. By the mid-1980s, the efficacy of the Keynesian monetary and fiscal instruments had declined drastically as a result. Federal and provincial governments began to heed the calls of Canadian capitalists for deficit and public-debt reduction. They gradually espoused the new right's theses about budgetary austerity and strict financial management, withdrawal of the state from various social programs, and the self-regulating nature of unimpeded market mechanisms. This situation was not without consequences for the cohesiveness of Canada's political institutions, as the federal government, increasingly under pressure from finance capital, had to devolve a number of financial and administrative responsibilities to the provinces, thus weakening its own claim to be a national government.

Quebec's own political economy can be understood against this general backdrop of Canada's economic history since the mid-nineteenth century. As a member of a larger, national capitalist framework, Quebec's socioeconomic fate has been inevitably and closely linked to that of Canada. But as a distinct and cohesive society within that broader political entity, increasingly bent on asserting more political autonomy, Quebec has also sought its own solutions to the country's economic transformations and predicaments.

Quebec's socio-political trajectory in the past three decades largely reflects this search for solutions adapted to its own concerns. Two parallel processes have triggered this search. First, the new international economic conditions that destabilized the Canadian economy and forced it into a reformulation of its orientation after 1970 brought many provinces to look for ways to promote their own local and regional economic interests, thus accelerating the polarization between increasingly incompatible national and provincial visions of the country.[2] Second, after 1960, there emerged within Quebec a new configuration of social and class forces, putting in a leading role a modernist, nationalist, francophone petite bourgeoisie prepared to insist on the political and administrative autonomy of Quebec.[3] These processes worked together to produce a Quebec-centred paradigm of sociopolitical existence (what we call here a "counter-paradigm").[4] Some observers believe that it is possible for Quebec to realize the objectives of this paradigm within Canada; others conclude that it can work to the best interests of the province only if Quebec opts out of the current Canadian political and institutional structures. This debate is still unresolved, but it is quite clear to a large majority of political and social actors in Quebec that whatever the solution to Canada's economic predicament, Quebec's particular interests must be foremost in Quebec.

As social forces developed in Quebec during the 1950s and 1960s, successive provincial governments encouraged the pooling and growth of indigenous sources of capital, which were then targeted to support the growth and expansion of an indigenous, principally francophone, business class.[5] Some elements of this class came into increased competition with capitalists based in other parts of Canada and in the United States. In addition, development of provincial-government institutions as part of the welfare state was accompanied by rapid unionization of public-sector workers. These workers added a dynamic element to the Quebec labour movement, pushing it to adopt a more radical, socialist position.[6] Simultaneously, the Quebec labour movement increased its autonomy from national labour organizations in Canada.

Both the emerging francophone bourgeoisie and the labour movement questioned in their own way the hegemonic sway of Canadian socioeconomic agents and political institutions, a questioning that appeared first in political struggles over language.[7] For indigenous capitalists, language policy became a tool in their competition with outside interests. Their increased social power was reflected in new policies that made French the language of business and government. For workers, language became a stake in their struggle with capitalists, particularly against those from outside Quebec. By gaining the right to work in French, not only did workers increase their power in the workplace, but they also added a specific Québécois element to their identity as workers.

The pressure to adopt French as the standard language throughout Quebec society opened additional areas of debate and reflection. The conceptual shift from considering French to be a defining characteristic of a nationality to that of a society led to a broadening of the perceived boundaries of that society. The passage from Canadien français to Québécois in everyday self-identification marked the transition from a homogeneous society based on ethnicity to a pluralist society based on territory. Within this reconceived society, a new understanding of relationships had to be developed between the francophone "majority" and the non-francophone "minorities."[8] By the mid-1980s, Quebec's distinctiveness as a society came to be redefined, at least theoretically, as the fortunate combination of this majority and associated minorities. In the process, the new Québécois identity represented a further challenge to the hegemonic paradigm and its conception of French Canadians as a minority within a bilingual, multicultural Canada.[9]

One of the central tenets of Canada's hegemonic paradigm – Canada is an indissoluble nation-state – soon began to be questioned as members of the Quebec francophone middle class faced barriers to economic and social advancement both within the private capitalist world in Quebec and in the federal public service outside Quebec. Throughout the 1960s, they wondered out loud whether their aspirations might be better met in a new (Quebec) nation-state. A formal alliance between the rural, traditional middle class and the new technocratic and professional classes of the cities led to formation of the Parti Québécois (PQ) in 1968. By the April 1970 election, the new political party had also attracted significant working-class support. Throughout the 1970s, the PQ served as the greenhouse for the nurturing of a paradigm countering that which was dominant in Canada.

This counter-paradigm had penetrated deeply Quebec's political culture and civic ethics by the time further changes in the Canadian regime of accumulation and the state took place in the 1980s. Under intense pressures from the staples fraction of the Canadian capitalist class, the federal government moved to secure better access to U.S. markets. Completion of the Canada–United States Free Trade Agreement in 1988 marked the formal end to the idea of a distinct and autonomous Canadian economy. The government had acknowledged that Canada was but one region among others in the larger continental economy.[10] In addition, following the lead of the Bank of Canada, federal authorities adopted a monetarist view of economic policy.[11] Eschewing even the half-hearted commitment to full employment characteristic of a "Canadian" Keynesian view, policy makers chose price stability as their principal macroeconomic objective.[12] Such a choice was hardly surprising, given the increasing size of the public debt. Large institutional investors, multinational banks, and international securities houses sought assurance that their holdings of government securities would retain their value. By their buying and selling behaviour, they indicated clearly that in the absence of a commitment to stable prices they would demand a premium in interest payments.

The adoption of price stability as a primary economic objective marked the removal of a central building block of the hegemonic paradigm: Canadian governments no longer had much flexibility in the use of fiscal policy to promote full employment, and they clearly deferred in monetary policy to the "autonomous" central bank. The abandonment of Keynesian policy making marked the demise of significant federal attempts to redistribute wealth between the rich and the poor. Throughout the 1980s and 1990s, the gap increased between the relative standard of living and disposable wealth of the capitalist and the labouring classes.[13]

Within Quebec, the reformulated Canadian accumulation regime based on continentalism and monetarism became increasingly contested by the nationalist coalition headed by the PQ. Throughout the 1980s, this coalition expanded its class base to include not only workers and the middle class but also a growing number of Quebec-based capitalists. After a change in the leadership of the party in the late 1980s, the PQ moved actively to revise and deepen the counter-paradigm developed during the previous two decades.

In a document made public in the spring of 1993, under the title *Le Québec dans un monde nouveau* – and published in English the following year – the PQ unveiled its new blueprint, purportedly to help Quebec face changing circumstances. The volume opens by establishing as given the increased interdependence of the world's economies: to succeed, a nation-state must look more and more to export markets and must rely on international economic institutions and trade agreements to protect access to these markets. Second, the transition to this more globalized economy has placed tremendous pressure on the social welfare state and such programs as unemployment insurance, social assistance, and universal health care. As these programs have suffered through program cuts, fissures in society have widened between the poor and other classes, between peripheral regions and metropolitan centres, and between ethnic and religious groups.

Faced with these two profound social changes, the party purports to reject the neo-liberal world-view increasingly dominant in the Canadian paradigm. It argues that governments should not stand aside; rather, they must actively formulate coherent adjustment strategies to maximize opportunities in the new economy. Also, they must protect as best they can the social safety nets. Finally, they must cultivate and promote social solidarity and mutual responsibility.

In response to this analysis of the socioeconomic consequences of the new accumulation regime, the PQ sees a key place for a strong, active, interventionist state. In fact, it is urgent that the state move quickly and undertake major reforms. For such action to occur in Quebec, the PQ adds, sovereignty is a virtual necessity. The Canadian federal system is so paralysed by overlapping responsibilities and inter-governmental bickering, and the Canadian state so lacks legitimacy in Quebec following failed constitutional discussions, that no effective state response is possible within existing arrangements. Only the Quebec state can assume this full role, and only when it becomes a new, sovereign member of the family of nations.

The PQ's attempt to articulate a social-democratic counter-paradigm is signalled further by its overriding commitment to job creation and achievement of full employment. Together, these commitments form the core objectives around which the PQ's societal plan is built. In sketching out this plan, the party moves away from the typical social-democratic Keynesianism of the 1960s and 1970s – that is, management of demand by manipulation of fiscal and monetary macroeconomic policies. Its social democracy rests on a strong, interventionist state to be sure, but one that acts on the supply side, using microeconomic policies. In this context, the need to build social solidarity and a sense of partnership among key societal actors is crucial and a major plank of the PQ's strategy of action, one in which the state does indeed loom fairly large, though in a way different from that which was in vogue in the 1960s and 1970s: "For a full employment policy to work, it is essential for all stakeholders in employment – government, business, the cooperative movement, trade unions, community groups and educational institutions – to participate and work together ... Here the public authorities have the role of orchestra conductor or catalyst: they ensure that cohesion and solidarity among economic stakeholders work to best advantage."[14] This notion of social partnership echoes the social corporatism of the similarly small European states of Norway, Sweden, and Austria. It also represents a long-standing goal of the PQ. While in power from 1976 to 1985, the PQ set up a framework for joint decision making by social partners in various sectors.

Again, the PQ stresses repeatedly that this revitalized social-democratic society can be created and sustained only if Quebec becomes a sovereign state: "Sovereignty will provide us with the conditions in which full employment can be achieved because it will, at long last, make possible reaching the crucial goal of coherence in our policies relating to economic development – job training policies, fiscal and

budgetary policies, industrial and agricultural policies, regional development policies."[15] Sovereignty is also considered crucial for social
solidarity because it gives "Quebec control over all the instruments it
needs to develop its cultural identity."[16] Hence it will allow anglophones and other minorities to dispense with competing loyalties to
Canada and Quebec and to commit themselves firmly to Quebec. It
will provide a new context for drawing up a "social contract" between
the government of Quebec and Aboriginal peoples. For the PQ, realization of its social-democratic vision for Quebec is possible only if
Quebec becomes an independent nation-state.

Clearly, within the Canadian context, Quebec society has become
the site of an intense debate between competing paradigms that pro-
pose alternative strategies for adjusting to the reconstructed capitalist
economy. This debate brings into question the established boundaries
of the Canadian nation-state, the role of the state, the future of wealth-
redistribution policies, and the identity of Quebecers.

Its ramifications within Quebec are no less significant. The success
of the counter-paradigm offered by Quebec's nationalist political elite
is premised largely on achieving a wide social consensus with regard
to public policy. Building and strengthening this consensus no doubt
constitute a major challenge to those who believe in Quebec sovereignty. It implies a collective social project to which a large majority
can rally. Thus the PQ's insistence on solidarity and partnership is
politically strategic: without a broad coalition, the counter-paradigm
cannot be achieved.

In an age of socio-political fragmentation, when the political dynamic
of modern societies is shaped mainly by particularistic demands for
recognition of the public place of singular identities, broad, collective
social projects may prove harder and harder to sell. History has shown
that the consensus on which societies rest is often defined and imposed
by socially or economically dominant classes or groups. It essentially reflects their hegemonic position and their inevitable desire to preserve
it. Consensus-driven societies often rest on forms of exclusion – a prospect now considered unacceptable in modern, pluralist, and democratic polities. Quebec then faces an interesting predicament: how
can it reach that consensus so necessary to the vitality of the counter-
paradigm without discarding politically and socially those who do not
accept or do not fit into the terms of the consensus? To varying degrees,
similar predicaments are emerging in other Western countries. For
political economy scholars, Quebec represents an important site in
which to observe the consequences of the unfolding of the international, liberal, monetarist economic order on domestic circumstances.

THROUGH THE LOOKING GLASS: SETTING
THE COUNTER-PARADIGM STRAIGHT

Quebec's counter-paradigm stems largely from the symbolic, but crucial, position held by the Quiet Revolution in the collective imagination. It was the fateful period in the first half of the 1960s, during
which progressive social and political forces seemingly broke the province free from the combined domination of the Catholic church, a
profoundly conservative petite bourgeoisie, and Anglo-Canadian capitalist interests. That experience has intimately shaped the perception
that successive generations of Quebec's political, economic, and social
decision makers have had of themselves, the whole Quebec community, and the general direction they think it should follow. Unsurpris-
ingly, the Quiet Revolution is also, for large segments of the Quebec
population, the main reference point in their conception of what
their society ought to be. The Quiet Revolution has instilled a strong
sense of self-confidence and turned French-speaking Quebecers – the
French Canadians of old – into heroes in their own right, social actors
in command of their own destiny.[17]

The symbolic place the Quiet Revolution occupies in Quebec's collective imagination rests on the highly positive values that it has come
to encompass. The Quiet Revolution was motivated by a spirit of collective and individual liberation and of rights enhancement and by a
welfare-driven, fairly inclusive sense of social solidarity and partnership among social classes and cultural communities. Understandably,
this vision continues to be expounded today and is part of the general
objectives pursued, at least in principle, by most political actors. As the
fiscal crisis and budgetary restraints of the past decade have dramatically narrowed the financial leeway needed to implement those objectives, however, difficult choices of social and economic management
have had to be made by the state. More often than not, they entail significant departure from the progressive ideals that guided the socio-
political transformations of the 1960s and 1970s. Quebec is not unique
in this regard; the delegitimization of the welfare state is a phenomenon with which most Western societies are currently confronted. But it
does take on a particular resonance in Quebec: as the lofty aspirations
of the Quiet Revolution have been gradually reoriented, toned down,
if not, in some cases, abandoned in the wake of the economic crisis of
the early 1980s, the dream of a modern, democratic, politically sovereign, economically self-reliant, and French-speaking nation has been
shattered in the eyes of many.

Though undeniable progress occurred, especially in the democratization of political and administrative practices during the 1960s and

1970s, the re-emergence and persistence of the very issues and problems of socioeconomic inequality that the policies of the Quiet Revolution sought to address become perplexing. Today, Quebec is the province with the highest proportion of poor people in Canada;[18] it continues to have a rate of unemployment that is constantly above the national average;[19] it has a disconcertingly high rate of high-school dropouts relative to other jurisdictions in North America; and most experts agree that current patterns of inequality push the poor, the young, women, and ethnic minorities further onto the margins of the economy and society.[20] Though Quebec's political and administrative elites often cite the province's record of democratic achievement as exemplary, what kind of democracy is it when some of its members who have fallen by the wayside or who cannot fit into a pre-established picture of what that society is or should be are excluded and pushed to the margins? This question becomes crucial to the future political economy analysis of Quebec.

Quebec is facing a difficult challenge. Though the socio-political aspirations of the Quiet Revolution still weigh quite heavily in the political scale of the province – if perhaps more symbolically than anything else – objective, societal conditions have made it virtually impossible to achieve them to any satisfying degree. In fact, pressures to turn away from those aspirations are great. In this regard, the PQ, for all that its members have been instrumental in defining the counter-paradigm that moved and shaped contemporary Quebec, is no more immune than any other party from giving in to these pressures.[21]

Quebec is caught between the Quiet Revolution's moral imperative to achieve a just society and economic, market-grounded "realities" which, in the mind of many a decision maker, justify the recourse to tough policy stances and the return to unfettered market mechanisms for the benefit of competitive, individual economic agents. This current, unavoidable fact of life in late capitalist societies gives a somewhat less glorious image to the counter-paradigmatic sense that some would like to impress on recent political and administrative actions of the Quebec government. Indeed, it is increasingly evident that Quebec's counter-paradigm leaves several issues unresolved:

- The counter-paradigm presupposes an active, interventionist state. How does this presupposition fit within the framework of international trade agreements, such as the North American Free Trade Agreement and GATT, which rule out many traditional policy instruments, including government ownership?
- The counter-paradigm stresses the building of social solidarity and a sense of partnership among social classes and cultural communities.

Such a proposal borrows and elaborates on the social corporatism found in smaller, European social-democratic states. These same states, however, have found it more and more difficult to sustain corporatist arrangements in a free-trade, monetarist world.

- The counter-paradigm emphasizes the retaining of and building of the Keynesian welfare state. This objective, however, stands contradicted by the actions of both the federal and Quebec governments, which are reducing and even eliminating key programs of the welfare state.

- Quebec has attempted to move away from an ethnic basis for defining identity and the objectives of society to a definition that encompasses diverse ethnicities. In doing so, nationalists have sought to redefine the nation-state to give Quebec sovereignty. How can they realize these changes while maintaining a dialogue with Aboriginal peoples, who never accepted the nineteenth-century nation-state framework in the first place and who never defined themselves in "Western" terms?

In short, it is not altogether clear whether the Quebec counter-paradigm, which is essentially a political construction, can be realized at all. Cynics might even question whether there remains the political will to see it through.

In fact, the recent literature on Quebec political economy reflects unequivocal disenchantment over the potential of realizing a counter-paradigm in Quebec. The referendum defeat of 1980, the perceived illegitimacy of the constitutional patriation of 1982, and the fruitless constitutional tribulations of Meech and Charlottetown all forced a reconfiguration of the political discourse in both Quebec and Canada. Though much of the debate around the future of Canada prior to the early 1980s had focused almost exclusively on unity problems and Quebec's national question, political concerns expressed in the wake of the 1982 entrenchment of a Charter of Rights and Freedoms in the Canadian constitution began to include broader and, in a way, more theoretical issues. These included the form and content of citizenship, individual versus collective rights, socioeconomic inclusion and exclusion within the public sphere, Aboriginal claims to self-determination, and the politics of identity. In this refocused political discussion, the Quebec question moved from the forefront of national debate, being gradually subsumed under a variety of diverse socio-political issues that vied for public attention.[22]

The scholarly literature on Quebec echoed this shift. Until a little more than a decade ago, most of what was written about Quebec by historians, sociologists, political scientists, and political economists was couched in an almost-obsessive eagerness to make sense of the national question. The same writings often sought unequivocally to promote a heightened nationalistic sense of Quebec's particular socio-historical circumstances. English-French relations – an implicit "us" versus "them" antinomy – and the unwavering certainty that the Quebec question ought to be understood first and foremost as a national/ethnic question loomed rather large.[23] More recently, the new social and economic realities, combined with the change in political discourse noted above, have forced a shift away from understanding Quebec through the lens of the national question to a view that is more encompassing.

Political economy analysis of Quebec has led this change. The issues and questions that have been at the centre of its concerns largely transcend a narrowly defined "Quebec question." In much recent scholarship the social and economic problems confronting Quebec are addressed in and of themselves, within their own societal logic, and no longer with a view to illuminating or solving the national question. A number of Quebec analysts have drawn on the works of French political economists gravitating around the École de la régulation, contributing occasionally to the theoretical development of this school of political economic thought. Modalities of Quebec's insertion in the continental and global economy, changes in the wage-labour relationship, and reconfiguration of the regime of accumulation within Canada and Quebec are more likely to be their focus than any of the issues that attracted preceding generations of social scientists.[24] Others who do not adhere to the *régulation* school have also produced works whose tenor and orientation break away from the national/ethnic purview of previous scholarship.[25]

A remarkable feature of these recent writings, whether within or outside the political economy tradition, is the absence of the traditional emphasis on the specificity or distinctiveness of Quebec society. Quebec is now approached intellectually as a society like any other, confronted like most Western social formations with the socioeconomic problems typical of late capitalism.[26] Some see in this growing interest in more universal, less Quebec-specific themes a revisionist quest for normality: Quebec is a modern, democratic, pluralist society whose history and development are not idiosyncratic but totally in line with the patterns of evolution experienced by other Western societies.[27]

In short, a number of Quebec intellectuals and academics – though by no means a majority – have unequivocally begun to take their distance from the counter-paradigm. In their view, it has failed to make good on its promise of a better society and shows little prospect of doing so. Though they cannot necessarily be lumped into a homogeneous school of thought or into a precise epistemological mould, they refuse to be trapped either in the discursive terms imposed by the formulators of the counter-paradigm or in the discourse supportive of Canadian federalism. Their positions are still somewhat tentative, but they are calling for a redefinition of Quebec's public debate in a way that would bring to the fore questions silenced, neglected, or improperly addressed by the counter-paradigm: democratic practice, sexual identity, gender relations, inter-ethnic and race relations, citizenship, the place of the citizen within the public sphere, environmental preservation, decentralization of administrative power, and local autonomy.[28]

Though the proponents of this emerging critique do not partake of the political economy tradition – their language is often closer to postmodernist theoretical and epistemological stances – they consolidate its critical dimension. They take issue with the whole configuration of social power implicit in the market bias underlying the socioeconomic strategies of the counter-paradigm. Theirs is an indictment of the capitalist market and of its constitutive social relations, but, most of all, by this indictment they mark their disapproval of the counter-paradigm's insistence on the market as a means of redemption for Quebec's socioeconomic ailments. Perhaps for the first time in recent Quebec history, some progressive intellectuals are wondering about the very idea of sovereignty for Quebec. They question not so much the political validity of the sovereigntist project, but the possibility and value of sovereignty in an era of increasing economic globalization. The current process of globalization, some feel, compromises the sovereignty of the nation-state by surrounding it with a new "architecture of power" that seriously limits its room to manoeuvre according to self-defined, internal, and subjective norms (Breton 1994). The nineteenth-century idea of sovereignty may have run its course; it is not a natural, or an eternal given. It reflects a certain understanding of power and authority, rooted in a particular, historically determined configuration of social relations and public space. As socio-historical conditions change, does sovereignty remain an adequate or desirable political objective? Some Quebec intellectuals are beginning to doubt that it is and believe it is time to re-examine and question past certitudes. Political economist Gilles Breton summed it up when he wrote: "Certainly we are living at a time that obliges us to imagine what might be new, rather than to repeat simply old truths."[29]

THINKING WITH AND AGAINST
THE COUNTER-PARADIGM

Whether Quebec's social scientists and political economists are ready to heed Breton's exhortation remains to be seen. Breaking away from the intellectual pull of the counter-paradigm, however flawed it may have become, may not prove easy. The counter-paradigm is largely a product of the same Quebec intellectuals who realize today that its political virtues have been overshadowed by its inability to address important social and economic issues. In the recent history of Quebec society, their own claim to fame has been intimately linked to its political attractiveness.[30] Rejecting it now would amount in a way to admitting to their own failure.

But, as noted above, there are new problems to face. Through the political and social institutions they have created in the past few decades, French-speaking Quebecers have amply shown their staunch attachment to democratic principles. None the less, their attitude towards manifestations of otherness is fraught with the ambivalence typical of a nation whose own future is uncertain, whose minority status within a wider, global socioeconomic context leaves it at the margins of history. They inevitably tend to oscillate between a laudable democratic impulse – which calls for socio-political inclusiveness and enlarged citizenship – and concerns over the possibility of losing parts of their historically determined identity, of seeing their community fall into political irrelevance. This ambivalence clearly came to light in the briefs and expert advice presented both to the Bélanger-Campeau Commission on Quebec's constitutional future in 1990–91[31], and to the roving commissions on Quebec sovereignty in 1995.

Quebec stands as an interesting test case for democracy in an age of heightened identity politics and multiple pleas for recognition of difference. The PQ's plan to create a nation-state dramatically poses the question of inclusion in the context of the increasing heterogeneity and pluri-ethnicity of contemporary societies. How can the claims of particularistic identities be met and satisfied without endangering the foundations of heretofore politically, socially, and culturally homogeneous societies? Such is the key challenge with which Quebec and, vicariously, the rest of Canada must wrestle. The history of the past three decades shows that Quebec's own will to self-determination has vigorously confronted the Canadian state with this issue. Paradoxically, today large segments of the Quebec population that cannot accept the hegemonic aspirations of French-speaking Quebecers are also challenging the Quebec state no less vigorously. They are demanding nothing less than reconfiguration of the public sphere – suggesting new criteria of governance, propounding a politics of identity and difference, and celebrating all manners of heterogeneous, polymorphous, and hybrid social models, which perforce negate the universalistic assumptions on which modern societies are predicated.[32]

Canada and Quebec are illustrations of this emerging reality. For five years, between 1987 and 1992, as they navigated the often murky waters from the Meech Lake to the Charlottetown Accord, Canadians collectively tried to redesign their constitution, but failed. The process collapsed on the reef of the 1992 referendum over the Charlottetown Accord. This failure reflected the inability of Canadians to agree on one common definition or conception of their political community – on one acceptable, unifying vision of their polity.[33] On the contrary, during those five years myriad voices were heard. Some were seeking in this constitutional exercise a means to promote or protect particularist goals, often in defiance of the structures and principles on which the Canadian state has historically rested.

The nationalism embodied in the Quebec counter-paradigm is essentially liberal, couched in universalistic, supposedly value-neutral political terms. In this sense, contemporary Quebec nationalism is truly modern and truly bourgeois. Just like the liberal discourse on which it feeds, it implies, despite repeated public declarations to the contrary, silencing of a number of socially grounded differences. Indeed, it implies eventual negation of socio-political expressions, cultural or otherwise, that do not or will not fit into the mould of the counter-paradigm – a mould essentially cast by members of the francophone community. As such, it is painfully at odds with the growing and irreversible heterogeneity of the social fabric of Quebec.

Recent waves of immigration into Quebec have brought increasing numbers of people from Third World countries.[34] More than half of the immigrants to land in Quebec in the past ten years originate from Asia. Large contingents of immigrants and refugees from the Caribbean, South America, North Africa, and the Middle East have also made Quebec their home. Quebec has always been open to immigration, but in the past two decades there has been a complete reversal of the trends in the origin and ethnocultural nature of immigrants. From a largely white and European constituency that easily merged into the mainstream of society, immigration has now become comprised of distinctly "visible" minorities with no mastery of French or English, whose ethnocultural background often has little in common with that of the host society. Issues of ethnic and racial discrimination in housing, employment, educational institutions, and relations with the police force are constantly raised and create a socio-political gap between minority groups and the host society, which public authorities are generally at a loss to address.[35]

Despite the manifest will of the Québécois to exercise sway over Quebec society, government policies related to immigration and intercultural relations did not amount to the overt marginalization of ethnocultural minorities.[36] Nevertheless, the prospects for a sound, convivial, and integrated multicultural society seem fraught with misunderstanding about what Québécois and other ethnocultural communities should expect of each other in creating a new public space.

Even with the best of intentions, interculturalism is not easily accepted. Recurrent problems – acts of rampant racism in the predominantly white, male, and French-speaking Montreal police force; increasingly vocal exasperation of growing segments of the Aboriginal population about non-resolution of land claims and non-recognition of self-government; social disenfranchisement and an attendant propensity for criminality among the youth of visible minorities; and public denunciations of civil authorities by representatives of ethnocultural communities – all indicate that the reality and implications of pluri-ethnicity and sociocultural diversity do not make for an easy fit between the Québécois and other groups. Paradoxically, as a 1993 survey by the Ministry of Immigration and Cultural Communities showed, a majority of Québécois claim to feel at ease with most ethnocultural groups and support openness towards immigration. Nevertheless, a majority of respondents confessed to feeling uneasy with members of ethnocultural groups displaying distinctive physical traits or clothing. Two in three respondents also admitted to being dissatisfied with what they saw to be insufficient efforts on the part of immigrants to "integrate" into the mainstream of Quebec society.

This ambivalence is entrenched in the whole set of policies devised by successive Quebec governments with regard to insertion of immigrants into Quebec society. The language legislation of the late 1960s and the 1970s, premised as it was on the will to protect and promote the language and culture of the French-speaking majority, perhaps inadvertently ethnicized the Quebec state. Throughout the 1970s and 1980s, other legislation and policies aimed at defining conditions of immigration and criteria of intercultural relationships in Quebec recognized the existence of so-called cultural communities. Though it was not their aim, those policies widened the divide between Québécois and other ethnocultural groups. Under the guise of fostering peaceful intercultural and interethnic coexistence, respect for cultural difference, and promotion of diversity, they contributed to separate formal cultural categorization and to identity formation alongside, rather than as part of, Québécois culture.

The policies implemented over the past decade or so have in effect dichotomized the Quebec population between the majority of Québécois (Us) and a minority, which is comprised of all other ethnocultural groups (Them). In everyday life, this dichotomization may not be experienced by individuals in a conscious way, but in the public sphere it has created implicit boundaries along ethnic, cultural, and even racial lines. It is a rather pernicious process, for if public discourse claims that being Québécois applies to everyone residing in Quebec, in reality access to Québécois culture is restricted to those who were born into it.[37] Speaking French does not automatically buy membership in the Québécois community, as the PQ White Paper on Cultural Development published in 1978 had assumed.

Quebec's cultural and immigration policies are the products of a fundamentally contradictory and ambiguous approach: while the state pretends to include, it excludes by pigeonholing people into ethnocultural categories, outside which their existence seems unjustified. Such policies proceed from an irrevocable tendency to typecast ethnocultural communities into socioeconomic roles. This essentialism results in increased political tensions between French-speaking Quebecers and others. Strengthened by the official recognition granted them, cultural communities feel vindicated in questioning and even opposing the monopoly that francophone Quebecers claim to have on the social and political definition of Quebec. While intercultural and interethnic relations in Quebec have not yet had severely destructive consequences, the potential for damaging, irremediable conflicts is real. The armed stand-off of the summer of 1990 between the Canadian army and Mohawk Indians at Oka remains a sad reminder of the fragility of pluri-ethnicity and pluri-culturalism in Quebec (and Canada).

Clearly, unless a new ethic of intercommunal relations is developed, unless Quebecers learn to construct a public space founded on the mélange of differences rather than on the basis of the socio-political priorities of one of society's constitutive parts (the francophones), the situation may increasingly bear witness to the socio-political inefficacy of liberalism, indeed to the inefficacy of the modern nation-state.

The issues raised by intercultural relations in Quebec are but one example of the changing dimensions of the exercise of power and power relations in modern societies. It is tempting for the liberal state to give in to various practices of social engineering in order to maintain the integrity of the bourgeois socioeconomic order in the face of new and seemingly disorienting societal challenges. It behoves political economy to address this reality. The problems and issues that these new circumstances underscore are unlike many of the questions that have traditionally caught the attention of the majority of Canadian political economists. At times this group may be at a loss to comprehend them with the intellectual tools that have been its for many years.

NOTES

1 Noël, "Jobs!"
2 Rocher and Salée, "Logique."
3 See Guindon, *Quebec*; McRoberts, *Quebec*; and Simard, *La longue marche*.
4 We refer to the idea of a hegemonic paradigm in Canada much in the way of Jenson, " 'Different.' "
5 A number of authors describe this phenomenon. See Bélanger and Fournier, *L'entreprise*; Fournier, *Le capitalisme au Québec*; Fraser, *Quebec*; Niosi, "New"; Niosi, *Canadian*; Pelletier, *La machine*; Vaillancourt and Carpentier, *Le contrôle*.
6 See Boucher, "Les syndicats"; Denis and Denis, "Quebec"; Fournier, *Solidarité*; Hébert, "La négociation"; Rouillard, *Histoire*.
7 See Coleman "Class" and *Independence*; Levine, *Reconquest*.
8 See Rocher and Rocher, "La culture."
9 Létourneau, "La nouvelle figure."
10 Rocher, "Canadian."
11 See Coleman, "Macroeconomic."
12 Chorney, *Deficit*.
13 See Gunderson and Muszynski, *Women*; McBride, *Not*; and McQuaig, *Wealthy*.
14 Parti Québécois, *Quebec*, 25.
15 Ibid., 20–1.
16 Ibid., 36.
17 See Létourneau, "Le Québec" and "La production."
18 According to the National Council of Welfare's recent data on poverty in Canada, in 1993 17.6 per cent of Quebec families lived below the poverty line, the worst situation in all the country. The national average is 14.8 per cent. Quebec came ahead even of Newfoundland, at 16.1 per cent. For persons living alone, in Quebec 45 per cent live in poverty, against a national average of 37.1 per cent – again Quebec is the worst province. Among the elderly (65 years of age and over), 21.4 per cent of males and 34.2 per cent of females in Quebec are poor; nowhere else in Canada do figures exceed 13.7 per cent for men and 24.9 per cent for women. Overall, one Quebecer in five lives below the poverty line, as opposed to one Canadian in six. See National Council of Welfare, *Poverty*.
19 This is not a new phenomenon. Since the 1960s, Quebec's rate of unemployment has always been higher than the Canadian average – for the past two decades, 2 to 3 per cent higher. See Statistics Canada, *Historical Labour Force Statistics*, Cat. No. 71–201, annual; and Noël, "Politics."
20 Langlois, *S'appauvrir* and "Anciennes."
21 As one observer of Quebec commented: "On economic and social issues, the Parti Québécois has moved closer to the Liberals' traditional territory:

both now extol the virtues of the market and call for a dramatic scaling down of the state. Both, most tellingly, have become zealous apostles of North American free trade. ... Though the PQ might protest that it has more of a social conscience than the Liberals, that its version of the new economic orthodoxy is both kinder and gentler than that of Bourassa and his business friends, this is cold comfort to those marginalized groups in society who are being left behind in the scramble to embrace the discipline of the market. In Quebec, the poor, the marginal, and the powerless are now effectively disenfranchised, as both of the major parties seem eager to sacrifice their needs to the new gods of competitiveness and globalization" (Tanguay, "Quebec's," 194).

22 Rocher and Salée, "Démocratie."

23 Coleman, "Political"; Létourneau, "La production"; Rudin, "Revisionism"; Salée, "L'analyse."

24 See, for example, Boismenu and Drache, *Politique*. Gérard Boismenu has been instrumental in the development of *régulation*-inspired work in Quebec. He and his colleagues of the Groupe de recherches et d'études sur les transformations sociales et économiques (GRÉTSÉ), based at the Universtité de Montréal, have produced over the past decade a variety of works, both empirical and theoretical, which are germane to Quebec but also transcend Quebec specificity.

25 This is readily apparent in a number of readers, anthologies, and textbooks published recently. See, for example, Daigle with Rocher, *Le Québec*; Dumont, ed., *La société*; Dumont, Langlois, and Martin, eds., *Traité*; Gagnon, *Quebec*; and Lachapelle et al., *Quebec*.

26 A manifestation of this reality is the recent publication of Daigle with Rocher, *Le Québec*, and Dumont, Langlois, and Martin, eds., *Traité*. Both contain an impressive number of articles written by leading social scientists analysing the entire range of social problems and issues confronting Quebec society. In these two volumes, Quebec appears clearly as a society with an internal logic shared by all modern societies.

27 Létourneau, "La production"; Rudin, "Revisionism."

28 Breton, Fecteau, and Létourneau, eds., *La condition*, reflects a critical, alternative vision of Quebec society. It is mainly this book that we have in mind when we refer to an emergent critique of the counter-paradigm.

29 Breton, "De la mondialisation," 37, authors' translation.

30 Létourneau, "La production."

31 Létourneau and Ruel, "Nous"; Ruel, "Entre."

32 Yeatman, *Postmodern*.

33 Rocher and Salée, "Démocratie."

34 This discussion borrows from Salée, "Multiculturalism."

35 The unemployment rates of the youth (15–24 age group) of so-called visible minorities reach staggering highs: 60 per cent among Jamaicans,

45 per cent for Haitians, close to 30 per cent for Vietnamese and Cambodians, and over 25 per cent for Latin Americans. By contrast, unemployment among young French-speaking Quebecers stands at 17 per cent. Also, nearly 90 per cent of all recent Quebec immigrants live in the Montreal region. This situation helps create a socio-geographical divide between Montreal and the rest of the province, which is essentially white and old-stock francophone and does not understand the new socioeconomic particularities of Montreal. See GRES, "Immigration."

36 Since 1975, Quebec has had its own Charter of Rights and Freedoms, which explicitly protects and promotes the expression of ethnocultural differences. The Ministry of Immigration and Cultural Communities regularly puts its employees to work to find appropriate ways to accommodate difference in public institutions and reduce public and private discriminatory practices. There are at least three government-funded major research units on ethnic studies and intercultural relations now in operation in Quebec universities. Immigrants with political-refugee status are fully supported by the state until their personal situation is settled. Various immigrant and anglophone lobby groups receive financial support from the state and are generally integrated in the consultative process on policy matters regarding immigration and intercultural relations. All this is in addition to a full range of health, welfare, and educational services financially supported by the Quebec state and to which everyone living in Quebec has access. Language courses, manpower training, anti-racist and anti-discriminatory measures, as well as various forms of accommodation, are regularly put in place. In the mid-1980s, the Quebec government officially recognized Aboriginal languages spoken on its territory and the existence of the province's Aboriginal communities as distinct nations.

37 Gagnon, *Echoing*.

REFERENCES

Bélanger, Yves. "Economic Development: From Family Enterprise to Big Business." In Alain G. Gagnon, ed., *Quebec State and Society*, 390–406. Scarborough, Ont.: Nelson, 1993.

Bélanger, Yves, and Fournier, Pierre. *L'entreprise québécoise*, Montreal: Hurtubise HMH, 1987.

Boismenu, Gérard, and Drache, Daniel, eds. *Politique et régulation: Modèle de développement et trajectoire canadienne*. Montreal and Paris: Méridien and L'Harmattan, 1990.

Boucher, Jacques. "Les syndicats: de la lutte pour la reconnaissance à la concertation conflictuelle." In Gérard Daigle and Guy Rocher, eds., *Le Québec en jeu*, 107–36. Montreal: Presses de l'Université de Montréal, 1992.

Breton, Gilles. "De la mondialisation: ses contraintes, ses défis, ses enjeux." In Gilles Breton, Jean-Marie Fecteau, and Jocelyn Létourneau, eds., *La condition québécoise: Enjeux et horizons d'une société en devenir,* 19–40. Montreal: VLB Éditeur, 1994.

Breton, Gilles, Fecteau, Jean-Marie, and Létourneau, Jocelyn, eds. *La condition québécoise: Enjeux et horizons d'une société en devenir.* Montreal: VLB Éditeur, 1994.

Chorney, Harold. *The Deficit and Debt Management: An Alternative to Monetarism.* Ottawa: Centre for Policy Alternatives, 1989.

Coleman, William. "The Class Basis of Language Policy in Quebec, 1949–1975," *Studies in Political Economy,* no. 3 (1980), 93–117.

– *The Independence Movement in Quebec, 1945–1984.* Toronto: University of Toronto Press, 1984.

– "Macroeconomic Policy: Dwindling Options." In M.M. Atkinson, ed., *Governing Canada,* 207–40. Toronto: HBJ, 1993.

– "The Political Economy of Quebec." In Wallace Clement and Glen Williams, eds., *The New Canadian Political Economy,* 160–79. Montreal: McGill-Queen's University Press, 1989.

Daigle, Gérard, with Rocher, Guy. *Le Québec en jeu: Comprendre les grands défis.* Montreal: Presses de l'Université de Montréal, 1992.

Denis, Roch, and Denis, Serge. "Quebec Unions in Politics, 1960–90." In Alain G. Gagnon, ed., *Quebec State and Society,* 2nd ed., 199–223. Toronto: Nelson, 1993.

Dumont, Fernand, ed. *La société québécoise après 30 ans de changements.* Quebec City: Institut québécois de recherche sur la culture, 1990.

Dumont, Fernand, Langlois, Simon, and Martin, Yves, eds. *Traité des problèmes sociaux,* Quebec City: Institut québécois de recherche sur la culture, 1994.

Fournier, Pierre. *Le capitalisme au Québec.* Montreal: Albert Saint-Martin, 1978.

– *The Quebec Establishment.* Montreal: Black Rose Books, 1976.

– *Solidarité Inc.* Montreal: Québec/Amérique, 1991.

Fraser, G. *Quebec Inc.* Montreal: Editions de l'Homme, 1987.

Gagnon, Alain G., ed. *Québec: État et société.* Montreal: Québec-Amérique, 1994.

– *Quebec State and Society.* 2nd ed. Toronto: Nelson, 1993.

Gagnon, Michelle. "Echoing in the Silence of Redemption: Discourses of Nationhood and Identity in Quebec." MA thesis, Communications, Concordia University, Montreal, 1994.

GRES "Immigration et relations interethniques au Québec: un pluralisme en devenir." In Gérard Daigle and Guy Rocher, eds., *Le Québec en jeu,* 451–82. Montreal: Presses de l'Université de Montréal, 1992.

Guindon, Hubert. *Quebec Society: Tradition, Modernity and Nationhood.* Toronto: University of Toronto Press, 1988.

Gunderson, Morley, and Muszynski, Leon. *Women and Labour Market Poverty.* Ottawa: Canadian Advisory Council on the Status of Women, 1990.

Hébert, Gérard. "La négociation collective: bilan." In Gérard Daigle and Guy Rocher, eds., *Le Québec en jeu*, 137–59. Montreal: Presses de l'Université de Montréal, 1992.

Jenson, Jane. "'Different' but not 'Exceptional': Canada's Permeable Fordism," *Canadian Review of Sociology and Anthropology*, 26 no. 1 (1989), 69–94.

Jenson, Jane, and Keyman, Fuat. "Must We All Be Postmodern?" *Studies in Political Economy*, 31 (1990), 141–57.

Lachapelle, Guy, et al. *The Quebec Democracy: Structures, Processes and Policies*. Toronto: McGraw-Hill Ryerson, 1993.

Langlois, Richard. *S'appauvrir dans un pays riche*. Montreal: CEQ/Saint-Martin, 1990.

Langlois, Simon. "Anciennes et nouvelles formes d'inégalités et de différencia-tion sociale au Québec." In Fernand Dumont, ed., *La société québécoise après 30 ans de changements*, 81–98. Quebec City: Institut québécois de recherche sur la culture, 1990.

Legaré, Anne. "La souveraineté: nation ou raison?" In Alain G. Gagnon, ed., *Québec: État et société*, 41–59. Montreal: Québec-Amérique, 1994.

Lesage, Marc, and Tardif, Francine, eds. *Trente ans de révolution tranquille*. Montreal: Bellarmin, 1989.

Létourneau, Jocelyn. "La nouvelle figure identitaire: Essai sur la dimension symbolique d'un consensus social en voie d'émergence." *British Journal of Canadian Studies*, 6 no. 1 (1990), 17–38.

– "La production historienne courante portant sur le Québec et ses rapports avec la construction des figures identitaires d'une communauté communi-cationnelle." *Recherches sociographiques*, 36 no. 1 (1995), 9–45.

– "Le Québec moderne: un chapitre dans le grand récit collectif des Québé-cois," *Revue française de science politique*, 43 no. 5 (1992), 765–85.

Létourneau, Jocelyn, and Ruel, Jacinthe. "Nous Autres les Québécois. Topiques du discours franco-québécois sur Soi et l'Autre dans les mémoires déposés devant la Commission Bélanger-Campeau." In Khadiyatoulah Fall, Daniel Simeoni, and Georges Vignaux, eds., *Mots représentations: Enjeux dans les contacts interethniques et interculturels*, 283–307. Ottawa: University of Ottawa Press, 1994.

Levine, Marc. *The Reconquest of Montreal: Language Policy and Social Change in a Bilingual City*. Philadelphia: Temple University Press, 1990.

McBride, Stephen. *Not Working: State, Unemployment and Neo-Conservatism in Canada*. Toronto: University of Toronto Press, 1992.

McCall, Christopher. "Identités, inégalités et territoires: une société à décons-truire." In Jean-Marie Fecteau, Gilles Breton, and Jocelyn Létourneau, eds., *La condition québécoise: Enjeux et horizons d'une société en devenir*, 41–60. Mont-real: VLB Éditeur, 1994.

McQuaig, Linda. *The Wealthy Banker's Wife*. Toronto: Penguin, 1993.

McRoberts, Kenneth. *Quebec: Social Change and Political Crisis*. 3rd ed. Toronto: McClelland and Stewart, 1988.

Magnusson, Warren, and Walker, R.B.J. "De-Centring the State: Political Theory and Canadian Political Economy." *Studies in Political Economy*, 26 (1988), 37–72.

Maillé, Chantal, and Salée, Daniel. "De la démocratie au Québec: enjeux et perspectives." In Gilles Breton, Jean-Marie Fecteau, and Jocelyn Létourneau, eds., *La condition québécoise: Enjeux et horizons d'une société en devenir,* 61–82. Montreal: VLB Éditeur, 1994.

Moreau, François. "La résistible ascension de la bourgeoisie québécoise." In Gérard Daigle and Guy Rocher, eds., *Le Québec en jeu*, 335–56. Montreal: Presses de l'Université de Montréal, 1992.

National Council of Welfare. *Poverty Profile 1993*. Ottawa: Supply and Services Canada, 1995.

Niosi, Jorge. *Canadian Capitalism: A Study of Power in the Canadian Business Establishment*. Toronto: Lorimer, 1981.

– "The New French Canadian Bourgeoisie." *Studies in Political Economy*, no. 1 (1979), 113–61.

Noël, Alain. "Jobs! Job! Jobs! The Political Management of Unemployment." In Alain G. Gagnon and James P. Bickerton, eds., *Canadian Politics: An Introduction to the Discipline*, 446–70. Peterborough, Ont.: Broadview Press, 1990.

– "Politics in a High-Unemployment Society." In Alain G. Gagnon, ed., *Quebec State and Society*, 422–49. Scarborough, Ont.: Nelson, 1993.

Parti Québécois. *Quebec in a New World*. Toronto: Lorimer, 1994.

Pelletier, Mario. *La machine à milliards: l'histoire de la Caisse de dépôts et de placements du Québec*. Montreal: Québec/Amérique, 1989.

Piché, Victor. "Le discours démo-politique au Québec: inclusion ou exclusion?" *Sociologie et sociétés*, 24 no. 2 (1992), 141–50.

Renaud, Gilbert. *A l'ombre du rationalisme*. Montreal: Éditions coopératives Albert Saint-Martin, 1984.

Rocher, François. "Canadian Business, Free Trade and the Rhetoric of Economic Continentalization," *Studies in Political Economy*, 35 (summer 1991), 135–54.

Rocher, François, and Rocher, Guy. "La culture québécoise en devenir: les défis du pluralisme." In F. Ouellet and M. Pagé, eds., *Pluriethnicité, éducation et société: Construire un espace commun*, 42–76. Quebec City: Institut québécois de recherche sur la culture, 1991.

Rocher, François, and Salée, Daniel. "Démocratie et réforme constitutionnelle: discours et pratique." *International Journal of Canadian Studies/Revue internationale d'études canadiennes*, no. 7 (1993), 167–87.

– "Logique d'État et fédéralisme canadien: l'improbable décentralisation." In François Rocher, ed., *Bilan québécois du fédéralisme canadien*, 93–123. Montreal: VLB Editeur, 1992.

Rouillard, Jacques. *Histoire du syndicalisme québécois*. Montreal: Boréal, 1989.

Rudin, Ronald. "Revisionism and the Search for a Normal Society: A Critique of Recent Quebec Historical Writing," *Canadian Historical Review*, 73 no. 1 (1992), 30–61.

Ruel, Jacinthe. "Entre la rhétorique et la mémoire: usages du passé et références à l'histoire dans les mémoires déposés devant la Commission sur l'avenir politique et constitutionnel du Québec (1990)." *Discours social/ Social Discourse*, 6 nos. 1–2 (1994), 213–42.

Salée, Daniel. "L'analyse socio-politique de la société québécoise: bilan et perspectives." In Gérard Boismenu et al., *Espace régional et nation: Pour un nouveau débat sur le Québec*, 15–49. Montreal: Boréal Express, 1983.

– "Multiculturalism and the Politics of Identity in Quebec." *Cultural Survival Quarterly*, 23 no. 3 (1994), 89–94.

– "Pour une autopsie de l'imaginaire québécois: regards sur la morosité postmoderne." *Canadian Journal of Political and Social Theory*, 10 no. 3 (1986), 114–23.

Simard, Jean-Jacques. *La longue marche des technocrates*. Montreal: Albert Saint-Martin, 1979.

Tanguay, A. Brian. "Quebec's Political System in the 1990's: From Polarization to Convergence." In Alain G. Gagnon, ed., *Quebec State and Society*, 2nd ed., 174–98. Scarborough, Ont.: Nelson, 1993.

Vaillancourt, François, and Carpentier, Josée. *Le contrôle de l'économie du Québec*. Montreal: Office de la langue française, 1989.

Yeatman, Anna. *Postmodern Revisionings of the Political*. London and New York: Routledge, 1994.

13 From the Postwar to the Post-Liberal Keynesian Welfare State

ISABELLA BAKKER AND
KATHERINE SCOTT

THE KEYNESIAN WELFARE STATE IN CANADA

There is probably no single institution more evocative of the post–Second World War political economy than the Keynesian welfare state (KWS). Touching the daily lives of all Canadians through its provision of health care and education, the KWS was thought to be a key mechanism for realizing what Pierre Trudeau called "the just society." Some twenty-five years later calls for a just society have been replaced by concerns about global competitiveness, government deficits, and how to minimize the role of governments in the economy. Canada's social programs are currently at a turning point: critics urge a cut in programs and benefits, while defenders have not come up with a viable long-term set of economic and social policies that address the new "value-for-money" attitude to public spending.

The KWS represents an amalgamation of political and economic strategies designed to resolve problems of harmonizing the production of wealth with its distribution.[1] Welfare states are one element of capitalist economic and political development. The nineteenth-century "nightwatchman state" was largely focused on soldiery and police protection of property and national frontiers. With increasing industrialization, gains from capitalist development became increasingly unequal among factory owners, older landowning and professional elites, and the working class. A range of political pressures led to the incremental growth of welfare states, pioneered in Germany in the 1880s by Bismarck and gradually adopted in all advanced capitalist countries. The growth impetus from the right of the political spectrum (Bismarck) saw provision of welfare as a form of "system-legitimation," while on the left reformist socialists such as George Bernard Shaw saw the possibility of using the state for redistributive purposes – "system modification."[2]

What do we mean when we talk about the welfare state, and where does Keynesianism come into the picture? The welfare state is generally defined to include both government expenditures on services such as education, health, social security and welfare, housing, community and other social services, and government cash-transfer expenditures on pensions, unemployment insurance, family allowances, and so forth.[3] Often left out in discussions of the welfare state, but equally important, is consideration of the size and progressivity[4] of the tax burden. "Expenditure on services" refers mainly to public provision of services and government employment; cash transfers reallocate income in the market. Both elements together represent a decision by the state to provide assistance and support for individuals unable to participate in the labour market enough to meet their basic needs.

In the aftermath of the Depression and the Second World War, the British economist John Maynard Keynes provided the framework for the postwar welfare state. As David Wolfe has noted, "Keynes' ideas represented an attempt to unite the principle of continued private control of the investment and production process of a capitalist market economy with public demands for a change in the market-determined pattern of employment and income."[5] In an elegant fashion, Keynes argued that during periods of heavy unemployment government should use its taxing and spending powers (fiscal policy) to offset the loss in private incomes. Conversely, during economic booms, government should contract its activity and accumulate a surplus to meet hard times. The KWS was to be a central instrument of fiscal policy in realizing the goal of continuous, stable development.

Although never warmly embraced in Canada, the KWS was tolerated as long as it was financed out of increased economic growth and higher marginal incomes; it was deemed acceptable and muted distributional conflicts among capital, labour, and regions. The Canadian welfare state was intended to ensure continuity of income over the ups and downs of the economy much in the same way as Keynesian macroeconomic policies were to secure smooth flow of profits during economic upswings and downturns. Through this dual approach, Keynesianism addressed the concerns of both labour and capital. The burden of the KWS was acceptable in the context of workers' rising standard of living and rising profitability stimulated by the high level of foreign demand for Canadian resource exports. The stable economic environment that had fostered this postwar development strategy, however, began to crumble in the late 1960s and early 1970s. In addition, the tax burden on corporations and the wealthy was beginning to be reduced through a series of tax measures that shifted the increased cost of the KWS onto working-class and middle-income earners. The resulting fiscal crisis has undermined the KWS.

To set the context of the current debate, we examine the distinctive features of the KWS in Canada and review explanations for its historical development.

Evaluating Welfare States

Typologies of welfare states usually categorize countries according to the ways in which they attempt to achieve some basic modicum of security for their citizens. The central question in creating typologies is how to define and measure a concept such as the welfare state. Gösta Esping-Andersen, a Danish sociologist, has developed one of the most influential approaches, based on T.H. Marshall's concept of "social citizenship rights."[6] For Esping-Andersen, the crux of a welfare state is social citizenship – that is, the character and degree of protection afforded to individuals or families from the capitalist marketplace in the event that wage-earners are unable to sell their labour – for example, because of illness or failure of a business. In this context, social rights "de-commodify" labour.[7]

Following from this, Esping-Andersen also evaluates the different processes of social stratification specific to a given welfare state. "Stratification" refers to how welfare states themselves order social relations through social policy and practice. Universalistic systems such as health care in Canada are based on the notion that all citizens should have equal rights, irrespective of class or market position. With working-class prosperity and the growth of the middle class, however, increasing numbers of citizens can turn to private insurance and fringe-benefit bargaining to supplement the comparatively modest universal system. This creates a dualism, as has been the case in Canada, where the poor must rely on the state and others can secure better provisions through the market.[8]

As well, Esping-Andersen's typology assesses the interrelationship between the state's activities and the role of the market and family in social provision and reproduction. The particular blend of public and private responsibility for essential human needs forms "the structural context of de-commodification, social rights, and the stratificational nexus of welfare state regimes."[9] Taken together, three broad groupings of "welfare-state regimes" are identified: social democratic, corporatist/conservative, and liberal.

Canada has a liberal system. In such a model, the welfare state is characterized in minimalist terms, providing a basic level of benefits and services, designed to encourage labour-force participation regardless of working conditions. This kind of welfare state is associated with a large private welfare sector, where the state encourages the market and families to meet needs outside public programs. As a consequence, the liberal regime "erects an order of stratification that is a blend of a relative equality of poverty among welfare-state recipients, market-differentiated welfare among the majorities, and a class-political dualism between the two."[10] This, Esping-Andersen argues, has implications for the permanence and character of the welfare state, since lesser universality elicits weaker support for the welfare regime.[11]

Feminist scholars have pointed out that welfare regimes also construct a stratification order that structures gender and racial inequalities – in the market, in the family, and within the state itself. Welfare states were institutionalized during a period when the dominant view of work and family life dictated strict division of labour between the sexes. Men were supposed to earn the market wage to provide for dependants; women were confined to the private, domestic sphere, taking care of the "personal" needs of the family. This particular model of social reproduction, as numerous scholars have noted, never captured the lives of working-class or non-white families. But its impact in the formation of policy, promoted aggressively by public institutions and social reformers alike, profoundly affected the development of all welfare states.

Consequently, women have tended to be treated either as mothers or as wives in the eyes of the state. The early Mother's Allowance program in Canada was a clear example of how women were identified with the social function of mothering, rather than in their individual capacity as citizens or as workers. The notion of the family wage – an integral part of the postwar compromise between capital and labour – also structured women's access to benefits. Adequate wages in the form of a family wage for male industrialized workers was recognized as critical to the viability of the social security system. Women were covered under provisions targeted to the "heads of households" and other subsidiary unemployment and pension benefits.[12] The extent to which women continue to be disproportionately represented in the secondary, means-tested stratum of income-security programs – predominant in the liberal model – and/or derive financial security only through access to a male wage-and-benefit package speaks to the gendered character of social rights provided under the auspices of the welfare state.

What then is the evidence to support the classification of the Canadian KWS as a liberal welfare regime? The next section addresses this question.

The KWS in Canada

The KWS developed in Canada in a piecemeal and incremental fashion as part of postwar reconstruction. Early welfare-state efforts were targeted at income security, through provincial provision of workers' compensation (1909–20) and mothers' allowances (1916–35), and dominion provision of means-tested pensions (1927), unemployment insurance (1942), and family allowances (1945). The rest, including health care, was left to negotiations between employers and unionized workers or to the private market for those able to afford the expense. Publicly funded income-security initiatives replaced the former system of private charity and municipal relief by the 1960s. Federal legislation to finance public health insurance was introduced in 1966, the same year that the Canada Assistance Plan was enacted, integrating all social-assistance programming across the country in a single, cost-sharing agreement.

All these efforts, as well as current attempts at reforming income security and job-creation initiatives, reflect ever-present tensions within the Canadian system, such as federal-provincial jurisdictional conflicts, an imbalance of resources and responsibilities between levels of government, and the constraining interpretation of the constitution forged before the provinces had significant resources and power.[13]

To what extent does this network of income-security programs and social services remove people's dependence on paid employment for meeting their basic needs? What is the welfare mix between private and public provision of income and services? What kind of stratification patterns – including gender patterns – have emerged from social policy initiatives?

Canadian social programs[14] provide people with two types of benefits: social transfer payments and "income in kind" (social services). The purpose of social transfer payments is to replace or supplement income from employment and other sources, so that if a person's income stops (because of unemployment, illness, or retirement, for example), social programs (such as Unemployment Insurance, social assistance, and Old Age Security) will replace a portion of that income. The income-tax system can also be used to deliver social benefits, through tax credits, exemptions, and deductions (for instance, the Retirement Savings Plan [RSP] and the Non-Refundable Child Tax Credit). Commonly referred to as "tax expenditures," these can reduce a person's taxable income and hence taxes paid to federal and provincial governments.

Social services are funded and delivered by governments (the public sector), the private for-profit sector, and the private non-profit (voluntary) sector. Some social services are free of charge, fully subsidized by the government, but others rely on payment of a full or partial fee, depending on the income of the recipient. Services, of course, cover a wide range of areas, from health care and education to subsidies for housing and employment-promotion activities.

There are four criteria of financial eligibility used in making decisions about who qualifies for assistance: universal payments, social insurance, income testing, and needs testing. Universal programs make payments to all people, regardless of income, within a specific category (such as the elderly). One crucial universal program of the postwar KWS was Family Allowances which was terminated at the end of 1992. The remaining large universal program – Old Age Security – is "no longer truly universal because the federal government has introduced a 'clawback' which takes back benefits from higher-income families and pensioners."[15] Social insurance programs such as the Canada and Quebec Pension Plans (C/QPP) and the federal unemployment-insurance program provide benefits to workers in the paid labour force who retire, become unemployed or suffer a work-related disability. They are financed through the contributions of employees and/or employers, with benefits depending on the amount of an employee's earnings. An income-tested program is there to help families and individuals who have incomes below a specified level. Needs-tested programs give assistance to individuals and families who are in need no matter what the cause may be; for example, provincial social assistance (welfare) programs are needs-tested.

For the most part, Canada has been classified as a liberal welfare state on the basis of its social transfer payments. It has relatively low social transfer expenditures compared to other countries, despite its high levels of unemployment.[16] While the Canadian welfare state recognizes the social right to protection against such basic social risks as unemployment, sickness, and old age, its programs typically have stricter rules of eligibility, lower levels of income replacement, and a shorter duration of benefits. On balance, Canada relies more heavily on poorly paid, income-tested, or means-tested benefits than do many other OECD countries. Esping-Andersen estimates that means-tested benefits accounted for 15.6 per cent, or one-sixth, of Canada's total public expenditure in 1980; by contrast, the corresponding figure for Sweden was 1.1 per cent.[17] This trend continued through the 1980s, as the Conservative government moved increasingly to direct income programs towards the most "needy."

Limited benefit coverage has spurred growth of private, market alternatives for income replacement as well as service provision. Transfers to the elderly, for example, do not perform well in replacing the income of average workers on retirement; as a consequence, limited coverage has encouraged growth of private, government-regulated savings plans that enjoy favourable tax status. Health insurance companies are now looking at the possibility of expanding in Canada, as the number of health services covered by provincial health plans is being reduced. Support services of all kinds are now offered on the private market, as governments move to privatize public services and encourage expansion of commercial service providers.

The emphasis on income- and means-tested programs and the growing significance of private savings and insurance plans and service provision are further entrenching the dualisms characteristic of the liberal regime. Two welfare streams are evident: one for those on the margins of the paid labour market – unemployed or in poorly paid, tenuous employment – and enriched benefits and services for those in well-paid, secure employment. Labour-market polarization foreshadows growing polarization in the welfare state itself.

We see this already in the disproportionate numbers of women on provincial social assistance, compared to the unemployment-insurance program, where men are the principal beneficiaries. Sixty-nine per cent of income transfers to single-parent families in Canada are in the form of means-tested payments, as compared with 93 and 63 per cent in the United States and Britain, respectively, 16 per cent in Germany, 45 per cent in Sweden, and 4 per cent in Norway.[18] In programs for seniors we find a similar pattern; women rely principally on public benefits (Old Age Security, Guaranteed Income Supplement, and the Canada/Quebec Pension Plan) for retirement income. While increasing numbers of women now derive benefits from c/QPP, reflecting growth in labour-market participation, fully 32 per cent collect benefits as surviving spouses, as opposed to former contributors. Pension income from occupational plans and RRSPs represented only 11.6 per cent of women's total income, compared to 23.1 per cent among men.[19]

The two programs that contradict this general categorization are primary education and health care. Given the size of social expenditure for health and education, some writers have argued that Canada does not neatly fit the liberal model.[20] Indeed, Julia O'Connor notes that Canada's civil consumption expenditure, which includes health and education, was above both the mean and the average OECD levels in 1983.[21] Both systems are almost entirely public; there are few private alternatives. Moreover, health insurance in particular enjoys broad popular support and a good measure of international acclaim.

The apparent contradiction in the structure of Canada's welfare system lies in the detailed history of its development. We now turn to debates about development of the KWS in Canada to identify the most important factors behind the current impasse.

UNDERSTANDING THE DEVELOPMENT OF THE WELFARE STATE

A broad body of literature now exists on welfare theory. Studies range from philosophical works on the nature of claims and obligation between individuals to reviews of state activity in the political economy literature. As in any effort to identify the distinctive features of a single policy or the differences between political systems, theory serves as a guide, directing our attention to specific features of the subject in question, and can help us establish causal relationships between one set of variables or factors and another. As such, theoretical perspectives differ in regard to levels of analysis, assumptions about the nature and dynamics of political life, and, in the study of politics, views of the state.[22]

These differences are evident in the study of the public policies, practices, and institutions that comprise the KWS. There are four "mainstream" approaches:

- the liberal-pluralist, which emphasizes economic growth, related demographic pressures, and interest-group competition;
- the structural Marxist, which assumes that the "needs" of the capitalist economic system drive welfare-state development;
- the "politics matters" or power-resource, which interprets social policies as distributional conflicts – principally between class actors – where outcomes are determined by the distribution of power in society;
- the state-centred, which views welfare states as outcomes of nation building.

We use the term "mainstream" here to distinguish the literature cited above from more recent critiques, such as the feminist or anti-racist, which centrally locate gender and "race,"[23] respectively, in social and political life. Where gender or "race" concerns have been addressed in the discipline, they have usually been cited as additional dimensions of inequality. Rarely have gender relations or racism been positioned as central. By contrast, feminist and anti-racist perspectives on the welfare state seek not only to question the extent to which welfare politics reproduces gender and racial inequality, respectively, but also the degree to which gender inequality and racial inequality, respectively, structure welfare politics in the first instance.[24]

We take up each of the four approaches in turn, reviewing how each has been used to interpret the development of the Canadian KWS. We confine our discussion of anti-racism to efforts in the feminist literature to identify the structures of oppression that cut across categories such as class and gender. To date, Canadian work on racism and the welfare state has been limited. Much remains to be done in understanding distinct and overlapping social identities and how they both structure and are affected by the KWS.

The Liberal-Pluralist Perspective

Early research on the welfare state was a reaction against the forces of the capitalist market economy. The resulting body of work traces the expansion of state activity to sustain and support working peoples and other "dependent" groups through the transition from agricultural to industrial economies. As the waged economy expanded and demand for productive (male) labour grew, greater numbers of people were expelled from the labour market. At the same time, democratic political institutions took root; popular groups mobilized to press governments to regulate and ameliorate the excesses of urbanization, industrialization, and population growth that accompanied capitalist development. The intention was not to challenge the operation of the capitalist system but rather to protect vulnerable groups with tenuous connections to the labour market, such as children and the elderly, and to promote a "traditional" view of family life and social harmony among the populace. Thus the twin processes of industrialization and democratization laid the basis for the emergence of the welfare state.

In the Canadian case, it has been argued that introduction of social security programs was precipitated by social dislocations created by industrialization and urbanization.[25] The search for economic security forced politicians and the populace to discard old ideas about self-sufficiency and the ethos of individualism. The experience of the Depression in particular fostered a collectivist ideology and the belief that the government could help protect individuals from unbridled capitalism. In the face of popular political pressure at the ballot box, governments responded with new social welfare programs and services.

For the most part, this work shares a liberal-pluralist view of the state as a neutral mechanism that operates in response to societal demands expressed through established institutional channels. The specific pattern of policy and program development within this framework flows from the indigenous pattern of industrialization – timing, political culture, institutions, and historical attitudes to the "poor."[26] The emphasis is on the scope and character of reform activity and the struggles to create a caretaker role for the state.

Not surprisingly, this literature also shares a failing common to liberal-pluralist approaches to politics. In so far as both characterize the state as a neutral mechanism, articulating and mediating the relatively equal competition of societal interests for influence and power, they deny the inherently political and economic nature of the state. They beg the question of why some groups have been more successful than others over time – indeed, why the Canadian welfare state never evolved beyond its minimalist origins, as welfare states in Europe did, despite demonstrated public need. Within its own frame of reference, liberal-pluralism does not explain why some initiatives such as the Canada Assistance Plan were introduced in the absence of any pressure from anti-poverty groups or other welfare organizations.[27] It ignores the power of competing economic classes and the resources at the command of the state in favour of a competitive view of politics, where changing constellations of interest groups articulating the social concerns of the day promote their interests in an essentially democratic political marketplace. It identifies ideas as policy determinants – attributing cross-national differences in welfare states, for instance, to distinctive national values of concerned interest groups or of political elites.[28]

The Structural-Marxist Perspective

In response to the hegemony of liberal-pluralism in political science, neo-Marxism has challenged the central assumption that the liberal state is neutral. Since the late 1960s, a new generation of state scholars has argued that the state, and welfare policies and programs in this case, exist to secure the reproduction of capitalist relations. Ian Gough is perhaps the best-known member, for his thesis that welfare states have served to underwrite the costs of capitalist accumulation and, concomitantly, have acted as mechanisms to secure the consent of the majority to continued subordination. The specific form that the welfare state takes is contingent on the specific needs of the capitalist economy at a given point in time.[29]

Influenced by structural Marxism, a number of Canadian authors have used this framework to explain struggles to introduce programs such as unemployment insurance. Looking at the history of this program in Canada, Marxists have argued that the state acted to ensure the long-term viability of the capital accumulation process and to secure social control over the working class – in the face of opposition from the capitalist class itself.[30] From this perspective, unemployment insurance becomes a mediating response on the part of the state during the period of intense conflict between capital and the working class in the 1930s and 1940s. Donald Swartz makes the same case for the introduction of public health insurance, arguing that "the state viewed health insurance as an economic concession to the working class in order to realize better the long-run political and economic interests of the capitalist class."[31]

The structuralist-functionalist variant of neo-Marxism draws our attention to the limits within which the state in capitalist societies can operate. It identifies conflict between social actors as the principal motor of systemic change. It positively states the importance of the relationship between democratic representative institutions and the institutions of the marketplace, highlighting the interrelationship of these two arenas of politics. Yet this perspective has been roundly criticized as being overly deterministic, reducing all social, political, and economic activity to the objective structures of capitalism and materially divergent interests of labour and capital. Moreover, its exclusive focus on economic cleavages of capitalist society negates both the importance of other structural cleavages in society that have shaped struggles over specific welfare-state policies and practices, including those of gender and "race," and the prominence of the state as an actor in its own right. The latter observation is the point of departure for state-centred approaches to welfare-state development.

The State-Centred Perspective

Liberal pluralists and structural Marxists locate the sources of change within and between social forces. State-centred theorists, conversely, argue that state structures and state managers are "relatively autonomous" from "society" and, consequently, must be considered as sources of change and persistence in their own right. The development of this approach has been largely attributed to Theda Skocpol. This neo-institutionalism emphasizes the process of state formation, the role of state managers in policy design, and the ongoing effect of past policy decisions in structuring deliberation and action.[32]

Leslie Pal has argued, in contrast to the structural-Marxist interpretation, that state bureaucrats played the definitive role in shaping Canada's unemployment insurance; its class-divisive design emerged more "because of the application of cold administrative reason than because of hidden class motives."[33] The other significant institutional consideration was federalism. Negotiation over the form and content of the legislation was insulated from social pressures by the federal structure of the Canadian state; Ottawa had to bargain with the provinces to secure their approval for a transfer of authority to the federal level in order to implement this program. Carolyn Tuohy makes a similar argument for health-care policy, arguing that federal institutions served to foster "social democratic" innovation in one province and then to export this model, via a federal-provincial cost-sharing agreement, to others. By contrast, the need to broker an agreement between Ottawa and the provinces acted as a brake on welfare innovation, in the absence of powerful social interests promoting progressive change.[34]

Neo-institutionalist work on welfare programs has focused on the internal dynamics of the state. This approach is particularly weak, however, in explaining the dynamics of change within a given welfare state. As a result of an almost exclusive focus on state structures, statist scholars playdown the forces of society. There is also an implicit assumption running throughout this work that state policy makers are rational actors, choosing and discarding policy options on the basis of established criteria. How then does one explain the timing of welfare-state initiatives? Why are welfare-state policies subject to cutbacks at different times? An institutional analysis would suggest that the welfare state, now well established in advanced capitalist societies, will remain intact despite social, economic, and political conflict. We explore this contention in the conclusion.

The "Politics Matters"/Power Resources Perspective

The previous two approaches can be loosely grouped as "structuralist" attempts to account for welfare-state development. In contrast, the "politics matters," or power-resources, school is "voluntaristic." Within this tradition, the welfare state emerges from distributional struggles among social interests, the outcome of which reflects the distribution of power within a given society. With the extension of suffrage, less powerful groups have mobilized their new political power "to modify the play of market forces."[35] The rise of labour movements and parties has particularly encouraged the emergence of the welfare state, as the working class has fought for social programs that insulate working people from the "whip" of the market.

Much of the research in this tradition has explained welfare-state development by the relative strength of competing classes in terms of organizational structure, power resources, and the socio-political context (specifically, the presence of social-democratic governments). Labour was most successful where it was able to inscribe its power inside the state, preferably in the form of direct control of government by labour or social-democratic parties.[36] "This perspective retains the traditional Marxist emphasis on the role of class and class struggle in explaining social change. But unlike most Marxist theories since Lenin [including structural Marxism, discussed above], it takes political democracy seriously."[37]

In Canada a small and fractious labour movement, a working class often hostile to organized labour, and a moderate social-democratic party with tenuous links to the labour movement did not offer the formula for producing an advanced version of a full-employment, social-citizenship welfare state. The working class was unable to mobilize political support to introduce more comprehensive, "decommodifying," universalistic reforms. The language of class-based politics did not take hold in Canada; rather, the political discourse that accompanied the rise of the KWS after 1945 was organized around nation building and long-standing problems associated with federalism. Whereas in Europe, social-democratic parties were central in advancing the idea of citizenship rights based on the contribution of workers to the well-being of the economy and nation as a whole, little new state activity in Canada "was founded in a class analysis nor was it rationalized in terms of class equality or even the social importance of producer groups."[38] The crisis of federalism provided the rationale for development of the KWS.

The "politics matters" perspective acknowledges the role of human action within the context of the objective structures of capitalism and democratic political institutions. It expands the parameters of welfare-state analysis to incorporate an understanding of the interrelationship between capitalist and democratic institutions in welfare provision. Moreover, it clearly stresses political mobilization and coalition building as causes of welfare innovation. The dynamic of change in this model rests in the course of conflict between significant societal forces. Welfare-state institutions forged in the process become settings for opportunities and constraints for social actors.

One of its chief criticisms, however, is that concepts such as class structure or coalitions, markets, and state do not capture all the properties of social citizenship and welfare-state development. There is no reason to assume that class is the only basis of political identity any more than region or nation, nor is there a necessary affiliation between the interests of the working class and a social-democratic labour movement. Other interests have been crucial in the welfare state's development, including social and health-care professionals, moral reformers and church officials, and client groups. These groups cannot be reduced to their class character; other social identities such as those of gender and "race" or ethnicity have framed expanded claims of citizenship and mobilized democratic struggle for change through institutions of state.

The Feminist Perspective

The difficulty in talking about feminist scholarship on the welfare state is that feminism spans many theoretical perspectives, including anti-racism, which vary in their views of women's oppression and their assumptions about the process of social and political change. Yet these perspectives in different ways all approach the question of "social reproduction" and its centrality in the diverse lives of women.[39] They start from the hypothesis that "the omission of a gender analysis distorts our understanding of the welfare state through many levels."[40] This omission in turn obscures the existence of policy, the reasons behind inconsistencies within welfare policy, and "the inequitable distribution and production [of income and wealth] that create the need for welfare programs in the first place."[41]

The first studies of women and the welfare state looked specifically at the differential character of social rights embedded in the KWS. At one level, they analysed how specific programs discriminated against women, in effect reproducing gender inequality in domestic and public life. Discrimination is evident in the practice of individual programs such as social assistance and public pensions. The rules governing the Quebec/Canada Pension Plan, for instance, while formally gender neutral, provide no credits for periods of unpaid caretaking as they do in Britain. And the period of contributions required for a full benefit is relatively long – forty years – a level difficult to reach for those who have had intermittent work.[42]

At a broader level, recent scholarship has identified the different ways in which women and men are "written into" the KWS. Men, for example, typically base their claims on the state on the basis of paid work; women, by contrast, who have different patterns of paid employment, make their claims based on familial or marital roles: "Governments have attached greater or lesser entitlements to women as paid workers, but the tendency has been ... to make a dichotomous choice between treating women as wives and mothers, or as workers, with the former predominating. This has meant first, that women's substantial contributions to welfare, particularly their unpaid contribution, have been ignored and with them the direct entitlements that should have been their due; and second, that women's needs have been defined in terms of motherhood as a social function rather than on the basis of individual need."[43]

While the pattern of white women's employment in the paid labour force is becoming increasingly similar to the male pattern,[44] women are disproportionately represented in residual programs such as provincial social assistance or the Guaranteed Income Supplement (GIS) that provide a limited version of Marshall's social citizenship rights. The consequences of women's disproportionate representation among clients of welfare programs is greater financial insecurity, because individuals or households that rely primarily on public transfers for income will be poorer than their counterparts in the labour market.[45]

Because the wage has been the definitive means of providing for the citizenry, women are faced with the prospect of tenuous employment in an increasingly polarized labour market or increased dependence on men in the domestic sphere.[46] Consequently, moves to cut back welfare services – a source of well-paid employment for women since the 1960s – threaten not only to block women's access to paid employment and the possibility of maintaining autonomous households but to reprivatize welfare provision and women's primary role as caregiver.

Some of the feminist scholarship has been criticized as functionalist, emphasizing the objective structures of the economy and the state. Feminist historiography has attempted to paint a more nuanced picture, stressing the role of women's groups in the development of the KWS.[47] New research on the history of women of colour has begun to identify the dimensions of racism and the welfare state, including ideas about the Black family, the role of women of colour as a reserve of cheap labour, and the link between immigration policy and welfare provision, as illustrated in the Live-In Caregiver Programme.

Conclusion

Clearly neither mainstream typologies nor the alternative feminist/anti-racist model are sufficient to characterize welfare states in their entirety. It is necessary to identify the strengths of different approaches to understand better the development of the Canadian KWS and its particular mix of liberal social-transfer programs and universal health care and education. We have identified several important factors:

- There has not been a strong working class, and only weak links have subsisted between labour and the social democratic party. By contrast, organized capital has enjoyed a close relationship with the dominant Progressive Conservative and Liberal parties.
- Canada has seen a weak commitment to redistribution and full employment.

- The federal structure of the political system has served to channel political activism around the welfare state, facilitiated innovation, and provided a venue for reform-minded bureaucrats. More recently, federalism has thwarted reforms in areas of joint federal-provincial jurisdiction.
- There has been a historic commitment to maintaining separate spheres and sustaining men as breadwinners and women as primary caregivers.
- Fiscal- and monetary-policy parameters are constrained by Canada's vulnerability to international markets and capital flows.

DIRECTIONS OF REFORM

Trends in Social Spending

Since 1945, Canada has constructed a modest network of income-security programs and social services. In total, such programs at the provincial and federal levels cost $102.9 billion in 1989–90, including benefits delivered through the tax system. When income taxes and clawbacks are taken into account, total direct social spending was $82.5 billion. An additional $20.4 billion was paid out in the form of federal and provincial tax expenditures.[48] Between the late 1950s and the early 1990s, social spending increased by 718 per cent in real terms and by 63 per cent over the 1980s.[49]

Growth in welfare-state activities in Canada has been marked in the postwar period, with one estimate suggesting an increase from 32 per cent in 1950 to 55 per cent in 1981.[50] Yet, by international standards, Canada is a relatively low social-welfare spender: public expenditure on income maintenance, health, and education as a proportion of GDP – 22.3 per cent in 1986 – remains below the OECD average of 24.7 per cent.[51] This low standing is in large measure the result of the comparatively impoverished status of the income-security system in scope of eligibility, systemic disincentives to eligibility, and the degree to which benefits approximate market earnings.

What has happened to social spending in the last few years? Over the last decade, social spending has been constrained, frozen, or reduced as part of a broader, neo-conservative approach to public-sector management at both levels of government. Overall levels of federal social spending[52] did not increase significantly from 1984 to 1991 and decreased slightly in real terms between 1987–88 and 1990–91. As Rice and Prince note, "In relation to Canada's overall economic activity as measured by the gross domestic product (GDP), federal social spending rose in the early 1980s due to the 1981–82 recession, peaked in

1983–84 at 12.3 percent of GDP, then – over the Mulroney years – declined from 12.1 percent in 1984–85 to 10.7 percent in 1990–91, indicating social spending was growing more slowly than the Canadian economy."[53]

In addition, federal transfers to other levels of government have declined, leaving the provinces in the paradoxical position of having less financial resources but needing to fulfill greater responsibilities, such as welfare assistance, because of recession and economic restructuring.[54] Since 1984, the most notable change in federal social spending has been the 6.1-percentage-point decline in transfers to other levels of government as a share of social expenditure, reflecting the drive towards a more decentralized system of fiscal federalism. The 1994 federal budget indicates that transfers to provinces under the Canada Assistance Plan will be cut back over the next three fiscal years. The Liberal government would appear to be staying the course of retrenchment.

It is important when looking at welfare-state activities to remember that modern governments have grown for many reasons, not just because of expansion of the KWS. For example, the demographic pressures of the postwar baby boom called for greater expenditures on public goods such as roads and sewers and services such as health and education. In Canada, public enterprises and services have historically absorbed many of the expenses that private corporations did not wish to pay, given the high start-up costs of infrastructural projects such as the Canadian Pacific Railway and the James Bay hydro-electric projects, or which otherwise would have had to be paid by the private sector as part of its costs of production. In addition to establishing the economic infrastructure required for the private sector, there are a number of other necessary functions performed by the public sector that have increased spending over time. Government absorbs the costs of creating a well-educated and technically trained labour force. Though business bears part of the taxation and spending burden, the incremental costs to employers are frequently outweighed by superior productivity of the labour force.

A number of more general socioeconomic factors have also been identified in the literature as expanding public expenditure. The growth in population and resulting demographic changes have influenced public spending in all OECD countries, not just Canada. In particular, health care, education, and pensions have expanded with the size and age of the population, and service and benefit levels have also increased. The degree to which coverage and benefits have expanded will depend on, aside from economic resources, political factors such as the strength of organized labour and other social movements concerned with improvement in the standard of living of the working population and the degree to which financing of social expenditures is centralized. In political systems where collective bargaining and allocation of resources are relatively centralized, such as Austria and Sweden, social-program coverage tends to be more generous and extensive.

Canada also has a regional dimension to redistribution, which has taken three main forms: federal equalization payments to the poorer provinces; federal income transfers to individuals who are vulnerable to seasonal unemployment; and industrial-assistance programs meant to subsidize businesses in economically depressed regions.[55] The growth in regional assistance partly reflects the historically lower fiscal resources of some regions such as the Maritimes, the desire to stem the outward flow of labour, and the reality of higher unemployment in an open economy such as Canada's.

Some have argued that government spending will increase over time because the demand for public expenditures rises with upward movement in real personal disposable income. Once basic needs are met, the theory goes, then public demand for "leisure" services such as parks and cultural facilities requiring government spending will increase. Inflation can also influence government spending levels. For example, if current dollars are "deflated" to take into account price increases, then the "real" rate of government expenditure growth declines significantly.

Finally, some analysts offer public-choice arguments that attribute the rise in public expenditures and the resulting tax increases on the expansionary tendencies of the bureaucracy and the "empire building" of individual bureaucrats. Public-choice theorists apply an abstract version of consumer and firm behaviour to voters and government and political representatives (the political market); political actors, much like economic ones, are guided by self-interest. Public-choice theorists conclude that from the perspective of public budgeting, public servants' goals are related to maximizing the size of their budgets rather than pursuing efficiency.[56]

The Current Debate

Despite Canada's comparatively low levels of social spending, the KWS bolstered federalism and the overall project of nation building. Income-security programs such as Old Age Security and unemployment insurance gave Canadians a sense of common citizenship rights; the health-care system "socialized" a basic service that came to be seen as the right of every Canadian; and attempts at regional and class-based income distribution sought to buffer the influence of economic fluctuations on actual distributions of income.

While such programs as equalization payments from Ottawa to the poorer provinces or income transfers to individuals may not have alleviated the disparities in income distribution, they do appear to have created stability over the last couple of decades.[57] In this sense, the redistributive role of the state has been an important source of financial stability for individuals and families.

Recent changes to the tax system that appear to be regressive (such as the Goods and Services Tax [GST], which falls heavily on lower-income groups) and the decline in federal social spending as a proportion of GDP (from a peak of 12.3 per cent in 1983–84 to 10.7 per cent in 1990–91, to 11.6 per cent in 1991–92 as a result of the recession) reveal a gradual shift in KWS initiatives. In addition to fiscal pressures on all levels of government, there is broader questioning of the role of the state versus the private sector in the meeting of basic needs. In political terms, citizenship rights appear to be constricting with the declining role of public provision. More conservative analysts such as those within the public-choice tradition argue that public budgets are out of control largely because of the self-interest of political and state actors. Social-democratic and progressive forces have responded in largely defensive terms, arguing for a "staying of the course" as set out more than three decades ago.

Those involved in the debate about the future of the KWS agree that significant changes in the economy and the domestic sphere have eroded the ability of the state to underwrite economic and social reproduction. Neo-liberals have seized the occasion to advocate a welfare state that subordinates "social policy to the demands of labour market flexibility and structural competitiveness."[58] This entails a move away from redistributive concerns, based on expanding welfare rights, towards cost saving. Proponents of neo-liberalism support continued emphasis on the elevation of the market and family in welfare provision, increased targeting of remaining public resources to the subsistence needs of the "poorest," and linking the receipt of public support to participation in the current labour market, in addition to measures to ease the transition from income-security programs to the low-wage labour market, often in the form of subsidies to low-wage employers.[59]

These themes or features have been associated with liberal welfare states and, as we have seen above, are characteristic of the welfare state in Canada. Today we find renewed emphasis on neo-liberal prescriptions. Many of the current proposals being considered by the federal Social Security Review incorporate neo-liberal elements. The Newfoundland government's proposal for a Basic Income Supplement, for example, has curried much attention. This program would combine funds available under the Canada Assistance Plan for social assistance and the unemployment-insurance fund to provide a guaranteed annual income of $3,000 per adult and $1,500 per child. The benefit would be reduced as family income from earnings increased, disappearing at $27,500 for an individual and at $42,500 for a family with one wage earner. In that the maximum benefit level is set significantly below minimum wage, individuals would be "encouraged" to find work at any price.

Opposition to the direction of neo-liberal reform has been mobilized. Groups that once criticized the authoritarian character of the welfare state have found themselves defending these same programs as conservative governments have taken the upper hand in pursuing neo-liberal goals. While there are different critiques of the forces undermining the KWS, progressive forces have come together around two central propositions: the continuing importance of the nation-state in economic management and welfare provision, and the bonds between citizens to promote the well-being of all members of the community. We have chosen to call this alternative "post-liberal Keynesianism."[60]

The referent for opponents of neo-liberalism has been the social-democratic vision of market and state crafted in Scandinavia. There, social-democratic governments successfully combined Keynesian full employment with a high and relatively egalitarian wage distribution, high levels of total employment, and high levels of income security available as a right of citizenship.[61] The social-democratic model broke down during the recession of the early 1990s. Yet the example continues to inspire what we are calling "post-liberal Keynesian" responses to the impasse of the Canadian welfare state. Key elements of this approach are the interrelationship of state, market, and family in economic and social reproduction; the critical role of the welfare state in redistribution of income and opportunity; active labour-market policies to facilitate the shift to a high value-added economy, crowding out low-wage employers; public programs to help families, women in particular, to participate fully in the paid labour market; provisions to ensure greater equality in public and private life; and fiscal and monetary policies that attempt to keep the proceeds of Canadian labour economic activity at home.

Both neo-liberalism and post-liberal Keynesianism approach the KWS from opposite directions, both intent on restructuring the welfare state in response to major changes in political, social, and economic life. Indeed, this is a time to reflect on the future of the KWS. Can there be a response that both reflects the positive characteristics enshrined in public action and recognizes the weaknesses of the old state forms?[62] Dealing with the state's limitations in a new and creative way, without negating the importance of the public sphere, is the balance that needs to be struck in going beyond the old dividing lines, where free-market advocates champion privatization and supporters of the KWS defend public subsidies and entitlements. The specific factors behind the development of the Canadian welfare state will surely influence the outcome of this transformative struggle.

NOTES

1 See Myles, "Decline?"
2 See Maddison, "Origins."
3 See Julia O'Connor, "Gender."
4 A progressive tax system is one in which the ratio of tax to income rises with income; the more one earn, the greater proportion one pays.
5 Wolfe, "Rise," 47.
6 See Marshall, "Citizenship."
7 Esping-Andersen, *Three*, 21–3.
8 Ibid., 23–6.
9 Ibid., 80.
10 Ibid., 27.
11 Two other types of welfare state are identified by Esping-Andersen: the corporatist and the social democratic.
12 Orloff, "Gender."
13 Strain and Hum, "Canadian."
14 This discussion relies on Hess, *Canadian*.
15 Ibid., 5.
16 See Julia O'Connor, "Welfare."
17 Esping-Andersen, *Three*, 69.
18 Smeeding, Torrey, and Rein, "Patterns," 111, cited in Tuohy, "Social," 283.
19 Galarneau, "Women," 29.
20 See Tuohy, "Social"; Olsen, "Locating."
21 Julia O'Connor, "Welfare," 133.
22 See Brooks, *Public*, 2nd ed., chap. 2.
23 We follow the practice of putting "race" in quotation marks to indicate that racial identity is socially constructed. As in the discussion in the feminist community about the use of the word gender, "race" here is distinguished from reference to biology.
24 See Williams, *Social*; Quadagno, *Color*.
25 See Guest, *Emergence*; Rice, "Politics."
26 See Rimlinger, *Welfare*.
27 See Haddow, *Poverty*.

28 See Brooks, *Public*, 2nd ed.

29 See Gough, *Political*; James O'Connor, *Fiscal*.

30 See Cuneo, "State, Class," and "State Mediation."

31 Swartz, "Politics," 335.

32 See Weir, Orloff, and Skocpol, *Politics*.

33 Pal, "Relative," 84.

34 See Tuohy, "Social."

35 Briggs, "Welfare," 228.

36 See Korpi, *Democratic*; Esping-Andersen, *Politics*.

37 Myles, "Decline?" 82.

38 Jenson, " 'Different,' " 82.

39 Williams, *Social*, 41–2.

40 Gordon, ed., *Women*, 10.

41 See ibid.

42 Myles, *Old*, 61.

43 Lewis and Ostner, "Gender," 25–6.

44 Women of colour have always had high participation rates in the paid labour market. They are often confined, however, to poorly paid employment that does not provide the welfare benefits characteristics of core-sector employment. This pattern is also true for men of colour. Data are not collected on the race of benefit recipients, with the exception of Aboriginal peoples.

45 See Rainwater, "Social."

46 See Nelson, "Origins."

47 See Koven and Michels, eds., *Mothers*.

48 Battle and Torjman, *Opening*, 2.

49 See ibid., 6.

50 Brooks, *Public*, 1st ed., 240.

51 OECD, *OECD*, 16–17.

52 "Social spending" refers to transfers to persons, cash transfers to other levels of government, other major social transfers, and transfers to Canada Mortgage and Housing Corporation and the CBC. See Rice and Prince, "Lowering," for a detailed discussion.

53 Ibid., 386.

54 "Economic restructuring" refers to the ongoing transformation of the economic system caused by for example, trade liberalization and rapid technological change. The result is the decline of old industries and the emergence of new forms of work (part-time).

55 Brooks, *Public*, 2nd ed., 205.

56 See Savoie, *Politics*, for a discussion of the applicability of public-choice to the Canadian case and critiques of the public-choice approach.

57 See Banting, *Welfare*.

58 Jessop, "Towards," 9.

59 See Myles, "Decline?"

60 We borrow the term "postliberal" from Bowles and Gintis. They describe their alternative future as a post-liberal democracy: "The promise of postliberal democracy is to ... continue the expansion of personal rights and thus to render the exercise of both property rights and state power democratically accountable." Bowles and Gintis, *Democracy*, 177.

61 Myles, "Decline?" 98.

62 For example, universal services and benefits have generally meant uniform provision that does not respect the needs and demands of a more hetero-geneous population marked by distinctive and new groupings. Calls to "reinvent government" or pressures for "democratic administration" reflect the lack of control, accountability, and visibility of government spending on services and programs. They also signal the profound alienation of citizens from a faceless bureaucracy that is unable, given the current administrative form, to meet appropriately the needs of increas-ingly heterogeneous "client" groups.

REFERENCES

Banting, Keith. *The Welfare State and Canadian Federalism*. 2nd ed. Montreal McGill-Queen's University Press, 1987.

Battle, Ken, and Torjman, Sherri. *Opening the Books on Social Spending*. Ottawa: Caledon Institute of Social Policy, 1993.

Bowles, Samuel, and Gintis, Herbert. *Democracy and Capitalism*. New York: Basic Books, 1986.

Briggs, Asa. "The Welfare State in Historical Perspective." *European Journal of Sociology*, 2 no. 2 (1961), 25–45.

Brooks, Stephen. *Public Policy in Canada*. 1st ed. Toronto: McClelland and Stewart, 1989.

– *Public Policy in Canada*. 2nd ed. Toronto: McClelland and Stewart, 1993.

Cuneo, Carl. "State, Class, and Reserve Labour: The Case of the 1941 Canadian Unemployment Insurance Act." *Canadian Review of Sociology and Anthropology*, 16 no. 2 (1979), 141–70.

– "State Mediation of Class Contradictions in Canadian Unemployment Insurance, 1930–1935." *Studies in Political Economy*, no. 3 (1980), 36–65.

Esping-Andersen, Gösta. *Politics against Markets*. Princeton, NJ: Princeton University Press, 1985.

– *The Three Worlds of Welfare Capitalism*. Cambridge: Polity Press, 1990.

Galarneau, Diane. "Women Approaching Retirement." *Perspectives* (autumn 1991), 28–39.

Gordon, Linda, ed. *Women, the State and Welfare*. Madison: University of Wisconsin Press, 1990.

Gough, Ian. *The Political Economy of the Welfare State*. London: Macmillan Press, 1978.

Guest, Dennis. *The Emergence of Social Security in Canada.* 2nd ed. Vancouver: University of British Columbia Press, 1985.

Haddow, Rodney. *Poverty Reform in Canada.* Montreal: McGill-Queen's University Press, 1993.

Hess, Melanie. *The Canadian Fact Book on Income Security Programs.* Ottawa: Canadian Council on Social Development, 1993.

Jenson, Jane. "'Different' but not 'Exceptional': Canada's Permeable Fordism." *Canadian Review of Sociology and Anthropology,* 26 no. 1 (1989), 69–94.

Jessop, Bob. "Towards a Schumpeterian Workfare State? Preliminary Remarks on Post-Fordist Political Economy." *Studies in Political Economy,* no. 40 (1993), 7–39.

Korpi, Walter. *The Democratic Class Struggle.* London: Routledge and Kegan Paul 1983.

Koven, Seth, and Michel, Sonya, eds. *Mothers of the New World.* New York: Routledge & Kegan Paul, 1993.

Lewis, Jane, and Ostner, Ilona. "Gender and the Evolution of European Social Policies." Paper presented to Workshop on Emergent Supranational Social Policy: The EC's Social Dimension in Comparative Perspective, Centre for European Studies, Harvard University, November 1991.

Maddison, Angus. "Origins and Impact of the Welfare State, 1883–1983." *Banca Nazionale del Lavoro,* no. 148 (1984), 55–87.

Marshall, T.H. "Citizenship and Social Class." In *Class, Citizenship and Social Development.* New York: Anchor, 1965.

Myles, John. "Decline or Impasse? The Current State of the Welfare State." *Studies in Political Economy,* no. 26 (1988), 73–107.

– *Old Age in the Welfare State.* Lawrence: University of Kansas Press, 1989.

Nelson, Barbara. "The Origins of the Two-Tracked Welfare State: Workmen's Compensation and Mothers' Aid." in Linda Gordon, ed., *Women, the State and Welfare,* 123–51. Madison: University of Wisconsin Press, 1990.

O'Connor, James. *The Fiscal Crisis of the State.* New York: St Martin's Press, 1973.

O'Connor, Julia. "Gender, Class and Citizenship in the Comparative Analysis of Welfare State Regimes: Theoretical and Methodological Issues." *British Journal of Sociology,* 44 no. 3 (1993), 501–17.

– "Welfare Expenditure and Policy Orientation in Canada in Comparative Perspective." *Canadian Review of Sociology and Anthropology,* 26 no. 1 (1989), 127–50.

OECD. *OECD in Figures.* Supplement to the *OECD Observer,* no. 158 (June-July 1989).

Olsen, Gregg. "Locating the Canadian Welfare State: Family Policy and Health Care in Canada, Sweden and the United States." *Canadian Journal of Sociology,* 19 no. 1 (1994), 1–20.

Orloff, Ann Shola. "Gender and the Social Rights of Citizenship: The Comparative Analysis of Gender Relations and Welfare States." *American Sociological Review,* 58 (June 1993), 303–27.

Pal, Leslie. "Relative Autonomy Revisited: The Origins of Canadian Unemployment Insurance." *Canadian Journal of Political Science*, 19 no. 1 (1986), 71–102.

Quadagno, Jill. *The Color of Welfare*. New York: Oxford University Press, 1994.

Rainwater, Lee. "The Social Wage in the Income Package of Working Parents." Working Paper No. 89, Luxembourg Income Study, 1993.

Rice, James. "Politics of Income Security: Historical Developments and Limits to Future Change." In B. Doern, ed., *The Politics of Economic Policy*, Research Studies for the Royal Commission on the Economic Union and Development Prospects for Canada, Vol. 40, 221–50. Toronto: University of Toronto Press, 1985.

Rice, James, and Prince, Michael. "Lowering the Safety Net and Weakening the Bonds of Nationhood: Social Policy in the Mulroney Years." In S. Phillips, ed., *How Ottawa Spends 1993–94*, 381–416. Ottawa: Carleton University Press, 1993.

Rimlinger, Gaston. *Welfare Policy and Industrialization in Europe, America and Russia*. New York: John Wiley & Sons, Inc., 1971.

Savoie, Donald. *The Politics of Public Spending in Canada*. Toronto: University of Toronto Press, 1990.

Smeeding, Timothy, Torrey, Barbara Boyle, and Rein, Martin. "Patterns of Income and Poverty: The Economic Status of Children and the Elderly in Eight Countries." In J. Palmer, T. Smeeding, and B. Torry, eds,. *The Vulnerable*, 89–120. Washington, DC: Urban Institute Press, 1988.

Strain, Frank, and Hum, Derek. "Canadian Federalism and the Welfare State: Shifting Responsibilities and Sharing Costs." In J. Ismael, ed., *The Canadian Welfare State: Evolution and Transition*, 349–71. Edmonton: University of Alberta Press, 1987.

Swartz, Donald. "The Politics of Reform: Conflict and Accommodation in Canadian Health Policy." In L. Panitch, ed., *The Canadian State: Political Economy and Political Power*, 311–43. Toronto: University of Toronto Press, 1977.

Tuohy, Carolyn. "Social Policy: Two Worlds." In M. Atkinson, ed., *Governing Canada: Institutions and Public Policy*, 275–305. Toronto: Harcourt Brace Jovanovich Canada Inc., 1993.

Weir, Margaret, Orloff, Ann Shola, and Skocpol, Theda, eds., *The Politics of Social Policy in the United States*. Princeton, NJ: Princeton University Press, 1988.

Williams, Fiona. *Social Policy: A Critical Introduction*. London: Polity Press, 1989.

Wolfe, David. "The Rise and Demise of the Keynesian Era in Canada: Economic Policy, 1930–1982." In M. Cross and G. Kealy, eds., *Readings in Canadian Social History*, 46–79. Toronto: McClelland and Stewart, 1984.

14 Displacing the Welfare State

LIORA SALTER AND RICK SALTER

INTRODUCTION

The New Infrastructure

Problems and contradictions within the welfare state seem insurmountable at a time when the welfare state appears to be crumbling. The situation looks like a "hollowing out of the state."[1] Globalization threatens to render nation-states impotent, it is argued. The right wing is ascendant, and its adherents never shared commitments to the welfare state. That they would eagerly abandon it at the first opportunity is not surprising. Nor do there seem to be any limits to the dismantling of the institutions of the modern welfare state, to privatization, liberalization, and deregulation. With the advent of new trading blocs such as the North American Free Trade Agreement and the European Union, the recent spate of mergers and acquisitions among major firms worldwide, the collapse of state-based economies in eastern Europe, and the emergence of a new world trade organization, it does seems as if the nation-state, and the welfare state more particularly, are increasingly not involved when important issues are at stake. When these developments are combined with the dismantling of universal social programs, the attack on unions, and the pervasive preoccupation with efficiency and competitiveness, it is easy to conclude that the welfare state is a relic of the past.

There is more to the story, however. Even while the welfare state is under attack, something new is being put in its place, especially in the case of state administration – regulatory boards and agencies. A reconstituted state is emerging, with new methods of administration, not quite under the auspices of government. Regulatory functions are being performed, but in ways that only minimally resemble the legal institutions long associated with the welfare state – for example, the Canadian Radio-television and Telecommunications Commission and the National Energy Board. The welfare state is not being abandoned, so much as its key institutions and provisions are changing, as are the roles for its key participants – the state, civil society, and capital. Unfortunately, it will not be easy to arrive at a picture of the newly emerging situation; this side of the story is much more difficult to see than the "hollowing out of the state."

Actually, "reconstituted state" is a poor choice of terminology. As becomes evident below, much of what is emerging to supplant the welfare state cannot be described as the state, even if governments continue to play important roles. Moreover, something more than government administration is involved. Perhaps the best word to to describe the new situation is "infrastructure," using the term in the same way that one would say that roads, garbage collection, zoning, and social services are the "infrastructure" of the modern city. Roads and so on represent the all-but-invisible organization that gives shape to and makes possible city life. When one speaks about reconstitution of the welfare state, or its replacement by something else, the reference is to the newly emerging infrastructure of social, political, and economic relations.

This chapter asks what is being put into place in the face of challenges to the welfare state. It follows two strategies to answer the question. First, it describes some elements of the new infrastructure, concentrating on a few case studies, because there are so few data yet to support a more comprehensive analysis. It focuses on examples of new forms of regulation replacing the conventional regulatory agencies. Examples include: (1) environmental regulation, where "stakeholder mediation" is increasingly being relied on to arrive at environmentally sound decisions; (2) broadcasting, where a traditional regulatory agency has undertaken to remake itself on a continuing basis; (3) telecommunications, where deregulation is in full force; (4) standard setting, where new relationships between public and private sectors are emerging; (5) and the Patent Medicines Prices Review Board, an agency created by a government intent on deregulation.

These five case studies of regulation are complemented by a different kind of example, that of Aboriginal self-government. Though self-government involves considerable regulation, we chose this example because it illustrates another aspect of the reconstitution of the relationships among state, civil society, and capital. In the instance of regulatory boards, the relations of power between state and capital are of primary importance and those between state and civil society less so. In the case of Aboriginal self-government, the relationships of the state to civil society are directly at issue, even with respect to new regulations in the self-government agreements. If the goal is to understand the new infrastructure, and the roles of the state and civil society within it, this example usefully complements more conventional studies of regulation.

The topic is vast; each of the six examples provided here is complex, and even they do not tell the whole story. So we adopt a second strategy as well, to identify the contours of the new infrastructure. We examine changes to social values, as these are reflected in the new infrastructure. The welfare state is associated with attempts to realize particular values: fairness, representation, and redistribution, in particular. By asking what happens to these values in the new infrastructure, and, more specifically, in each of the six cases described in this chapter, we can gauge some larger implications of the change.

Issues in Political Economy

Problems and contradictions of the welfare state are now high on the agenda for political economists, but the issue of regulation is not, nor has it ever been.[2] The focus in political economy has traditionally been on the "mechanisms through which governments' social and economic policies help to stabilize the dynamics of the process of capitalist accumulation."[3] From this perspective, it is not surprising that little attention has been paid to administrative tribunals or regulatory boards. There would be little reason to single out tribunals, which represent only one among many such mechanisms. Alternatively, if one adopts Marchak's formulation of political economy as "the study of power derived from or contingent upon a system of property rights ... ,"[4] administrative tribunals, or regulation as it is commonly understood, might be somewhat more interesting to political economy, inasmuch as tribunals do alter the system of property relations in quite significant ways.[5] But recognizing this fact about tribunals requires quite a detailed understanding of what regulators do, and of the implications of their decisions.

To the extent that political economists have dealt with regulatory boards and tribunals at all, it has usually been only to see them as "captured" by the industry they are supposed to regulate.[6] The focus on "capture" has led political economy down a blind alley. Of course, regulatory boards and tribunals are captured. They are set in place precisely to fashion compromise; they are often created by request from industry; they establish regimes of co-management.[7] Regulation loses its legitimacy only when one or other party to the compromise is no longer satisfied with the benefits (such as reduced competition) derived through regulation and, consequently, finds the rules (even the regulations it helped set into place) to be coercive and burdensome. None the less, regulatory regimes are often established at the instigation of industry, and specific regulations are normally negotiated with those bodies being regulated. The intimate relationship between the state and capital easily observed in dealing with regulatory boards is one that is freely admitted to by both parties.

More promising for political economy has been Mahon's analysis of regulation,[8] which does draw attention to the negotiations and compromises within the state reflected in the creation of any new regulatory board or agency. By extension, her analysis also offers some clues about the current political situation, about the recent rejection of regulation by its previously strongest supporters. There has been a shift in the balances of forces within the state; not surprisingly, this change is reflected in different attitudes towards regulatory boards on the part of both state and capital. What Mahon's analysis did not offer originally was an appreciation of the implications of the kinds of decisions made by regulators, as opposed to other state officials. Why was regulation their "chosen instrument"?[9] What did this state institution accomplish specifically for the state and capital that was not achieved through other means?

Until very recently, political economists have paid little attention to the design of any state institution, not just to regulation, preferring to concentrate instead on the role of state policies in shaping the economy. This omission has been short-sighted. Regulatory boards are interesting precisely because they constitute an important venue for routine, ongoing interactions not only between the state and various fractions of capital but also – because of their reliance on public hearings – between the state and civil society. With regard to the latter, one need draw attention only to the active involvement of advocate organizations such as the National Action Committee on the Status of Women and poverty or Aboriginal groups before regulatory boards.

Observing the actions of a regulatory board is roughly comparable to watching a labour negotiation in process or to being the proverbial "fly on the wall" in a corporate boardroom when merger discussions are under way. Embedded in the routines, the discourse, and the most seemingly mundane decisions of regulatory boards are the data necessary for finely drawn studies of power. Furthermore, in regulation, most of these routines, discourses, and decisions are reasonably accessible because of the public records accompanying much regulation.

In Clement and Williams's *The New Political Economy* (1989), Bartholomew and Boyd speak about the ways in which law and legal institutions mediate the relations of power.[10] Regulatory boards are especially interesting as legal institutions because, unlike courts, they bind state, capital, and civil society together in a sustained relationship focused on particular problems (such as the environment) or sectors (such as telecommunications) and because they provide a relatively open window on the intricate, but often mundane mediation involved.

There is a new urgency to studying regulatory boards. Whatever else is implicated in the welfare state, it is characterized by its reliance on regulation. The pressures on it are manifested immediately by changes in regulation. Its problems and contradictions have been under discussion even within regulatory boards for some time. It may seem as if regulation is being dismantled, and dismantling of regulation is often seen as synonymous with dismantling of the welfare state. Something else is occurring, however: a reshaping of this particular legal institution and of the relationships mediated through it. Paying attention to regulation may illuminate the broader issues implicated in the reconstitution of the state and its many relationships with capital and civil society. With this in mind, we should look at some examples.

CASE STUDIES

Broadcasting

The Canadian Radio-television and Telecommunications Commission (CRTC) deals with broadcasting, telephones, and, to some extent, the new information technologies. It fits the classic model of a regulatory agency. In this, the CRTC is unusual in the Canadian context.[11] The CRTC has its own legislation. It reports to a minister but is not part of a government department. It holds public hearings, not just on applications for broadcasting licences but also on matters of broad general interest. It has a large staff and relatively expert commissioners. It issues decisions that, though they can be pre-empted or overturned by government, are usually final. The CRTC is often used as the example of a regulatory agency being used to effect social policy; its current chair is very concerned about violence on television, for example. The CRTC is also frequently used as the example of the burdensome nature of regulation, to make the point that governments should stop playing "big brother" to their citizens.

In 1991, a new Broadcasting Act replaced the legislation governing the CRTC since 1968. Surprisingly, given the number of public attacks on the CRTC, the new act set in place an even more comprehensive social mandate for the agency. Reference in the new act was made not only to the new information environment and technologies but also, for example, to supporting community, multi-ethnic, and Aboriginal broadcasting.[12] The scope and powers of the agency were strengthened, not diminished, in spite of the prevailing deregulatory rhetoric.

Yet something quite fundamental has changed. First, the CRTC has been linked much more directly to government. Not only can the cabinet now set its general direction, but it can overturn decisions, require the CRTC to deal with specific matters, and, generally speaking, supervise the CRTC's actions before as well as after its licensing decisions. Second, the CRTC has been given permission to withdraw from regulating where it considers that competitive market forces are sufficiently strong.

The first development – linking the agency more directly to government – came only after considerable pressure had been exerted to make the CRTC accountable. The argument had been advanced that, because no one elects the commissioners, they fall outside the ambit of democracy.[13] Tying the CRTC more closely to government, it was claimed, would ensure that matters of public importance remain under the control of the legislature, where they belonged. What this argument misses is the way in which the CRTC was already accountable directly to the public, through its public hearings and its public, record.[14] Also cast aside was the traditional justification for regulation: the need for a body independent of government to make decisions about technically complex matters in which powerful interest groups might be involved. The new situation may increase the CRTC's accountability to government, but the CRTC is an agency now without much protection from the whims of members of Parliament, cabinet, political lobbyists, and powerful interest groups. In effect, the CRTC can now make decisions after public hearings based on a public record, only to have these same decisions rendered irrelevant after closed-door sessions of cabinet. In the name of accountability, the agency has become more politically oriented.

Giving the CRTC power to withdraw from regulating particular matters has resulted in the agency's having considerably more power over and flexibility in how it conducts its business. Furthermore, the CRTC now has more recourse to monetary fines and to the courts, even in situations where previously it could only issue its own decisions and solicit voluntary compliance. To be sure, the new legislation, the pressures on the agency, and the mind-set of its commissioners all converge on the desirability of deregulation, but this is not the point. A traditional rationale for regulation – that companies being regulated were inevitably going to become monopolies and thus needed governments to act as proxies for the marketplace forces otherwise absent – has only ever applied to a small part of the broadcasting sector, and the CRTC's efforts at deregulation extend far beyond the realm where this rationale is applicable. Rather, the questions of whether, what, and how to regulate have been turned over to the regulator, whose job it is now to take stock continually of both the environment and the state of the industry in the broadest sense. In this context, the CRTC holds hearings even about whether its own legislative mandate should be substantially rewritten – in other words, about its own law, framework, and rules of operation.[15]

Deregulatory in orientation, the CRTC conforms to few of the conventional stereotypes of deregulation. Notwithstanding its withdrawal from some traditional areas of regulation, the CRTC remains a highly activist agency, mandated to oversee something akin to an industrial strategy for the communications sector.

Telecommunications

Much rhetoric about deregulation is associated with airlines, but deregulation's most significant impact has been on telecommunications. Less than ten years ago, competition was the exception and monopoly was the rule in provision of telephone services. In all but a few countries, governments owned and operated the telephone systems. Today, governments everywhere are selling off the telephone companies to private interests[16] and considering whether even local telephone service might be provided by more than one company operating in a single community or neighbourhood. The telecommunications sector – which includes telephones and new data services – is considered to be one of the most dynamic and potentially competitive of all.

As in broadcasting, it is easy to miss the significance of these developments for regulation and thus to see them as an exemplar of deregulation in practice. Absent from this picture is the degree to which the regulator was always dependent in the past on the industry for its every initiative. The conventional picture of regulation, which equates it with government intervention and interference, has always been partly fiction, because regulators always have had to negotiate with those they regulate about the approach to be taken, about specific decisions, and about compliance. Regulated firms, especially those that provide necessary services on a monopoly basis, have considerable influence: they can threaten to withdraw their services, fail to live up to "the spirit of the regulation," work to rule, fail to innovate or cut costs when new technologies are available, and so on.[17] The best way to describe the situation of regulation is as co-management, because governments and industry together negotiate the rules of the game for those operating in the sector (and to keep competitors out).

Governments have now mostly withdrawn from active engagement in the detailed management of the regulated firms, and thus from the kind of negotiations that previously characterized regulation. Co-management has not diminished, nor have governments ceased to play a major role. The state's role has changed, and efforts at co-management now take new directions. The state is important within the management of the sector because governments are often the major users of the services. They exercise market clout. This is especially true in the new communications technologies, where government and military use constitutes a critical bloc within the emerging markets. More significantly perhaps, emphasis has moved away from managing firms to managing markets. Considerable efforts are made by regulators (plus government departments and the courts) to deal with perceived imbalances and unfairness in the market, with abuse of market dominance by the major, established companies.[18] Finally, even if regulators no longer play a direct part in governing activities within the sector, other arms of the state take up the slack. Government departments actively fashion industrial policies involving government investment or grants to particular firms in the industry. Governments bring new consortia into being and provide the money for the research they undertake.[19] When complaints arise, matters are now often turned over to the courts, which have taken over much of the dispute resolution formerly done by the regulatory agency. In short, one would be hard pressed to argue that the state has removed itself at all from co-management, notwithstanding the very significant withdrawal of formal regulations in sectors such as telecommunications.

Standards

In the health and environmental fields, standards are the actual numbers used to indicate how much pollution and so on should be considered safe. For industrial products, the standards reflect agreements about how the products will perform – how many rotations per minute should be completed, for example. In the telecommunications industry, standards describe amount of noise on the line, availability of area codes, ability of one telephone system to connect with another, and so on. In information technology, different standards mean that a disc initialized on one computer will not necessarily work on another.

Standards are agreements concerning the technical or other qualities of any product, system, or industrial process – acceptable levels of safety, performance, or compatibility.

Historically, these agreements have been developed mainly within industry, or by government engineers and bureaucrats, or in small (and all-but-invisible) government-industry organizations.[20] Safety considerations and social benefits have been traded off against technical feasibility and cost in closed-door sessions. The vast majority of standards have been developed locally, then reviewed and approved nationally and internationally. The international standards organizations, which have been active for many decades, have mainly been forums for making contacts within industry and between governments and for exchanging information among erstwhile competitors. So slow and cumbersome was their process for arriving at any standard that the international organizations only recognized decisions already taken at the national or firm level.

National standards have always been non-tariff barriers to trade; international standards have been used mainly to further the market strategies of multinational companies. In a fully globalized economy with fully liberalized trade rules, however, there would be little room for non-tariff barriers to trade nor for incompatible products. The information age requires that everyone be able to communicate, without barriers, with everyone else; trade with everyone else; and produce products for any market on demand. In this context, international standards should become much more important than local or national ones; indeed, they should be supplanting national standards completely, removing non-tariff trade barriers in the process.

The degree to which international standardization has actually taken place is, however, hardly an encouraging sign for globalization. The pace of standardization, along with that of the internationalization of standards, is a good indicator of how little and how unevenly globalization and the "information economy" have actually spread. Incompatibility still exists everywhere; national standards are still major non-tariff barriers to trade; and the standards organizations still fight a losing battle to set establish their right to set the necessary standards for the new information society. This poor prospect for standards illustrates how thoroughly infused with rhetoric the debate about the new economy really is.

Yet relationships are changing among state, capital, and civil society. If the rhetoric about the new economy is put aside, standards can be seen as a new form of regulation. Their real significance lies in their role in the new trade alliances – for example, the European Union and NAFTA. Even if the European Union negotiations are not fully successful, there has already been significant integration of European industry, effected mainly through agreements about technical standards. Whatever NAFTA will eventually mean in geopolitical terms, its impact will be significant when the technical standards of Canada, the United States, and Mexico (and other countries in the Americas) are harmonized, as indeed they will be very soon. In other words, a new infrastructure is being created within and consonant with the new trading blocs, quite independent of any political developments. This new infrastructure has little to do with the political arrangements laid out in the treaties, and even less to do with the movement of companies across borders to avoid regulations or gain profits. It is instead bound up with harmonization of technical requirements for industry and for environmental, health, and occupational safety. This harmonization is effected through seemingly mundane decisions about standards, but this new infrastructure will have the same effect as did roads and railways in a previous era. It will provide the designated pathways for relations among state, capital, and civil society, forcing everyone to orient themselves accordingly.

Furthermore, especially in the European case, a new kind of regulation is evolving in conjunction with the setting of technical standards – one that is highly compatible with privatization. In this new form of regulation, the supranational government (the European Union) develops general policy guidelines (called "essential requirements") for matters previously or potentially subject to national regulation. These requirements are then turned over to private-sector organizations, which develop the actual "rules" or technical agreements. The private-sector organizations are partly funded by the European Union to carry out specific work; their members include government administrations as well as major firms. They operate with a formal mandate and charter quite similar to a legislative act. In other words, the state has certainly not withdrawn from regulation. But the main technical work is now being done by voluntary organizations, not government regulators. The state is formally cast in the role of participant-like-any-other in negotiating the technical agreements that will constitute standards. The whole process is underwritten financially by the state, but it is intended to produce voluntary, industry-driven standards.

What happens to these technical standards once they have been developed by voluntary organizations? In theory, they become the European Union's rules or regulations, and all member-countries are required to adopt them. In theory also, the European courts mediate disputes. In practice, it remains for individual national governments to adopt the standards as regulations and to carry out whatever enforcement they deem important. There is a good deal of slippage between reaching an agreement about the standards and enforcing compliance in each country. Though the trade agreements construct a new relationship among state, capital, and civil society, the nation-state continues to have much more power, at least in this instance, than is implied by "the hollowing out of the state."

To speak of a new form of regulation, using Europe as one example of a trading bloc, is to speak of a complex system of interlocking parts, some public and some private. Regulation is, in some sense, a misnomer because much of this system remains voluntary. Interest-group negotiation is the prevailing form of interaction, and the state is one among many interest groups represented in forums designed to be industry-led. Policy making and enforcement remain tasks of the state, but the complexity of the system leaves much room for conflict to develop within the state. National governments remain important, not because of the particularity of their standards or regulations, but because they control the adoption and enforcement of the newly harmonized standards.

Stakeholder Mediation and Environmental Regulation

Environmental assessment now occurs in every province in Canada and also for projects coming under federal jurisdiction. Government departments devote vast resources to identifying "priority substances" – chemical products deemed potentially dangerous and worthy of scrutiny.[21] The review process for approving new pesticides, and reassessing old ones, has been revised several times. Occupational health and safety standards deemed to be flawed in some respect are regularly brought to attention and subjected to multi-level review. Risk assessment, a method for dealing with potentially dangerous products, has now become the norm, as have other complex method in aid of decision making.[22]

Risk assessment and other environmental-assessment processes all appear to conform to the conventional view of government regulation. Someone (or several people) is empowered to act as commissioner, to review the data, and to arrive at decisions. Various groups are invited to make their views known. Lawyers and expert witnesses are brought in. Public hearings are scheduled. Questions about procedural fairness combine with highly technical debates. Only a small portion of potentially dangerous substances is ever deemed worthy of scrutiny. Only some developments, usually those with significant government funding or involvement, are subject to review. The pesticides reviewed in Canada are rarely developed or even fully tested in Canada, and all have been evaluated abroad before they are considered for approval.

Yet risk assessment and environmental regulation constitute the more-or-less independent, formal, and participatory process that people expect when they speak about regulation.

Environmental regulation has now become so cumbersome, so litigious, and so bogged down in procedural wrangling that it renders the process unworkable. In the last few years, especially given widespread preoccupation with deregulation, efforts have been directed at simplifying, quickening, and easing the burden of regulation while producing adequate and timely decisions. "Stakeholder mediation" is now in vogue and involves bringing together the various interest groups – including the public and environmental advocacy groups – to negotiate an agreement that all can accept. The stakeholder groups meet behind closed doors. Their mandate is to find solutions that take each group's interests into account. It is assumed that the groups are themselves expert and that among the matters to be negotiated is agreement about the scientific issues. Formal procedures, expert witnesses, even lawyers are cut out of the process. Stakeholder mediation seldom fully replaces the regulatory process, but it can short-circuit it, rendering public hearings unnecessary and allowing governments to arrive at decisions in a relatively speedy manner.[23]

One would be hard pressed to defend the classic model of environmental regulation as being the best way to arrive at decisions about waste management, forestry policy, or new hydro dams. Far too often, legal wrangling replaces genuine debate, and those with the resources to remain engaged over the life of the hearing process (and to call the highest-paid experts) win, notwithstanding the emphasis given to public participation. In some cases – for example, in waste management – it seems impossible to make any decision at all, which is a back-handed tribute to the power of the advocacy groups but does not get rid of the waste. In this area, stakeholder mediation has been as warmly welcomed by the public-interest groups and environmental advocates as it has by government and industry.

Yet no one should discount the significance of the change. Conceiving of the public as "stakeholders" is akin to viewing members of the public only in terms of how they fit within one or other interest group.[24] The idea that there is, and should be, an overarching public interest, which everyone shares regardless of their affiliation with particular groups, is rejected. In stakeholder mediation, if no group exists or comes forward to represent the public interest, it is deemed not to exist. Imagine what would have happened prior to the 1970s in negotiations about forestry policies or new hydro dams. Without an environmental movement and active advocacy groups, environmental concerns would have been entirely ignored. At the very least, when a legislative mandate governs a traditional regulatory agency, and when this mandate includes the phrase "in the public interest," it has been possible to identify issues of overarching concern, irrespective of the existence or capabilities of the advocates who appear before the tribunal.

Stakeholder mediation is not a public process, even though advocacy groups are involved. Whatever the benefits of the agreements reached behind closed doors, they do little to stimulate public debate about important issues. Moreover, the public aspect depends entirely on the advocacy groups to participate. Not all such groups are wise, or hold any broad notions of their public purpose. It is all too easy, especially given the closed doors, for such groups to become focused on the narrow interests of their own members (for example, the "not-in-my-backyard" syndrome), as opposed to a more comprehensive societal or environmental interest. Cooptation is an ever-present danger, because it is especially difficult for such bodies to remain accountable when the negotiations are likely to be confidential. In short, stakeholder mediation is not just a useful complement to traditional regulation but a means by which the discourse and content of such regulation are changed.

Patent Medicines

Despite so much talk about deregulation, very few agencies have been shut down, and some new ones have been created. The new agency many have only superficial resemblance to the old, however. The Patent Medicines Prices Review Board is an excellent example.[25] Its origin was not particularly unusual. It was created in the mid-1980s in the heat of a political controversy about whether government would extend patent protection to the big, multinational drug companies operating in Canada, jeopardizing the fortunes of domestic generic drug companies in the process. The argument for supporting the multinationals was that only they conducted research and developed new drugs. But generic drugs were invariably cheaper for the consumer, and, when the patents of the multinationals were extended, consumer savings were likely to disappear.

The controversy was intense; the government was feeling the pressure. Its response was to create an administrative tribunal to handle the situation, to reduce the controversy to a matter of routine supervision and co-management of the sector. That this agency supported the dominant multinationals goes without saying; the board was intended to effect a compromise by ensuring that price increases were reasonable and that there would be social benefits for Canada (in the form of research and development within the sector) as a result.

The legislation creating the board reflected the traditional compromise to be expected from regulation and involved rhetorical integration of all the concerns expressed throughout the controversy. Among other things, it placed an annual limit on price increases for drugs, in response to the argument that these companies would use their market dominance and monopoly to engage in price gouging. The board was given the powers to turn back the price increases if, in its view, they were unreasonable and unjustified. The multinational drug companies were formally integrated into the government's industrial strategy. They were mandated to spend a proportion of their Canadian earnings on research and development, thus contributing to the Canadian consumer indirectly through promoting economic development. A board was created to oversee the process.

The Patent Medicines Prices Review Board is similar to others in many respects. It has appointed commissioners, a professional staff, money for research, and the capacity to hold hearings and render decisions. But some things are different about it. First, little effort was made to disguise the political reasons for having established the board. Indeed, the board was required to report regularly to government. Second, public hearings were intended to be only a measure of last resort, not to canvass issues in public (as with the CRTC). The board was more like a court, using hearings to deal with problems of compliance after the fact. The hearings represented failure on the part of board and industry to reach agreements on voluntary compliance, and they were designed to ensure that the companies received their legal right to a defence before any punitive action was taken by government. The hearings were also intended to be public only in the way that a court is public. The data submitted by the companies were confidential, as were the studies conducted by the board's own staff and consultants (who were required to sign a confidentiality statement), and so no public record was created, except as data were read into the hearing record.

All the regulatory effort was directed to the pricing of drugs, which was assessed in the same manner as auditors might regard pricing, as opposed to being canvassed in open hearings. The issues to be determined were exceptionally narrow in focus. On the research side, reporting was voluntary, "regulations" were guidelines, and relatively little effort was made to conduct full assessments of how research money might be spent (for example, whether it had been spent on buildings rather than research) so as to meet the industrial-strategy goals of the legislation.

From the outside, the whole situation looks very much like a cosy deal among the government, the multinational drug companies, and the proposed regulators. None of the participants has taken pains to portray the situation otherwise. That the board is new regulation, in an era of deregulation, seems to evoke no surprise. The answer probably lies in the fact that the board is different from traditional regulation agencies in important respects.

A CONTRASTING EXAMPLE: ABORIGINAL SELF-GOVERNMENT

Introduction to the Agreements

The new self-government agreements for Aboriginal Canadians can be read as handbooks on regulation. Each agreement sets into place a variety of boards, councils, and other legal institutions designed to implement the broad principles of the agreement. These new bodies do not look like regulation as traditionally practised in the welfare state; they openly incorporate the idea of co-management, for example. The agreements represent significant attempts to reconstitute the relationships between state and civil society. How regulatory functions are handled is only one aspect of the new relationships, but it provides a different perspective on responses to the pressures on the welfare state.

Each instance of Aboriginal self-government is unique. With some Aboriginal communities, agreements set in place something akin to a municipality based on the reserve. In others, self-government takes a back seat to land-claims negotiations, and the primary goal is adequate financial compensation for Aboriginal land alienated during the past hundred or more years. In Yukon, however, self-government is the primary preoccupation and subsumes both a new relationship among governments (with the Aboriginal peoples constituting a third order of government in Canada) and the administrative and regulatory infrastructure to be put into place throughout Yukon for both Native settlement lands and Native involvement in the territory more generally.[26]

The Yukon self-government agreements have only recently become law, and thus it is too early to know what they will mean in practice. Yet their most important aspect is the manner of their creation. Just as something fundamental was changed when large, independent administrative tribunals made up of disinterested experts were put in place early in this century in the United States or when environmental and broadcasting regulation was established three decades ago in Canada, so too the Yukon agreements represent a new way of conducting the business of governing and regulation.

History and Impact

Before describing this new way of governing, it is worth looking at the context for the Yukon self-government agreements. Like many other First Nations, Yukon's Aboriginal peoples have an understanding of their relations with the governments of Canada and Yukon very different from that which is commonplace within government or in media accounts. Unlike the general population, First Nations have not looked on the welfare state very positively, nor have they found in its regulatory functions the kinds of protection or administration they desire. The dismantling of the welfare state represents a relatively straightforward victory for First Nations peoples; its contradictions and problems have been all too evident for a long time.

There were originally no formal treaties in Yukon, but there were many individual formal agreements between the First Nations and the state. These might as well have been written in different languages, given how differently the same words are understood by each party to them. There is little shared understanding about the characteristics of the welfare state as it has affected First Nations. When self-government and land-claim negotiations began more than two decades ago in Yukon, the first step was to establish a common language about the history and meaning of all the previous agreements, about the meaning of existing agreements, and about the task to be undertaken. Not surprisingly, this process took many years.[27]

Like many other places, Yukon has several quite different First Nations, each with its own language, culture, and still-discernible clan structure. Years of colonial administration and residential schools had worn away at the fabric of the clan structure, but there remained the outlines of a cultural and political system within and among First Nations, which serves as the basis for different modes of governing. Because of the enormously disintegrating pressures introduced through European–Aboriginal contact, the task of recouping the knowledge on which new modes of governance could be built is immense, and even after two decades of negotiations much work remains to be done.

Because there were no treaties signed in Yukon, and perhaps also because Yukon is a territory (with far more extensive links to the federal government) and not a province, the clear demarcation between Native and non-Native communities that often exists elsewhere is less evident there. Racism exists, and distinctions are commonly made between what governments like to call "government for everyone" and "Native government." However, levels of cooperation and joint responsibility for shared resources are possible in Yukon that might not be attainable elsewhere in Canada. There is also ample evidence of an existing Aboriginal subsistence economy, comprised of active engagement in hunting, fishing, and trapping. It is still quite feasible to foster an economy that owes more to First Nations' history and culture than to the urban industrial economy. Yukon communities are small and located far from major urban centres; elders are actively engaged in many cases; and Aboriginal knowledge has not been lost.

The Negotiating Process

Traditionally in Canada, land-claims negotiations have taken place in Ottawa and major urban centres because usually high-priced lawyers, consultants, and vast numbers of government bureaucrats are involved and the negotiations are deemed too technical for most people to follow in detail. Aboriginal political organizations have given ample direction to their negotiators, and they have reviewed agreements in progress from time to time. At the end of the process, the expectation has been that all First Nations people will be given the agreements to review and that they will either ratify or reject them. While many land-claims negotiations have taken place far from local communities, and have engaged the services primarily of professionals, it has been assumed that First Nations peoples will make the final determination about the agreements.

This was indeed the process that led up to the Yukon land-claims agreement brought before a general assembly of Yukon First Nations in 1984. The agreement was rejected. Notwithstanding the good efforts of the negotiators and the competent leadership of Yukon Native organizations, matters of critical importance to the local communities had been compromised in the inevitable give and take of negotiation. As is always the case when agreements are brought before the people for ratification, the claim was made that the 1984 agreement was "the best that could be accomplished," and, as usual, there was some measure of truth to this assertion. But when the 1984 agreement was rejected, it became clear to everyone that something fundamentally different would have to be done if any acceptable agreement was to be reached in the future.

First, all negotiations would have to take place within the local communities. It was unreasonable to expect that people could absorb, let alone accept, a complex arrangement, negotiated mainly by outsiders, that they had seen, perhaps for the first time, in the general assembly where the ratification vote took place. That this might involve the legions of government officials travelling to "out of the way" places in the most difficult of weather was a small price to pay and might well have the benefit of bridging the language barrier attendant on the different understandings of all previous agreements.

Second, no aspect of any agreement was to be considered too technically complex for local people to understand. After all, what was being discussed were the intimate facets of life in the communities, and even complex taxation systems had to be understood in terms of how they might impinge on community life. If the experts could not render their views in an accessible form, perhaps they should not be considered expert in matters of importance to the First Nations.

Third, elders had to play a role, which they could do only if they could be made an integral part of the negotiation process. Furthermore, negotiators needed to remain accountable to the local communities even as they engaged in the give and take of negotiations. This meant not only conducting negotiations in public in the local communities, but also having a caucus of people who would meet with the negotiators in a side room to discuss each position before it was tabled for discussion. Even with this highly participatory model, it was understood that some negotiations would take place in Ottawa and many more in Yukon's capital, Whitehorse. Members of the caucus had to travel to these places, to meet in the side rooms of whatever fancy hotel had been pressed into service. As well, because complex issues were involved, members of the caucus had to be part of the working groups alongside outside experts before positions on particular issues were formulated.

Previous agreements had been considered final documents to be ratified and signed. In the new approach, any agreement was considered to be only one element in a continually evolving and iterative process. It would take time, much time, for the various parties to hear properly the concerns raised by others. Account also had to be taken of the changing public discourse about Aboriginal government and lands, within and outside First Nations. First Nations people had to arrive at a point where they felt that they "owned" the agreements, and this could never be achieved quickly. But most important, the agreements themselves were a moving target, responsive to ever more deeply entrenched concerns that would become apparent only after the initial level of agreements had been reached. There was no end in sight to the self-government and land-claim negotiations, nor could there ever be. To be sure, sub-agreements of considerable importance could be reached and ratified, but once this was done, the path was only cleared for the next level of negotiations. It would take a major effort on the part of all concerned to educate everyone to this fact.

The Content of the Agreements

Land-claims and self-government agreements are treaties. As treaties, they are intrinsically about the relationships between the First Nations and the rest of Canada, between the state and the formal legal institutions of civil society. At the same time, treaty making engenders a somewhat artificial distinction between First Nations and others. All the agreements establish Native lands and jurisdiction; all involve some level of third-party rights or access to the land or its resources; and all establish new constitutions and governing bodies within the First Nations.

But the agreements fail if they do not also engage First Nations people with the larger territory within which they reside. The Yukon agreements have among their first principles that not just institutions on First Nations land, but also institutions within the territory more generally, should be reconfigured to take account of First Nations people. This requirement might mean creating a different kind of hospital, serving everyone but also responsive to the specific needs of its First Nations clientele. It might mean establishing joint environmental resource boards dealing with matters outside First Nations territory. It might mean new arrangements for school boards, as well as, in some case, First Nations schools. What had to be negotiated was a two-way relationship between the institutions of the First Nations and those of the territory more generally. The goal was not "separate but equal," but self-sufficiency and mutual influence. The First Nations had to become a presence not only on their own, newly recognized, First Nations territories but in the wider community in which they also held full status as members.

It would be mistaken to view the land-claims and self-government negotiations as exclusively local in orientation, though this was their special contribution. Nothing can be accomplished about self-government without major changes in Canadian public discourse about resources, economic development, environment, and Native issues. The agreements depend on active engagement of First Nations people in politics. Local negotiations are complemented by continuing lobbying in Ottawa and Whitehorse, by conversations with ministers of governments, by public statements and meetings, and so on. The land-claims and self-government process is and must be oriented to politics in the most conventional sense of the term.

The Yukon negotiations are continuing, even though several levels of agreement have been ratified and legislation has been passed in Ottawa and Whitehorse. Much attention now is being directed to the local communities, which were not directly involved in some of the earlier community negotiations, and to the vast array of further negotiations required if hospital boards, school boards, environmental assessment, and similar territory-wide institutions are to be transformed as a result of active participation by the First Nations. Meanwhile, negotiations are looking at implementation – how actually to govern and regulate in a new mode.

THE NEW INFRASTRUCTURE:

The six case studies of regulation outlined above obviously differ from each other. Some involve only Canada; others are international. Some involve traditional regulatory agencies; others, new modes of governing, where regulation is simply a by-product, not a central concern. The self-government story is different yet again. Yet taken together, these situations provide some indication of the shape of the new infrastructure being put into place even while the welfare state is under attack. They do indicate something about how the relations among state, civil society, and capital are being reconstituted.

What story do they tell? What do these very different cases and examples have in common? The answers can only be surmised, presented as possible trends and implications. None the less, if the new infrastructure is to be understood, if an early glimpse of the reconstitution of the key relationships of state, civil society, and capital is to be had, it is worth stretching the analysis beyond what the data yet support to see how the situation is evolving.

First, all the case studies, including that of First Nations self-government, seem to reflect efforts to decentralize functions previously associated with central governments in nation-states, territories, or provinces. Institutions of the state are no longer expected to perform all the roles previously associated with the welfare state, but the roles have not disappeared or even necessarily been diminished. Rather, other bodies, including such different groups as First Nations and industry-led standards organizations, have been delegated to perform tasks that had resided within the purview of the state. When functions traditionally associated with the state are decentralized to other groups, some of which lie outside the state, it appears as if the functions no longer exist. It looks as if deregulation has taken place and the state itself has been diminished. But deregulation, in this instance, means only the substitution for the central state of other bodies that may, or may not, have other levels of state involvement.

Second, all the case studies illustrate an increasing preoccupation with questions of process. This is true in such very diverse instances as the Patent Medicines Prices Review Board and Yukon self-government.

How decisions are being made, by whom, and with what kind of involvement or representation seem to have become as important as the decisions themselves. This does not necessarily mean that members of the public are better represented, though in a few instances they are. On the contrary, members of the public may be excluded, or the public may have been reduced to the status of interest group or potential party to a legal dispute. In the First Nations, concern for process has rendered the search for self-government highly participatory, but, ironically, stakeholder negotiations and the Patent Medicines Prices Review Board, seem to exclude the public, even while they deliver an administratively or politically attractive solution to the state.

Third, in all cases regulation is now much closer to the political process. Whether in the name of accountability (broadcasting), or because lobbying is essential (self-government), or because the board is on a "short leash" from government (patent medicines), or because the regulatory agency itself gets to participate in developing new legislation (broadcasting and telecommunications), those involved in regulation work hand in hand with elected legislators. The much vaunted independence of regulation from the legislative process was probably always part fiction; today it is not very highly valued.

Fourth, a strong link now exists between regulation and the industrial policies of government. Regulation is justified in a deregulatory age if, and only if, it can be connected to industrial development. The mechanisms of regulation – boards, standards organizations, or whatever – are compatible with promoting industry-led economic development, and the mandates of the new regulators include explicit reference to how they will promote industry and competitiveness. This point applies even to the First Nations agreements. Self-government is not separate from land claims, and both are designed to further economic relations. In the Yukon case, the conception of economic relations is quite different from that envisioned by the state in its dealings with new forms of regulation in the Patent Medicines Prices Review Board, but the Yukon case is the exception rather than the rule. In many other self-government agreements, relations between state (in this case, the "state" represented by the First Nation) and capital bear all-too-close resemblance to that generally being instituted.

Fifth, all these cases, contain a complicated mix of public and private functions. What has changed may be only a matter of appearance. As suggested above, regulation has always involved a relationship of co-management, with state and capital each playing important roles. In the current context, however, regulation is no longer seen as the prerogative of the state, and many of the functions (such as assessment) previously assigned to the state have now been devolved to others.

Sixth and finally, there has been a change in how regulation is understood. The presence of interest groups in dealing with regulatory boards has always been strong, but regulation itself was once conceived of as something other than a negotiation of interest groups, as involving a determination of the public interest, as well as a compromise among the interests involved in any decision.

The public interest has disappeared or, rather, been reconceived as simply the end-product of agreements negotiated among various interest groups. The discourse has changed radically. Members of the public, representing Natives, for example, are now conceived of only in terms of their specific interests (as a Native interest group). Issues of concern to everyone, such as the environment, are understood to be only the interests represented by environmental advocacy groups. Whatever finds no expression in the form of an interest group finds no expression at all in public discourse, more particularly in regulation. Thus business is an interest; consumers are an interest; women are an interest group; Natives are an interest group. Civil society has been recast as a collection of interest groups. The state is an interest group too. It is no longer understood to reflect the needs and concerns of everyone but is relegated to the status of interest group like any other.

SOCIAL VALUES INHERENT IN THE NEW INFRASTRUCTURE

As a means of revealing the significance of the forces of change, proposed above to examine the fate of social values in the new forms of regulation and in the reconstitution of the relationships among state, civil society, and capital. Of particular interest are values associated with the welfare state. The focus in this chapter has been on regulation, as a key element of the welfare state; and consequently the values of concern are those associated with its regulatory functions: redistributive justice, representation, equity, fairness, and protection of people and their environment. How do these values fare in the examples of the new infrastructure briefly surveyed in this paper?

Fairness and Representation

The verdict on fairness and representation is mixed. In some cases, the new infrastructure reflects more attention being paid to both representation and fairness; in others, it appears that the new infrastructure is less responsive to public needs and concerns than was the welfare state. Aboriginal self-government is an example of the strengthening of representation. So is the new legislation governing broadcasting, which recognizes groups previously silenced within the political process and, more particularly, in broadcasting. The Patent Medicines case is hardly reassuring in this regard, however; nor is stakeholder mediation. Placing disputes in the purview of the courts can reflect increased emphasis on fairness, but usually it does not, as Bartholomeuw and Boyd so clearly indicated in Clement and Wiliams's *The New Political Economy* (1989).

Protection of People and the Environment:

The final verdict on protection of people and the environment is still not available. There are grounds for suggesting that dismantling of traditional regulation, which was conducted through seemingly independent regulatory agencies, will diminish public protection. A case can be made, for example, that the public is not well protected by the Patent Medicines Prioces Review Board. Yet one can argue that stakeholder mediation will deliver decisions more protective of the environment than were usually generated in the cumbersome environmental assessment processes. It is unlikely that it will produce a veto on a new economic development, as a more conventional environmental assessment might. But such vetoes have always been rare.

Whether, over the longer term, competition in telecommunications and broadcasting will protect consumers remains to be seen. Whether the technical standards produced now are better or worse at protecting the public is difficult to say. Whether North American environmental and health and safety standards will be harmonized at the most or least stringent level is yet to be determined. The effect of harmonizing standards on Mexico is as yet only conjectural. It is too easy to be romantic about the past, about the degree of protection that traditional regulatory agencies afforded the public or the environment. It is too soon to predict with much confidence whether the reconstituted relationships among state, civil society, and capital are better or worse than has been the case for protecting human or environmental health.

Redistribution and Equity

About redistributive justice and equity, unfortunately, there is far less question. The new infrastructure seems to lack the capacity even to encompass a discourse about general benefits to society. Equity and redistribution are no longer key concepts in public discourse. It is likely that some redistribution will result from the self-government agreements, but even this depends on who is involved and their intentions.

Whatever the failings and contradictions of the welfare state, it reflected a commitment (often more important rhetorically than practically) to some measure of redistribution and equity. What now threatens to supplant it – the decentralized, politically oriented, process-oriented mix of public and private functions – is unlikely to effect significant redistribution precisely because it is highly decentralized and involves much more than the state and capital as traditionally understood. Nor is there much indication that those who now take up the tasks previously assigned to the welfare state have any strong commitment to equity.

NOTES

1 Held, "Democracy."
2 For example, regulation was omitted as a category in Drache and Clement, eds., *The New Practical Guide to Political Economy*. Regulation has a new currency in political economy in conjunction with the regulation school. In this chapter, however, "regulation" is used in its more commonplace sense as referring to administrative tribunals and boards and to deregulation.
3 Clement and Williams, eds., *The New Canadian Political Economy*, 6.
4 Marchak,"Canadian," 673.
5 Regulating common-property resources, such as fishing, through use of quotas, makes it possible to invest it with something akin to private property relations. This observation has not yet been developed into a full argument in the literature.
6 The classic argument accepted among political economists – that regulatory agencies are captured – was first made by Kolko, *Railroads*.
7 This argument is developed further in Albo, Langille, and Panitch, eds., *Different*, 87–101.
8 Mahon, "Canadian."
9 Trebilcock, *Choice*.
10 Bartholomew and Boyd, "Toward."
11 Most Canadian agencies only make recommendations to governments, hold hearings only in special cases, and have limited autonomy. The general view of regulation is taken from the United States, where powerful administrative agencies constitute a "fourth branch of government." For further discussion, see my "Accountability."
12 Broadcasting Act 1991 c. 11 s. 89.
13 For examples of this argument, see Janisch "Policy" and "Independence" Kernaghan, "Political" and Vandervort, *Political*.
14 This argument is developed in Salter "Experiencing."
15 Convergence hearings began 6 March 1994 in Ottawa.

16 Mansell, *New*.

17 For a development of this argument see Salter, "Capture."

18 The intentions and mandate for regulation are laid out quite clearly in the order in council calling for hearings on the new "information highway." PC, 1994-1689 October 1989.

19 Ruby and Salter, *Standardization*.

20 Salter, *Mandated Science*.

21 This argument is developed further in Salter, "Housework."

22 Chociolko and Leiss, *Risk*.

23 Ibid.

24 This argument is developed further in Salter, "Commentary."

25 Patented Medicines Prices Review Board, Sixth.

26 Canada, House of Commons, Bill C-33 and Bill C-34.

27 The negotiations took twenty years to reach the stage of a ratified and legislated agreement.

REFERENCES

Albo, Gregory, Langille, David, and Panitch, Leo, eds. *A Different Kind of State? Popular Power and Democratic Administration*. Toronto: Oxford University Press, 1993.

Bartholomew, Amy, and Boyd, Susan. "Toward a Political Economy of Law." In Wallace Clement and Glen Williams, eds., *The New Canadian Political Economy*, 212–39. Montreal: McGill-Queen's University Press, 1989.

Bentkover, J.D., Covello, V.T., and Mumpower, J., eds. *Benefits Assessment: The State of the Art*, Vol. 1, *Technology, Risk and Society: An International Series in Risk Analysis*. Dordrecht, Holland: Kluwer Academic Publishers, 1986.

Brunk, Conrad G., Hayworth, Laurence, and Lee, Brenda. *Value Assumptions in Risk Assessment: A Case Study of the Alachlor Controversy*. Waterloo, Ont.: Wilfrid Laurier University Press, 1991.

Canada, House of Commons. Bill C-33. An Act to Approve, give effect to and declare valid land claims agreements entered into between Her Majesty the Queen in right of Canada, the Government of the Yukon Territory and certain first nations in the Yukon Territory, to provide for approving, giving effect to and declaring valid other land claims agreeements entered into after this Act comes into force, and to make consequential amendments to other Act. Ottawa, 1994.

– Bill C-34. An Act Respecting Self-Government for first nations in the Yukon Territory. Ottawa, 1994.

Chociolko, Christina, and Leiss, William. *Risk and Responsibility*. Montreal: McGill-Queen's University Press, 1994.

Clement, Wallace, and Williams, Glen, eds. *The New Canadian Political Economy*. Montreal: McGill-Queen's University Press, 1989.

Drache, Daniel, and Clement, Wallace, eds. *The New Practical Guide to Canadian Political Economy*. Toronto: James Lorimer, 1985.

Harrison, Kathryn, and Hoberg, George. *Risk, Science and Politics: Regulating Toxic Chemicals in Canada and the United States*. Montreal: McGill-Queen's University Press, 1994.

Held, David. "Democracy, the Nation-State and the Global System." *Economy and Society*, 20 no. 2 (1991), 138–72.

Janisch, H.N. "Independence of Administrative Tribunals: In Praise of Structural Heretics." *Canadian Journal of Administrative Law and Practice*, 1 (1987), 1–19.

– "Policy Making in Regulation: Towards a New Definition of the Status of Regulatory Agencies in Canada." *Osgoode Hall Law Journal*, 17 no. 1 (1979), 46–106.

Kernaghan, K. "Political Control of Administrative Action: Accountability or Window Dressing." *Cahiers du droit*, 17 (1976), 927–34.

Kolko, G. *Railroads and Regulation*. Princeton, NJ: Princeton University Press, 1965.

Krimsky, Sheldon, and Golding, Dominic, eds. *Social Theories of Risk*. Westport, Conn.: Praeger, 1992.

Mahon, Rianne. "Canadian Public Policy: The Unequal Structure of Representation." In L. Panitch, ed., *Canadian State: Political Economy and Political Power*, 165–98. Toronto: University of Toronto Press, 1977.

Mansell, Robin. *The New Telecommunications: A Political Economy of Network Evolution*. London: Sage, 1993.

Marchak, Patricia. "Canadian Political Economy." *Canadian Review of Sociology and Anthropology*, 22 (1985), 673–709.

Patented Medicine Prices Review Board. *Sixth Annual Report for the Year Ended December 31, 1993*. Ottawa: Patented Medicine Prices Review Board, 1994.

Richardson, Mervyn L., ed. *Risk Assessment of Chemicals in the Environment*. London: Royal Society of Chemistry, 1988.

Ruby, Peter, and Salter Ammon. *Standardisation and Strategic Alliances*. Ottawa: Department of Communication Standards Program Office, 1993.

Salter, Liora. "Acountability and Capture of Agencies: Proposals for Change." In C.E.S Franks et al., eds., *Canada's Century: Governance in a Maturing Society*, 278–97. Montreal: McGill-Queen's University Press, 1995.

– "Capture or Co-management: Democracy and Accountability in Regulatory Agencies." In Gregory Albo, David Langille, and Leo Panitch, eds., *A Different Kind of State? Popular Power and Democratic Administration*, 87–101. Toronto: Oxford University Press, 1993.

– "Commentary on Stanbury and Vertinsky." In Thomas J. Courchene, ed., *Technology, Information and Public Policy*. Kingston, Ont.: John Deutsch Institute, Queen's University, 1995.

– "Experiencing a Sea Change in the Democratic Potential of Regulation."
  In L.F. Seidle, ed., *Rethinking Government*, 124–71. Montreal: Institute for
  Research on Public Policy, 1993.
– "The Housework of Capitalism." *International Journal of Political Economy*,
  23 no. 4 (1993), 105–33.
– *Mandated Science.* Dordrecht, Holland: Kluwer Academic Publishers, 1988.
Trebilcock, M.J. *The Choice of Governing Instrument.* Ottawa: Supply and Services
  Canada, 1982.
Vandervort, L. *Political Control of Independent Administratve Agencies.* Ottawa: Law
  Reform Commission, 1980.

Public Discourse and the
Structures of Communication

TED MAGDER

Communication is a symbolic process whereby reality is produced,
maintained, repaired, and transformed.[1]

Freedom of the press is guaranteed only to those who own one.[2]

All social formations, from the most basic (such as the family) to the
most elaborate (such as representative democracy), are predicated on
the ability to share and exchange information, ideas, attitudes, and
values. "What we call society," as Raymond Williams once noted, "is
not only a network of political and economic arrangements, but also
a process of learning and communicating."[3] How societies choose to
communicate – in particular, how they organize and regulate their
systems of public communication – is of fundamental importance. If
communication is a social process that affects our very understanding
of reality, there is good reason for paying close attention to the ways
and means by which we make and remake our sense of ourselves and
the world within which we live.

It should come as no surprise that democratic political systems place
considerable value on the development of an open and comprehensive system of public communication. Citizens in a democratic state
are entrusted with the responsibility of articulating, directly or indirectly, their collective interests and of ensuring that state institutions
properly reflect those interests: to do so, individuals must have access
to a communication system that promotes a wide range of information and opinions about public life. Indeed, the relationship between
politics and communication is an old theme. Aristotle wrote that the
ideal size of any state was a function of the largest number of citizens
who could assemble together and "be taken in at a single view."[4]
For Aristotle, legitimate political rule was grounded on a process of
unmediated public communication: a mutual gaze between rulers and

ruled. Citizens – native-born, property-owning men, in the case of the Greek city state – had to engage in frequent public meetings to determine the contours of public life. Good government was to be conducted on the basis of ongoing dialogue between office holders and citizens.

The legacy of the Greek city state is something of a benchmark against which the contemporary relationship between politics and communication can be measured. Obviously, much has changed since Aristotle's time. For one thing, political systems have come to encompass far more citizens than can be taken in at "a single view." In democratic political systems, the principles of representative government were designed to replace (and approximate) the unmediated encounter between rulers and ruled that characterized the Greek polis. A second significant change concerns the nature of public communication itself. In Aristotle's time, political communication was oral and face to face. In political systems today, the communicative relationship between rulers and ruled is far more abstract. As John Hartley remarks: "Contemporary politics is *representative* in both senses of the term: citizens are represented by a chosen few, and politics is represented to the public via the various media of communication."[5] The age of electronic communications, which began with the telegraph in the mid-nineteenth century and has since seen the emergence of telephones, radio, television, and satellites and, more recently, application of computers as a means of producing, retrieving, storing, and manipulating communication "data," is the era of near-instantaneous, long-distance communication. Public communication is no longer primarily a face-to-face encounter. The public domain has no material centre; rather it exists in the intersection of mediated forms of communication, on the pages of newspapers and magazines, through speakers and over screens. Moreover, public discourse is now channelled through individuals who practise communication as a vocation: journalists, writers, media consultants, press and publicity agents, advertisers, graphic designers, and a whole range of occupations associated with the production of public drama (from producers, actors, and directors to gaffers, focus pullers, and special-effects craftspeople). Finally, the organizations within which these "professional communicators" ply their trade are more often than not driven by commercial considerations. Public communication is not only a discourse, it is also a business.

In the 1940s, one of Canada's leading scholars of the history of communication, Harold Innis, turned to the role of media of communication in the establishment and maintenance of political systems.[6] His work suggests that all political systems, whether democratic or not, must work out solutions to two overriding problems: first, how to maintain (and often augment) the geographical territory under their control; and second, how to promote a system of values and attitudes – culture, in its broadest sense – that constructs a sense of identity and commonality among their citizens. For Innis, the media of communication (everything from the papyrus of Egypt, through the parchment of Rome, to the newspapers and radio of Canada and the United States in the first few decades of the twentieth century) were determinants of the state's ability to reproduce itself.

Innis's work is a reminder that communication media are about more than just exchange of information; they are also intimately connected to the dynamics of order and control, both political and social. But for Innis, the structure and organization of public communication were to be measured not only in terms of their utility as a mechanism for political control; ultimately, he argued, communication systems had to be evaluated in terms of their ability to create the "conditions favourable to creative thought." Unfortunately, Innis's analysis of the history of communication revealed that moments of vibrant, creative expression were fleeting. More often than not, communication systems degenerate into "monopolies of knowledge," where diversity of thought and expression are either marginalized or suppressed outright.[7] The history of communication is not simply the story of successive triumphs, of an ever-broadening forum for freedom of expression. The conditions favourable to creative thought have to be constantly reworked and rethought. Each era, each political and social system, has its own tendency to reduce public communication to a mechanism of social control.

Innis's critical scrutiny of the communications media and their relationship to politics includes a stinging indictment of the First Amendment of the American constitution, which states that "Congress shall make no law abridging the freedom of speech, or of the press." Given the importance to democratic systems of public discussion and debate, of disclosure of information and diversity of opinion, freedom of the press and of other forms of expression is regarded as sacrosanct by adherents of democratic politics. Innis's critique was not levelled at the principle itself, but at the structures and practices of the u.s. press that were protected by a formalistic reading of the constitution. Innis saved some of his most vitriolic language for his assessment of the modern newspapers. Because of their desperate attempt to increase advertising revenues by increasing circulation, newspapers had turned public discourse into a cacophony of sensationalism, sentimentalism, and an "obsession with the immediate."[8] The First Amendment provided legal protection to unscrupulous press barons, whose alleged credo – "you cannot aim too low" – had become the basis for the emergence of a whole range of new media practices. There is, it needs to be said, an elitist tone to Innis's critique. Like many critics of mass communication, from Matthew Arnold to Neil Postman, Innis seems at times to disparage all forms of mediated communication that have broad popular appeal.[9]

But there is still some value in pursuing Innis's project – in particular, his desire to assess critically the structure and practices of the media of communication in terms of their contribution to the vibrancy of public discourse and to nurture communication systems that expand democratic public life.

NEWS MEDIA AND PUBLIC DISCOURSE

When the First Amendment was drafted in the late eighteenth century, the overriding issue was the threat posed by governments to freedom of expression.[10] During this period, in Britain, in the American colonies, and in Canada (indeed in most of the world), state institutions carefully regulated the content of newspapers and other forms of public communication (such as pamphlets and billboards). Publishers and editors were often fined, put out of business, or jailed for printing material deemed inappropriate to the public interest, defined primarily in terms of the interests of the state itself and its ruling elite. Undaunted by the threat to both livelihood and person, a number of publishers and editors challenged the limits of state tolerance. In Halifax in 1835, Joseph Howe, publisher of the *Novascotian*, printed a letter signed "the People" that accused local political authorities of fraud and, for good measure, mocked the appearance of Nova Scotia's lieutenant-governor. Howe was charged with seditious libel. At Howe's trial, the crown needed only to prove that the article in question had been published; the truth or accuracy of its content was irrelevant. Howe defended himself and asked the jury "to leave an unshackled press as a legacy to your children."[11] The judge instructed the jury to find Howe guilty of libel. In an act of pure defiance, the jury took no more than ten minutes to acquit Howe.

The verdict did not guarantee press freedom in British North America, but it was one of the pivotal moments in the struggle to establish an independent press. Howe's acquittal demonstrated that the state's heavy-handed regulation of newspaper content – and hence of public discourse – was losing its legitimacy. The case for freedom of the press and freedom of expression generally was gaining momentum.[12] No less important was a shift in the economic structure of newspapers. Until the mid-eighteenth century, newspapers in British North America were financially dependent on government patronage and/or support from political factions – a dependence that tended to breed editorial conservatism and caution. By the mid-nineteenth century, advertising revenues were becoming their chief source of income. Not surprisingly, increasing financial independence gave publishers, editors, and journalists a firmer foundation on which to establish the independence of newspapers.

But the growing reliance on advertising revenues had a number of unforeseen consequences. Newspapers began to compete more directly against each other in an effort to boost circulation (the economics of newspapers is such that typically only a small advantage in circulation translates into a large advantage in advertising revenue). This competition led to dramatic new overhead costs in the production of newspapers: new "hot-metal" mechanical typesetters (linotype machines) were introduced, as were improved techniques for reproducing photographs. Editorial content changed as well. Newspapers began to offer "softer," human-interest stories and a steady flow of stories about crime and scandal. In most papers, the space for hard, political news was reduced. The competition for larger readerships led not only to a change in the type of news reported, but to the style of writing. Journalists began to perfect narrative techniques that gave the impression of "objectivity" and "impartiality."[13]

By the early twentieth century, newspapers began to look less and less like small, publisher-owned and -operated endeavours and more and more like modern business undertakings. As readerships peaked, competition for larger audiences led to a series of corporate takeovers. Over the last seventy years, independently owned and controlled newspapers have all but disappeared, to be replaced by large, integrated newspaper chains. The two most significant chains in Canada are owned and operated by the Thomson Corporation and Southam Inc. Between them, Thomson and Southam control 59 per cent of daily newspaper circulation in Canada.[14] There are also important regional chains, such as the Irving group, which controls most of the papers (and broadcast outlets) in New Brunswick, and the Armadale newspapers (and radio stations) in Saskatchewan. Independent papers – those not affiliated with a chain or media conglomerate – comprised 7 per cent of daily-newspaper national circulation in 1992.

Given the historic importance of newspapers as a source of information, their consolidation into large chains has been cause for concern. In 1970, the federal government's Special Senate Committee on Mass Media (known as the Davey Committee) concluded that the level of concentration had reached alarming proportions. Its principal argument contrasted the public's interest in diversity of expression with the industry's increasing emphasis on economies of scale and "bottom-line" profitability: "The more separate voices we have telling us what's going on, telling us how we're doing, telling us how we *should* be doing, the more effectively we can govern ourselves. ... The more suggestions there are from below, the better will be the decisions made at the top. The big trouble with this assumption, the notion that media diversity equals a higher polity, is that it happens to be in flat defiance of economics. More voices may be healthier, but fewer voices are cheaper."[15]

In 1981 a second government-sponsored report documented further consolidation and an alarming trend towards cross-media ownership (Maclean Hunter, for example, which started as a publisher of magazines, has extensive holdings in broadcasting, cable television, and newspapers).[16]

Both studies made recommendations designed to curb newspaper concentration and cross-media ownership, including enforced divestment of newspaper monopolies, tax incentives for journalistic excellence, and a Press Rights Council to monitor newspaper performance and to hear public complaints. Against a chorus of newspaper editorials depicting the measures as a threat to freedom of the press, the government backed away from legislative action.[17]

One way of assessing the impact of chain ownership is to examine specific cases. In 1980, Thomson Newspapers purchased FP Publications, which included among its holdings the *Globe and Mail*.[18] For better or worse, the *Globe and Mail* is Canada's newspaper of record; its *Report on Business* is the most significant source of business news in the country, and it is the one newspaper read (and clipped) by most of the country's top political officials. Among North American newspaper chains, Thomson has a reputation as a "bottom-line," profit-maximizing publisher; pre-tax profits of its newspapers are close to double the industry's average.

Under the stewardship of Roy Megarry, the *Globe*'s publisher from 1978 to 1992, Thomson's new newspaper underwent a makeover. In 1982, budgets were cut in almost every department; news space was reduced by more than 30 per cent, freelance budgets were cut by 20 per cent, and fifty employees were laid off. These cost-cutting measures were accompanied by Megarry's plan to rid the *Globe* of about 50,000 lower-income readers (sometimes referred to as "waste circulation") and to replace them with a new group of "middle and upper income, managerial and professional Canadians."[19] Three tactics were employed to achieve this objective: first, the *Globe* stopped home delivery to a number of rural communities in the outlying Toronto region; second, it "repositioned" itself in the Canadian market as a "national" newspaper, with same-morning, satellite delivery to significant urban centres throughout the country; third, its content was altered to reflect (even more) the interests of Canadian business and the managerial and professional Canadians so sought after by up-scale advertisers. The departures of columnists such as June Callwood, Linda McQuaig, David Suzuki, and Thomas Walkom and elimination of the labour beat (which focused on the activities of organized labour) from the *Report on Business*, are indicative of the narrowing of viewpoints.

Ownership patterns and corporate strategies are not the only factors that influence production of news. As noted above, public discourse is now channelled through the activities of professional communicators, such as publishers, editors, and journalists, individuals who help determine both the broad contours of public communication and, at any given time, the issues for public discussion and debate. Social scientists who study the news often argue that it is "manufactured by journalists" or that it is a "social construction of reality."[20] This is not meant to demean the activities of journalists or to suggest that the news is somehow fake or even necessarily biased; rather, the news, as a form of public discourse, has a set of common narratives, rules, and practices. Though it is new each day, it is very much the product of predictable journalistic and organizational routines. The literature on the social construction of news is voluminous. For our purposes, some pertinent findings will have to suffice.

There is an old saying that while "dog bites man" is not news, "man bites dog" is. This adage points to the problem of determining, from the infinite number of daily occurrences, which will become news. It also offers a solution: unexpected events, which constitute a break from prevailing norms, are news. Journalists need to have a sense of what is normal, of "cultural givens," and of what is deviant, the values and actions that are socially reprehensible. Journalism is thus as much about articulating a sense of social order as it is about providing the facts of public life. As Richard Ericson, Patricia Baranek, and Janet Chan suggest: "In effect, journalists join with other agents of control as a kind of 'deviance-defining elite', using the news to provide an ongoing articulation of the proper bounds to behaviour in all organized spheres of life."[21]

Journalists do not work alone. Indeed, an important element of news gathering involves use of sources: individuals and organizations from whom journalists regularly get the news.[22] The most important sources are bureaucratic and political institutions: in the case of news about crime, police institutions play a formative role in defining the news for journalists; other sources, such as community groups and criminologists, must typically work within the framework set by police sources. Given the pressure of daily deadlines, use of sources helps minimize the anxiety of producing the news. Unfortunately, journalists can easily become source dependent; scheduled media events, press releases, and off-the-record comments can become a substitute for independent inquiry and assessment. Sources can further this dependence by adopting strategies that maximize their ability to influence the final product; for example, government sources can schedule a press release or news conference for late afternoon, giving television journalists as little time as possible to file their story for evening news broadcasts. Finally, not all sources of news are equal; certain sources, such as high-ranking government officials, major corporate figures, and, to a lesser extent, public celebrities enjoy routine or habitual access and are aided in their quest for media attention by press agents and media consultants, while other sources – whom journalists often refer to as "special-interest groups" – must struggle to gain notice.

While "source journalism" characterizes both print and television news, there are important distinctions. Television newscasts are greatly restricted in terms of time, and they place inordinate emphasis on use of visuals. Stories rarely run longer than two minutes, and without visual coverage events stand little chance of getting to air. These factors serve to limit both the absolute number and the type of stories that television news covers. Complicated public-policy issues are not common fare on nightly newscasts. Ongoing stories, such as environmental degradation, are not covered unless there is a discrete event that fulfils the criteria of newsworthiness (for example, the oil-spill from the *Exxon Valdez* represented only a small fraction of all the oil that routinely "leaks" into the world's oceans, but these routine leaks are not news). Moreover, because of the costs involved in gathering good visuals, television newscasts tend to provide a very poor representation of international events. As media analysts have detailed, the international component of Canadian television news is restricted to the activities of the major Western industrialized nations; the rest of the world is covered in so far as particular events are meaningful or important to North Americans, and even then the focus is on moments of violence, social disruption, and environmental disaster. When Canadian television news strays from the Western industrialized countries it focuses primarily on "coups, earthquakes and hostages."[23] Cost considerations prompt it to make heavy use of reports from foreign news organizations, primarily u.s. and, to a lesser extent, British agencies.[24]

While television news may suffer from constraints of time and over-dependence on visuals, survey after survey has shown that North Americans regard it as more trustworthy and more credible than print news. Use of visuals undoubtedly helps to explain part of this phenomenon ("seeing is believing"), but television news also relies heavily on the role of the anchor and the news set itself to establish its legitimacy and credibility.[25] Consisting of banks of monitors and information technologies of all kinds, the typical set is designed to connote a constant, up-to-date connectedness, a technological hub that can gather, assess, and disseminate information in an instant – a stage to all the world. In the midst of this command centre sits the anchor, who must assume the role of pilot and sage; all-knowing and all-seeing, the anchor projects stability and honesty amid a world in turmoil and flux. In direct contrast to print journalism, where journalists are faceless unless they write opinion columns, television news establishes its professional objectivity through visual identification with a charismatic personality.

The emergence of television as an important source of news and information has forced most newspapers to adjust their corporate strategies. Some papers have responded by changing radically their format in an effort to reflect the narrative style of television news. The most obvious example is *USA Today*, which had its début in 1982 and now boasts a daily readership of 6.6 million. *USA Today* incorporates the more staccato visual style of television into print journalism; it makes abundant use of colourful images, charts, and graphics and replaces analysis with "fact boxes," summaries, and digests. It is to news what McDonald's is to food. In a recent essay, Shawn Berry has examined how the *London Free Press* (London, Ontario) has incorporated many of *USA Today*'s innovations. For Berry, these changes have reduced the newspaper's ability to provide meaningful and contextualized exploration of events and issues. Newspapers so transformed have difficulty avoiding what Berry refers to as "superficiality" – "pointless graphics, surveys on trivial topics, light features at the expense of comprehensive local-news coverage, and unduly short articles lacking in much-needed context."[26]

Television has also affected coverage of election campaigns and the strategies of political parties.[27] Modern campaigns are driven by carefully crafted media strategies; speeches, events, even candidates, are carefully managed by media consultants and press agents to project the best possible image. To a large degree the politics of image has replaced the politics of substance; parties now make heavy use of marketing research techniques – focus groups, polling, and pyschodemographic profiles – to tailor campaigns in which political advertising itself plays a most significant role. While the Canada Elections Act limits the amount of money that parties can spend on campaign advertising, it also partially subsidizes broadcast advertising for the established parties and thereby promotes "image politics." The news media themselves have contributed to this trend by focusing increasingly on leaders and their image strategies and measuring public reaction through constant reference to polling figures.

THE CULTURE INDUSTRY: COMMERCIALIZATION AND MARKETING

The concentration of ownership and the pressures of commercial competition discussed above are not features unique to the newspaper industry. All sectors of the media are typified by similar economic trends. The history of feature films, for example, is in large part the history of Hollywood's economic dominance over the international marketplace.[28] In the 1920s, the major Hollywood studios (such as Columbia, M-G-M, Twentieth-Century Fox, and Warner Bros.) consolidated their hold over the domestic market by purchasing, or aligning themselves, with theatre chains. This vertical integration was complemented by development and marketing of a "star" system and near-constant technical innovations (sound, colour, panavision, 3-D, and special effects), both of which drove up the cost of film-making and often distinguished Hollywood from its international competitors. The sheer size of the American domestic market permits Hollywood to amortize most of the costs of film-making at home and thus reap surplus profits in the international marketplace. Film industries in countries such as Canada are at a constant economic disadvantage.[29]

Hollywood's transformation of film-making into a lucrative, international business is one of the foremost examples of the commodification of culture in the twentieth century. In recent decades, Hollywood's global success has been paralleled by the development of large, diversified, transnational media corporations. Perhaps the most stunning example was the 1989 merger of Warner Bros. with Time Inc. The combined assets of Time-Warner are valued at over $18 billion (U.S.) and include book and magazine publishing, sound recording, cable-television systems and pay television, and, of course, feature film production. The company has subsidiaries in Asia, Australia, Europe and Latin America and likes to boast that it is "the world's leading direct marketer of information and entertainment."[30]

One Canadian company is in the stratosphere of global media giants. The Thomson Corporation is ranked somewhere near fifth-largest in terms of revenue (approximately $6 billion in 1992).[31] Thomson controls over 150 daily newspapers in Canada and the United States and over 23,000 trade and professional products, including magazine and book publishers. Thomson has also ventured into the marketplace for electronic information services. It now derives close to half its revenue from specialty databases in such fields as financial services, science and engineering, educational and library, and medical and health care.

In the winter of 1994, the Canadian trend towards media consolidation reached new heights when Rogers Communications Inc. completed a hostile take-over of Maclean Hunter Ltd. At that time, Maclean Hunter ranked as the third-largest Canadian media empire, with revenues of $1.7 billion in 1992. Known primarily for magazine publishing (it controls five of the ten top-selling Canadian magazines and publishes 200 periodicals in ten countries), it also owns 35 cable systems (with 9 per cent of national subscribers), 21 radio stations, and three television stations. It also has a 62 per cent, controlling interest in the *Toronto Sun* newspaper chain (eight dailies, with 11 per cent of national circulation) and a 14 per cent interest in the CTV network. Rogers Communications is Canada's leading cable-systems operator, with control over close to 25 per cent of national subscriptions. Rogers is also one of two major shareholders in Unitel Communications (long-distance telephony) and owns Cantel (the country's largest cellular-telephone company), 16 radio stations, and a multilingual television station in Toronto; it also bas stakes in specialty cable channels Canadian Home Shopping Network Ltd., Viewer's Choice, and YTV. In defending his company's take-over of Maclean Hunter, Ted Rogers suggested that he was protecting Canada's media from foreign media giants such as Time-Warner. He remarked: "If we're to maintain a distinctive Canadian voice, it's essential we build companies of comparable scale and sophistication."[32]

For Ted Rogers, if his rhetoric is to be trusted, media corporations are about more than production and distribution of goods and services. On this point, there is little disagreement. But is the Rogers take-over of Maclean Hunter such an obvious boost to maintenance of a distinctive Canadian voice? To answer this question we must explore in more detail the scholarly literature on the commercialization of culture and communications in the twentieth century.

One way of assessing the impact and the influence of media corporations is to examine the individuals who own and operate them. Owners of large media corporations are often referred to as "barons" or "lords," which imply a rather feudal level of power and influence. There is no doubt that if one wants to influence the flow of public discourse, then being at the top is better than being at the bottom, and there are numerous examples of owners who modify, and sometimes dramatically alter, the editorial line of a newspaper or the production priorities of book publishers or film and television companies.

It is also possible to chart the complex, inter-corporate and inter-elite alliances that are facilitated by careful selection of boards of directors and other links. As James Winter and Amir Hassanpour note, the board of directors of Power Corporation, one of Canada's largest conglomerates, includes former Ontario Premier William Davis and Pierre Trudeau's former secretary to cabinet, Michael Pitfield. Former Prime Minister Brian Mulroney now works in Power's long-time Montreal law firm, Ogilvy Renault, and the daughter of Prime Minister Jean Chrétien is married to the son of Power Corporation's owner, Paul Desmarais, Sr.[33] Power Corporation has significant media holdings, including Montreal's *La Presse*, three television and eighteen radio stations in Ontario, Quebec, and New Brunswick, and a major stake in the Southam news chain. While it is possible to outline further examples of what John Porter once termed this "confraternity of power," it is all too easy to make erroneous deductions about the level of direct influence actually exerted on day-to-day operations.[34] Indeed, scholarly work on the dynamics of public communication is more insightful when it turns to the process of media commercialization – and the commodification of culture itself – as the main source of influence on media content.

We noted above, for example, how the shift to dependence on advertising revenue affected the structure and practices of newspapers and how Hollywood's rise to global prominence was in part a function of production costs and market size. Individual firms (and owners) do adopt different corporate strategies, but these strategies are constrained by the exigencies of the marketplace for particular media products. As Canadian scholar Dallas Smythe put it, the principal task of the media is "to mass produce audiences and sell them to advertisers."[35]

Over time, media that rely on the sale of audiences to advertisers have developed elaborate strategies to maximize potential audiences. U.S. network television, which, like Hollywood, is a dominant world player, covets large audiences and spends an almost obscene amount of money researching, developing, and pre-testing new programs that will appeal to the largest possible number of viewers. With self-promoting rhetoric, the networks argue that all this research gives people what they want, that sale of audiences to advertisers makes the system democratic. But the effort to maximize audience ratings and audience share, and to maintain the loyalty of advertisers, has led network television to produce a steady diet of inoffensive, "middle-of-the-road" programming. Inoffensive, for network television, does not typically mean that there is much sensitivity to violent, or sexist, or stereotypical narratives; rather, it means programming that will not unduly upset the normal viewer. So *Cheers* is a place where everybody knows your name, but no one ever really gets too drunk or seriously abusive; and families – the staple institution of network television – while often unstable are rarely sites of domestic violence and real generational dysfunction. Violence on television is "out there," in the streets (which might make staying at home and watching television more appealing), and though the violence on television has reached epidemic proportions, the forces of law and order typically prevail.

The dire need to maintain audience levels also leads to an endless cycle of "tried-and-true formulae," "copycat" programming, spin-offs, and repeats.[36] Obviously, if large audiences can be delivered at low cost to the network, so much the better. "Trash television" – including "reality-based" programming, such as *America's Funniest Videos, A Current Affair,* and *Toplops,* and game shows, such as *Wheel of Fortune* – is also cheap, delivering audiences to advertisers at a fraction of the cost of dramatic programming. Despite the high-minded rhetoric of network executives, it is probably more accurate to conclude that television gives audiences what they are most willing to watch (or what they are least likely to turn off) than what they most want to watch.

Advertising not only influences media practices, it is also in its own right a significant form of communication. In a world increasingly dominated by advertising (and ubiquitous commercial promotion), consumer goods become the currency of public life. Style is everything: who you are is what you buy, what you wear, and what you use to construct your "personal environment." And the cycle is endless. As Stewart Ewen notes, advertising promotes a culture of "conspicuous consumption" and "dynamic obsolesence," where packaging (of goods and individuals) is everything – a culture of waste, which more and more uses history as a way of selling a fleeting presence.[37] Through the discourse of advertising, the "consumer" has replaced the "citizen" as the focal point of public life.

Advertising's influence, and the whole ethos of marketing, have permeated almost every aspect of public life. Professional (and world-class amateur) sports have become significant sites for promotion and extension of consumer goods and style. Indeed, the ubiquity of advertising as public discourse is perhaps nowhere more apparent.[38] Almost everything connected with sport – from the clothing of athletes to the arenas and fields themselves – is saturated with commercial messages. Televised sport adds a further dimension, as the viewer is inundated with promotional messages and sponsorships attached to every conceivable facet of the broadcast – from the graphics and the scoreboards to the interjections of announcers, who must attach a corporate dimension to the play itself ("this pitching change is brought to you by … ").

Slowly but surely televised sports is constructing a seamless flow between advertising and the program itself.

The extension of a culture of marketing has made significant inroads into all facets of cultural production. Hollywood feature films, for example, have become sites of advertising messages, through a practice known as product placement.[39] In an effort to defray the exorbitant overhead costs of feature film production, studios have begun to sell "spots" in their movies. If a scene calls for the star to drink a soft drink, perhaps Pepsi or Coke will pay for the privilege of being consumed (and displayed) prominently. Brokerage houses have been established to "rationalize" the process, analysing scripts scene by scene and mediating between the studios and prospective advertisers. Not content with getting their products into a movie, advertisers have also begun to negotiate "tie-in" promotional campaigns. For the studios, these campaigns serve as additional publicity. Of course, this phenomenon does more than reduce the overhead costs of film-making. The film itself (or the scene itself) must meet the expectations of the advertiser – somehow it must elicit a "feel-good" response in the viewer. Heroes and happy endings are a must.

The Hollywood films that have used product placement and promotional tie-ins to the fullest extent have been aimed at children or family audiences. As Stephen Kline has shown, over the last two decades the market for children's toys has become integrated into the production of culture (television shows, movies, and books) for children.[40] Saturday-morning television programming, in particular, is part of a carefully orchestrated marketing strategy. The programs themselves promote an imaginary world that children can re-create for themselves if they can convince their parents to make the right purchases. For Kline, the most damaging consequence of this phenomenon is that children's play itself is increasingly patterned after the imaginary worlds (both stereotypical and Manichaean) designed by marketing strategists.

The triumph of this type of total marketing has not been lost on other sectors of the cultural industry. The corporate mergers noted above are driven partly by the desire to apply a strategy known as "synergy" to the production of cultural goods. By owning companies involved in every aspect of the cultural marketplace – from film and television production, through cable systems and specialty and pay-per-view channels, book and magazine publishing, sound recording, and video games, to theme parks – a corporation such as Time-Warner can maximize the returns on any project it undertakes. The net effect is to narrow further the range of cultural material that enters the public realm and to expand the role of marketing in cultural production.

THE PROMISE OF NEW COMMUNICATION
TECHNOLOGIES?

There is another trend taking shape in the realm of public communication that for many onlookers, holds out the promise of extending and deepening both the range and quality of public discourse.
It would seem that we are in the midst of a revolution in public communication, driven by the marriage of computers and telecommunications.[41] It is now possible to create, store, manipulate, and transform
all manner of information at break-neck speeds. For those who have
the right tools, communication at a distance has never been easier.
Moreover, the much-vaunted "information superhighway" promises
to establish a multi-layered dialogue among and between citizens and
institutions. Old broadcasting systems, even newspapers themselves,
were characterised by a top-down process of communication: there
were few senders of messages, and many receivers. The public was
addressed by professional communicators, but for the most part it did
not have the opportunity to talk back. To many optimistic observers,
the "interactivity" of newer forms of electronic communications, perhaps most notable in the emergence of internet virtual communities,
will once and for all break down the structures and practices that promote monopolies of knowledge, mass communication, and the uses of
media power itself as a form of social control.

Previous revolutions in communication technologies (such as the
printing press and the telegraph) brought forth similar optimism, if
not euphoria. More recently, introduction of cable as a television delivery system was accompanied by a great deal of rhetoric about its democratic potential. In Canada and the United States in the early 1970s,
cable was seen not merely as a way of improving television reception
and modestly increasing the number of available channels but also as a
means by which audiences could be given their own voice through
community or access channels.[42] The Canadian Radio-television and
Telecommunications Commission (CRTC) first encouraged and then
obliged cable companies to provide facilities for local, community-
based television production and to promote fair and balanced access
for all groups within the community. In theory, the policy of community programming was a breakthrough for democratic communication
and an expansion of public discourse; in practice, community channels have too often become a banal outlet for multicultural boosterism, local sports events, and local council meetings. Cable companies
themselves are legally responsible for all programming on community
channels, and most have developed "better safe than sorry" programming; risqué, alternative programming is rarely encouraged.

The electronic superhighway could easily go the way of community television. In the United States and Canada, a wave of corporate mergers and pilot projects are under way to deliver interactivity. In January 1994, Groupe Videotron announced that a $750-million system called UBI (Universal, Bi-directional, and Interactive) would be up and running in the Saguenay region of Quebec by 1995. UBI will provide users with pay-per-view movies, interactive sports coverage, home shopping, and home banking. UBI's partners include Loto-Quebec, the National Bank of Canada, and Canada Post. Canada Post hopes to use UBI as a means of testing and launching the first direct-mail consumer service on the information superhighway. As Mark Surman notes, the language of UBI and other corporate systems in the planning stage is that of consumerism: "the kind of democracy that really excites superhighway visionaries [is] the right to choose between a large selection of products."[43] Indeed, application of computer technologies to the process of communication makes it feasible to establish a complex fee structure based on the amount of time (or storage capacity) used to obtain information and/or the quality or popularity of the information sought. Digitization of information facilitates commodification of communication and culture.

While media corporations vie for the privilege and the challenge of building and operating these new services, the Internet represents one of the last frontiers of grass-roots, alternative public communication. It is a network of networks, the product of a maze of data lines owned by private companies and public institutions. During the Gulf War, the Internet was one place where information was available that had not been cleared by the Pentagon. At its best, the Internet resembles a series of global coffee-houses, where the chatter is stunningly diverse and informative; at its worst, it can be sexist and technocentrist. Its strength comes from the lack of commercialism. Unfortunately, access is still primarily a function of access to an institution (universities, in particular) that is "on-line." The Internet is not the "superhighway." The crucial issue at this moment is whether the Internet model of free public access will be adopted by the systems that reach directly into the home.

While most of the attention recently has been focused on the prospects for new forms of public communication (and marketing), there is another dimension of the information revolution that is equally noteworthy. New communication technologies are also adaptable as surveillance technologies.[44] In the workplace, employees who use communication technologies as an integral component of their work (encompassing a board range of information services, from telephone operators to ticketing and insurance agents) can (and do) have their performances routinely monitored. Private information networks can gather and transmit a wide range of information regarding individual and household spending patterns. While the federal Privacy Act restrict use and flow of information about individuals within and between government departments, it does not apply to the private sector. The new technologies make surveillance so easy that it is difficult to resist the temptation to watch, listen, and record. While each application of new surveillance systems can perhaps be justified, the net effect may be a fundamental shift in the way we treat and respect the privacy rights of individuals.

FINAL THOUGHTS

Constitutional provisions are not a sufficient guarantee of freedom of expression or democratic public life. The commercialization of culture over the last century has had serious consequences for the development of a robust and diverse public forum. Advertising, in particular, has affected not only the practices of those media institutions that are in the business of selling audiences to advertisers, but also public speech in the broadest sense. Politics itself is more and more shaped by the language of marketing and a focus on "image management." As Andrew Wernick has remarked, we live amid a "vortex of promotional signs" – an endless circulation of messages and images in which virtually every aspect of social life has become part of a sales pitch.[45]

Over the course of the twentieth century, democratic governments have helped etablish institutions and regulations that have protected public speech from the dynamics of the marketplace. In Canada, a wide array of policy measures have facilitated production of Canadian culture and provided reasonable access to a diverse range of public expression (from public libraries, the Canadian Broadcasting Corporation, the Canada Council, and postal subsidies for Canadian magazines, to Telefilm Canada).[46] None of these measures has been without contradictions, but they do indicate willingness to support forms of expression that would otherwise have little chance of survival in a wholly privatized system of social communication. Unfortunately, over the last decade and a half, there has been a notable shift in the fundamental objective of Canadian cultural and communication policy, towards emphasis on private enterprises that can compete in the international marketplace. In other words, cultural policy in Canada has become something of an industrial policy.[47]

The future, however, is not yet determined. If democratic public life is to flourish, we need to recommit ourselves to the basic principles of access and diversity, and we must understand the pitfalls of a culture that substitutes promotion for creative expression. The new communication technologies may be our last hope. But if freedom on the information superhighway is guaranteed only to those who can afford the on-line costs, if there is an increasing gulf between the "information rich" and the "information poor," democratic public life will surely wither. Now is the time to shape the new technologies into a system that will reduce information inequality, greatly extend freedom of expression, and facilitate a renewed and revitalized public forum.

NOTES

1 James Carey, as quoted in Horace Newcomb and Paul Hirsch, "Television as a Cultural Forum," in H. Newcomb, ed., *Television: The Critical View*, 4th ed. (New York: Oxford University Press, 1987), 457.

2 A.J. Liebling, *The Press* (New York: Ballantine Books, 1964), 30–1

3 Raymond Williams, *Communications* (Harmondsworth: Penguin, 1962), 11.

4 As quoted in John Hartley, *The Politics of Pictures: The Creation of the Public in the Age of Popular Media* (London: Routledge, 1992), 94.

5 Ibid., 35.

6 See Harold Innis, *Empire and Communication* (Toronto: University of Toronto Press, 1950), *The Bias of Communication* (Toronto: University of Toronto Press, 1951), and *Changing Concepts of Time* (Toronto: University of Toronto Press, 1952). See also James Carey, *Communication as Culture* (Boston: Unwin Hyman, 1988), chap. 6.

7 Innis, *Empire and Communication*, 9.

8 Innis, *The Bias of Communication*, 185.

9 See Alan Swingwood, *The Myth of Mass Culture* (London: MacMillan, 1977). See also Neil Postman, *Amusing Ourselves to Death* (New York: Penguin, 1985).

10 See Wilfred Kesterton, *A History of Journalism in Canada* (Toronto: McClelland and Stewart, 1967), and Paul Rutherford, *The Making of the Canadian Media* (Toronto: McGraw-Hill Ryerson, 1978). See also James Curran, "Capitalism and Control of the Press," in J. Curran et al., eds., *Mass Communication and Society* (London: Edward Arnold, 1977), 195–230.

11 As quoted in Kesterton, *History*, 22.

12 Freedom of expression became an important tenet of liberal theory by the mid-nineteenth century. See especially J. S. Mill, *On Liberty*, first published 1859 (Harmondsworth: Penguin, 1976).

13 See in particular Michael Schudson, *Discovering the News* (New York: Basic Books, 1978); Gaye Tuchman, *Making News* (New York: Free Press, 1978); and James Curran, "The Impact of Advertising on the British Mass Media," *Media, Culture and Society* (Jan. 1981), 43–69, also in R. Collins et al., eds.,

Media, Culture and Society: A Critical Reader (London: Sage, 1986), 309–35.

14 See James Winter and Amir Hassanpour, "Building Babel," *Canadian Forum*, no. 826 (Jan./Feb. 1994), 10–17.

15 Government of Canada, Special Senate Committee on Mass Media, *The Uncertain Mirror*, Vol. 1 (Ottawa: Queen's Printer, 1970), 3.

16 Government of Canada, Royal Commission in Newspapers, *Report* (Ottawa: Supply and Services, 1981).

17 See Rohan Samarajiwa, "The Canadian Newspaper Industry and the Kent Commission: 'Rationalization' and Response," *Studies in Political Economy*, no. 12 (fall 1983). During the 1970s, and into the 1980s, the industry did establish "voluntary" press councils to hear complaints from the public.

18 This discussion is based on Geoff Heinricks, "Business Circles the Globe," *This Magazine*, 23 no. 3 (Sept. 1989), 14–21, and Joan Tinter, "Hostile Makeover," *Ryerson Review of Journalism* (summer 1993), 14–18, 20–1.

19 The quotations are from memoranda drafted by Roy Megarry, as quoted in Heinricks, "Business," 16. In 1982, Megarry told the Canadian Media Directors Conference: "By 1990, publishers of mass circulation daily newspapers will finally stop kidding themselves that they are in the newspaper business and admit that they are in the business of carrying advertising messages" (ibid).

20 Michael Schudson, "The Sociology of News Production Revisited," in J. Curran and M. Gurevitch, eds., *Mass Media and Society* (London: Edward Arnold, 1991), 141. See also Robert Hackett, "Decline of a Paradigm? The Concept of Bias and Objectivity in Media Studies," *Critical Studies in Mass Communication*, 1 no. 3 (Sept. 1984), 251–73.

21 Richard Ericson, Patricia Baranek, and Janet Chan, *Visualizing Deviance: A Study of News Organizations* (Toronto: University of Toronto Press, 1987), 3.

22 See Richard Ericson, Patricia Baranek, and Janet Chan, *Negotiating Control: A Study of News Sources* (Toronto: University of Toronto Press, 1989), and James Curran, "Culturalist Perspectives of News Organizations," in M. Ferguson, ed., *Public Communication: The New Imperatives* (London: Sage, 1990), 114–34. See also references cited in note 20.

23 Robert Hackett, "Coups, Earthquakes and Hostages? Foreign News on Canadian Television," *Canadian Journal of Political Science*, 22 no. 4 (Dec. 1989), 809–26.

24 Deborah Clarke, "Constraints of Television News Production: The Example of Story Geography," *Canadian Journal of Communication*, 15 no. 1 (winter 1990), 67–94.

25 See Margaret Morse, "The Television News Personality and Credibility: Reflections on the News in Transition," in T. Modleski, ed., *Studies in Entertainment* (Bloomington: Indiana University Press, 1986), 55–79.

26 Shawn Berry, "*USA Today, The London Free Press*, and the Rationalization of the North American Newspaper Industry," *Canadian Journal of Communication*, 19 no. 2 (spring 1994), 173–87.

27 The 1991 Royal Commission on Electoral Reform and Party Financing supported extensive research into the relationship between the mass media and elections. For a review of some of the findings and a discussion of political communication in general, see Fred Fletcher, "Media, Elections, and Democracy," *Canadian Journal of Communication*, 19 no. 2 (spring 1994), 131–50.

28 Tino Balio, ed., *The American Film Industry*, revised ed. (Madison: University of Wisconsin, 1985).

29 Ted Magder, *Canada's Hollywood: The Canadian State and Feature Films* (Toronto: University of Toronto Press, 1993), and Manjunath Pendakur, *Canadian Dreams and American Control* (Toronto: Garamond, 1990).

30 As quoted in Ben Bagdikian, "The Lords of the Global Village," *Nation*, 12 June 1989, 807.

31 Winter and Hassanpour, "Building Babel." See also John Hannigan, "Canadian Media Ownership and Control in the Age of Global Megamedia Empires," in Benjamin Singer, ed., *Communications in Canadian Society*, 4th ed. (Toronto: Nelson, 1995), 311–31.

32 "Who Will Have Access to the King's Highway?" *Toronto Star.* 13 March 1994, C2.

33 Winter and Hassanpour, "Building Babel." For a brief discussion of different theoretical approaches to the study of media power, see Ted Magder, "Taking Culture Seriously: A Political Economy of Communications," in W. Clement and G. Williams, eds., *The New Canadian Political Economy* (Montreal: McGill-Queen's University Press, 1989), 278–96.

34 John Porter, *The Vertical Mosaic: An Analysis of Social Class and Power in Canada* (Toronto: University of Toronto Press, 1965), 522.

35 Dallas Smythe, *Dependency Road* NJ (Norwood, NJ: Ablex, 1981), xiv.

36 See, for example, Todd Gitlin, *Inside Prime Time* (New York: Pantheon, 1983).

37 Stewart Ewen, *All Consuming Images* (New York: Basic Books, 1988), 233, 23. See also William Leiss, Stephen Kline, and Sut Jhally, *Social Communication as Advertising*, 2nd ed. (Toronto: Nelson, 1990), 1, 5.

38 See Varda Burstyn, "The Sporting Life," *Saturday Night* (March 1989), and David Guterson, "Moneyball! On the Relentless Promotion of Pro Sports," *Harper's*, (Sept. 1994), 37–46. See also Michael Real, *Super Media* (London: Sage, 1989), especially chap. 8.

39 Mark Crispin Miller, "Hollywood: The Ad," *Atlantic* (April 1990); Janet Wasko, Mark Phillips, and Chris Purdie, "Hollywood Meets Madison Ave.: The Commercialization of US films," *Media, Culture and Society*, 15 no. 2 (April 1993), 271–94.

40 Stephen Kline, *Out of the Garden: Toys and Children's Culture in the Age of Marketing* (Toronto: Garamond Press, 1993).

41 Useful introductions to the information revolution include David Lyons, *The Information Society: Issues and Illusions* (London: Polity, 1988); Vincent

Mosco, *The Pay-per Society* (Toronto: Garamond, 1989); and Vincent Mosco and Janet Wasko, eds, *The Political Economy of Information* (Madison: University of Wisconsin Press, 1988).

42 See Kim Goldberg, *The Barefoot Channel* (Vancouver: New Star Books, 1990), and Dot Tuer, "All in the Family: An examination of Community Access Cable in Canada," *Fuse* (spring 1994), 23–9. See also Thomas Streeter, "The Cable Fable Revisited: Discourse, Policy and the Making of Cable Television," *Critical Studies in Mass Communication*, 4 (1987), 174–200.

43 Mark Surman, "Staking a Claim in Cyberspace," *This Magazine*, 28 no. 1 (June 1994), 13–16. See also "Feeling for the Future: A Survey of Television," *Economist*, 12–18. Feb. 1994, 1–18.

44 See Oscar Gandy, *The Panoptic Sort: A Political Economy of Personal Information* (Boulder, Col.: Westview, 1993), and David Lyon, *The Electronic Eye* (Minneapolis: Univeristy of Minnesota Press, 1994).

45 Andrew Wernick, *Promotional Culture: Advertising, Ideology and Symbolic Expression* (London: Sage, 1991).

46 Magder, "Taking," 288–92.

47 Jody Berland and Will Straw, "Getting Down to Business: Cultural Politics and Policies in Canada," in Benjamin Singer, ed., *Communications in Canadian Society*, 4th ed. (Toronto: Nelson, 1995), 332–56.

16 The (Real) Integrated Circus: Political Economy, Popular Culture, and "Major League" Sport

DAVID WHITSON AND
RICHARD GRUNEAU

One of the most intriguing titles in Canadian political economy belongs to Pat Marchak's recent book, *The Integrated Circus*. For Marchak the title serves as a useful metaphor. It recalls the spectacle associated with the globalization of financial markets in the 1980s, when developers and stock traders achieved popular notoriety and corporate takeovers formed the storylines of Hollywood films. It can also remind us of the barker's rhetoric that was used to convince Canadians about the merits of free trade. In Marchak's view, this economic "circus" is closely connected to new possibilities arising from changing information technologies. She explores the effect of these technologies in several manufacturing industries and argues that they have facilitated new kinds of global corporate integration, as well as a lucrative trade in "services" that is dominated by transnational firms. By the late 1980s the postwar era of increased international trade was giving way to a post-national economy in which the effective power of governments to control transnational capital was diminished. This change was facilitated by public discourses that aggressively celebrated the role of markets and consumer choices in the delivery of a better life.

Yet Marchak offers virtually no analysis of the leisure and entertainment industries – the actual business of creating diversion and spectacle. This omission is striking because these industries became increasingly significant components of transnational capitalism in the period that she describes. They have also, arguably, helped generate popular consent for the current gospel of free trade, deregulated markets, economic competitiveness, and the privatization of public goods and services. Indeed, it is precisely in leisure and popular entertainment that people's self-chosen identities as consumers have most forcefully come to rival other, older forms of personal identification, such as "national" identity.

The industries that have grown up around the provision of leisure and entertainment in the late twentieth century are wide-ranging. They encompass advertising, popular music, films, video products, sports, radio, and television – all of the most familiar and visible forms of popular culture. They also include the tourism and holiday-property industries, in which sports such as skiing and golf are transforming landscapes around the world, and the fast-food and beverage industries, where major corporate brand names such as McDonald's and Molsons have made themselves ubiquitous features of the rhythms of leisure, both at home and on vacation. One can also add the sports-equipment and leisure-wear industries (the original distinction now largely erased), as well as the booming industry in the audio-visual technologies – cameras, televisions, camcorders, CD players, and VCRs – which enable people to enjoy all the above activities in their homes. This list is not exhaustive. It simply draws attention to some of the merchandise and experiences that the leisure and entertainment industries have turned into objects of almost universal knowledge and desire, a populist vision of "the good life" in the late twentieth century.

Marchak's silence on these industries – and the popular cultures of consumption that support them – is by no means unusual in Canadian political economy. At best there has been only passing interest in the production and consumption of popular culture.[1] The work done has generally focused on two areas. First, political economists have engaged popular culture in studies of cultural dependence and underdevelopment, typically through research on the impact of popular U.S. commercial entertainment on Canadian culture in general or on specific "cultural industries."[2] Second, certain key areas of popular culture – for example, news media and television – have occasionally been discussed in analyses of dominant ideologies in Canada and the legitimation of capitalist social relations.[3] Brief references to popular culture appear in studies of class and the capitalist labour process, the functions of the capitalist state, and social-democratic struggles associated with the workplace, gender relations, and "new social movements." But almost all political economy perspectives have dealt with popular culture in a perfunctory way. There has been very little sustained analysis, and much of what exists is static and pessimistic and reduces matters of culture solely to economic and technological determinants.

A significant alternative can be found in the comparatively new, interdisciplinary field of cultural studies. Over the past three decades, this field has developed primarily in response to intellectual traditions in Western life that have celebrated the cultural preferences of educated elites (for instance, "classical" and "modern" art and literature) while devaluing mass-produced cultural goods (such as comics, romance fiction, and television shows) that have become so popular in the twentieth century. Cultural studies was also a response to political economy's reductionism and pessimism about popular culture. The result has been a groundswell of critical studies of popular cultural forms and practices, from country music to soap opera, which treat popular culture as a major dimension of human experience and, in some cases, as a site for counter-ideological expression and political struggle – contested terrain rather than a sphere of mere diversion or ideological containment.

The work in cultural studies has been remarkably diverse. In some hands, it has taken the form of historical analyses or ethnographies of working-class cultures, including cultural assimilation and resistance among ethnic minorities.[4] In others, it has involved investigating the various meanings and practices associated with film and television.[5] In its early, and especially its British variants, cultural studies gave considerable attention to the role of popular culture in the formation of class and regional solidarities and to how changes in the soccer and music industries, for example, helped break down these traditional anchors of identity in favour of a more fluid and mobile individualism based in consumer and life-style choices.[6] Though much of this research developed in reaction to perceived limitations of neo-Marxist political economy, it shared a concern for class relations and the ideological means by which capitalist relations of production were sustained and reproduced.

More recently, cultural studies has shifted away from some of the traditional concerns of political economy and towards discourse analysis and semiotic "readings" of vernacular culture (such as advertising, clothing, television, and shopping malls).[7] This change has coincided with a movement away from class issues in favour of attention to ethnicity, race, gender, and sexual orientation. In turn, there has been a corresponding de-emphasis on class politics (seen as struggle over those forms of power that follow from economic resources) and a focus on struggles over "voice," sexuality, and the body – in general, an "identity politics" in which economic issues and interests are less central. As a result, much recent work has examined issues of subjectivity, meaning, and the politics of signification, rather than changes in the social and economic production of popular cultural forms and their role in the ideological struggles that variously challenge and sustain capitalist consumer cultures.[8]

We associate ourselves wholeheartedly with the cultural studies project of legitimizing critical analysis of popular cultures. Still, without dismissing the importance of issues of voice, subjectivity, and meaning, we want to insist on the continuing value of the political economy tradition. In a whole series of industries, changes in cultural form and content, as well as in marketing and distribution, have been shaped by political-economic processes and strategies. These changes include the quest for new cultural commodities and global markets opened by information technologies and computerization, an increasingly sophisticated appreciation of market segmentation and customization, the relentless push for deregulation and the privatization of (formerly) public services, and the concentrated, yet mobile and nomadic, character of capital. In the dynamic and more deregulated business environment of the 1990s, transnational and national corporate mergers, often across different sectors of the leisure and entertainment industries, can confer enormous advantages on corporate giants with the means to achieve a continental or global market presence.

These tendencies in the commercial production of popular culture now fuel a seemingly limitless proliferation of cultural goods and styles, thereby creating an unprecedented global field of sources for consumer satisfaction and identity formation. But, at the sametime, these sources of satisfaction become ever more closely tied to the market, to the need to find meaning through consumption. Moreover, the global expansion and integration of cultural industries – primarily Western cultural industries – also harbour new and changing hierarchies of consumption. Notably, there is intense promotion of a variety of so-called world-class entertainment products and services that compete for public money with less glamorous social programs and services and threaten to marginalize popular cultural practices that cannot promote themselves on a global scale.

If political economy assists us in the study of popular culture, it is also true that popular culture is important to political economy. First, leisure and entertainment are now among the fastest growing and most publicly visible industries in the world.[9] This is not simply a matter of empirical importance; it may also be a matter of theoretical significance. In recent years a number of researchers have argued that the leisure and entertainment industries may now play a defining role in a new phase of capitalist accumulation – variously described by terms such as "postfordism," "postmodernism," "disorganized capitalism," and "new times."[10] It is argued that, the production of images and the marketing of pleasures have become so significant that political struggles centred in and through popular culture may now be as crucial as the more traditional struggle against class domination at the workplace or in state policy. Expansion of new sectors of information, cultural, and service workers has helped to fragment and realign older blocs of class alliances and has given the category of "the popular" a much greater role in the struggle over power in Western life. The current prominence of cultural and media politics, the fragmentation of political agendas, the micropolitics of "single issues" (such as peace and the environment) and other "local" concerns, and the politics of identity can all be seen as expressions of – and constitutive features in – the changing social and cultural world of contemporary capitalism.[11] While such arguments are by no means universally accepted either in political economy or in cultural studies, they have stimulated much-needed debate about the relevance of the political economy of popular culture.

In the remainder of this chapter we explore some of the arguments and issues noted above in North American "major league" sport. We argue that the sports industry – like the manufacturing industries studied by Marchak – is also undergoing integration and restructuring. This has implications for a wide range of issues, from the shifting meanings of sports consumption to the instability of major league franchises in Canadian cities. We begin with some historical background on the emergence of the modern sports industry and the making of "national" and "continental" popular cultures in North America, before we consider the current integration and restructuring of major league sport.

POPULAR CULTURES AND THE MAKING OF THE MODERN SPORTS INDUSTRY

Modern sport in Canada has its roots in the nineteenth century in a wide range of local folk games, masculine physical contests, and gaming activities practised at fairs, picnics, taverns, social clubs, and community outings. As Canada became a more industrial and urbanized market society after the 1870s, sport became commercialized, haltingly at first, through periodic, scheduled challenge matches and events sponsored by local groups across the country. Early commercial sporting events such as horse races, prize fights, baseball games, and rowing races generally attracted male audiences and were often surrounded by gambling and drink. Venues varied, depending on available facilities and the possibility of disruption by the police; money may or may not have been collected at the gate.[12]

By the end of the first decade of the twentieth century the commercialization of sport had become much more broad-ranging and systematic. Promoters were offering regularly scheduled events on weekends in response to the emergent rhythms of paid work and leisure in industrial towns and cities and the weakening of religious prohibitions against playing games on Sundays. Many athletes were receiving payment for their services, and a large number of professional and semi-professional teams and leagues – primarily in baseball, lacrosse, and hockey – had started up across the country. Spectator sport quickly became one of the most commercially successful forms of popular urban culture, largely because it organized and celebrated skills and passions that had long been familiar features of male recreation. Sport also played to inter-community rivalries, as teams and athletes from clubs in different communities competed against one another. The early commercialization of sport – like many areas of commercial popular culture – offered Canadians a more professional and packaged version of their traditional leisure practices.[13] But the price was a culture of leisure that was less and less controlled by local participants and more influenced by a growing Canadian-u.s. network of promoters and facility owners. In addition there was strengthening popular identification with the market as the most able supplier of sporting entertainments, goods, and services.

With the development of professional leagues and regularly scheduled professional games, the relationship of sports teams and players to their home communities began to alter. The earliest competitive sports in Canada involved recreational or "amateur" teams whose performances became closely linked to community pride. As long as teams were made up of local players, popular mythology held that a team's play said something about its home community and the qualities of its people. The growing quest to field competitive teams in a market society, however, opened the door to the hiring of professional outsiders. The older sense of community solidarity, with citizens supporting the athletic efforts of friends and neighbours, gave way to a relationship more like that between a local business and its loyal customers, while civic pride was rearticulated in the more commercial language of civic boosterism.[14] Sports "clubs" (the older term was maintained, with its residual connotations of membership) fulfilled their obligations to their supporters by fielding the best sporting "representatives" local money could assemble. But appeals for fans support continued to invoke the language of civic duty, the subtext here being that a community's ability to support a winning team was a marker of its character and collective wealth.

Between the 1890s and the 1920s professional teams and leagues in several sports were formed in resource towns, farming communities, and industrial cities across Canada, but most of them lasted only a few years. Professional teams were organized in markedly varying ways and played in communities with significantly differing resources. In hockey, for example, some teams emerged out of amateur clubs, others were controlled by rink owners, and still others were controlled by former players or affluent local entrepreneurs. Few teams made much money: they played in small arenas, and unfettered competition for the best players often led to wild escalations in player salaries.

These developments both expressed and dramatized the wide-open, entrepreneurial atmosphere of Canadian capitalism in the early years of the century. New lumber, mining, and banking tycoons were attracted to professional sport as an aspect of popular culture well suited to their own restless, entrepreneurial energy and ambition. These people typically wanted to bring winning teams to their home communities as well as to make money. But in many of the smaller resource centres this was proving to be impossible. Professional, semi-professional, and amateur leagues competed with each other for the best players, and there was also often unrestricted competition within each league. Many sports promoters and owners soon realized that the most profitable way to organize the developing sports industry was to create effective monopolies, whose members would honour one another's contracts, restrict access to the business, and work (more or less) collectively to secure the best markets and drive competing leagues out of business.

The gradual consolidation of these monopolies was helped by broader economic pressures and political policies that were centralizing corporate power in a handful of major industrial centres in Canada and the United States. Again, professional hockey provides a useful example. In the years before the First World War good professional hockey was played in the Maritimes and in western Ontario, and during the 1920s the Western Hockey league competed with the eastern-based National Hockey League (NHL) for players and status as the "best hockey league in the world." But uneven development undermined the ability of "peripheral" centres in the Maritimes and the west to sustain professional teams capable of building arenas large enough to compete with cities such as Toronto and Montreal. Moreover, as U.S. investors began to see the potential of hockey as a complement to boxing and other indoor sporting events, they built arenas with massive seating capacities, making it clear that, in addition to Toronto and Montreal, the future home of "the best hockey" would be in eastern U.S., big-city markets.

Similar patterns of development characterized U.S. baseball and football. Teams sprang up in many small manufacturing centres as well as in the major cities, and both sports had regional leagues whose claims to superior status were seldom clear-cut. Good players moved regularly to teams prepared to offer them more money, while owners were equally quick to move their teams in search of larger markets.[15] Just as in Canadian hockey, the most prosperous, big-city clubs in each sport eventually united in one league and built league-wide agreements designed to guarantee exclusive access to the best markets and to control players' recruitment, mobility, and salaries. There was competition from minor professional leagues, but the owners in the major cities were easily able to buy the best players and to constitute themselves as the "big league" in the public mind. This pattern – cartelization, stable monopoly as national institution, and incorporation of potential competitors through mergers and/or expansions – has characterized every "major league" sport in North America.

Clearly, major leagues in all professional sports are now best understood as combines of team owners whose perspective on the "good of the game" has less to do with national or civic traditions than with the prospects of their businesses, individually and collectively. The very idea of major league sport is a historical promotional construction: it is a description whose credibility depends on a league's maintaining its monopoly with respect to the purchase of players' talent and the selling of sporting contests. Status as a major league sport has also depended on that sport's presence in the biggest and most important cities and on media coverage that makes league games into objects of popular attention, not just locally, but also across Canada and the United States.

Media coverage has undoubtedly shaped the North American sports industry and helped make major league sport one of the most visible elements in Canadian and u.s. popular cultures. In the early decades of the twentieth century – when newspapers and radio were bringing new leisure "interests" to popular awareness – enthusiasm for professional sports far exceeded individuals' opportunities to attend games or events in person. In the extensive North American coverage that was accorded to events such as title fights and the World Series, and to athletes such as Babe Ruth and Joe Louis, the news media made sports championships into "national" events and sports heroes into national and international figures.[16] In the pre-game speculation and post-game analysis that became a standard feature of sports journalism, a star-centred style invested leading athletes with heroic, almost mythic qualities. The serial narrative that developed around the professional sport season, moreover, helped sustain public interest over many months, while the popular sense that teams represented their cities also meant that sports coverage naturalized the idea of civic identities. Not unlike the business sections of major newspapers, the sports pages presented their subjects as grand spectacle, complete with swashbuckling heroes. In addition, by relating local events and standards to those elsewhere and simply by keeping readers abreast of national and international results, each offered its readers a sense of membership in larger communities of interest.[17]

The advent of radio further boosted popular interest in "nationally important" sports events, by making it possible for people to follow them from homes, cars, and hotels across the continent. In addition, the large male audiences for sports broadcasts quickly convinced advertisers in Canada and the United States that sports were among the best of vehicles for the promotion of national brand names in products targeted at male wage earners. With the formation of national commercial radio networks in the United States in the late 1920s, companies such as General Motors and Gillette sponsored national broadcasts of major sports events, and this helped to make events such as the World Series and the Rose Bowl national institutions, along with the sponsoring corporations. In Canada, the Canadian Broadcasting Corporation's (CBC's) radio coverage of NHL hockey from the 1930s through the early 1950s had an even more profound effect, raising hockey to the level of a national passion and Saturday night ritual and carving out a central place in Canadian popular memory for the NHL. These developments in both countries also to increased popular attention to *all* major league sports and pushed professional sport to the forefront of popular discussion. Canadian media were quick to cater to the interest that their audiences showed in major league sport, and, as Paul Rutherford comments, "especially in the cities, Canadians became wedded to the idea that a continuous supply of American entertainment and sports was their birthright."[18] Just as major leisure brand names such as Coke and RCA sought to make themselves synonymous with the new pleasures that were part of North American progress and prosperity, so too did the major Hollywood film studios and the major professional sports leagues create their own places in a Canadian popular culture that was increasingly both continental and commercial.

The examples noted above underline how nationalization and continentalization of symbolic production in Canada and the United States served as necessary conditions for the making of a North American popular culture that prominently featured major league sports and star athletes. A wide range of technological and organizational developments in communications through the twentieth century created unprecedented possibilites for mass-producing audiences; examples include increasing corporate concentration in newspapers, the advent of national wire services, the rise of national advertising agencies, and the growing power and visibility of the major U.S. radio and television networks.[19] The resulting mass audiences created expanded markets for mass consumption, which ultimately played a key role in a postwar North American economic boom.

NEW DIRECTIONS IN THE POSTWAR SPORTS INDUSTRY

This was the context in which organizations such as baseball's National and American leagues, the National Hockey League (NHL), and the National Football League (NFL) consolidated their positions as the sporting equivalent to other nationally branded products and flourished in the major North American manufacturing and financial centres: cities such as New York, Chicago, Boston, Detroit, Pittsburgh, Toronto, and Montreal. In most instances, teams in these major leagues played in landmark urban sports stadiums and arenas built in the 1920s or 1930s. With low labour costs, the teams also tended to be very profitable; they generally had loyal fans; and the teams came to be viewed as civic fixtures. But as early as the mid-1950s there were important signs of change, beginning with the moves of the major league baseball Giants and Dodgers from New York to California and of the Boston Braves to a new, publicly financed stadium in Milwaukee.

These moves drew strong criticism from people who still believed strongly in the established notion of "representative" ties between local teams and their fans. It soon became evident, however, that widespread local fan support was no longer enough on its own to keep a team in any given "home" community, even in the most prosperous industrial cities. It was also clear that the demand for major league sport in new markets could not be fully satisfied by the transfer of existing teams. Much of this demand was arising in response to subtle changes in the North American economy: in particular, to the gradual shifts of wealth and population away from the older industrial centres of the northeast and Great Lakes and into the American west and south. By the 1960s, resource industries, such as oil and gas, combined with aerospace industries, finance, and tourism, were contributing to growth in Dallas and Houston, Denver, Seattle, and Atlanta, as well as, of course, California.

As these regions began to boom, their affluent suburban populations constituted obvious new markets for professional sports, and there were wealthy local entrepreneurs anxious to buy and move existing teams or secure new franchises. Still, the established major league monopolies were cautious about expansion in the 1960s and early 1970s, so much so that in football and hockey rival leagues were formed by entrepreneurs in cities that were left out of initial expansions. These produced brief but costly bidding wars and led in each case to the original league's absorbing the strongest franchises from the rival group into a renewed major league monopoly. For the established major league teams, the combined effects of expansion and the absorbtion of successful teams from rival leagues brought in immediate revenues (in the form of franchise fees) while re-establishing monopolies and cornering new markets for television advertising.

The major league expansions of the 1960s and early 1970s can be usefully viewed as exercises in revenue creation through franchising. Just as in the fast-food business, franchising in sports involves selling the rights to offer a national brand-name product (such as NHL hockey or NFL football) in a given market area. Indeed, expansion in major league sports in the 1960s and early 1970s coincided historically with the unprecedented growth of franchising in other businesses (such as McDonald's, Burger King, and Pizza Hut) and the eclipse of many kinds of independently operated local businesses at the hands of nationally promoted, brand-name goods and services. Expansion in major league sports was thus entirely consistent with postwar developments in commerce, which saw leading, eastern-based retailers in the United States and Canada move into booming suburban locations across North America, with local manufacturers being either taken over or marginalized by heavily promoted national brands. All these phenomena contributed to standardizing of consumers' opportunities and continued undercutting of local and regional differences.

While franchising brought in significant revenues, the longer-term objective for all major league sports in the 1960s and 1970s was to secure and retain national television contracts, especially with the major U.S. networks.[20] Through the 1950s and early 1960s it had become self-evident that television was vastly increasing the numbers of people actively or casually interested in professional sports. Television technologies allowed audiences to see things they often missed in the arena or stadium, while commentary sought both to explain play and to make it more exciting than it often is. Television also brought athletes' faces into living-rooms – it helped to "personalize" major league sport – and this played no small role in turning pro athletes (and even sometimes broadcasters) into celebrities. The effects of this were to make sports television programming of interest to new audiences beyond the core of already knowledgeable male fans and to make the major leagues more widely watched and talked about than ever before.

At the same time, large weekend audiences of viewers with a predictable demographic composition – still mostly men – meant lucrative advertising revenues, which fuelled an upward spiral in the amounts that networks were willing to pay for exclusive rights to televise major league games.[21] The major leagues developed formulae for splitting television revenues among member teams, and these revenues increased profits. Meanwhile, players were struggling to increase their share of these revenues by mounting court challenges to the leagues' restrictive labour practices. They also began to improve their individual bargaining positions by hiring agents, while bargaining collectively through increasingly militant player associations. In addition, many owners' desires to sign "marquee players" to sell teams in new markets further increased players' salaries.

Television was not, of course, directly responsible for all these developments, but it helped change the dynamics of professional sports. It especially accelerated a delocalizing tendency, the effects of which would be unevenly felt.[22] Popularization of successful major league teams often occured at the expense of local loyalties, creating continent-wide followings for teams such as the Dallas Cowboys and the Chicago Bulls. Television opened up the market for sports entertainment by bringing new options to viewers in regions where these sports were not part of local culture. It became the ultimate medium for pursuit of continental audiences in all the major league sports, and those that used the medium most effectively – for example, the NFL and later the National Basketball Association(NBA) – would vastly increase followings for their respective products. Even more notably, television was a catalyst for intensified competition among sports for market share, in which promotional resources and savvy would be important, and regional traditions no guarantee of continued fan loyalty, especially among the young.

Sports that did not increase their continental profile risked losing their regional fan base to more actively promoted and trendier rivals. This is one reason why the Canadian Football League struggled for some years and felt compelled to expand to the United States. It is also why the NHL must now compete with the NBA for the interest of young Canadians, and why the NHL has recently followed baseball and football's earlier expansion into the U.S. sunbelt. Of course, Toronto and Montreal have long been the most successful NHL hockey franchises, and with the growth that both cities enjoyed in the 1970s, they also were able to secure expansion major league baseball franchises. Vancouver – long Canada's "third city" – was finally granted an NHL franchise in the late 1960s, but only after public outcry when the NHL's expansion placed a team in California rather than on the Canadian west coast.

By the 1990s, NBA franchises were awarded to Toronto and to Vancouver, which had experienced economic diversification and an influx of wealth since the 1980s. By contrast, smaller Canadian cities such as Edmonton, Calgary, Winnipeg, and Quebec, are simply not considered major league markets by American standards, which factor in the size and spending power of the surrounding television market as well as the size of the city and the suitability of its stadium or arena. In hockey, all four cities had high-quality professional teams in the 1920s. And all four regained professional teams in the 1970s, when the NHL absorbed its short-lived postwar competitor, the World Hockey League. In an era when gate receipts were still the biggest source of revenue, these centres were large enough and affluent enough to generate audiences that could support NHL hockey. Indeed, in the aftermath of the oil boom, the two Alberta clubs played to sell-out crowds and were consistently successful on the ice. But by the late 1980s the changing dynamics of the sports industry were conspiring against these "small-market" teams, making their survival unlikely without continual increases of public subsidies.

MAJOR LEAGUE SPORT AND THE MARKETING OF "GLOBAL" POPULAR CULTURE

Public money has been crucial in the past twenty-five years in bringing major league sport franchises to "small-market" Canadian cities, and to many larger U.S. centres as well. Though private investors have paid the franchise fees, most expansion teams since the late 1960s have played in publicly financed facilities, which socialized one of their major costs. In the 1970s, public money built Northlands Coliseum in Edmonton, the Saddledome in Calgary, and the Olympic Stadium in Montreal, as well as numerous expansion facilities in the United States. More recent and spectacular instances have been Toronto's SkyDome, the new St. Louis football Stadium, and the Coors Stadium in Denver.[23]

These most recent examples of public subsidization should be understood against the background of greater national and international mobility of capital in an area of new information technologies, free trade, and more flexible industrial work processes. In addition, there has been significant fragmentation and globalization of markets and audiences for manufactured goods and popular entertainment, along with rapidly changing consumer tastes and preferences. Such circumstances have intensified what British geographer, David Harvey calls "the entrepreneurial city," in which civic (and provincial, and state) authorities feel more and more need to offer infrastructure and other incentives to attract new businesses – or just to keep existing ones. Growing and declining cities alike now compete more self-consciously and intensely for every kind of investment and the jobs that come with

it. They have long done so for manufacturing, of course; but with manufacturing jobs declining in many centres, civic leaders now campaign
for information-processing and telecommunications functions and for
shopping complexes, entertainment venues, and other consumption-
and tourism-related investment.[24] This situation underlines the growing role of leisure and entertainment in the North American urban
economy and the perceived importance of investment in civic image
and the entertainment infrastructure (stadiums, arenas, concert halls)
that can sustain a city's reputation as a "big league" player on the
national and international stage.

These dynamics now give owners of major league sports franchises
unprecedented leverage, allowing them to play municipalities off
against each other to secure better deals. In 1993, for example,
the Edmonton Oilers' ownership entered into negotiations with both
Hamilton and Minneapolis, in order to exert pressure on local politicians for a more favourable arena lease agreement. At the same time,
the owners of the Calgary Flames were pushing for renovations to add
luxury boxes to the Saddledome. These are two Canadian examples of
the increased demand now faced by local governments across North
America for stadium improvements and luxury boxes, for one-sided
leases and concession agreements, and even for complete control of
the stadium. All such deals give owners rights to make more money –
from other events, from advertising, even from selling the name of
the facility – from a venue built or renovated at public expense. Reno-
vation and management deals were eventually concluded in 1994 in
Edmonton and Calgary, while demands for new arenas hastened the
departures of NHL teams from Quebec City and Winnipeg. More recently, the lure of new stadiums with heavily subsidized lease arrangements in St Louis and Baltimore has prompted the defections of
National Football League (NFL) teams from large and well-established
markets in Cleveland and Anaheim.

Civic and corporate leaders in today's entrepreneurial cities fight
hard to keep their major league sports teams – or conspire to lure
teams to their cities – because of the depth of popular appeal of major
league sports, their alleged economic value, and their role as signifiers
of civic prosperity and ambition. Still, recent trends point to a precarious future for major league sport in smaller centres, especially in Canada. Public subsidy may well help "small-market" franchises in the
short term, but the markets that really interest the major leagues
are both larger and wealthier. These encompass older metropolitan
centres with numerous corporate head offices and large media markets (New York, Chicago, Boston, Toronto), but also the newer centres
of money in the American sunbelt – most recently, in southern Florida

and North Carolina, as well as California, Atlanta, Dallas, Phoenix, and Denver. These places are where the most recent expansion franchises have been granted in all pro sports, because they offer the greatest possibilities for new and bigger revenues in sports and related entertainments.With the corrent jostling of contenders for major league teams, franchise placement in pro sport is likely to be volatile for the foreseeable future, even in the largest U.S. centres, where some teams still play in older stadiums and arenas.

Meanwhile, public subsidies for major league sports teams are coming under much closer scrutiny. In Winnipeg, for example, community groups were angered by a 1992 decision by the Manitoba government and Winnipeg city council to underwrite the Winnipeg Jets' losses until 1997 – which some critics claimed would run to $30 million – when the Winnipeg food bank was supplying 33,000 clients a month and all levels of government were plagued by massive debt.[25] Private-sector proposals to link a partially subsidized new arena to downwtown redevelopment garnered a great deal of popular support, but they also became a touchstone for political opposition by people seeking more emphasis on social revitalization and less on "world class" sports. Similarly, a number of U.S. cities have been shown in referenda to be highly divided on the merits of public subsidies to pro sports teams. In 1995 in Seattle, for example, a referendum on building a new, tax-supported stadium for the Mariners baseball team was defeated by a narrow margin, but the issue was kept alive by local boosters, who took the case to the state government.

Opponents of public subsidies for major league sports teams face a difficult struggle with business and political leaders who argue that public spending on "world-class" sport is simply a matter of economic and cultural "common sense." This claim has considerable popular appeal, and it is supported by the way that major league sport has become so thoroughly integrated into broader promotional circuits, which market the virtues of business culture at the very moment that they work to sell individual commodities within it. In the media-oriented world of capitalism today, virtually every cultural event, every public communication, has come to have promotional messages and public-relations purposes built into it.[26] Formerly linked, but discrete endeavours – middle-class civic boosterism and urban development, the marketing of professional sport, and the use of sporting events, athletes, and sports facilities to promote other products – are becoming seamlessly united.

These "synergies" become more evident in the new "revenue streams" that now influence the political and economic dynamics of major league sport. The most visible of these derives from the licensing and promotion of merchandise bearing "official" team or league insignia. Team caps and jerseys were historically a small source of additional revenues for the most popular teams. In the 1980s, however, the NBA and the NFL, in particular, showed that a more aggressive approach to the licensing of insignia for reproduction, combined with vigorous promotion of team apparel as fashion items, could yield enormous new revenues while also making team logos and colours part of a familiar repertoire of popular symbols and meanings, especially among teens. The NHL was slower to offer licensed merchandise, but a measure of the market potential can be seen in claims that league revenues from this source have increased from $100 million in 1989 to over a billion dollars in 1994.[27]

New revenue also comes from more intensive exploitation of the arena or stadium. Owners may maximize revenues from other dates and control marketing of the facility for other events (in the case of publicly owned facilities). They may also sell advertising on rink boards, dasher boards, and electronic scoreboards and even lease the stadium or arena name (for example, to General Motors in Vancouver or United Airlines in Chicago). Owners may also increase revenues by allowing more and or more lucrative concessions (wine and premium ice cream, as well as more expensive beer and hotdogs) and restaurants. Most of all, they offer premium seating: club seats and luxury boxes; luxury boxes and corporate entertaining have boosted the profits of major league teams.

"Company tickets" have long constituted a major portion of season subscriptions in many major league venues. But the "Skybox" phenomenon demonstrates that luxury suites can bring in much more revenue that the bleachers they typically replace. This is why otherwise-fine hockey arenas have been replaced in Montreal and Chicago and why teams such as Calgary could demand that what was a state-of-the-art (publicly funded) facility less than ten years ago be reconfigured with more luxury seating. Still, the size and wealth of the local corporate sector ultimately determine how many boxes can be sold, and at what kinds of prices. Cities with growing economies and head offices will inevitably be the best markets.

The largest "revenue streams" will probably flow from new television technologies. For most of the last thirty years large network contracts have provided dependable and rising revenues, which have been divided fairly equally among member clubs. Network contracts will arguably continue to be big revenue suppliers, but it is unlikely that they will be the golden goose they were from the 1960s through the 1980s. The major networks have faced sharply increased demands from the major sports leagues at a time when their own dominance of television is threatened by the growth of cable and satellite. Because of the local market penetration achieved by cable operators, as well as the niche marketing facilitated by specialty sports channels, cable advertising has become more cost effective than its network counterpart, especially for local businesses (such as car dealerships and furniture and appliance stores). Local and regional cable coverage has thus proved lucrative for some teams, and the proceeds do not have to be shared with other teams. The fragmentation of television coverage produces even greater disparities, however, because the value of advertising on the New England Sports Network, for example, or the Prime Network (in southern California) is commensurate with the size and affluence of their audiences.

The new revenue sources identified here will heighten the advantages enjoyed by teams in large and affluent markets. These teams will sell more merchandise around the world, and the revenues they receive from every kind of advertising, whether in the facility or on local television, will be greater. At the same time the more numerous large corporations in affluent cities will rent more luxury boxes, at higher prices, than is ever possible in cities such as Edmonton, Winnipeg, and Quebec.

We need also to consider a broader set of underlying tendencies that are part of the integration of sports with modern marketing – cross-ownership, cross-marketing, and globalization. Cross-ownership is the increasing ownership of sports teams by large, integrated corporations, which also have substantial interests in related leisure and entertainment businesses: beer, films and videos, leisure and sports wear, theme parks, and television and radio. It extends in a strategic direction an existing tendency towards corporate ownership that contrasts with older traditions of ownership by collections of local business leaders or flamboyant entrepreneurs such as George Steinbrenner and Peter Pocklington. Affluent individuals are not going to disappear from major league sport; the lure of owning prominent teams with star players, and the high profile that it provides, will probably continue to attract big egos. But large, integrated corporate owners have distinct competitive advantages, including capital, increased lobbying power with local governments, more developed and geographically diversified marketing programs, and the ability to cross-market professional teams with other members of the corporate family.

The most traditional version of cross-marketing involves ownership of sports teams by breweries, whose beer sales are promoted by their association with the team (Busch in St Louis, Coors in Denver, and Labatts in Toronto). Another profitable "synergy" links sports teams with cable-television operators, which provide regular exposure for the team while the team provides popular prime-time and weekend programming. We see this connection with Viacom and Madison Square Garden, with the Turner network and the Atlanta Braves, and again with the Blue Jays and the Canadian all-sports cable network TSN (where beer, television, and baseball all promote each other). Similarly, Comsat Video Enterprises, a Maryland-based communications and entertainment group, paid $75 million to purchase the Quebec Nordiques and move the franchise to Denver. Comsat, which already owned the NBA's Denver Nuggets, wanted an NHL team as another attraction in the arena it was building in Denver and for further programming on satellite television.[28] This offer further illustrates the interest that large media and entertainment conglomerates now have in "sports entertainment properties." Control of such properties may well provide advantages in the burgeoning competiton among sattelite television, telephone, and computer companies for home delivery of information and entertainment. This is one reason why the incidence of professional sports teams run by integrated entertainment corporations is increasing.[29]

Cross-marketing also extends to promotional synergies at the conceptual stage, when different entertainment products in a corporate empire are carefully designed and marketed so as to enhance each other's presence and fashionability in popular culture. Promotion of toys and video games in conjunction with television shows and children's accessories offers the most familiar and controversial examples of this (from Strawberry Shortcake to Teenage Mutant Ninja Turtles).[30] Disney has been an especially sophisticated practitioner of cross-marketing in its strategic promotion of films, toys, children's fashions, theme parks, and new sports, all in ways that reinforce their individual and collective visibility. Its move into professional sports, its promotion of its second *Mighty Ducks* film, and its involvement in POGS (children's collector discs carrying licensed images of NHL players and Disney film characters) point the way towards new forms of integration between professional sports and other leisure and entertainment products. Other practitioners of innovative and sophisticated cross-marketing include Blockbuster Video (four southern Florida sports franchises, a theme park, and sports videos) and Nike (sports equipment, sports clothing, sports celebrities, and sports themselves). In December 1994 Nike offered $545 million for Canstar sports, Montreal-based manufacturer and distributor of the leading North American brands in hockey and roller-hockey equipment (for example, Bauer, Cooper, Lange, and Mega) and holder of the rights to manufacture and sell NHL-insignia clothing in Europe and Asia.

These examples of the involvement of major international corporations suggest a new stage in the political economy of North American major leagues sports in which the ultimate audiences are global. Today, even though the initial efforts of the NFL to expand into Europe have met with only partial success – just like those of professional soccer to expand into America and Japan – it is clear that most of the U.S.-based major leagues are considering how best to expand globally. Indeed, the NFL's huge new television contract with the Fox network makes sense to the broadcaster (a part of the transnational Murdoch communications empire, which includes satellite broadcast networks in Europe, Latin American, and Australia) only if Fox can develop global audiences for the product and associated merchandise. The NBA "Dream Team" at the Olympics in Barcelona in 1992 demonstrated just how successful the league (and Nike) have been in promoting themselves and basketball in European popular culture, while the NHL has talked for some years about how to capitalize in Europe on its name recognition as world hockey's premier league. Today, all the major professional sports seek to demonstrate to transnational advertisers that they can attract global audiences, in the manner of the Olympics. For those that succeed, the potential revenues from merchandising, television, and related promotional ventures are almost unlimited.

There is nothing to suggest that local, regional, and national cultures will somehow be swallowed up whole by such globalizing popular cultural practices. Generations of Canadians did not lose their identity simply because they were passionate about the Boston Bruins or the New York Yankees, just as years of following German football has in no way undercut the national culture of the Danes. Indeed, one of the unanticipated effects of increasing globalization appears to be intensification of popular senses of "difference," as people feel more compelled to assert their distinctiveness and make their voices heard in the face of economic and cultural homogenization. This push for distinctiveness ensures continued support in some quarters for state regulation of culture, and it often supports vibrant local circuits of media production and distribution that serve specialized markets (as in "underground" or regional magazines, local popular music scenes, and community radio and television). Still, a number of older correspondences between culture (as "way of life") and place have been subverted, especially in response to global franchising and the global competition to provide more and more "up-market" consumer choices.

In this respect, the expansion of the NHL into the American sunbelt and of the NBA into Canada is not all that unlike the spread of sushi and cappuccino bars into up-scale malls around North America. The range of consumer options is expanded for those who can afford them, but the resulting monoculture of signs and symbols has more to do with gentrification, boutique capitalism, and the marketing of "difference" than with any genuine interest in other cultures.[31] Yet the language in which these new cultural possibilities are promoted routinely celebrates the role of globalizing markets in making available new and more cosmopolitan kinds of identities. In the optimistic hyperbole that so often announces the arrival of the "global village," there is an implicit claim that "as people gain access to global information, so they develop global needs and demand global commodities thereby becoming global citizens."[32] In this kind of promotional discourse, and indeed in the promotional culture that it exemplifies, identity is less a matter of geographical or social location, let alone the political solidarities that once followed from this, than a construct of consumer sovereignty, of product preferences, and "life-style choices."

This near-obsession with consumers' sovereignty – with people's identities and even "rights" as consumers – has emerged as a legitimating element of the globalizing thrust of capitalism. It frames and deflects a wide variety of frustrations and popular criticisms of the central political-economic tendencies in contemporary life. A particularly graphic example arose in the "framing" and diffusion of the widespread anger and frustration among Canadian sports fans caused by the strike in major league baseball in 1994–95, the bitter lockout in NHL hockey, and the threat that NHL teams might abandon Edmonton, Winnipeg, and Quebec. What was at issue for many men, and for growing numbers of female fans, was a seemingly final assault on the romantic ideal that sport is (or ought to be) different from other commodities that are produced for circulation and exchange in the market. Hence the widely voiced complaint that "greedy" owners and players "are ruining sports" by pursuing their own interests over "the good of the game." Behind these public declarations of disgust lurks an implicit set of more sweeping critical ideas – for example, that some areas of life are contaminated when they are driven by nothing more than the logic of economic growth and expediency, that some cultural practices may require protection from the vagaries of completely deregulated markets, and that some community traditions ought not to be "for sale" to the highest corporate bidder.

All these ideas stand as a significant ideological counterpoint to current trends in Canadian and U.S. consumer cultures. But rarely have they surfaced in any conscious way in public criticisms of major league sport. Popular criticisms of the sports industry are almost never viewed as overtly "political" and are rarely extended to encompass a broader critique of current patterns of economic accumulation and the corporate and state policies that sustain them. Instead, they are much more likely to be draped in nostalgia and blended with the language of individualized consumer "revolt"; today's apparent greed and corruption are contrasted to the "good old days," a mythical time when owners were sports people first and entrepreneurs second, professional franchises more deeply anchored in their home communities, and players happy just to play the game. Implied is a threat of popular resistance: if owners and players are not careful, the fans – the consumers – just might not be so quick to run out and buy tickets, purchase licensed merchandise, or watch sports on television.

Widely threatened fan revolts in sports, however, have typically been no match for the combination of widespread popular demand and the monopoly power of major league suppliers. They rarely have any organizational basis, and their ideological focus tends to be self-contradictory. Refusing to see themselves as "political" in any way, they generally draw their energy from populist sentiment, echoing a suspicion of "big business" and "big unions" and championing the rights of individuals as consumers. Yet this emphasis on the rights and needs of individual consumers is itself part of the economic and ideological condition that is promoting current trends and conflicts in the sports industry. People's interest in having the greatest possible range of market choices, including access to "world-class" events, goods, and services, is perfectly compatible with the interests of monopoly suppliers of sporting entertainment and their unceasing quest for new markets and revenues. This now includes a growing market for major league "heritage" products – "classic" team sweaters, television rebroadcasts of "classic" games, and popular "coffee-table" book histories of famous teams and players.

Popular conceptions of the "good old days" typically celebrate the major leagues and their "traditions." But the popular construction of tradition here tends to be highly selective, and the sepia-tinted images usually tell us little about the changing political-economic pressures and limits that permitted development of sports cartels and about their role in the constitution of national and continental popular cultures. In the absence of an adequate historical and political-economic analysis, it is difficult to discern what is new in major league sport in the 1990s and what is primarily an extension of older economic and cultural patterns and tendencies. It is even harder to conceive how sport might serve as an additional organizing point for resistance to the broader pressures and limits shaping Canadian life in the 1990s.

CONCLUSION

We can best understand the changes and tensions in major league sport today – expansions into new markets, explosions in franchise values and players' salaries, labour struggles, and increasing cross-ownership and cross-marketing – as extensions of older commercial dynamics and as products of a newer political-economic environment that has been forming since the mid-1970s. The industries that produce and promote popular cultural goods and consumption styles have become the real "integrated circus" in Canada and around the world. There is still a great deal of work to be done to clarify exactly what is old and what is new about the apparent restructuring of these industries and the promotional discourses that sustain them. There is also a need to examine when and how current forms and practices of symbolic production in these industries sustain ideology – mobilize meaning on behalf of dominant interests – and when they do not.[33]

We have only touched lightly on the question of ideology in the forms of symbolic production associated with major league sport. There is now a substantial literature on sport and ideology in capitalist societies, but there has not been enough research that examines how popular discourses produced around sport either sustain or challenge the new economic and political orthodoxies of our age.[34] The range of possible issues for examination is broad. To cite just one example, most of what people have read and heard about trade unions in recent years has been conveyed through the intense media coverage of the strikes and lockouts in hockey and baseball. But these "unions" in sports are vastly different from most trade unions. Their collective agreements set the framework within which individual "workers" negotiate private contracts, rather than the wage scales and agreements on work conditions that are felt collectively across an industry or workplace.[35] Moreover, sports "unions" are not engaged in broader forms of political work, like many other unions. Yet these differences get lost in media coverage of labour disputes in sports. Meanwhile, populist anger at the actions of seemingly "greedy" players, who already make huge salaries, seems easily extended to tacit condemnation of trade unions in general.

The problem of ideology needs to be explored, particularly in the promotional discourses of team owners, civic boosters, and media commentators. Sports promoters and media commentators work to construct an imaginary "us" around professional sports, as if everyone shares in the benefits that teams bring to their "home" cities. Yet as players' salaries and ticket costs have risen, regular attendance at major league sport is now out of reach for most working-class and even middle-class fans. Popular celebrations of the benefits of "world-class" sport tend to gloss over an increasing polarization of many of our cities – between the business and professional classes, for which the attractions that make a city such as Toronto or Vancouver famous are a regular feature, and the growing numbers of people who can only look on from a distance.[36] Still, we need more research about who actually attends games, as well as about the material ways in which the business and professional classes benefit from "world-class" entertainment – for example, through increases in property values and from tax-deductible corporate entertaining.

We also need to understand how the lives of poorer citizens, of women, and of various racial and ethnic groups are affected by public-sector cutbacks that erode community services while spending on sports and entertainment megaprojects proceeds. How are the forms of exclusion and vulnerability experienced by people who cannot readily present themselves as "buyers," when the buying public is the only public that counts? This kind of information is surely necessary before people can evaluate whether public subsidies to the venture capitalists and corporations that own Canadian-based major league franchises really are a good long-term economic and social investment. Several scholars have begun this task, but we need more research on the costs, as well as the benefits, of major league sport, to civic and provincial economies.[37] These are simply a few issues associated with the restructuring of the modern sports industry that a political economy of popular culture can help us see more clearly.

NOTES

1 A word about definitions. There is a considerable literature on the problems of defining "popular" culture versus "elite" or commercial "mass culture." However, too often attempts to define popular culture are unnecessarily static and abstract. We favour a view that defines the terrain of "the popular" in historical and sociological terms, recognizing that debates over the borders among popular, elite, and mass cultures have always referred to competing interests and differences in power. Useful discussions of this view can be found in Mukerji and Schudson, eds., *Rethinking*, chap. 1, and Hall, "Notes."

2 See Innis, "Strategy," for a classic study. More radical early interpretations include some of the essays in Lumsden, ed., *Close*, and Laxer, ed., Canada. More recent studies include Audley, *Canada's*, and Pendakur, *Canadian*.

3 See the discussions of media and ideology in Clement, *Canadian*, and Hackett, "For."

4 Willis, *Learning*; Foley, *Learning*; and Hall et al., *Resistance.*

5 Hall et al., *Culture*; Ang, *Watching*; Fiske, *Television*; and Morley, *Family.*

6 On soccer, see Critcher, "Football"; on rock music, Frith, "Industralisa-
   tion"; on mobile privatization, Williams, *Towards.*

7 See Wernick, "American," and the more detailed discussion in Gruneau,
   Power, chap. 1.

8 For example, see Hall's discussion of the theoretical legacies of cultural
   studies in "Cultural."

9 Useful data on the global scale of these industries can be found in "American's Hottest Export: Pop Culture," *Fortune*, 31 Dec. 1990; and "The Entertainment Industry," *Business Week*, 14 March 1994.

10 Jameson, "Post-Modernism"; Harvey, *Condition*; Lash and Urry, *End*; Hall
   and Jacques, *New.*

11 This argument is discussed in detail in Witheford and Gruneau, "Between."

12 Most of the material in this section is discussed in much greater detail in
   Gruneau and Whitson, *Hockey.*

13 For a more general discussion of this point see Bourdieu, "Sport," 828.

14 See Gruneau and Whitson, *Hockey*, chaps. 4 and 9.

15 Ingham, Howell, and Schilperoort, "Professional," 428–35.

16 For a more developed discussion, see McChesney, "Media."

17 See Rutherford, *Making*, 60–1; and Gruneau and Whitson, *Hockey*, 83–5.

18 Rutherford, "Made," 265.

19 This point is developed more fully in Leiss, Kline, and Jhally, *Social.*

20 See Bellamy, "Professional."

21 For a more detailed discussion see Jhally, "Spectacle."

22 Euchner, *Playing.*

23 See Sage, "Stealing," and Kidd, "Toronto's."

24 Harvey, "Flexible"; Gruneau and Whitson, *Hockey*, chap. 10.

25 "It's Millions for Jets Set; Handouts for City's Poor," *Vancouver Sun*, Thurs-
   day 30 March 1995, A8.

26 Our discussion here is indebted to Wernick, *Promotional.*

27 J. McLaughlin, "Hot Ice," *New York Times*, 10 April 1994.

28 *Edmonton Journal*, February 21, 1995

29 For more on this point see *Financial World Magazine*, 10 May 1994.

30 See Kline, *Out.*

31 See Zukin, *Landscapes*, chap. 7.

32 From Theodore Levitt, *The Marketing Imagination*, as cited in Robins,
   "Tradition," 28.

33 There are countless discussions of the meaning of the term "ideology"
   in modern social thought. Our use of the term here is influenced by
   Thompson, *Ideology.*

34 The most detailed analysis of sport and ideology is in Hoberman, *Sport.*
   Useful summary treatments can be found in Hargreaves, "Sport," and
   Jhally, "Cultural."

35 We are indebted to Wally Clement for bringing this example to our attention.

36 See Murdock, "New"; Harvey, "Flexible," and Gruneau and Whitson, *Hockey*, chap. 10.

37 See Baade and Dye, "Sports," and Kidd, "Toronto's." Some of the most detailed work on this has been done by the Winnipeg community coalition, Thin Ice; see, for example, "Winnipeg Jets Hockey Club and a New Arena", prepared for Thin Ice by Errol Black and Joe Dolecki, Department of Economics, Brandon University. We are indepted to Jim Silver, Department of Political Science, University of Winnipeg, for bringing this report to our attention.

REFERENCES

Ang. I. *Watching Dallas*. London: Methuen, 1985.

Audley, P. *Canada's Cultural Industries*. Toronto: James Lorimer, 1983.

Baade, R., and Dye, R. "Sports Stadiums and Area Development: A Critical Review." *Economic Development Quarterly*, 2 (1988), 265–75.

Bellamy, R., Jr. "Professional Sports Organizations: Media Strategies." In L. Wenner, ed., *Media, Sports, and Society*, 120–33. Newbury Park, Calif.: Sage, 1989.

Bourdieu, P. "Sport and Social Class." *Social Science Information*, 17 (1978), 819–40.

Clement, W. *The Canadian Corporate Elite*. Toronto: McClelland and Stewart, 1975.

Critcher, C. "Football since the War." In J. Clarke and C. Critcher, eds., *Working Class Culture: Studies in History and Theory*, 161–84. London: Hutchinson, 1979.

Euchner, C. *Playing the Field: Why Sports Teams Move and Cities Fight to Keep Them*. Baltimore, Md.: Johns Hopkins University Press, 1993.

Fiske, J. *Television Culture*. London: Methuen, 1987.

Foley, D. *Learning Capitalist Culture: Deep in the Heart of Tejas*. Philadelphia: University of Pennsylvania Press, 1990.

Frith, S. "The Industrialisation of Music." In J. Lull, ed., *Popular Music and Communication*, 49–74. Newbury Park, Calif.: Sage, 1987.

Grossberg, L. et al., eds. *Cultural Studies*. New York: Routledge, 1991.

Gruneau, R. *Power and Spectacle*. Cambridge: Polity Press, forthcoming.

Gruneau, R., and Whitson, D. *Hockey Night in Canada: Sport, Identities, and Cultural Politics*. Toronto: Garamond, 1993.

Hacket, R. "For a Socialist Perspective on the News Media." *Studies in Political Economy*, 21 (fall 1986), 141–56.

Hall, S. "Cultural Studies and Its Theoretical Legacies." In L. Grossberg et al., *Cultural Studies*, 277–86. New York: Routledge, 1992.

– "Notes on Deconstructing 'the Popular.'" In R. Samuel, ed., *People's*

History and Socialist Theory, 227–39. London: Routledge and Kegan Paul, 1981.

Hall, S., Hobson, D., Lowe, A., and Willis, P., eds. *Culture, Media, Language*. London: Hutchinson, 1980.

Hall, S., and Jacques, M., eds. *New Times: The Shape of Politics in the 1990s*. London: Lawrence and Wishart, 1989.

Hall, S., and Jefferson, T., eds. *Resistance through Rituals: Youth Subcultures in Post War Britain*. London: Hutchinson, 1976.

Hargeaves, J. "Sport and Hegemony: Some Theoretical Problems." H. Cantelon and R. Gruneau, eds., In *Sport, Culture and the Modern State*, 103–40. Toronto: University of Toronto Press, 1982.

Harvey, D. *The Condition of Postmodernity*. Oxford: Blackwell, 1989.

– "Flexible Accumulation through Urbanization: Reflections on 'Post-Modernism' in the American City." *Antipode*, 19 (1987), 260–86.

Hoberman, J. *Sport and Political Ideology*. Austin: University of Texas Press, 1984.

Ingham, A., Howell, J., and Schilperoort, T. "Professional Sports and Community: A Review and Exegesis." *Exercise and Sport Science Reviews*, 15 (1988), 427–65.

Innis, H. "The Strategy of Culture." In Eli Mandel, ed., *Contexts of Canadian Criticism*. Toronto: University of Toronto Press, 1971.

Jameson, F. "Post-Modernism; Or the Cultural Logic of Late Capitalism." *New Left Review*, 146 (1984), 53–92.

Jhally, S. "Cultural Studies and the Sports/Media Complex." In Larry Wenner, ed., *Media, Sports, and Society*, 70–93. Newbury Park, Calif.: Sage, 1989.

– "The Spectacle of Accumulation: Material and Cultural Factors in the Evolution of the Sports/Media Complex." *Insurgent Sociologist*, 12 no. 3 (1984), 41–56.

Kidd, B. "Toronto's SkyDome: The World's Greatest Entertainment Centre." Paper presented at "The Stadium and the City" Conference, Göthenburg, Sweden, 1993.

Kline, S. *Out of the Garden: Toys and Children's Culture in the Age of TV Marketing*. Toronto: Garamond, 1993.

Lash, S., and Urry, J. *The End of Organized Capitalism*. Cambridge: Polity Press, 1987.

Laxer, R., ed. *Canada Ltd.: The Political Economy of Dependency*. Toronto: McClelland and Stewart, 1973.

Leiss, W., Kline, S., and Jhally, S. *Social Communication in Advertising*. 2nd ed. Scarborough, Ont.: 1990.

Lumsden, I., ed. *Close to the 49th Parallel Etc.: The Americanization of Canada*. Toronto: University of Toronto Press, 1970.

McChesney, R. "Media Made Sport: A History of Sports Coverage in the United States." In Lawrence Wenner, ed., *Media, Sports, and Society*, 49–69. Newbury Park, Calif.: Sage, 1989.

McLaughlin, J. "Hot Ice." *New York Times*, 10 April 1994.

Marchak, P. *The Integrated Circus: The New Right and the Restructuring of Global Markets*. Montreal: McGill-Queen's University Press, 1990.

Morley, D. *Family Television: Cultural Power and Domestic Leisure*. London: Comedia, 1986.

Mukerji, C., and Schudson, M. *Rethinking Popular Culture*. Berkeley, Calif.: University of California Press, 1991.

Murdock, G. "New Times/Hard Times: Leisure, Participation, and the Common Good." *Leisure Studies*, 13 (1994), 239–48.

Pendakur, M. *Canadian Dreams and American Control: The Political Economy of the Canadian Film Industry*. Toronto: Garamond, 1990.

Robins, K. "Tradition and Translation: National Culture in Its Global Context." In J. Corner and S. Harvey, eds., *Enterprise and Heritage: Crosscurrents of National Culture*, 21–43. London: Routledge, 1991.

Rutherford, P. "Made in America: The Problem of Mass Culture in Canada." In D. Flaherty and F. Manning, eds., *The Beaver Bites Back? American Popular Culture in Canada*, 260–80. Montreal: McGill-Queen's University Press, 1993.

– *The Making of the Canadian Media*. Toronto: McGraw-Hill Ryerson, 1978.

Sage, G. "Stealing Home: Political, Economic, and Media Power and a Publicly Funded Basball Stadium in Denver." *Journal of Sport and Social Issues*, 17 (1992), 110–24.

Thompson, J. *Ideology in Modern Culture: Critical Social Theory in the Era of Mass Communication*. Stanford, Calif.: Stanford University Press, 1990.

Wernick, A. "American Popular Culture in Canada: Trends and Reflections." In D. Flaherty and F. Manning, eds., *The Beaver Bites Back? American Popular Culture in Canada*, 293–302. Montreal: McGill-Queen's University Press, 1993.

– *Promotional Culture: Advertising, Ideology, and Symbolic Expression*. London: Sage, 1991.

Williams, R. *Towards 2000*. Harmondsworth Penguin, 1985.

Willis, P. *Learning to Labour*. London: Gower, 1977.

Witheford, N., and Gruneau, R. "Between the Politics of Production and the Politics of the Sign: Post-Marxism, Postmodernism, and 'New Times'." *Current Perspectives in Social Theory*, 13 (1993), 69–91.

Zukin, S. *Landscapes of Power*. Berkeley: University of California Press, 1991.

17 Contested Terrains: Social Space and the Canadian Environment

IAIN WALLACE AND ROB SHIELDS

Canada's staple resource industries are in retreat. The east coast cod fishery has been overexploited to the verge of extinction. In British Columbia, the salmon fishery has been severely reduced by mismanagement and environmental degradation; the forest sector is encountering serious constraints on the availability of woodfibre; and the minerals industry has met with government refusals of projected developments. Electricity no longer comes cheaply in central Canada. Hydro-Québec has been obliged to postpone indefinitely its plans to dam the Grande Baleine River basin, and Ontario Hydro has formally abandoned its overambitious plans for constructing nuclear power plants. On the prairies, a decade of low grain prices, exacerbated by "subsidy wars" between the United States and the European Union, has seen wheat farmers increasingly turn to alternative crops – a move likely to accelerate now that the Crow's Nest freight-rate subsidy has been terminated. Canadian mining firms are investing in new projects in Latin America and the Pacific Rim, rather than at home. Only the oil and gas sectors can be said to be relatively prosperous, but their fortunes are not immune from international price fluctuations, and conventional oil reserves continue their steady decline.

There is more to this retreat of the staples economy, however, than quantitative measures of reduced output or decelerated growth. The past several decades has witnessed a sea change in most Canadians' conception of their natural environment. From being regarded as an almost unlimited storehouse of *resources* – a perspective that has had currency from the earliest days of European commercial interest in the country – it has come to be viewed as a treasured *resource* in itself, one directly threatened by its exploitation as a cache of staple commodities.[1] This change of sensibility, which has deep cultural roots and profound political and economic implications, is part of a wider rediscovery of "Nature" in a world that is nevertheless as strongly shaped by the forces of capitalist markets and industrial technology as it is by those of "post-industrial" and "postmodern" values.[2] As an advanced industrial nation and yet, unlike most of its counterparts, a large country containing many resources, much "wilderness," and (in addition to its urban majority) significant numbers of Native people still living on and from "the land," Canada has experienced this revolution in popular perception and valuing with more ambiguity than countries of greater cultural and environmental homogeneity. Nowhere was this more obvious than in the province of British Columbia in the early 1990s.

"B.C. Chooses Green over Copper," proclaimed the headline in the *Globe and Mail*, announcing the 1993 decision of the NDP provincial government not to permit development of the Windy Craggy project, a $550-million scheme (claimed to yield $8.5 billion in revenues) that would have mined one of the largest untapped copper deposits in North America.[3] Instead, a 9,600-sq-km region surrounding the project was declared a provincial wilderness park (the Tatshenshini-Alsek), to be nominated as part of a United Nations world heritage site. This decision, together with the government's prior attempt to find an acceptable compromise to MacMillan Bloedel's bitterly contested proposal to log in Clayoquot Sound, and its subsequent disallowal of previously approved clearance for Alcan's Kemano Completion hydro-electric project, crystallized the novel and uncomfortable situation faced by the NDP, rooted in the unionized workforce of the province's staple forest sector, forming a west coast government. For even after major workforce restructuring from the early 1980s on, the province's forest and mining industries remain major sources of employment and revenue, especially in the hinterland.

We say "West Coast," because if "Nature" has been rediscovered of late, so too has "place," both as a particular environment (shaped jointly by the social and the natural elements) and as an analytical category. One cannot appreciate the intensity of conflict around values and visions concerning the BC natural environment without recognizing, following Joel Garreau, that the province forms part of a distinct cultural region on the west coast of North America. Whether labelled "Ecotopia,"[4] or more prosaically "Cascadia," this "SuperNatural"[5] region, sharing mountains, "majestic" coastal forests, ocean vistas, and a mild climate, has nurtured a culture (to a significant degree a counter-culture) whose values have formed the "leading edge" of contemporary environmentalism. It is not surprising that Greenpeace started life in Vancouver (nor that the Sierra Club originated further south in this region). The characteristic life-styles that have evolved around the Georgia Strait, influenced more by California than by central Canada, have provided fertile ground for counter-cultural social movements spearheading the shift from "industrial" to "environmental" politics. This has been reflected not only in the confrontation between economic and bioethical priorities in the coastal forests, but also in contested visions of urban society, as between boosters of traditional economic growth and those who see the city as a "post-industrial" place for convivial social interaction. Vancouver, the business hub attaching Canada to the dynamic Pacific Rim economy, the city of Expo '86, the stunningly situated metropolis with scarcely a freeway, is a fascinating laboratory of these ambiguities.[6]

In addition to being a zone where resource-intensive economic development has encountered the social carriers of new environmental values, British Columbia is also the place within Canada where the priorities and practices of industrialized Euro-Canadian society are being most pointedly challenged by engagement with Native peoples, who have their own long-standing and nuanced relationship with nature. Belated moves to end the history of malign neglect of Indian land claims, in the province where no treaties extinguishing Aboriginal title were ever signed, have rightly been perceived by many non-Native citizens as a potential threat to their security of title and proprietary rights of resource exploitation. They have certainly acted as a brake on expansion of conventional resource industries.[7] But Native people, for whom the forests and the coastal regions are a home and a resource, not an aestheticized "wilderness," have proved no more certain to promote an externally scripted environmentalist agenda than to advance one written by multinational forest or fish-canning companies.

The interactions between the three social forces introduced above are threads that interweave throughout this chapter. Contemporary Canadian political economy reflects the interests of a dominant industrial and urban economy, which profoundly transforms nature. But these traditional forces are being challenged by a culture increasingly sensitive to more holistic environmental values, which seeks to preserve nature. Meanwhile, as Native peoples assume a more prominent place within national life, their distinctive modes of engagement with the natural environment frequently disrupt the categories in which nature is discursively constructed within mainstream society. The interplay of these forces is not confined to British Columbia, but it has created some of the most clearly defined conflicts within that province.

The balance, and the geography, of forces differ elsewhere. In the industrial heartland of southern Ontario and Quebec, the "tail-end" of the production process, generating solid waste, hazardous materials, and acidic precipitation, generates more immediate environmental concern than does extraction of natural resource inputs.[8] There, too, interactions between the metropolitan economy and surrounding rural areas raise complex environmental questions. How far is the prosperity of industrialized commercial agriculture based on ecologically unsustainable practices, and to what degree should rural environments be protected against encroaching residential and recreational development?[9] Across much of the prairies and of Newfoundland, limited opportunities for livelihoods that do not derive from traditional staple production, even when allowance is made for tourist development, can lead to a much different perception of desirable economic and environmental initiatives than those espoused by middle-class professionals in Toronto or Vancouver.

"NATURAL RESOURCES," OR "NATURE" AS RESOURCE?

Exploitation of Canada's natural resources has always been driven by the demands of external markets. First, Europeans sought fish, furs, and lumber from Atlantic Canada and the "empire of the St. Lawrence." By the mid-nineteenth century, the emergence of a rapidly growing and industrializing United States created a new magnet for forest products and selected minerals, promoting the westward extension of Canada's resource frontier. By the 1930s, development of the prairies as a granary for Europe, of the Shield as a major source of new industrial inputs (pulp, electricity, refined metals) for North America, and of coastal British Columbia as the last and best lumber frontier spread resource-based, single-industry communities across most of southern Canada outside the agricultural and urban core of the Quebec City–Windsor corridor.

The postwar boom (1948–73) in the global economy greatly intensified demand for natural resources from the Canadian hinterland. Railways penetrated northwards into the Shield and into central British Columbia to tap mineral and forest resources for American and overseas markets. The energy needs of the Canadian economy and of the fuel-deficient northern United States were met by development of the Alberta oil- and gas-fields and the vast expansion of hydro-electricity generation on the Columbia, Peace, Nelson, and Churchill and on the many northern rivers of Ontario and Quebec, culminating in the James Bay project. Towards the end of this period, Japan's economic growth and emergence of newly industrializing countries elsewhere on the Pacific Rim created a new set of markets that stimulated further resource exploitation, particularly in British Columbia.

Throughout this history of staples-based industrialization, the predominant image of Canada held by Euro-Canadians has been that of an "empty" land of boundless resource potential. Initially and in part, this view reflected accurately the relative abundance of space and natural resources, compared to the countries from which the immigrant communities had come. It was greatly reinforced, however, by prevailing cultural values within Western industrializing societies, which defined "progress" in terms of the triumph of "Man" (an unequivocally gendered agent) and his technology over a wild "Nature" (equally and oppositely gendered, usually explicitly), which it was his mission to tame and render "productive." This world-view, whose technocratic and utilitarian visions became grander in scale as the capacity to implement them increased, persisted longest in those institutions whose culture was most directly shaped by it and whose interests it most directly served. Hydro-Québec's visions of harnessing the Grande Baleine drainage basin, and private-sector engineering consultants' often-canvassed proposals for massive water diversions from northern Canada to the arid u.s. southwest have embodied this approach. So too, in their own context, have those agents who have pursued "factory fishing" and indiscriminate clear-cutting of forests. But many would argue that no citizen of Canada's consumer society is unimplicated.

The emergence of other-than-utilitarian attitudes towards the natural environment among the settler societies in North America dates from the early nineteenth century. A different social construction of nature, focusing on the wilderness as a realm unsullied by the degrading impact (moral as much as material) of an urbanizing, industrializing, profit-seeking society, was articulated by such u.s. writers as Thoreau and Emerson. Their romantic vision, of the essentially spiritual character of wilderness as a source of healing and moral uplift, was elaborated later in the century in terms of the recreational opportunities that nature offered to an increasingly affluent and mobile society. John Muir's advocacy of national parks, to protect wilderness areas from transformation by frontier society, was echoed in Canada once the Canadian Pacific Railway had provided ready access to the mountains of the west. The Rocky Mountain Parks Act of 1887 served to keep public control over development of the hot springs at Banff and over the scenic landscape and habitat for wildlife in the surrounding area.[10]

Ambiguities within the concept of 'wilderness' have become clearer over the past century. The spectrum of values associated with this expression of nature, and hence of forms of activity judged compatible with it, is broad, and emphasis has shifted. Conflicts of purpose and interest among preserving nature from human penetration, conserving areas of valued natural resources for human use or "passive" enjoyment, and facilitating consumption of nature through the varied outdoor recreational pursuits of an increasingly leisure-oriented society have marked the evolution of parks policy, both federal and provincial. Disputes over whether any logging should be permitted in Algonquin Park, or tourist infrastructure expanded at Banff, or hiking permits rationed on the Pacific Coast Trail and about whether wilderness preservation at the expense of potential employment in resource industries or tourism represents an elitist and socially regressive policy testify to this.

But for Canadians, wilderness has had deeper cultural significance than as merely an antidote to the pressures and pathologies of a commercialized, urbanized society. Part of the self-definition of Euro-Canadians in the nineteenth and early twentieth centuries was their habitation of a northern land, whose extensive wilderness terrain and harsh climate presented character-building challenges to the society that built its civilization by (successfully) accepting them. So "the true north strong and free" expressed both a cartographical positioning – at one scale, Canada as the frontier society north of the United States; at another, the Shield and the Arctic as the wilderness beyond the urbanized society of southern Ontario and Quebec – and a projected mapping of moral social space (a concept elaborated below).[11] The north became the source of images and myths that were interpreted as symbolizing Canadian cultural identity: its rugged and pristine beauty captured the essence of all that was admirable in the society that was emerging through encounter with it. Significantly, however, the Native peoples who actually lived in the north were largely absent (certainly as autonomous actors) from this land of the southern imagination.

The cultural and political transformations that have brought concern for the "health" of the natural environment into the mainstream of Canadian life and consciousness really date from the 1960s.[12] By that time, the "success" of the industrialized economy that, with the aid of the welfare state, was spreading wealth and material well-being widely across the Western world began to reveal some of its environmental costs. Advances in science and technology were seen to yield not only undeniable benefits but increasingly also threats. These might come in the form of radiation fall-out from Cold War nuclear-weapons testing; or discovery of the build-up of toxic chemicals in the agri-food production system; or experience of the environmental damage (such as from oil-spills and atmospheric contaminants) associated with expanding resource consumption; or recognition of the destruction of natural and social environments entailed in continual expansion of urban and transportation infrastructures. No matter what the source, the basis for a changed awareness of society's relationship with nature steadily accumulated. Triggering events – such as the first images of "Spaceship earth," the Club of Rome's report *Limits to Growth*, and the energy crisis of 1973 – and increasingly vocal and effective campaigns by new or revitalized social movements, focusing attention on threatened species and indigenous communities, destroyed habitats, and industrial practices that were damaging the environment, helped to heighten public, media, and government attention. Canadian examples of these threats were not hard to find – the polluted Great Lakes, acid rain from smelter emissions at Sudbury, the *Arrow* oil-spill in Chedabucto Bay, neighbourhood destruction by the Spadina Expressway in Toronto, pipeline construction in the north, and logging in British Columbia.

More extended attention is given below to the forces behind this change of public awareness. What is pertinent here is that the valuing of the natural environment as more than simply a storehouse of resources has come to acquire much greater political salience than ever. Canada's resource-based industries have thus been confronted, in effect for the first time, with a world-view and a constituency that fundamentally question the legitimacy of their operations. The political economy of traditional staples production has been transformed, most clearly in British Columbia, where environmentalism has its strongest appeal. But while this shift in public attitudes is to a large degree common across the advanced industrial nations, Canada has felt the impact most directly. In addition to threatening the commercial interests of a major segment of the economy, the revaluing of nature has reinforced the revaluing of those seen to have lived most harmoniously with it – the Native peoples. Already, the conscience of Canadian settler society was awakening to the injustices perpetrated on the original inhabitants of the land, creating growing political support for moves to renegotiate the relationship between the state and Native communities. The manner in which Thomas Berger conducted the inquiry into plans for a pipeline along the Mackenzie Valley in the mid-1970s, and the thrust of his report, gave strong momentum to this movement[13] Conflicts of interest and vision surrounding the future of resource extraction and the desirability of environmental preservation have thus come to involve not only the traditional actors (the state, capital, labour), but also environmentalists and, in most hinterland contexts, Native peoples.

ENVIRONMENTALISM, THE ECONOMY, AND "POST-INDUSTRIAL" CULTURE

The computer models in *Limits to Growth* predicted that, given projected population growth, the global economy would soon be disrupted by shortages of raw materials and by the pollution that their consumption created.[14] Depletion of non-renewable resources, particularly oil, was of more immediate concern than the sustainability of renewable resources, such as agricultural land, forests, and fish stocks. As a resource-rich nation, Canada could be expected to benefit from this scenario, enjoying rising demand and prices for its natural resources as their global availability shrank. Federal industrial-development strategy reflected this thinking as late as 1981, seeing resource-based megaprojects as the engine of growth.[15] Expansion of oil output from Alberta's tar sands, of coal production from new fields in northeastern British Columbia, and of electricity production from schemes such as James Bay promised to spread prosperity across the nation and promote the growth of Canada's stunted capital equipment–supply industries. At the same time, rising global food demands would ensure steady incomes to domestic farmers and the fishing industry, particularly given expansion of Canadian coastal waters to 200 miles in 1977.

In the mid-1980s, the Macdonald Report, on Canada's economic development prospects, saw constraints on resource-industry output as being primarily organizational, harming international competitiveness, rather than as arising out of physical scarcity, though it expressed concern about the continued adequacy of timber supply.[16] It acknowledged the need to integrate economic and environmental decision making but failed to identify environmentalism as a significant threat to expanded output by resource industries. Native land claims were scarcely mentioned in this context.

The surge in environmental awareness that was detected in national opinion polls in the late 1980s and early 1990s was attributed to a number of changes in Canadian society.[17] A period of economic expansion and reduced unemployment was seen to have addressed the most pressing issues of concern to Canadians, releasing their energies for attention to other matters. Such a post-materialist phase suggests that once basic subsistence requirements are assured people give priority to "quality of life." Popular support for action to protect the environment and restore polluted ecosystems was accumulating through the 1980s.[18] Concern over specific environmental problems in Canada, such as acid rain, soil degradation, and loss of wetlands and old-growth forest, was given added urgency by the dissemination of evidence pointing to potential global warming (which would disproportionately

affect high-latitude countries such as Canada) and the dramatic thin-
ning of the stratospheric ozone layer, which posed a direct threat to
human health. The federal government offered its *Green Plan* of 1990
against this background.

As well, changes in the sectoral composition, occupational profile,
and geographical location of the Canadian workforce have brought a
shift in cultural hegemony. The proportion of the population whose
livelihoods depend on resource-based production has been steadily declining since 1945. The farm population numbered 867,265 in 1991
(3.2 per cent of the total), and employment in logging, mining, and
fishing has shrunk to 2.2 per cent of the labour force. Neither in politics nor in popular culture does this segment of society exert its former
influence. Today's dominant social class comprises urbanized professionals,"knowledge workers" rather than producers of material goods,
who engage with nature as part of a life-style (shaped by post-materialist values, but also by the consumption of commodified recreational
and/or aesthetic experiences) rather than in the manner of those who
labour in and with it.[19]

Among this articulate and influential group, support for curtailing
environmental exploitation by Canada's staple resource industries, in
the name of a higher ethic than profit and a longer time-horizon than
the business cycle, is growing. It can be advocated with great single-
mindedness at little personal cost, which statement is meant not to
question its motivation but simply to recognize that it emerges in a different "place" from the one where its human consequences are played
out. Those who live and work in the resource hinterland, where non-
farm employment is dominated by large, resource-transforming firms,
are naturally more sensitive to the ambiguities of society's continuing
resource dependence in a post-material age. But their assessment
of the tension can too readily be devalued as simply an expression of
threatened material interest.[20] Exploitation of hinterland resources by
Native peoples tends to be accorded greater moral legitimacy in contemporary discourse, as it is judged to involve a more organic link between society and its environment, with less taint of corporate profit
seeking.

For the majority of Canadians concern for the environment is part
and parcel of a post-industrial culture that puts a high value on non-
materialist dimensions of human experience. This culture finds expression in other advanced industrialized societies, with national variations in its form and strength. Environmental values have begun to
influence economic policies in all these societies, and attempts to rec-
oncile often-conflicting priorities give substance to the search for
patterns of "sustainable development."[21] The history of resource

exploitation in Canada, especially in the renewable sectors, provides clear evidence that past practice, driven by capitalist industry and supported by the state, was and is not sustainable. Calls for significant changes in the scale and operations of these industries are far more than mere expressions of environmentalist fundamentalism on the part of remote urban elites. But unlike those European nations (in particular) that have become eloquent critics of Canada's environmental record, Canada remains a relatively resource-rich country. Yet its hinterland offers limited economic options, with potentially sustainable resource extraction being one of them. There is therefore less justification for purist environmental policy making in Canada than may be the case elsewhere (as in Germany); but negotiating a wise (sustainable) and politically viable set of resource-development policies in a post-industrial era is a major challenge to all parties involved.

THE CHALLENGE TO THEORY

Glen Williams has acknowledged that the absence of a chapter on the environment in *The New Canadian Political Economy* reflected the inadequate theorizing by Canadian political economists of the transformation of traditional staples concepts.[22] Laurie Adkin has identified problematic silences even in Williams's attempt to account for the omission.[23] There is obviously a need to revisit the classic interpretations of the evolution of the Canadian economy, particularly given new post-industrial and postmodern attitudes towards the environment.

Innis's account of the development of Canada's staples industries focuses on application of the metropole's advanced technology to the relatively abundant natural resources of the hinterland. The capacity of that technology (financed by foreign capital, first from Britain and later primarily from the United States) to exhaust localized natural endowments rapidly in the name of supplying external markets resulted in a mobile frontier of exploitation, even of so-called renewable resources. This dynamic was seen clearly in the early fur and lumber trades but was not confined to them. Cumulative depletion of regional forest biomass, by extraction that has exceeded regeneration rates, has characterized twentieth-century lumbering in coastal British Columbia and the pulp and paper industry's assault on the wide swath of economically accessible boreal forest, leading most recently to exploitation of the "final" pulpwood frontier in northern Alberta.[24] Inadequately regulated access to the fisheries of the east and west coasts, with high-technology fleets going farther and farther afield off Newfoundland, has had even more devastating results. Depletion of the natural fertility of prairie soils by a century of industrialized agriculture has been no less evident, albeit somewhat offset by rising applications of agrochemicals, and has contributed to the continued expansion of the farming frontier in the Peace River area. Paradoxically, the inevitable exhaustion of specific, localized, non-renewable resources has resulted in expansion of the mining frontier over the past two hundred years, but without so far leading to the crises of sustainabilty that face other sectors.

This history of staples extraction is seen by Williams as evidence of the "eco-hostility" of North American capitalism. He contrasts the disregard for, and damage done to, nature by producers of resource-based commmodities with the "rational, social planning for production and consumption" of environmental resources that would express a broadly defined public interest. However, the state in Canada has occupied a profoundly ambiguous postion (aggravated by the messy federal-provincial division of powers with respect to the environment)[25] and in most situations has been (by design or default) fully complicit in the eco-hostility.

As capitalist states, Canada and its constituent provinces have depended on the continued success of private accumulation to provide the means for carrying out their varied and often conflicting functions of governance and legitimation. At least until the 1940s, staples were the foundations of the Canadian economy, and the state at both levels had a direct revenue interest in their prosperity. This did not preclude conflict with resource-industry capital, especially where the latter's continentalist interests challenged nationalist industrial development, but it ensured that state regulation created no serious obstacle to expansion of the staples economy. Post-1945 diversification saw no basic change, as expanded resource exports to the United States become a significant component of growth.

As Williams argues, the emergence of widespread and increasing concern about the quality of the Canadian environment, which dates from the early 1970s, was initially cast in a regionalized or nationalist framework, rather than into a critique of the capitalist exploitation of nature. The environmental problems that first attracted public concern were ones encountered in the national heartland of southern Ontario and Quebec, rather than in the resource hinterland, and were symptoms of resource consumption, rather than of resource extraction. Pollution of the Great Lakes, and the damage to forests and structures caused by acid rain, were clearly products of industrial activity on both sides of the border; but it could be convincingly argued in each case that the greatest contribution came from U.S sources.[26] Ottawa could thus take a strong line, as guardian of the Canadian environment, in its attempts to pressure Washington into taking remedial action, while leaving to the provinces (notably Ontario) the much more ambiguous dealings between the state and domestic polluters over phased reductions in emissions. The James Bay energy proposal, however, made by an agent of the provincial state (Hydro-Québec), confirmed for the growing social movements forming around environmental and Native issues that the "staple state"[27] was still fundamentally aligned with capitalist resource exploitation. The federal National Energy Program (1980), while wrapped in the nationalist flag and anathema to the transnational oil companies, was in fact another, massive state subvention to frontier resource exploitation (at the expense of equivalent development in Alberta).

In brief, to Canadians increasingly sensitized to environmental and social-justice (primarily Native) movements, neither capital nor the state has presented itself in a good light. Growing awareness since the mid-1980s of the environmental record of the former state-socialist societies in central and eastern Europe has certainly given no support to notions of the industrialized state as a protector of nature.[28] Evidence from European social democracies of more enlightened environmental policies negotiated between the state and the private sector (as in Scandinavian forest management or German solid-waste reduction) is not widely known, and much of it has been denigrated in North America, by both business and the culture of right-wing populism, as involving excessive state intrusion.[29] As Adkin observes, one of the most distinctive political thrusts of the new social movements is their push for genuine democratization, because environmental sustainability and institutions of local accountabilty are seen to be correlates.[30] In contrast, the strategies whereby the state and capital have sought to mute and co-opt radical revaluing of social priorities and practices reveal the inertial strength of modern society's commitment to resource-consuming economic growth.[31] For increasing numbers of articulate people, traditional, class-based conflict over how that growth is to be distributed is not perceived as the central issue, for life and health are seen to be directly threatened by the environmental degradation that it causes.

To explain this shift in priorities, one has to draw not only on the bio-ethical and post-material social revaluation of Nature, and the changing occupational profile of society that more readily accommodates it, but also on the eclipse of confidence in an economy of science-based technology as the harbinger of a better future ("progress"). As Ulrich Beck argues, there has been a profound loss of public trust in this paradigm and set of social forces, which increasingly appear as a source more of harm than of well-being.[32] The economic and political imperatives that have permitted the pervasive spread of technologically grounded hazards, putting increasing numbers of people unwittingly at risk through various forms of pollution, threats of exposure to nuclear radiation, loss of environmental security, and so on, have increasingly lost legitimacy. While there is a good case for arguing that this phenomenon is further developed in densely populated and heavily industrialized Europe than in a North America still conscious of having "wide open spaces" and real "wilderness," the geography of Canada's largest metropolitan regions is decidedly "European" in this respect, and national elites and two-thirds of the population live there.

The distrust of science, recognized much more widely now (as it was not in the 1960s) as a socially constructed discourse that has usually been harnessed to serve the ideology of economic growth, is reflected in popular demands for absolute elimination of risks – such as by a moratorium on uranium mining, or requirements for no discharge of organochlorine from pulp mills (both legislated in British Columbia). Having been used by the liberal state as much as by private capital, in conjunction with status-quo methods such as cost-benefit analysis, to promote unwarranted technocratic confidence and frequently socially regressive outcomes, technical and scientific expertise is increasingly suspect, especially regarding exploitation of environmental resources. New expressions of culture, and new social movements whose priorities challenge the world-views and goals of prevailing political and technological projects, further complicate the challenge facing theory in political economy.

CHANGING TIMES, CHANGING PLACES

These new social movements and the cultural climate that nurtures them do not take shape in the abstract: they arise in particular places, out of specific configurations of lived experience, and involve reinterpretation and reappropriation of both "natural" and built environments. For example, Gibbins[33] has shown that the "traditional political agenda" of western Canada, rooted in a form of territorially defined alienation strongly shaped by disenchantment with Ottawa over economic and linguistic policies, is being challenged by a "new political agenda" reflecting the post-materialist priorities of environmentalism, feminism, and (we would add) respect for Native or New Age spirituality.

Obviously, the power of a traditional regional ideal such as freight-rate equity is based on the place-specific experience of prairie grain farmers. In contrast, the "new political" values are essentially universal, and their appeal is not confined to western Canada. Yet they are not free-floating, homeless values: they become culturally sanctioned, institutionally embodied, and politically charged in particular places or regions and not others. This involves a process of "social spatial-ization,"[34] or the dialectical creation of "social space." Lefebvre[35] iden-tifies three elements to this process: representation of locations as specific types of region endowed with a character, perhaps moral (character building), or ludic (involving a place for play and relax-ation); a reflexive moment in which these representations, or "space myths" influence individuals' vision of the behaviour appropriate or permissible in the region, given its putative character; and finally a mo-ment of praxis, in which the spatialization takes on an embodied, per-formative character as "practices of space" engaged in by those who live in or visit that place. This process, and some of its ambiguities, are well illustrated in the discursive construct of the region of Cascadia.

The utopian image of a Pacific Northwest society, stretching from Oregon to Alaska, depicts people as pursuing their post-industrial livelihoods in a natural wonderland of forests, mountains, sunny shel-tered waters, and "livable" cities[36] that sustains all sorts of healthy and healing recreational pursuits. It captures, and is grounded in, precisely that emergence in a specific place of a distinctive set of social practices conceptualized above. It embodies the prominence given to aesthetic experience in postmodern culture,[37] so that the beauty and "natural-ness" of the region become the dominant motifs and are represented as infusing the lives of its citizens. The myth of "Cascadia" is associated with wilderness and a spiritual closeness to nature – themes expressed, for instance, in the material practices of "the hopeless romantics and urban refugees" who have settled in the Queen Charlotte Islands since the early 1970s;[38] in the thriving economy of New Age services in Kitsi-lano (on Vancouver's West Side);[39] and in the successive challenges, in places such as the Carmanah Valley, Meares Island, and Clayoquot Sound, to conventional forest-industry practices that value only wood-fibre and not the forest as a holistic environment of ecological and spiritual values. The arrival of wealthy Asians, able to ensure that influ-ences such as *feng shui* – traditional Chinese geomancy that attempts to ensure good fortune through the harmonious alignment of habita-tions with local topography and cardinal directions – are incorporated into the workings of the regional real-estate and design professions, has reinforced this dimension of Cascadian culture.[40] But this utopian discourse suppresses questions that might probe more critically the un-derlying political economy. It ignores the unresolved Native land claims that express a prior call on how the natural environment might be perceived and used and the economic and social predicament of fami-lies in single-industry communities whose livelihoods are at risk. The character of the "space myths" that come to prevail, in other words, expresses the differential social power of those who shape them.

The selective silence of the Cascadian myth is equally well demonstrated in the tensions that exist within the built environment.
Vancouver has emerged over the past twenty years as an archetypal,
second-tier "world city." Employment in its traditional staple-based
industries has shrunk drastically, to be replaced by a growing concentration of producer-sevice employment, associated with the city's
emergence as a centre of Pacific Rim trade and finance and a major
beneficiary of entrepreneurial emigration from Hong Kong.[41] The
city's successful hosting of the Expo '86 World's Fair and its development, with outposts such as Whistler, of a flourishing recreational and
cruise-shipping industry have firmly stamped it as one of those post-
industrial metropolitan centres prospering as a centre of life-style and
leisure-oriented consumption.[42]

But the rapid economic growth and the influx of off-shore wealth
have changed the place in less appealing ways. Astronomical housing
costs, increasing polarization of household income, suburban sprawl,
growing incidence of automobile-induced smog, and political paralysis
in the face of these challenges paint less than a utopian picture.[43]
Nor is the myth exposed only in Vancouver. Despite the vaunted environmental responsibility of Cascadians, Victoria continues to dump
untreated sewage directly into the ocean; rapid population growth on
Vancouver Island, fuelled by "life-style" and retirement migration from
the rest of Canada, has led to the emergence of adults-only "clear-cut
condo" developments;[44] and Banff National Park teeters on the edge
of having its environmental integrity finally destroyed by the human
activity taking place within it.[45]

Whereas the culture of the Cascadian space myth undoubtedly epito-
mizes in Canada the creation of postmodern social space, the phenomenon is not restricted to the west. A gentler version of the "back
to nature and to rootedness" culture is revitalizing the economy of
parts of the Maritimes, such as the South Shore and Annapolis Valley
of Nova Scotia. Footloose professionals from metropolitan Ontario,
drawn by the sea and a simpler, more community-focused life, are making homes and starting small businesses there. Yes, property is generally cheaper (unlike in the west), and faxes and modems prevent total
isolation from peers and contracts in Toronto; but the revaluing of
places that until recently were viewed as rural backwaters is nevertheless very marked.[46] Environments of "country charm" are fragile, however. When Prince Edward Island's government attempted to register
Anne of Green Gables as a trademark, to develop better the appeal
of the island to Japanese tourists, it was opposed by the family of
L.M. Montgomery, which wanted to keep Anne's image "pure and not
tacky" (unlike, it was claimed, much of the immediate environment of

Cavendish).[47] And questions of the political economy of space myths lurk beneath the surface in the east, as they do in the west. To many local residents of Louisbourg on Cape Breton Island, the reconstructed fort and town site have become "a 1700s Disneyland by the Sea" – an elite amusement park, from which the local "peasants" are banished by a despotic Canada Parks Service bureaucracy.[48]

CONCLUSION

At the United Nations Conference on Environment and Development at Rio de Janeiro in 1992, Canada committed itself to stabilizing emissions of "greenhouse gases" at the 1990 level by 2000. Implementation of the National Action Plan to do so, however, has foundered (as of mid-1995) on the danger that reduced emissions of carbon dioxide are perceived to represent to Alberta's fossil fuel–based economy. The provincial minister of the environment opposed any regulatory or fiscal mechanism to achieve compliance and insisted that only voluntary measures to reduce emissions are acceptable. She emphasized, moreover, "the need to balance environmental and economic objectives ... the uncertainty of science ... the lack of hard information about emissions, a conviction that technology can beat emissions problems ... and unwavering optimism." Her most vocal antagonist was the BC environment minister, who called for "tough, environmentally astute and progressive" fiscal and regulatory measures to achieve the national target.[49] He claimed that the shrinkage of the salmon population of BC rivers was partly attributable to warmer water and was ample evidence of the suspectibility of biophysical resources to modest environmental change. Canada's derisory efforts appear to confirm the strength of the social forces supporting the traditional "staple state," particularly where they are aligned with popular consumption. Yes, Canadian automobiles are considerably more fuel-efficient and free of chlorofluorocarbons than they were in the early 1970s, but neither industry nor the average citizen seems keen to pursue environmental standards that seriously disturb prevailing patterns of behaviour.

Outside the energy sector, where we are all immediate consumers, the story is somewhat different. The environment, as 'Nature,' has itself become a staple, to be enjoyed or (supposedly) non-destructively consumed. Appeals to preserve wilderness and wetlands, to protect habitats and endangered species, to recycle garbage, prohibit pollution, and restore (or re-create) cultural heritage can draw on considerable support from a public that has much to gain (in terms of its quality of life and moral comfort) and seemingly nothing directly to lose by opposing the interests (whether capital, the state, or labour) that would gain by exploiting these resources consumptively. Moreover, this public is not confined to Canada. The internationalization of environmental movements now matches that of the resource-based corporations, such that Greenpeace, for instance, has actively campaigned among German and Californian publishers to boycott MacMillan Bloedel for its Vancouver Island logging practices. The role of the media and its stars in advancing environmentalist causes is a telling sign of the new cultural climate. The poster of Brigitte Bardot posed next to a baby seal was one of the definitive images of the 1980s. It captured both the power and the lack of local accountability of an externally manufactured image of social spatialization.

At home, the ground has undoubtedly shifted throughout the country in favour of greater sensitivity to the environmental impact of human activity.[50] But the degree to which the state, particularly provincial governments, acts in support of the new staple, 'Nature,' depends on what is at stake, economically and politically. Hence the divergence between "places." British Columbia will continue to face the most pronounced cleavages between post-material values of Ecotopia and the traditional Social Credit (now Reform) goal of progress. The political culture and energy industry of Alberta will resist further state intervention imposed in the name of environmental policy. Central Canada will see long-standing cleavages between provincial heartlands and their resource-based hinterlands assume new guises (as in the configuration of protagonists that focused on proposed disposal of Metropolitan Toronto's garbage in abandoned mines at Kirkland Lake).[51] Clashing interpretations of the cultural environment as staple, seen in the ambiguities of the cult of Anne of Green Gables, are likely to appear more widely through Atlantic Canada, especially with the decline of the traditional fishing economy.

At the same time, as in other spheres, the province will not necessarily be the most relevant scale of "place." Just as economic restructuring has increased the permeabilty of national and provincial boundaries and forged more immediate links between the global and the local, so pervasive cultural shifts in post-industrial society are finding particular expressions in specific places. This is clearly evident with respect to Canada's Native peoples, as their emergence from under a common bureaucracy of dependence facilitates a variety of expressions of more autonomous development, grounded in local environmental contexts.[52] It is also discernible in the range of responses to the vulnerabilities of single-industry resource towns that have emerged with the contraction of former staple employers. In Nelson, British Columbia, for instance – a distinctively Cascadian "place" – closure of the sawmill, the railyard, and (less typically) the postsecondary educational institution fostered emergence of a local economy much more marked by domestic, cooperative, and environmentally sustainable ventures. In these, women have played a leading role, in contrast to the prior dominance of masculinist capital/labour relations in the traditional staple industries.[53] Across all these scales of analysis, gradual infiltration of environmental priorities into economic decision making, and the more advanced emergence of disparate social carriers of a postmodern culture,[54] are providing new terrains of contestation in the evolution of Canadian political economy.

NOTES

1 Haley and Leitch, "Future," 49. They claim that "exponential growth in public concern for the impact of industrial timber harvesting on other forest values" was the most challenging issue identified by the BC Forest Resoures Commission Report.

2 The intellectual history and frequently ambiguous usage of these terms is carefully dissected by Rose, *Post-modern*.

3 See *Globe and Mail*, 23 June 1993, B1.

4 Garreau, *Nine*, Garreau names the west coast region "Ecotopia" after the 1975 novel by Ernest Callenbach, which depicts life in a separatist Pacific Northwest, constituted as an ecological utopia set apart from the corrupted and polluted United States.

5 "Cascadia," named after the mountain range, has been embraced as the popular label to focus the emerging regional consciousness. More formal institutional expressions include the Pacific Northwest Economic Region organization, created in 1989 by the premiers of British Columbia and Alberta and the governors of Alaska, Washington, Oregon, Idaho, and Montana, and the Pacific Corridor Enterprise Council, a private-sector equivalent. Implementation of the Canada–United States Free Trade Agreement, with its objective of dismantling cross-border barriers to trade, certainly nurtured the business orientation of the Cascadian concept, but Garreau rightly identifies the deeper cultural dimensions of this "region of the mind." See *Globe and Mail*, 25 Jan. 1992, D1; *Report on Business Magazine* (Jan. 1995), 32. "SuperNatural British Columbia" has often been used in promotional material marketing the province as a tourist destination.

6 See Ley, Hiebert, and Pratt, "Time?"

7 See *Globe and Mail*, 11 Feb. 1995, A1, and 29 May 1995, A11. The gap of expectations between (overlapping) Native claims to 110 per cent of the land area of the province and the NDP government's stance of suggesting

5 per cent as an appropriate target for a final settlement remains substantially unresolved despite the interim claim agreement reached with the Nisga'a. See *Globe and Mail*, 13 Feb. 1996, A1.

8 This is not to ignore conflict over logging of provincial forests in Ontario, notably in the Temagami region, but the environmental issues that have most sustained attention are of the sort identified here.

9 Quebec legislation of 1978 embodies a distinct ideology of the appropriate agricultural and social "vocation" of rural areas; see McCallum, "Effect." In Ontario, planning commitments to preserve quality agricultural and rural environments have proved quite permeable in the face of localized development pressures, especially in areas such as the Niagara Escarpment.

10 Taylor, "Legislating."

11 Shields, "True."

12 Macdonald, *Politics*.

13 Berger, *Northern*.

14 Meadows, *Limits*.

15 Phillips, "New."

16 Whalley, *Canada's*.

17 Bakvis and Nevitte, "Greening."

18 By the early 1990s, Canada was estimated to have over 1,200 environmental non-governmental organizations. See Mowat, *Rescue*.

19 Bakvis and Nevitte, "Greening."

20 Reed, "Implementing."

21 Hoberg and Harrison, "It's."

22 Williams, "Greening."

23 Adkin, "Environmental."

24 Novek and Kampen, "Sustainable."

25 See examples reviewed by Vanderzwaag and Duncan, "Canada," 8–15.

26 Munton and Castle, "Continental."

27 Clark-Jones, *A Staple*.

28 The pervasive environmental effects of industrialized societies of all ideological stripes suggest that explanations of environmental problems must involve more than just modes of production. As Tester argues, "the western world has much to learn from indigenous [pre-capitalist] populations" on this score, but modern technology and the institutions in which it is embedded cannot just be wished away, as some commentators appear to think. See Tester, "Canada," 410.

29 The political strength of the green (environmentalist) movement in continental Europe is related to the presence of electoral systems that allow minority parties to gain representation.

30 Though see Reed, "Governance," concerning the co-opting of local decision making in the hinterland by special interests.

31 "By encouraging Canadians to think that they can have environmental protection without economic sacrifice, the Green Plan denies the difficult choices that are called for today if we are ever to achieve a sustainable economy"; Hoberg and Harrison, "It's," 135. The gutting of Environment Canada, as part of the Liberals' "downsizing" of the federal government announced with the 1995 budget, indicates where real priorities lie when the chips are down.

32 Beck, *Risk*.

33 Gibbins, "Another."

34 Shields, *Places*.

35 Lefebvre, *Production*.

36 In 1976, the Greater Vancouver Regional District released its "Livable Region Plan," which was designed to bring about by 1986 "a region of complete communities – livable cities in a sea of green." Quoted in Ley, Hiebert, and Pratt, "Time?" 263.

37 Harvey, *Condition*.

38 *Globe and Mail*, 24 Nov. 1993, A1.

39 Mills "Social."

40 Ley, Hiebert, and Pratt, "Time?"

41 Barnes et al., "Vancouver."

42 Ley and Olds, "Landscape."

43 *Globe and Mail*, 15 April 1995, D1.

44 Ibid., 8 Aug. 1992, C2.

45 Ibid., 24 Dec. 1994, A1.

46 Ibid., 25 Sept. 1993, D1.

47 Ibid., 13 March 1993, D2.

48 Ibid., 26 Jan. 1993, A19.

49 Ibid., 20 Feb. 1995, A1.

50 Brown, "Target?"

51 A proposal to ship garbage by rail from Metropolitan Toronto, where disposal sites are at a premium, to abandoned iron ore mines at Kirkland Lake, where there was strong community support for at least holding an environmental impact assessment of the scheme, was ruled "unthinkable" by the NDP provincial environment minister. (Such rail-based disposal systems are well established in Europe, and no adequate alternative strategy for Toronto was identified by the minister.) The whole affair provided an intriguing insight into how a doctrinaire form of urban environmentalism turned the usual not-in-my backyard dynamic on its head, to the detriment of hinterland interests and of strategic urban management in the heartland. See *Globe and Mail*, 4 April 1991, A14.

52 Native people's determination to forge their own modes of satisfying their economic needs while maintaining the environmental integrity that characterizes their traditional societies has produced a growing diversity of local

solutions. Many of the activities being pursued by Native groups attract criticism, and even opposition, from exponents of the "post-industrial," environmentalist values of mainstream society in Canada (and perhaps even more virulently in western Europe). Condemnation of Native involvement in the fur trade and of the revival of restricted ceremonial hunting of whales, and denigration of Natives for their success as business people (and hence for being untrue to the approved image of "nativeness" constructed within mainstream discourse), reflect the cultural imperialism inherent in dominant "space myths."

53 Mackenzie, "Neglected."

54 For an excellent critical treatment of this topic, see Wilson, *Culture.*

REFERENCES

Adkin, L.E. "Environmental Politics, Political Economy, and Social Democracy in Canada." *Studies in Political Economy,* 45 (1994), 130–69.

Bakvis, Herman, and Nevitte, Neil. "The Greening of the Canadian Electorate: Environmentalism, Ideology and Partisanship." In Robert Boardman, ed., *Canadian Environmental Policy: Ecosystems, Politics and Process,* 144–63. Toronto: Oxford University Press, 1992.

Barnes, Trevor J., et al. "Vancouver, the Province, and the Pacific Rim." In Graeme Wynn and Timothy Oke, eds., *Vancouver and Its Region,* 171–99. Vancouver: University of British Columbia Press, 1992.

Beck, Ulrich. *Risk Society: Towards a New Modernity.* London: Sage, 1992.

Berger, Thomas R. *Northern Frontier, Northern Homeland: The Report of the Mackenzie Valley Pipeline Inquiry: Volume One.* Ottawa: Supply and Services Canada, 1977.

Brown, M. Paul, "Target or Participant? The Hatching of Environmental Industrial Policy." In Robert Boardman, ed., *Canadian Environmental Policy: Ecosystems, Politics and Process,* 164–78. Toronto: Oxford University Press, 1992.

Clark-Jones, Melissa. *A Staple State: Canadian Industrial Resources in Cold War.* Toronto: University of Toronto Press, 1987.

Garreau, Joel. *The Nine Nations of North America.* Boston: Houghton Mifflin, 1981.

Gibbins, Roger. "Another New West: Environmentalism and the New Policy Agenda." In Frances Abele, ed., *How Ottawa Spends 1991–92: The Politics of Fragmentation,* 107–26. Ottawa: Carleton University Press, 1991.

Haley, David, and Leitch, Jeanette. "The Future of Our Forests – Report of the British Columbia Forest Resources Commission: A Critique." *Canadian Public Policy,* 18 (1992), 47–56.

Harvey, David. *The Condition of Postmodernity.* Oxford: Blackwell, 1989.

Hoberg, George, and Harrison, Kathryn. "It's Not Easy Being Green: The Politics of Canada's Green Plan." *Canadian Public Policy,* 20 (1994), 119–37.

Lefebvre, Henri. *The Production of Space.* Trans. D. Nicholson-Smith. Oxford: Blackwell, 1991.

Ley, David, Hiebert, Daniel, and Pratt, Geraldine. "Time to Grow Up? From Urban Village to World City, 1966–1991." In Graeme Wynn and Timothy Oke, eds., *Vancouver and Its Region*, 234–66. Vancouver: University of British Columbia Press, 1992.

Ley, David, and Olds, Keith. "Landscape as Spectacle: World's Fairs and the Culture of Heroic Consumption." *Society and Space*, 6 (1988), 191–212.

McCallum, Charlotte A. "The Effect of Quebec's Agricultural Preservation Law on Agriculture and Rural Land Use near Sherbrooke." MA thesis, Carleton University, Ottawa, 1994.

Macdonald, Doug. *The Politics of Pollution: Why Canadians Are Failing Their Environment.* Toronto: McClelland and Stewart, 1991.

Mackenzie, Suzanne. "Neglected Spaces in Peripheral Places: Homeworkers and the Creation of a New Economic Centre." *Cahiers de géographie du Québec*, 31 (1987), 247–60.

Meadows, Donella H., et al. *The Limits to Growth.* New York: Universe Books, 1972.

Mills, Colin. "The Social Geography of New Age Spirituality in Vancouver." MA thesis, University of British Columbia, Vancouver, 1994.

Mowat, Farley. *Rescue the Earth! Conversations with Green Crusaders.* Toronto: McClelland and Stewart, 1990.

Munton, Don, and Castle, Geoffrey. "The Continental Dimension: Canada and the United States." In Robert Boardman, ed., *Canadian Environmental Policy: Ecosystems, Politics and Process*, 203–23. Toronto: Oxford University Press, 1992.

Novek, Joel, and Kampen, Karen. "Sustainable or Unsustainable Development? An Analysis of an Environmental Controversy." *Canadian Journal of Sociology*, 17 (1992), 249–73.

Phillips, Paul. "New Staples and Mega-Projects: Reaching the Limits to Sustainable Development." In Daniel Drache and Meric S. Gertler, eds., *The New Era of Global Competition: State Policy and Market Power*, 229–46. Montreal: McGill-Queen's University Press, 1991.

Reed, Maureen G. "Governance of Resources in the Hinterland: The Struggle for Local Autonomy and Control." *Geoforum*, 24 (1993), 243–62.

– "Implementing Sustainable Development in Hinterland Regions." In Bruce Mitchell, ed., *Resource and Environmental Management in Canada*, 2nd ed., 335–57. Toronto: Oxford University Press, 1995.

Rose, Margaret A. *The Post-modern and the Post-industrial: A Critical Analysis.* Cambridge: Cambridge University Press, 1991.

Shields, Rob. *Places on the Margin.* London: Routledge, 1992.

– "The True North Strong and Free." In Rob Shields, *Places on the Margin*, 162–99. London: Routledge, 1992.

Taylor, C.J. "Legislating Nature: The National Parks Act of 1930." In Rowland Lorimer et al, eds., *To See Ourselves/To Save Ourselves: Ecology and Culture in Canada*, 125–37. Montreal: Association for Canadian Studies, 1991.

Tester, Frank J. "Canada and the Global Crisis in Resource Development." In Daniel Drache and Meric S. Gertler, eds., *The New Era of Global Competition: State Policy and Market Power*, 399–414. Montreal: McGill-Queen's University Press, 1991.

Vanderzwaag, David, and Duncan, Linda. "Canada and Environmental Protection: Confident Political Faces, Uncertain Legal Hands." In Robert Boardman, ed., *Canadian Environmental Policy: Ecosystems, Politics and Process*, 3–23. Toronto: Oxford University Press, 1992.

Whalley, John. *Canada's Resource Industries and Water Export Policy*. Toronto: University of Toronto Press, 1986.

Williams, Glen. "Greening the New Canadian Political Economy." *Studies in Political Economy*, 37 (1992), 5–30.

Wilson, Alexander. *The Culture of Nature: North American Landscape from Disney to the Exxon Valdez*. Toronto: Between the Lines, 1991.